In telling the story of Charles C
light a long neglected, but imp
Scottish history. Industrialist, philanthropist, politician, churchman and Christian, Charles Cowan lived life to the full. His role in the foundation and consolidation of the Free Church of Scotland is a particularly important story that has long deserved to be told. In telling this tale, Macleod has vividly brought to life the story of a man who was gregarious and generous. This book is a splendid example of the best kind of history, because from its pages emerges a flesh and blood figure who touched the lives of many of his contemporaries.

ALEXANDER (SANDY) FINLAYSON,
Professor of Theological Bibliography & Director of Library Services,
Westminster Theological Seminary, Philadelphia, Pennsylvania

Charles Cowan was a significant actor in the most important event of Scottish history during the nineteenth century, the Disruption of the Church of Scotland that in 1843 created the Free Church, free from state interference in its mission of preaching the gospel. Cowan, a prosperous paper manufacturer, was returned as M. P. for Edinburgh, defeating the famous man of letters T. B. Macaulay and becoming the voice of the Free Church in parliament. Don MacLeod has used a wealth of primary sources, including diaries and the press, to recreate the life of a leading lay champion of the Free Church of Scotland.

DAVID BEBBINGTON
Professor of History, University of Stirling, Stirling

Don Macleod navigates an ocean of detailed evidence with consummate skill, deep contextual knowledge and commendable narrative drive, bringing us a major, holistic, insight into the life and times of a Scotsman whose life typifies a complex and deeply serious age, as yet too little understood. A page turner and eye-opener.

SAM MCKINSTRY
Professor of Business and Financial History
University of the West of Scotland, Paisley

Donald Macleod has done us a great service in this biography. Well researched, using fresh material...Readers of biography are in for a treat, and students of church history will see the Disruption for what it was: a church crisis that absorbed and impacted the lives of real people.

Iain D. Campbell
Minister, Point Free Church of Scotland, Isle of Lewis

Much of the biographical writing on those involved in the Scottish Disruption of 1843 has been concentrated on ministers. Now Dr. A. D. Macleod helps to redress the balance by writing on a prominent layman who gave so much of his time and money to support the Free Church. This is a fascinating account by a skilled biographer, who highlights the many aspects of Cowan's life — family man, paper manufacturer, politician, and devoted churchman. It gives a completely fresh look at the issues at the Disruption and the subsequent Free Church history. What is now needed is other similar biographies to fill in the picture of religious life in mid to late 19th century Scotland from the point of view of non-clerical participants. This book, with its detailed yet highly readable story, sets the pattern for others to follow. It is high-class biography, accurate and broad in scope, yet immensely interesting and informative.

Allan Harman
Research Professor of Old Testament,
Presbyterian Theological College, Melbourne, Australia

A Kirk Disrupted

Charles Cowan MP
and the
Free Church of Scotland

A. Donald Macleod

MENTOR

Epigraph excerpt from *Listening last poems*
by Margaret Avison McClelland & Stewart, Toronto.

Enter, Within (pages 24-25) © Estate of Margaret Avison
And used by permission of Random House.

ISBN 978-1-78191-269-0

Published in 2013
in the
Mentor Imprint
by
Christian Focus Publications,
Geanies House, Fearn, Ross-shire,
IV20 1TW, Scotland.

www.christianfocus.com

Cover design by Daniel Van Straaten

Printed and bound by Bell and Bain, Glasgow

Contents

To the memory of
Margaret Elizabeth Pamela Shone (1909 – 1985)
A woman of faith and integrity

Only child of Charles Cowan Newnham (1871 – 1957)

Only grandchild of
Anna Thompson [née Cowan] Newnham (1840 – 1909)

At full or at
ebbing tide, the welcomed One
has His own in and
outflowing purposes.
Already we are bonded. Nonetheless the eternal
Person is
willing to
watch with me, listen, look
ahead, knowing
His host must joyfully in
time
yield to some not
yet visible to me
design.

Margaret Avison

Abbreviations

AC	Alexander Cowan
AV/KJV	Authorized or King James Version Bible (1611 translation)
CC	Charles Cowan
CathC	Catharine Cowan, Charles' wife
ElizaC	Elizabeth Hall Cowan, Alexander's first wife
Letters	Isabel Buckoke, Ed *The Cowan Letters*
LLLM	*Life and Letters of Lord Macaulay* by George Trevelyan
NAS	National Archives of Scotland, Edinburgh
PDGAFCS	*Proceedings of the Free Church of Scotland General Assembly*
SNIC	Scottish National Insurance Company
SUIC	Scottish Union Insurance Co. Edinburgh
TC	Thomas Chalmers

Preface

It is almost twenty years ago since Robert Morris and Graeme Morton asked the question 'Where was nineteenth-century Scotland?'[1] They spoke of the fragmentation of that period and the difficulty of moulding a coherent narrative. As a biographer researching the life and labours of Charles Cowan I can heartily concur. Cowan's life revolved around so many diverse interests: social, entrepreneurial, religious, political, philanthropic, intellectual, and even sporting. With fourteen children and a large family network, he was linked to a fascinating range of individuals who helped shape nineteenth century Scotland.

'Read no history: nothing but biography, for that is life without theory,' Charles Cowan's nemesis Benjamin Disraeli advised in one of his novels.[2] The relationship between history and biography is always a subject for discussion but one does not need to go as far as Lytton Strachey when he said that 'Human beings are too important to be treated as mere symptoms of the past. They have a value which

1. Morris, Robert and Morton, Graeme. 'Where was nineteenth-century Scotland?' *Scottish Historical Review* vol 73, No 195, 5.

2. Disraeli, Benjamin. *Contarina Fleming, A Psychological Auto-biography*. New York: J & J Harper, 1832. 96.

is independent of any temporal process – which is eternal, and must be felt for its own sake.'[3] That aphorism came to mind as I wrote. The biographer and the historian: have different roles, different commitments, but shared values and common objectives. My life of Charles Cowan is a biography of a man not a history of his times.

I acknowledge indebtedness to two professors from student days, At McGill there was Scottish historian Stanford Reid (1913–1996) and at Harvard David Edward Owen (1898–1968) who taught a memorable course on Victorian Britain. I am grateful for the encouragement of two church historians at New College, Edinburgh: the ever-gracious Alex Cheyne (1924–2006) and the faith-full David Wright (1937–2008). The ever-gracious Professor David Bebbington, University of Stirling, has been a helpful critic.

When I started the research for this biography I found many helpers in Edinburgh: the staff at National Archives of Scotland, the (former) West Registry House, and New College Library, Edinburgh as well as then Principal Donald MacLeod of the Free Church College and Iain H. Murray. Carrubbers Close Christian Centre, Edinburgh, provided generous hospitality.

Among helpful Cowan family members, I cite Isabel Buckoke, Lymington, Hampshire; Ali Cowan and his sister Pat Kennedy, both of Penicuik; Katherine Derrick, Halifax, Nova Scotia; Elizabeth ('Meme') Errington, Elie, Fifeshire; Humphrey Errington; and Peter Smail, Edinburgh. Others I thank include Richard Wakeford of the British Library, London; Sheriff David B. Smith, Troon, Ayrshire; from Penicuik South Church of Scotland elders James A McClean and Bill Bruce; Dr. Roger G. Hipkin, Honourary Fellow, Grant Institute, University of Edinburgh, and particularly Roger Kelly, Valleyfield, Penicuik, whose passionate interest in local history (and specifically the Cowans) has been an inspiration. Anna Stone, Group Archivist at Aviva, Norwich, has provided assistance with the SNIC records, as has Gerald W. Hall of Peterborough, UK. I am grateful to Professor Don Carson for that contact.

I acknowledge the encouragement and help of our Tyndale Seminary Dean, Janet Clark as well as Hugh Rendle and Jennifer Spencer

3. Strachey, Lytton. *Eminent Victorians*. New York: G.P. Putnams, 1918. 1.

in the Library. Without the support of former Tyndale Librarian Sandy Finlayson, now at Westminster Theological Seminary, Philadelphia, I doubt I would have persevered in getting the manuscript to press. The staff at Christian Focus also deserve great credit for the production of this book: Willie MacKenzie, Martin MacLean, and Daniel Van Straaten.

Above all, thanks are due my wife, a true Cowan, whose roles in the composition of this book were many and varied: family resource, editor, and critic. In token of my gratitude this book is dedicated to her mother Margaret Elizabeth Pamela Shone, daughter of Charles Cowan Newnham, grandson of the subject of this book. I only wish she was here to read it.

A Donald MacLeod,
Research Professor of Church History,
Tyndale Theological Seminary,
Toronto, Ontario, Canada M2M 4B3
Website: adonaldmacleod.com
Email: adonaldmacleod@gmail.com

GENEALOGY

GEORGE COWAN (1695- 1775) m 1727 ISABEL GOW

CHARLES COWAN (1735-1805) m MARJORIE FIDLER (1734-1819)

ALEXANDER COWAN (1775-1859) and thirteen other siblings

ELIZABETH (1751-1827) m 1771 JOHN CHALMERS

THOMAS CHALMERS (1780-1847) and thirteen other siblings

m (1) 1800, ELIZABETH HALL (1781-1829)

- CHARLES (1800-1829)
- GEORGE (1804-1831)
- ALEXANDER ('SANDIE' (1806-1875)
- HELEN m Prof ALLAN MENZIES (1806-1875)
- MARJORIE ("Madge") m HARRY SIMPOSN (1808-1887)
- ELIZABETH ("Bissie") m. ALEX THOMPSON (1810-1887)
- DUNCAN (1812-69)
- SIR JOHN BT m 1. JANE GILLESPIE 2. JANE CURRIE (1814 – 1900)
- JAMES m CHARLOTTE COWAN (1815-1895)
- LUCY ("Pussie") m THOMAS CONSTABLE (1818-1881)
- SUSANNA (1820-2)

m (2) 1830, HELEN BRODIE (1796-1865)

- JANET m ROBERT BOOG-WATSON (1831-1864)
- GEORGE m MARY FORBES (1832-1885)
- ISABELLA (1833-1908)
- JANE (1836-41)
- MARY m. C A McVEAN (1837 - ?)
- JOSPEPHINE (1839-1905)
- SUSANNAH m Wm - MACKENZIE (1840-1889)
- CHARLOTTE (1842-72)

CHARLES m. Catherine Menzies (1799 – 1872) 29 October 1824

- JEAN MENZIES m THOMAS CHALMERS (1825-1864)
- ELIZABETH HALL m Rev R H LUNDIE (1827-1921)
- HELEN HALL (1828-45)
- ALEXANDER (1829-3)
- WM. (1831)
- CATHERINE ("Kate") m CHARLES WAHAB (1832-1887)
- CHARLOTTE m. HENRY J WILSON MP (1833-1921)
- CHARLES WM. m. MARGARET CRAIG (1835-1920)
- JESSIE (1832-8)
- MARJORIE ("Mabel") m Hugh Cleghorn (1838-1887)

JEAN MENZIES and THOMAS CHALMERS:

- MARGARET MENZIES (1840-1934)
- ANNA THOMPSON m. EDWARD GEORGE NEWNHAM (1842-1909)
- JOHN JAMES m. SOPHIE GILLESPIE (1846-1936)

Introduction

Nothing could have kept Charles Cowan away from Edinburgh on 18 May 1843. The traditional levee at Holyrood Palace, hosted by the Lord High Commissioner, the Queen's personal representative to the General Assembly of the Church of Scotland, held only scant interest. He left without entering because it was too crowded. He had other things on his mind. In his diary entry for the day there is a palpable air of understated excitement. He knew that this would be a day like none other in Scotland. Thomas Carlyle's brother John was also anxious to be a witness to history but rain and mud made the eighty-mile journey from Ecclefechan impossible. 'He meant to go to Edinburgh,' his brother reported to a friend on the continent the day before, 'and see the old venerable Kirk commit suicide herself – like a noble old Kirk, accepting death rather than dishonour; a highly tragic operation.'[1]

18 May 1843: did the old venerable Kirk commit suicide? The Church of Scotland, since the accession of a Scottish King to an English throne, and particularly after the Union of the two

1. Thomas Carlyle to C. K. J. Bunsen 17 May 1843; DOI: 10.1215/lt-18430517-TC-CKJB-01; CL 16: 168-169. (http://carlyleletters.dukejournals.org) accessed 20 January 2013.

kingdoms a century later, had helped define national identity. That unity was now shattered beyond recovery. The Disruption of the Established Church that day aroused intense passions. For some it was a schism that squandered the legacy of the Scottish Reformation, for others it was its vindication and preservation. Some saw it as a challenge to legitimate authority, others a principled response to intolerable interference by the state in the life of Christ's church and kingdom.

On that spring afternoon, the clouds having just parted, four hundred and fifty ministers and elders walked out into the sunlight, turning their backs on status, a guaranteed and generous income for life, and a capacious house rent free, to go into an unknown future. It is scarcely a mile north from St Andrew's Church in central Edinburgh to Tanfield Hall in Canonmills, but the distance they travelled was immeasurable. Appropriately for those abandoning all vestiges of wealth and prestige, the site of a bankrupt oil-gas factory had been chosen as the venue for the birth of the new denomination. The retreating clerics and elders proceeded along George Street through Edinburgh's New Town. The crowds that had gathered since dawn lined the street, watching in solemn silence.

Towards the end of the procession, among the Irish and English fraternal delegates, Charles Cowan, scion of a prominent Edinburgh paper-manufacturing family, joined the line. The 1843 General Assembly would have been his seventh as a commissioner but he had been excluded by regional nominators because of his reputation for subversion. The Presbytery, dominated by loyalists to the Church of Scotland, was rightly suspicious because of his close identification with his father's first cousin, Thomas Chalmers. It was Thomas Chalmers, more than any other, who had brought the Church of Scotland to this point in its history.

Thomas Chalmers' conversion as a young cleric became a part of subsequent Free Church lore: how the cold formalism of a recently ordained and ambitious minister was transformed. The 'treacherous grounds' of legalistic Christianity (as he later described it) were replaced by 'the firm foundation of "Believe in the Lord

Jesus Christ and thou shalt be saved".[2] Perhaps it was during a visit as a boy to Chalmers' Kilmany Manse that Charles Cowan was first introduced to a personal faith. His teenage diaries suggest an intense and preternatural adolescent piety, recording daily hour-long Bible readings. The young Charles Cowan was a child of the warm and non-legalistic spirituality that birthed the Free Church of Scotland.

Thomas Chalmers, in the front of the parade, was witnessing that day the final collapse of his vision of Scotland as a Christian commonwealth, a covenanted nation in which the preaching of the Word informed a nation guided by Christian values of mutual support and sharing. What lay ahead was unknown: in three years he would be dead. The leadership of his church would pass to less experienced men. The so-called 'worthies' of the Disruption were young, untried and at times impetuous. They were passionate about their faith and the rightness of their stand for justice and truth. One of them, the fiery pulpiteer Robert Candlish, was Charles Cowan's chaplain of choice from the moment he was called to Edinburgh's prestigious St George's Church more than a decade earlier. Though remaining an elder in his own congregation, Cowan would frequent the city church, carefully summarizing Candlish's sermon and text in his diary and judging all other preachers by that high standard.

Back in 1841, as that year's General Assembly was about to adjourn, Robert Candlish reminded the departing commissioners that, as a result of the costs of litigation, the church had incurred an indebtedness of £2000. Charles Cowan, impulsive and generous as always, immediately stood to his feet and appealed to a hundred businessmen present to each contribute twenty pounds to pay off the obligation. For a church not used to making financial demands on congregants, it was a new and novel challenge. The 'worthies' might inspire but it was members of the rising middle class, among them Charles Cowan, deeply committed to the principles of the new Free Church, who would take practical steps to ensure that the rhetoric of the pulpit was supported by the generosity of the pew.

2. Hanna, William. *Memoirs of Dr Chalmers* vol 1. Edinburgh: A Fullarton & Co., 1852. 189.

In November 1842 Charles Cowan had attended a Convocation of five-hundred clergy, strategizing for the inevitable separation. As he heard clergy speak he thought, as he later recalled, 'that the time had come for the eldership to express their confidence in the ministers, and assure them of our warm support.'[3] He invited a dozen elders to join him at his home, 16 Melville St., the following afternoon. Only three attended. Cowan was all for an immediate declaration of financial support but Alexander Dunlop (as a lawyer) insisted on caution: 'They must be left to decide wholly for themselves,' he urged. Charles concluded: 'The sacrifice was all the grander that there was nothing in the shape of worldly inducement, but on the contrary, most serious loss and suffering to themselves and their families, which, as faithful ministers and loyal subjects, was their sole alternative when they took the grave and momentous step which was before them.'[4] Dunlop was unable to attend a follow-up breakfast the next morning, but a draft that he had drawn up was approved.

It was only after Convocation agreed to a final break that Dunlop's draft was presented to a cross-section of thirty-two businessmen, farmers, the military, medical professionals, and two tradesmen, a representative cross-section of the lay leadership of the nascent Free Church of Scotland. The careful wording of the motion prepared the way for the Disruption:

'Considering that the conflict in which, in the inscrutable providence of God, the Church is now involved ... the severance of all connection between that portion of the Church which holds the great scriptural principles she is now contending for and the State, and in consequent loss of the means thereby provided for the support of a Gospel ministry; and also considering, while we earnestly trust and pray that the ministers of the Church may to the glory of God be kept in the path of duty, what loss and sufferings soever they may expose themselves to, that it is our duty likewise so far as in our power, to lighten that loss and diminish those sufferings, and to make worldly sacrifices on our part also, in order to the maintenance in this land, in truth and purity, of the Church of our fathers, when

3. Charles Cowan. *Reminiscences*. Printed privately, 1877. 302.

4. *Reminiscences*, 304.

deprived of the benefits of an establishment on account of adherence to those very principles in respect of which, and for the perpetuation of which, that establishment was ratified by the Statutes of the Realm, and guaranteed by solemn treaty, – do contribute the amount attached respectively to our signatures to a fund for the support of the ministers of the Church left in consequence without their present means of subsistence.'[5]

At the time of the Disruption the total annual income of the Church of Scotland for religious, charitable and missionary purposes, was estimated by Charles Cowan at £20,000.[6] In Tanfield Hall Thomas Chalmers was able to report to its first General Assembly that the Free Church of Scotland had raised £223,028. The stewardship of the fledgling denomination in the next half-decade was astonishing: 730 new churches, 400 manses, 500 schools, as well as a new theological college.[7] The Free Church had inherited all of the mission work of the Church of Scotland, necessitating a new educational facility in Calcutta. And, unlike its counterpart in Ireland, the Scottish Highland potato famine did not, in itself, force starving émigrés overseas thanks to Free Church charity.

It was particularly in its Sustentation Fund that the Free Church of Scotland pioneered a new principle of clergy compensation in which all inducted ministers received the same amount from a common pool. Called by Thomas Chalmers, its initiator, 'the sheet-anchor of the Free Church,' the Sustentation Fund surprised even its creators by its stunning success. 'I am sure,' Cowan later commented of his 'cousin-german,'[8] 'he had no expectation that from the people of all ranks would come to so hearty a response and growing liberality, strongly indicating the high value placed by the people on their religious privileges.'[9] By creating a fund to insure that each minister

5. *Reminiscences*, 305-6.

6. *Reminiscences*, 391.

7. As cited by Stewart J. Brown 'Religion and Society to c.1900' in Devine, T. M. and Wormald, J. *The Oxford Handbook of Modern Scottish History*. (Oxford: Oxford University Press, 2012) 92.

8. 'Cousin-german' was the name Cowan used to describe his relationship to Thomas Chalmers, i.e. the son of a first cousin of the father. *Reminiscences*. 168.

9. *Reminiscences*, 320.

of the Free Church received adequate and equal compensation Chalmers had tapped into 'that unworked mine which was deep in the heart and affections of the people of Scotland'.[10] From the time of its inception, for over thirty years, Charles Cowan, as a longstanding and founding member of the Sustentation Fund Committee, was its tireless (and one suspects at times tiresome) advocate.

The Free Church had little time for self-congratulation before the shrill voice of its critics could be heard denouncing the Disruption as an attack on civil order and rational behaviour: 'it was a Church nurtured in revolution'[11] was one of the milder comments and others were less guarded in their denunciations. Cartoonists were savage in their mockery: 'Pope Thomas I issueth his bull' and 'Thomas Chalmers and friends in the bog' were among their offerings.[12] Being identified with the fledgling Free Church of Scotland was initially thought to be a liability when the political neophyte Charles Cowan was asked to stand for Parliament in the election of 1847. His opponent was none other than the illustrious Thomas Babbington Macaulay. Macaulay could barely hide his contempt for this Free Churchman.

Not noted for his ability to listen to his constituents, Macaulay should have known better. His father Zachary had been one of the Clapham Sect, a group of socially prominent evangelicals who had been determined to impact society through a single-minded commitment to Christian principles. But like many of the second generation Claphamites, Thomas was in severe reaction, embarrassed by his pedigree. He had rebelled after being sent at the age of ten to an academy outside Cambridge taught by a curate of Charles Simeon, the Clapham Sect's great mentor. Simeon, who summered at Moulin near Pitlochry, and had stirred Scotland in 1796 and again in 1798, was an ideological parent of the Free Church.

When Charles was importuned to let his name stand on the ballot running against Macaulay, Macaulay dismissed his opponents

10. *Reminiscences*, 320.

11. See page 174.

12. See Brown, S. J. and Fry, Michael. *Scotland in the Age of the Disruption.* Edinburgh: Edinburgh University Press, 1993. Between pages 62 and 63.

as united 'in nothing except in their holding their particular religion as the scriptural and therefore the only safe, criterion of fitness for public duty.' Lord Cockburn, Macaulay's agent, continued: 'The gentleman who introduced Mr. Cowan to the electors at his first public meeting recommended him on the expression ground that "Christian men ought to send Christian men to represent them".'[13] That opprobrium continues to this day: the most recent biographer of Macaulay identifies the man who beat him at the polls, simply and namelessly, as 'an ornament of the secessionist Free Church of Scotland.'[14]

For the rest of his life Charles Cowan would be identified as 'the man who beat Macaulay', a nomenclature with which he was not altogether happy, retaining a great respect for the virtuosic historian. Cowan's own thirteen-year career in the House of Commons was undistinguished but to the Free Church, as he reported to them at each General Assembly, he was their voice at Westminster. He was also the voice of Scotland, faithfully representing his constituents' concerns. The House of Commons was not really his *métier*: he felt more at home at the family's paper mills in Penicuik, in the counting house, on the curling rink, or with his large and growing family. In Scotland he was a familiar figure, known and respected. Allowances were made for his volatility and unpredictability. At his fortieth and final General Assembly in 1877 the minutes record that he spoke 'inaudibly' so that 'with difficulty he could be heard. He was understood to give an account of meetings of the eldership, held at the time of Disruption, to consider by which the ministry could be supported in the crisis.'[15] He was the old soldier recalling the glory year of 1843, showing his battle wounds, and making a final appeal for the Sustentation Fund as a true monument to Thomas Chalmers, much more appropriate, he said, than the one then being erected on George Street.

By then his wife of forty-eight years had long been gone. Catharine Menzies was a woman nurtured by a warm piety. Her father, for

13. Cockburn, Henry. *Journal of Henry Cockburn; being a continuation of the memorials of his time, 1831-1854* Edinburgh: Edmonston & Douglas, 1874. 189.

14. Sullivan, Robert E. *Macaulay The Tragedy of Power*. Cambridge, MA: Harvard University Press, 2009. 269.

15. *PDGAFCS*, 1877, 146.

forty-four years pastor of Lanark parish church, had been a doughty defender of the new evangelicalism. Catharine was unbending in her concern that the family adhere to the faith of the Free Church, in spite of the fact that her own father and two brothers, clergy all, did not go out at the Disruption. 'Try to frame your walk and conversation toward us and all the world upon the principle of love to God,' she admonished her daughters.[16] She became increasingly feeble in mind and body and the full measure of her steadying influence on her husband, whose earlier convictions had waned, became apparent in her absence.

By that time both Charles Cowan and the Free Church had moved on. He was no theologian, personal loyalties rather than dogmatic convictions mattered more. The theological lines were never clear-cut from the beginning of the Free Church (in spite of the protestations of loyalists), the boundaries blurred, and coalitions formed as the Free Church became mired in controversy and conflict. Charles was one of the first to abandon Chalmers' almost lifelong commitment to the establishment principle, arguing for voluntaryism and unsuccessfully advocating union with the United Presbyterians. Subsequently he chaired the Scottish Disestablishment Committee. But the old piety was still there: he was a sponsor of the Moody-Sankey revival meetings and his family was profoundly affected. His pastor at the Barclay Church, James Hood Wilson, who had invited the American evangelist to Scotland, epitomized both the strengths and the weaknesses of the evolving Free Church of Scotland in the late nineteenth century. As moderator of the 1895 General Assembly James Hood Wilson accepted without complaint the new realities of a church in theological transition.

Two things accelerated change during the nineteenth century for the Free Church of Scotland: increasing prosperity and the premium placed on academic and intellectual achievement. Until the collapse of the City of Glasgow Bank in 1878 Charles Cowan was a wealthy man. He was also intellectually curious and like many Scots, particularly of his generation, had a reverence for learning.

16. Wahab, Catharine. 'Catharine Menzies' handwritten memoir in the possession of Judith A MacLeod. 5.

The irascible Sir David Brewster, whose mature response to new scientific discovery might well have been followed by other men of faith, was an unrepentant Free Churchman for the rest of his life, an encourager of Cowan's insatiable curiosity. Cowan joined the Brewster-initiated British Society for the Advancement of Science. He was also a member of the Royal Society of Arts and the National Association for the Promotion of Social Sciences. But there was another side to this quest for knowledge: Cowan was an active advocate and sponsor of William Robertson Smith, the theological professor whose adoption of Old Testament Higher Criticism shook the very foundations of the Free Church.

The scene in Tanfield Hall on 18 May 1843 made photographic history. David Brewster had engaged twenty-one year old Octavius Hill and his teenage assistant Robert Anderson to assemble a montage of calotypes of commissioners shown witnessing the signing of the Deed of Demission using technology just discovered. 'The Picture,' the sales pitch for the finished product announced, 'is intended to supply an authentic commemoration of this great event in the actual sittings, in as far as these can be obtained, of the most venerable fathers, and others of the more eminent and distinguished ministers and elders.'[17] Four hundred and fifty-five single portraits were placed on a large canvas, five foot by eleven feet four inches, which instead of the two years originally promised took two decades to complete. That canvas was distributed all over the English-speaking world, hanging in Free Church vestries throughout the Empire. To the right of the Moderator a standing Charles Cowan can be clearly seen as an active participant and founding father.

Charles Cowan's life thus far had been a preparation for this hour. His stand that day would inform the rest of his life. His story, as it will unfold, is the narrative of Scotland in the nineteenth century, of how the Free Church, started in a blaze of glorious self-renunciation, struggled to maintain its original vision, and of the seismic changes in a Scotland that bore scarce resemblance at the end of his life to what it had been at its beginning.

17. As quoted on http://iainthepict.blogspot.ca/2012/05/david-octavius-hill.html, accessed 22 January 2013.

Chapter 1

'Fiddlers and Fules'

Born on the threshold of the nineteenth century, the choice of a name for Charles Cowan reflected the century just completed. Two men named Charles had dominated that century for the family of the infant son. The one was his grandfather, born in 1735, who was now nearing the end of his life, having almost reached his allotted three score and ten.

The other Charles was the Bonnie Prince, the Young Pretender, whose six weeks in Edinburgh at the head of a Highland army, caused great excitement in the city. One person smitten with the Prince was eleven-year-old Marjory Fidler, who was presented to the self-styled James VIII at a ball in Holyrood Palace, his ancestral home, where he had set up residence. He kissed her on the cheek, and she was infatuated for the rest of her long life.

Charles Edward Stuart elicited more than sentimental support. Marjory's father provided practical aid for the Prince. As Remembrancer Clerk in the Scottish Court of Exchequer, he handed over funds he considered to be the lawful property of the Young Pretender. It was also claimed that Fidler raised a troop and joined the clans in the Forty-Five Rebellion.[1] As with so many, disillusionment came

1. Boog-Watson, Charles Brodie *Alexander Cowan of Moray House and Valleyfield – His Kinsfolk and Connections*. Perth: D Leslie (Watson & Annandale), 1915. 7.

quickly: defeat at Culloden brought the Jacobite fantasies of William Fidler and many others to a tragic end. When order was restored by the dull Hanoverians, William Fidler was attainted by an Act of Parliament. Summoned to Edinburgh Castle, he listened as the bill of attainder was read out, along with all the names of those found guilty of treason. The list was long and at the very end was his own. The first-named, the Earl of Kellie, is reported to have exclaimed, 'Oh! Is not this a wise government, to begin wi' a fule, and end wi' a fiddler?'

The fiddler named Fidler soon fled for refuge to the continent with his daughter Marjory and his new wife, her stepmother. The three settled in Dunkerque under an assumed name and survived, but in very straightened circumstances. Marjory was given a convent education and acquired a facility in French. When William Fidler died in 1760, his widow joined Marjory, who had already returned to Scotland. In desperate poverty, they made an appeal to the exiled Pretender. In response, Marjory's mother received a gracious note, expressing thanks for Fidler's services and enclosing thirty pounds, twice the annual salary of a day labourer or servant at the time.

Marjory had already set up a brisk trade in lace and tea among wealthy families, working out of a shop she rented in Leith, Edinburgh's port. 'My grandmother,' grandson Charles Cowan recalled over a hundred years later, 'was said to be a first-rate "man of business".'[2] Pictures of Marjory suggest a feisty, no-nonsense woman, good-looking, with a set to her jaw. You would not want to disagree with Marjory Fidler, as she always had the last word. Her robust personality was fortunately moderated by a strong sense of humour and an inability to take herself too seriously.

*****

Enter the second Charles, surname Cowan, who had arrived in Edinburgh two years before Marjory. This Charles came from the picturesque town of Crail on the Fife coast. He was the son of George Cowan and his wife, born Isabel Gow, both of whom were in service to Sir David Scot, a substantial local landowner. George had risen through the ranks from footman to factor (property manager).

2. *Reminiscences*. xxvii.

Isabel was a chambermaid. The Scots were substantial landowners in the East Neuk of Fife. Reminders of their presence, such as the late medieval Scotstarvit Tower two miles south of Cupar, the county seat at the geographic centre of Fife, occupied by them from 1612, remains to this day.

The Scots' manor house nearby, Thirdpart, where George and Isabel Cowan worked, has since been torn down. There the Scots family raised the Cowan children as their own and gave them educational opportunities beyond the ordinary reach of parents in their social position. Fifteen-year old Charles Cowan, their son, was ambitious, earning a salary of twelve pounds per quarter, as usher (administrative instructor) at the local grammar school. Four years later he left for Edinburgh to improve his prospects, leaving a generous donation for the poor to the local church.

Among the young people flocking to Edinburgh, it did not take Charles long to find Marjory Fidler. They were married on 27 January, 1757. It was a dynamic union, a match of complementary opposites: Charles, steady and calculating, determined to get ahead, the perfect foil to Marjory, the venturesome, mercurial, and canny entrepreneur. One story perfectly illustrates the nature of their relationship. A hard worker, Marjory was not above joining the servants as they gardened or did domestic chores. One day, true to form, she was in the vegetable patch with the hired help. She was holding a lapful of cabbages, which she had been picking for dinner, when her husband walked by with an unknown gentleman. Nothing fazed, Marjory curtsied, and said, 'Your servant, Mr Charles,' thus saving him any embarrassment over his wife doing domestic chores. Two hours later, she appeared in the parlour, decked out in silk and satin, her identity as the garden worker unrecognisable, as she sparkled among the guests.

The twenty-one-year-old groom and the twenty-two-year old bride set up housekeeping over the shop in the Tolbooth Wynd in Leith. During their first six years of marriage, Charles and Marjory buried four infants. Leith and Edinburgh, with their drains and open sewage, were unhealthy place to raise a family. The anxious parents developed the practice of sending their children out of the city to Crail, along the Fife coast, until they reached the age of five. There they were raised by a local woman, Betty Anderson, in a cottage overlooking a pond belonging to an ancient sea mill. The sea breezes and the bracing country air provided a healthy start in life and also allowed both father and mother to be involved in the business, but at a cost: 'In consequence,' as a grandson reflected years later on his father's growing-up years, 'there was too little intercourse, or even acquaintance, between parents and children.'[3]

Of the fourteen children of Charles and Marjory Cowan, only four daughters and two sons survived into adulthood. The older boy, Duncan, born in 1771, was later described as 'Honest Duncan the papermaker' in Sir Walter Scott's *The Fortunes of Nigel.* The other, Alexander, was born as the American War of Independence was commencing. On his seventieth birthday Alexander recalled to his New York business agent, 'I don't know whether you are aware that I was born on the day the battle of Bunker Hill was fought.'[4] As a Scottish subject who made much of his money in America, the American connection was very important. Alexander Cowan's life ended as John Brown attacked Harper's Ferry, his years thus spanning the birth, growth and division of the United States.

Alexander showed early promise. Sent away to Fife as an infant, as were his siblings, he eventually returned to Edinburgh, attended the Royal High School, and then matriculated at the University with a degree, first in chemistry in 1793, and then another in physics two years later. Gaining practical business experience as a clerk at Kinnear's Bank, he joined his father and his brother Duncan in the family business in 1795.

*****

As Alexander was growing up, that business expanded. Originally it dealt in imported wine and tea, capitalizing on Leith's location as a seaport. Soon Marjorie's business acumen proved invaluable as Charles started to branch out into paper sales. In 1779 Charles responded

3. *Reminiscences*, xxviii.

4. AC to A. O. Brodie NY 1 Feb 1845. National Archives of Scotland, GD311/2/43 Letter 360.

to an advertisement in the *Caledonian Mercury*: 'To be let or sold: An assignment to the Tack of the Paper Mill and dwelling-house at Pennycuick, 9 miles south from Edinburgh, lately possessed by Mr T. Boswell now deceased; with the garden, dove-cote, coach house, stables with stalls for ten horses, &c, and any quantity of ground inclosed, from 16 to 25 Scots acres; and the property of the whole Machinery of the Paper Mill, on which a considerable sum has been lately laid-out.'[5]

The mill went back to the beginning of the eighteenth century: high quality 'Penicuik Blue Paper' was among items used for trading in the ill-fated 1698 Darien expedition. The mill was subsequently bought by the King's Printer and then sold to Richard Watkins. Watkins was prosecuted for fraud in 1742 and stripped of his title as King's Stationer that same year. His nephew Adrian then took on the business, and it went through several owners before Charles Cowan bought it in 1779. For the next hundred and eighty-two years, the Cowan name would be linked with the town of Penicuik.

The year he bought the mill Charles Cowan was described for the first time in the *Edinburgh Directory* as a paper-maker and paper-stainer (i.e., wallpaper manufacturer), his location given as Kincaid's Lane. Fourteen years later the company was described as 'Charles Cowan and Son papermakers and tea dealer' and the address of the office given as the British Linen Court, Canongate. The location was significant: for many years after the family was based at Moray House where the British Linen Court had had its premises since 1752, conducting both banking and warehousing out of the building. For the next fifty-two years the Cowan family and business were headquartered in one of the historic sites of Edinburgh. Moray House gained its name when the daughter of the woman who built it married the fourth Earl of Moray. The link with the British Linen Bank proved mutually beneficial: the Cowans provided banknote paper for the British Linen Bank and depended on the Bank operation for capitalization.

In 1802 Charles Cowan turned over his business to his sons, and following his death three years later the company became 'Duncan and Alexander Cowan.' Duncan, as the older brother (by eight years)

5. Quoted in http://wc.rootsweb.ancestry.com/cgi-bin/igm.cgi?db=kosmoid&id=I3318&op=GET accessed 11 May 2011.

took on merchandising and sales out of 172 Canongate. Charles was responsible for the Penicuik operation, which now included Bank Mill, a former corn mill bought in 1802 that turned out high quality papers. Alexander maintained an Edinburgh office at 17 Princes Street that was the hub of the business for over a century.

*****

Alexander's choice of a wife maintained a family tradition of marrying cousins. In about 1748, Lucy Cowan, Charles' sister (and Alexander's aunt), had come back from London, where she had been at finishing school, with a husband, George Hall.[6] The family set George up as a wine merchant in Crail, and he prospered in that business. George and Lucy had two children: the older, a son George, like his father was a wine merchant.[7] George married Helen Nairne, a name which would surface later in the family genealogy. Their other child, a daughter named Elizabeth, married in 1771, John Chalmers, a merchant, burgh bailie, and provost in Anstruther, a town about five miles along the Fife coast west from Crail, Thomas Chalmers was the sixth of their fourteen children.[8]

On 20 May 1800, Alexander married Elizabeth Hall, the granddaughter of Lucy and George Hall. Names in the Cowan genealogy were often recycled: she had the same as her mother. Thus she would have been Alexander's first cousin german (that is, first cousin once removed). In his long and happy life (Alexander Cowan lived to be eighty-three) he had two happy marriages. Elizabeth and Alexander were married twenty-eight years. Eighteen months after her death he remarried, this time Helen Brodie, sister of Duncan Cowan's wife. They were married for a further twenty-eight.

*****

6. Lucy Cowan was born in 1728 and married George Hall 'before 1763'. She was the grandmother of Thomas Chalmers.

7. George married Helen Nairne in 1780. He later left Scotland to make his fortune in London. George is buried in Bath. It was his firstborn, Elizabeth, that was Alexander Cowan's first wife, married in 1800, and the mother of Charles Cowan.

8. John Chalmers (1740–1818) merchant in Anstruther and Elizabeth Hall (1750–1827).

'Mr Cowan was of the great race, a natural king of men,' the *Scotsman* stated after Alexander Cowan's death. 'He walked about with the leisurely, free, great air of an Old Testament patriarch, or shepherd king; and we miss from our streets his massive person in his surtout, and his constant umbrella held at his back, with his calm, searching eyes, looking out.'[9] His family was in awe of Alexander Cowan and paid tribute to him on his second twenty-fifth wedding anniversary.

'Though never seen upon a public platform, or in any place of concourse save the house of God, he was always ready to lend a helping hand to every worthy object. His voice was not heard in the streets, yet he went about continually doing good. In the view of those most near to him he seems – with reverence be it said – to deepen his Redeemer's footsteps; and though in all their retrospect of memory not one dark spot is to be seen, his death has thrown a life-long shadow on their path.'[10]

Alexander Cowan's deathbed advice summarized his way of life. 'Were we and all our fellow-mortals good and amiable, there would be no trials. *It is part of our stock in trade* as Christians to have friends with faults and failings, and our talents and powers are the means by which we can remove these defects or lessen them in some degree.'[11] When he died an editorial tribute in the *Scotsman* observed 'that for many years he spent quite as much in works of love and kindness as in all other expenses of a personal or family nature.' One example given was his generosity 'in establishing persons in business and in aiding the unfortunate'.[12]

This was the person who more than anyone shaped the character of his firstborn. For fifty-eight years, his son Charles Cowan – even when an MP and a successful businessman – stood in the shadow of his father. In his letters to his son, Alexander seemed anxious and proud, generous but also critical, loving but stern. Charles sometimes chafed at the closeness of their relationship in a family

9. 'The Late Mr Alexander Cowan,' *The Scotsman*, 4 June 1859. 2.

10. Untitled and without an author's name, memoir of the late Alexander Cowan, 'printed for private circulation' which, according to *The Scotsman*, appeared in 1859. 1-2.

11. 'The Late Mr Alexander Cowan,' *The Scotsman*, 4 June 1859. 2.

12. 'The Late Mr Alexander Cowan,' *The Scotsman*, 4 June 1859. 2.

business dominated by his father. But he knew that he owed much to his father's example, reputation, faith, generosity, and business skills.

When he published his *Reminiscences* twenty years after his father's death, Charles placed as the frontispiece of the book an inscribed photograph of a stern and unbending seventy-six-year-old Alexander Cowan. Dated 19 April 1851, the inscription below speaks volumes about the complex relationship between father and son with its mixture of parental pride, self-conscious affection, and perhaps even surprise. Charles had reached the peak of his career both as a paper-maker and parliamentarian. To be a judge at Prince Albert's great exposition was no small achievement. To be a Member of Parliament was an equally significant accomplishment. Alexander Cowan writes: 'We shall be with you in thought on Thursday both at the Chrystal [*sic*] Palace and before the Speaker. Your affectionate father, A Cowan.'[13]

'Alexander Cowan and Sons, Co. Ltd.' – as his company became known – was not just the trademark of a leading Scottish paper manufacturer. The 'Sons' knew that they had inherited from their father more than just a name. Alexander Cowan set a high standard of integrity, high ideals, generous stewardship, strong Christian faith, and sound business practice. Three of his sons survived to manhood and ran the family business as partners. John, born 1814, was more his mother's child, sensitive, warm, and dedicated to his family. James, born almost two years later, was mercurial, a maverick who tended to be both lovable and quick-tempered, and took years to mature. And then there was Charles, born in 1801 and thus almost of a different generation. Fifty-eight when his father died, senior partner until 1875. Charles held both family and company together. He will be the main concern of this biography, as he was the centrepiece of his large clan.

13. It appears opposite page xxviii in *Reminiscences.*

Chapter 2

Papermaker's Pedigree

'I was born,' Charles Cowan wrote with characteristic puckish humour, 'upon what I have always regarded as good authority – though I am not aware that there is a register of the fact in any record of kirk-session, on 7 June 1801, in 12 or 14 South Charlotte Street Edinburgh.'[1]

While the city was his birthplace, the first ten years of his life would be spent largely in Penicuik, eight-and-a-half miles south of Edinburgh in the Pentland hills. Indeed, throughout his life, the town of Penicuik played a significant role. Shortly after his death, in a book titled *The Annals of Penicuik*, the author described Charles, in extravagant prose, as 'one whose name was a household word in Penicuik parish, and whose stately presence was familiar to all within its borders.'[2] After 1779, with a brief interruption during the Napoleonic Wars when the mill was unable to operate, Penicuik was known as a company town. For six generations, the Cowan family dominated the community, and when the paper works were sold to the international conglomerate Reed Paper Group in 1965, it marked the end of an era. The mill, which was

1. *Reminiscences*, 1.

2. Wilson, John J. *Annals of Penicuik*. Edinburgh: T & A Constable, 1893. 207.

once the thriving hub of the community, has been demolished and replaced with a tasteful housing subdivision. Penicuik is now an Edinburgh dormitory town with regular buses into the city.

As with all Scottish towns at the start of the nineteenth century, Penicuik was dominated by two individuals: the schoolmaster and the parson. Neither, as Charles Cowan recalls, were impressive individuals. Schoolmaster Thomas Muir was apparently more successful at farming than in instruction. At harvest time, he would summon the older children to go and work on his acreage 'an occupation tending much to promote vigour of body and intelligence.' The schoolhouse was the parish church, the pews provided opportunities for unobserved play beneath them, and the lack of a floor allowed the pleasure of wiggling bare feet in the sandy soil. 'To me the remembrance is one of wild liberty and pleasure, and I hope I am daily thankful in ascribing it to the enlightened economy of the heritors, in the mode of providing cheap sitting for the congregation, with a playground for the bairns on the floor safe from intrusion or pursuit.'[3]

The incumbent at the historic St Mungo's Parish Church, in the centre of town, was pivotal in shaping Charles Cowan's ideas of what a clergyman should *not* be. In his *Reminiscences,* he gave only the man's initials, which provided him with the freedom to describe his conduct in unflattering terms: '[A] more careless man was never intrusted with the duties of the pastoral office. A more indolent man could scarcely be imagined, nor one more regardless of his personal appearance.'[4] Thomas Coulston was born in Dunfermline in 1763 and licensed by the Presbytery of Kirkcaldy on 5 May 1796.[5] He was presented to the congregation by the trustees on behalf of the local heritor and squire Sir George Clerk of Penicuik, Bart., and was ordained on 12th March 1799.[6] He died unmarried

3. *Reminiscences,* 9.

4. *Reminiscences,* 4.

5. Thomas Coulston (1763–1829)

6. Scott, Hew, Ed. *Fasti Ecclesiae Scoticanae* Volume 1 – Synod of Lothian and Tweedale. Edinburgh: Oliver and Boyd, 1915. 345. Thomas Coulston was ordained as assistant and successor to David Ritchie who demitted the charge in October 1799 after twenty months to become minister of St Andrew's Edinburgh and subsequently from

on 13 March 1829, not only without issue, but also without surviving family.

In Cowan's view, Coulston was marked by an overweening vanity and arrogance, describing himself as 'the star of the Dalkeith Presbytery'. At one service in 1824, much to Cowan's annoyance, Coulston singled out his new white great coat from the pulpit at a service of worship. In retaliation, the usually generous Charles pilloried him as both lazy and indolent. He recalled that he was late harvesting his glebe (the land allocated to clergy for farming) and used to spend his morning – inappropriately dressed – gossiping outside the manse with passers-by. But Charles' charitable instincts then prevailed for, he said, the man 'had a "mind diseased," and could not be fairly held responsible for his actions; if so, he was more entitled to pity than censure.'[7]

Coulston was a Moderate, a party that had dominated the Church of Scotland since the last quarter of the eighteenth century. The name is thought to have come from a statement by William III at the 1690 Scottish General Assembly as quoted by Macaulay: 'Moderation is what religion requires, neighbouring churches expect from you, and we recommend to you.'[8] However, Moderate influence was starting to wane during Coulston's incumbency in Penicuik[9] but not before its chilling effect was felt throughout the Church of Scotland.[10] The visceral reaction of Charles Cowan to Thomas Coulston – unusual for a man generally charitable and forgiving – was not merely personal.

1808 to 1836 Professor of Logic at the University of Edinburgh.

7. *Reminiscences*, 18.

8. Macaulay, T. B. *The history of England from the accession of James II.* (vol. 3) (Philadelphia: E H Butler, 1856) 542.

9. The 1805 appointment of John Leslie to the mathematics chair at Edinburgh University marked their first defeat. Moderates had nominated one of their own clergy for the position but were roundly defeated. Their final collapse came in 1833 with the last Moderate moderator of the General Assembly.

10. Cf Stewart J. Brown's 'Beliefs and Religions,' chapter 4 in *A History of Everyday Life in Scotland, 1800 to 1900* (Griffiths and Morton, Eds.) Edinburgh: Edinburgh University Press, 2010, 116-146. In providing a somewhat unsympathetic portrayal of Presbyterian and Reformed faith in Scotland, Brown surprisingly fails to put it in the context of, and in reaction to, the Moderate dominance in the Church of Scotland that existed until 1834. The Evangelical wing of the Church of Scotland was providing a warmly Biblical, pastoral, and Reformed alternative to both Moderatism and the hyper-Calvinist legalism which Brown describes.

As he wrote: 'The evil caused by the appointment of an unworthy man like this is, I am convinced, perpetuated for generations.'[11]

As a foil, Coulston was significant in Charles Cowan's religious development. His vibrant evangelical faith as a young man and his esteem of clergy who took their calling seriously, was, in part, direct reaction to his own parish minister. Coulston's behaviour also convinced him of the evil of heritors, not the congregation, having the final right of appointment to a pulpit, and this provided a powerful motivation for Charles to identify with the Free Church of Scotland in 1843. He had observed at first hand the devastating impact of a man who had been forced on an unwilling congregation, many of whom – referring to some of his own mill employees – had gone to alternatives on offer. The Burgher and Antiburgher congregations of Bridgend and Howtown profited from Coulston's inability to provide spiritual nourishment for his flock.[12] They flourished in the wake of his depredations.[13]

His incompetence had its ironies. Even the wife of the laird who nominated him to the living, Lady Clerk, once responded to his boast of having on file several hundred sermons with the brief repartee, 'Texts, you mean Mr. Coulston.'[14] Her comment indicated a general perception that his preaching was little more than a sham. Another story was told of how after a service a parishioner followed him into the manse to compliment him on the amount of work that must have been involved in the preparation of his sermon. 'Trouble Sir,' Coulston replied, thumping his desk, 'There lies the

---

11. *Reminiscences*, 8.

12. The Burgher and Antiburgher congregations were the result of a 1747split among those who had left the Church of Scotland as to whether they could take the oath required of holders of political office which stated their support of 'the religion presently professed in this kingdom.' They further divided into 'Licht' and 'Auld Licht' factions.

13. The North Parish Church of Scotland Penicuik is the former United Presbyterian congregation. The United Presbyterian denomination joined in 1900 with the Free Church (in Penicuik now the South Parish Church) to form the United Free Church of Scotland. In 1929 they then re-entered the Church of Scotland, which in Penicuik is now St Mungo's Parish Church in the centre of town.

14. *Reminiscences*, 5.

Bible, I haven't opened it for three months.'[15] In Charles Cowan's estimation, Coulston was the opposite of the Scottish ideal of the pious Reformed minister-scholar, spending mornings in his study preparing sermons of high intellectual and moral content and out among his people in the afternoons, visiting and catechizing.

*****

The first decade of the nineteenth century was a challenging time for all Scottish businessmen but particularly for paper manufacturers. The Napoleonic Wars had isolated the continent from trade with Britain, and the importation of rags, the major ingredient in paper in those days, declined precipitously. Then in 1810, the government expropriated the Valleyfield mill as well as the Cowan's home, also named Valleyfield, above the valley. The family had to leave Penicuik. Alexander (cannily, it later turned out) retained the water rights, ensuring that he would have free access to water without which the mill could not operate. When negotiations for the government takeover were completed, Alexander Cowan's immediate concern was for his now unemployed workmen. 'He hurriedly called his foreman to him,' Charles later recalled, 'told him to get his hat, and in the course of a four-mile walk, gave such instructions as enabled him to provide for *everyone*. His generalship, or faculty of commanding men judiciously, and keeping his people usefully employed, was quite remarkable.'[16]

The expropriation of the mill was necessitated by the need for the government to find a place at a distance from the continent for the thousands of prisoners who had been captured during the wars then raging. In 1803 some had been sent to Greenlaw (later Glencorse Barracks) but, as numbers grew, by 1811 more accommodation had to be found: first briefly in the Esk Mills half a mile upstream from Penicuik, then from March that year in the commandeered Valleyfield mill. In all, 9500 prisoners-of-war were quartered at Valleyfield, some mere children of nine or ten but others over sixty

15. Wilson, John J. *Annals of Penicuik*. Edinburgh: T & A Constable, 1893. 91.

16. *Reminiscences*, 458.

years of age. The Navy Board of Transport, which had responsibility for the camp, built two new houses – one for the prison chaplain and the other for the doctor. Valleyfield became a prison hospital, and the rag-sorting huts and paper stores served as dormitories with double tiers of hammocks suspended from cast iron columns.[17]

Of the prisoners secured at Penicuik (only a minority of whom were actually French) 309 died. Fifteen years after Waterloo and the repatriation of the survivors, Alexander Cowan commissioned a monument to those who died which is still standing. An inscription was composed by his second son Sandie: 'Certain inhabitants of this parish, desiring to remember that all men are brethren, caused this monument to be erected in the year 1830.' The 'certain inhabitants' was a fiction: Alexander had solicited five shillings from the local watchmaker for the monument to ensure that his generosity would remain anonymous. Throughout the time the government occupied Valleyfield, the Cowan family kept a wary eye on their former property and demonstrated Christian compassion for the prisoners.

Alexander Cowan left for Edinburgh, taking up residence for the next three years at 5 St John Street, next door to Moray House where his brother Duncan and mother were ensconced. In October 1811, he enrolled his oldest child in the Royal High School. Charles had qualified for either the third or the fourth class, but he chose the fourth in order to be out of school a year earlier. Thus a year or two younger than his classmates, he early learned to stick up for himself.[18] The Royal High School was a prestigious institution, the oldest high school in Britain, and the model in 1820 for the English High School in Boston, the first of its kind in the United States. When Charles Cowan attended, 'there were boys from Russia, Germany, Switzerland, the United States, Barbadoes, St. Vincent,

---

17. There are many sources for this information, particularly Wilson, John James *Annals of Penicuik*. Edinburgh T & A Constable, 1891. 121. See also the commemorative historical plaque next to the monument in Penicuik. Lodged with the Penicuik Historical Society.

18. Unlike Thomas Guthrie, the renowned Edinburgh preacher and founder of the ragged schools whose statue stands on Princes Street, Cowan passed as Edinburgh. Guthrie, only twelve when he came to Edinburgh to attend university in 1815, was mocked for his northern Brechin accent and had to defend himself against a tormentor in a bloody encounter in the schoolyard. (*The Autobiography of Thomas Guthrie*. London: Daldy, Isbister & Co.,1877. 40-41.)

Demerara, the East Indies, besides England and Ireland.'[19] Cowan would walk over from his home along Holyrood Road and the Cowgate to the school which was located on Infirmary St., a fifteen minute journey. In 1828 the school moved to Calton Hill where it remains an Edinburgh landmark, though today no longer used as an educational institution. The curriculum at the Royal High School was heavily weighted toward the classics, and Latin and Greek were both requirements. Cowan's first teacher was a Mr Gray, and for his two final years, he was fortunate to have the rector, James Pillans, who in 1820 began a forty-three-year career as Professor of Humanity and Laws at the University of Edinburgh.[20] The monitorial system, modelled after English public schools, had just been introduced, and Cowan's monitor was Walter Scott, son of the novelist, himself an alumnus.[21]

*****

Charles' more informal education was enhanced by frequent contacts with his father's first cousin Thomas Chalmers, who was becoming widely known. Chalmers was minister in Kilmany in Fife, in country familiar to the family. He visited the Cowans in Valleyfield as they were about to leave for Edinburgh in the summer of 1811, and Charles Cowan remembered that, as a ten-year-old, Chalmers taught (or, as he added modestly, 'perhaps only attempted to teach'[22]) 'various problems on an astronomical globe.' Astronomy was a particular interest of Chalmers: four years later, on his first arrival in Glasgow, he published six discourses on the relationship between theology

19. William C. A. Ross, *The Royal High School.* Edinburgh: Oliver and Boyd. 1934. 74.

20. James Pillans (1778-1864) best known as the inventor of the blackboard and coloured chalks.

21. Sir Walter Scott (1771–1832) was at the High School of Edinburgh 1779 to 1783 when he entered the University of Edinburgh. His son Walter was remembered 'as a tall, handsome officer, very frank and pleasant in manner, who used to appear wearing a uniform I thought very grand, with gold epaulets and clanking sword. Walter was a fine, good-natured young man, but wholly without literary tastes or any special mental advantages.' ('Sir Walter Scott's Children' *New York Times,* 14 June 1896, quoting F. M. K. Skene 'Some Episodes in a Long Life' *Blackwood's,* June 1896).

22. *Reminiscences,* 169.

and astronomy titled *Astronomical Discourses*. It helped establish his reputation as no Evangelical lightweight.

That theological identity did not come cheaply. Chalmers' theology had shifted dramatically. Through serious illness, a failed courtship, and the friendship of several Evangelical clergy friends, his preaching acquired a new urgency. The year 1811 was the watershed: the previous eight years he had preached moral reformation, but after his conversion, for his four remaining years in Kilmany, he was a different man in the pulpit. 'All the vehemence with which I urged the virtues and the proprieties of social life had [not] the weight of a feather on the moral habits of parishioners,' he reflected as he was about to leave Kilmany in 1815. 'It was not till the free offer of forgiveness through the blood of Christ was urged upon their acceptance ... that I ever heard of any of those subordinate reformations which I made aforetime ... the ultimate object of my earlier ministrations.'[23]

'Tom Chalmers is now here,' Alexander wrote on 3 June 1814 to his brother-in-law, John Hall, then trading in Lisbon, '& is very popular as a preacher, being attended by immense crowds. Your Mother [Alexander's mother-in-law] went to hear him yesterday & was much pleased.'[24] In June 1815 Charles and his mother (his brother James having been born just the month before) walked the five miles from Cupar to the Kilmany manse. Chalmers was already in Glasgow, having been called to the Tron Church, but they were greeted by his wife Grace Pratt, whom Chalmers had married three years earlier, and their infant daughter Anne.[25] Charles was fascinated

---

23. Chalmers, Thomas. 'The Duty of Diligence in the Christian Life,' *Sermons and Discourses*. New York: Robert Carter & Bros, 1877. Vol. 2, 205.

24. AC to John Hall, 3 June 1814, NAS, GD 311/2/37. 16.

25. Anne Chalmers (1813–1891) was the oldest of Thomas Chalmers' six daughters. In 1836 she married Rev William Hanna (1808-1882) then minister at East Kilbride, Lanark. He was Chalmers' biographer, and a frequent celebrant of various Cowan family events. On 18 August 1847, less than three months after Chalmers' death, Hanna officiated at the wedding at Valleyfield of Thomas Chalmers (Thomas Chalmers' nephew) to Cowan's oldest daughter Jean Menzies. Hanna was involved in Cowan charities such as the Edinburgh Association for Improving the Condition of the Poor. At the annual meeting on 6 April 1869 Charles Cowan was appointed to the Committee of Management and Dr Hanna was made treasurer. Anne and William Hanna had an interesting theological odyssey far from her father.. On 30 May 1882

by the gas retort and pipes that Chalmers had fixed up in the house with the confidence that 'gas was to be the light of the future.'

Cowan would be in thrall to Chalmers for the next thirty years, and there is evidence to suggest, in their correspondence now preserved in New College, Edinburgh, that Chalmers regarded him almost as the son he never had. Charles' next encounter was in London on 14 May 1817 while en route to Geneva where his father had sent him to study. Cowan records that 'before breakfast, I went and called for Dr. Chalmers; found him at breakfast, and just going to preach in Southwark.'[26] Chalmers had arrived the night before, having taken a month to travel in a relaxed manner from Glasgow. A few hours later, he would be speaking to peers of the realm, cabinet members, MPs, and a cross-section of London society, receiving their adulation. Though by this time a celebrity, yet he made time for the teenage son of a cousin, demonstrating once again his legendary and magnetic common touch. 'He was from the first,' one contemporary noted, 'a man of original genius, one of those men, whom nature has marked out as extraordinary by faculty and character, and likely to be extraordinary in their lives.'[27]

*****

In 1814 Charles Cowan went up to the University of Edinburgh. His Greek professor was George Dunbar,[28] whose lectures he described as 'grave, dry, and without interest.'[29] At the end of that academic year, the family moved out of Edinburgh, this time to Melville, where in

---

Charles Cowan was a chief mourner at his funeral conducted by Alexander Whyte.

26. CC. 'A Journal of Travel to and Residence at Geneva' transcribed by Charles Boog-Watson and deposited in the Edinburgh City Library. 16. In a 17 May 1817 letter to her husband Eliza says 'I am glad that you are to meet & have met Dr. & Mrs. Chalmers sometimes–there is nothing talked of here but him.' Buckoke. Ed. *The Cowan Letters*, 9.

27. Quoted by Sara Stevenson in *Facing The Light: The Photography of Hill & Adamson*. Edinburgh: National Portrait Gallery, 2002. 25.

28. George Dunbar (1774-1851), employed in youth as a gardener, assistant of Andrew Dalziel, the Professor of Greek at Edinburgh University. On Dalziel's death, 1806, Dunbar was appointed successor, and filled the chair until his death on 6 December, 1851 (*DNB*, vol. xvi. p. 153.)

29. *Reminiscences*, 20.

1808 his father, to continue his business, had acquired St Leonard's Mill, working it with Bank Mill. At this time Alexander also bought Low Mill in Penicuik established in 1749. For the next two years as Charles Cowan studied at the university he either made the trip into Edinburgh or stayed with family in the city.

It was on one of those occasions, when boarding with his uncle Duncan at Moray House that he had dinner with Walter Scott, the novelist. Scott was greatly indebted to Joseph Pitcairn, the guest of honour that evening and uncle of Duncan's wife Janet Brodie, for his help in editing the *Edinburgh Register*.[30] Scott delighted Charles by addressing him by name and describing a new block-making machine. Cowan recalled in old age that 'I shall always regard this condescension to a young boy with gratitude and admiration, and as highly honourable to one of the most gifted and noble-minded of our Scottish heroes.'[31]

Joseph Pitcairn was a colourful figure: though a Scot by birth, he had become a naturalized American while working for his uncle David McCormick in New York City shortly after the thirteen colonies gained independence. He returned to Europe, became an arms dealer for the United States in Paris, and was then appointed American consul in Hamburg during the War of 1812. He had married the colourful Pamela, Lady Edward Fitzgerald, in a brief fling of passion, and they had a child, though the marriage did not last. He was now en route back to the United States, where he went on to invest capital very profitably for Alexander.

Alexander (whose second wife would also be a niece of Pitcairn) had already written to Joseph, then in Hamburg, about his son's future:

'My eldest, Charles, whom you will recollect, will be 15 next summer, has already got as much Latin & Greek, as is sufficient for his prospects, & he also knows a little French & Mathematics; it is to the last, that I would wish his attention particularly directed, for two or three years, & I also wish to have him from home, for some

30. Because of the Napoleonic Wars Walter Scott had found it difficult to get information and Pitcairn's help, as an American consul, had proved invaluable in relaying information to him from Hamburg.

31. *Reminiscences*, 21.

time. Now it happens, that there is no place in Scotland, so far as I know, where mathematics are made the principal object, not in England except Cambridge, & some of the military schools, to both of which I have objections, on account of the expense, & for other reasons. France would do for Mathematics, but not for morals in my opinion. I therefore turn my eyes to Germany & am willing to think that a situation might be had there with some respectable Protestant Clergyman, where Charles might preserve the classical knowledge he has & also acquire a sufficient acquaintance with French & German & more mathematical science, than young men in this country generally obtain. It is unnecessary almost to say, that a situation where his morals would be carefully attended to would be a *sine qua non* – one thing more I wish to mention that as my views for him are moderate, I should wish that nothing in his situation, should tend to make him think too highly of himself, & that his entertainment should be in all respects plain, his time well filled up, & himself kept under proper subjection. I should be disposed to send Charles over any time within 18 months, that would be considered best – as I could if necessary keep him pretty fully occupied for that period at home.'[32]

The interest in mathematics was another influence from Thomas Chalmers. In 1805 Chalmers had allowed his name to go forward as mathematics professor at Edinburgh but lost the nomination. His fascination with numbers is well known: statistics often helped him make whatever case he was advancing. Thomas Malthus, for whom mathematics supported his theories about political economy and population growth, described Chalmers as his 'ablest and best ally'.[33] Mathematical processes suggested to Chalmers order and symmetry in the Creator's world, a powerful evidence for faith. One of Cowan's better academic experiences in 1815 and 1816 were the mathematics classes he attended under Walter Nichol 'from which I derived great pleasure and advantage',[34] describing Nichol as 'an admirable teacher and greatly beloved'.

32. 23 Nov 1815 AC to Joseph Pitcairn, Hamburgh (*sic*) NAS, GD 311/2/37, page 20-1.

33. Thomas Robert Malthus (1766–1834) whose *Essay on the Principle of Population* (1798) greatly influenced Thomas Chalmers.

34. *Reminiscences*, 28.

At the same time, Charles was participating fully in the family business. A series of letters from February 1816 which he wrote to his father, who was away on a business trip in London, bear testimony to the seriousness with which he took his tasks. He wrote that an employee at the mill had promised a hundred reams of London demy, an order which would have been impossible to meet 'if the fine winds had not come two nights back, which made a great change.'[35] The ice had broken up the previous Wednesday, damaging a wooden bridge, and young Charles had assumed responsibility for replacing it with iron pillars. Ten days later he cites an order from his uncle Duncan Cowan for '50 reams of Pot No 3 which we will perhaps send off next Tuesday.'[36] He went on: 'Owing to the great scarcity of Sorted Seconds, we must make some alteration in the 1, 2, or 3, or 4th Vats. However I shall defer till I see Uncle tomorrow evening.' He informed his father about the wellbeing of an employee, 'the boy Pollock,' off work for eight days threatened with Iliac Passion, an intestinal blockage. Each letter is signed 'Your dutiful Son.'

It was a happy home and a good marriage: Charles' mother sent a letter to his father, indicating theirs was a real love match: 'I received your delightful letter yesterday, my dearest Alexander, with the greatest pleasure. I cannot tell you how often I have read it, & how often I have wished I could be with you, from 10 to 12 in the evening, to help you to arrange for the following day – & to tell you how much I love you & with what delight we shall all welcome you again – you seem to propose coming by the middle of March – I scarcely expected you so soon & think there is no chance, by that time, that I shall have a little stranger to present to you.'[37] James Cowan actually arrived on 12 March 1816. It is not known if Alexander had returned from his business trip in time for the birth. 'I should have preferred that it were over before you come home,' she writes, 'partly to save you some anxiety & as it would be a quieter time.'

*****

35. CC to AC, 16 February 1816, lodged with the Penicuik Historical Society.
36. CC to AC, 27 February 1816, lodged with the Penicuik Historical Society.
37. Elizabeth Hall Cowan to AC, 27 February 1816.

In the end, Charles was sent not to Hamburg but to the post-secondary Auditoire of Geneva, in common with many middle-class British (and particularly Scottish) young people at the time. Geneva was regarded by anxious parents as a 'safe' place for a broadening educational experience. Alexander set off on 6 May 1817 with Charles, his tutor and friend of the family Daniel Ellis, and Cowan's school classmate John Stewart Wood. Alexander accompanied the travellers to Southampton and then, taking leave, the group crossed the Channel in a storm. Everyone was seasick, according to an earnest and rather juvenile account of the journey that Cowan wrote for his parents. They arrived in Paris on 24 May. 'The people here do not like the English at all,'[38] he observed. Two years after Waterloo what did the young man expect? He turned up at the Église de la Madeleine, on Sunday, 15 June, his first time in church since he and his companions had left Edinburgh. 'The sermon might be very good for what I know, but I understood little. The minister seemed quite toothless.' He later recalled the fortnight in Paris as 'the most miserable period of my life.'[39] Mr Ellis hired a *voiturier* (stage coach driver) to take them to Geneva in eight days, taking a challenging journey through the Jura mountain range.

There was 'general joy throughout the whole family' when his first letter was received. 'We thank God for your preservation upon mount Jura,' his father wrote on 30 June. '[W]e trust that the life he has saved will be spent usefully and honourably. I do not wish you to be neither profuse or niggardly in your expenses – the way to be rich & independent is to have no ideal wants – whatever you require you will receive, & while I wish you to want nothing that is necessary or that becomes your present situation, I wish you to remember that you are one of a large family, all of whom may one day require the same expense being incurred upon their account, which is now necessary for you.' He went on: 'I should like an account of a days employment now & then. I would recommend your rising early, & fixing upon a particular time, early morning, for writing your Diary,

38. CC. 'A Journal of Travel to and Residence at Geneva' transcribed by Charles Boog-Watson and deposited in the Edinburgh City Library. 31.

39. *Reminiscences*, 35.

& for your religious duties. And if 7 o'clock should be your hour you may have the pleasure of thinking that at that time your mother & sisters are similarly employed.'[40]

Unfortunately there were problems at the boarding house in Geneva. Madame favoured her son, their tutor, who five minutes into their lessons fell asleep and then snored loudly. Amid a general lack of cleanliness, the suppers were 'meagre', and the coffee watered down with four-fifths milk. Alexander passed on these complaints to Mr Ellis, adding that 'Charles meant to write to me upon the subject, which I am pleased to hear. I have no secrets from him, & hope he will have as few as possible from me.'[41] Ellis responded by finding another boarding house, this time with a *prédicateur*, a cleric Charles respected and who remained a lifelong friend.

On the same day he wrote to Charles' tutor, Alexander also communicated with his son: 'I hope & have little fear of you both getting your examinations creditably, you must still enter as *Étudiants* even if you are obligated to attend the whole courses of the particular department of philosophy. You will both be quite at home in the Mathematics & Natural Philosophy. You will have a busy winter, my dear Charles if you do your duty, but if you do, you will find it a very happy one, & I trust that we shall all have every reason to be satisfied, with your progress.'[42]

The anxious father went on to reflect on Charles' future study options. 'It will be time enough again at New Year,' Alexander continued, 'to decide whether you are to remain one or two years. I shall probably allow it to depend a great deal upon your own sense of what is right. You say you are to have 6 months vacation in October, you mean weeks I suppose.' Then the request: 'You may send us your journal, when you hear of an opportunity.' This comment would suggest that the astonishing daily chronicle of discipline and devotion the teenaged Charles Cowan left to his heirs in his diaries is somewhat compromised by the reality that as he wrote, he knew an anxious (and critical) father would later read the entire script.

---

40. AC to CC, 30 June 1817, NAS, GD 311/2/37. 32-33.
41. AC to Daniel Ellis, Geneva, 21 July 1817. NAS, GD 311/2/37. 33.
42. AC to CC, 21 July 1817. NAS, GD 311/2/37. 34.

The Alexander Cowan that emerges from the correspondence is a striking figure, though typical of many fathers of his era. He is anxious for his firstborn, not a little proud of his accomplishments and independence, but also determined that the new freedom his son had experienced would not be compromised by the libertinism of the age. As the son of Marjory Fidler he is remarkably straight-laced, almost to the point of prudishness, but also assured and confident in the values he is trying to communicate to Charles. Religion plays an important part, though the piety is very measured and full of common sense and practical wisdom.

After a trip in the Bernese Oberland – too late in the season for safe mountain climbing – they returned to the Auditoire of Geneva for the beginning of the academic year. Geneva offered an outstanding postsecondary educational experience: so well-regarded that twenty-five years earlier, America's third president Thomas Jefferson, then in Paris, had suggested moving the entire school to Virginia. Teachers at the university had an international reputation, among them, particularly significant for Charles, the professor of Mathematics Simon Antoine Jean L'Huillier. He was being challenged both intellectually but also linguistically: both his French and his mind were developing.

As his studies continued, so did counsel from Scotland. In October, Alexander complained that 'a recent letter showed some disrespect to your mother when you mentioned to her your complaint that her letters often gave you the same information twice or even thrice in the same letter. I am not sure dear Charles that we have educated you with sufficient attention in impressing on your mind sufficient respect for your parents, especially towards your Mother & I rather think that this is more attended to upon the Continent.' He adds: 'Let me also recommend to you to pay a little more attention to your writing, as you are to be in business it is of great importance.'[43]

The advice continued: 'Fill up your spare time in the way you mention, in the first place take what is necessary for your private Mathematics which I wish you to consider as your first object, & devote the rest of Dancing Constituency & your Flute as you find

43. AC to CC, 20 October 20, 1817. NAS, GD 311/2/37. 38.

agreeable. I would much recommend your adding Dancing to the list from which you would afterwards derive much comfort as well as pleasure. When upon this subject allow me also my dear Charles to recommend attention to your manner which has hitherto been rather neglected, by manner I mean what is generally understood by address, ease and a constant readiness to do what is agreeable to others, as well as an innate desire to oblige & what I would call a spirit of humanity to all others, & I may acknowledge you are now in pursuit of a disposition to sacrifice selfish feelings, all which perhaps mean nearly the same thing.'

He enunciated for his son his own Reformed view of calling as vocation: satisfying work that pursued more than the accumulation of money. 'I suppose you still feel disposed to be a papermaker. If you have any wish to give it up, you will have my consent to any pursuit that is honourable & useful. You will not certainly as a papermaker merely require all the knowledge you are now in pursuit of, but I wish that your every thought should not be devoted to the acquisition of wealth, but that you should also be a well educated & well bred gentleman, zealous in the pursuit of knowledge, & in making your servants & all about you happy. Now my idea of the way in which all this may be best attained is that you come home in May, that you occupy the next & the following summer working in the Mill here, & also in teaching your Brothers & Sisters a little mathematics.'[44]

So it was decided for Charles that a single year in Geneva was enough. Alexander had careful instructions for the route home: the paper mills at Annency and in Holland were not 'worth a papermakers notice.' 'I don't wish you to hurry yourself on the journey, but look about leisurely, & with profit if you can' and 'inquire as to whether young men could be placed in other parts of Switzerland where they would have the advantages, & good manners, good German, & good Education, particularly in the Mathematical department.'[45] On 20 April 1818, Charles set out with his tutor Ellis and his schoolmate Wood to return to Scotland, travelling through the Rhineland and going on to Belgium, seeing a brutal beheading in Brussels, and the

44. AC to CC, 20 October 20, 1817. NAS, GD 311/2/37. 38.

45. AC to CC, 4 March 1818. NAS, GD 311/2/37. 46-7.

battleground of Waterloo. In Rotterdam, he caught a schooner to Leith. He was soon home.

On his arrival from the Continent a new confidence was observable. He returned from his year on the Continent with a stronger sense of vocation and purpose informed by his Reformed faith. Acquiring a second language had broadened his outlook. He had developed an appetite for travel, which would stay with him throughout his life, an intellectual curiosity, an ability to be stimulated by fresh encounters and new experiences, courage to ask important questions about a world rapidly changing. At only seventeen, but with a seriousness enhanced by being the oldest of nine children (soon to be joined that summer by a tenth, Lucy), a large responsibility rested on his shoulders. Paternal expectations for the first-born were high. He had received an expensive education: now it was time to demonstrate his mettle. He was keen to learn the family trade, which had given his father a comfortable income but was not without risk.

With Napoleon Bonaparte safely in St Helena, the new Europe as defined by the French Revolution, and now ordered by the Congress of Vienna, was a place of opportunity and trade. The British looked beyond the Continent: global expansion, a second empire, was on the horizon. The United States, with whom the country was no longer at war, provided fresh scope for venture capitalists such as Alexander Cowan. The Regency was drawing to an end.[46] The air was alive with excitement and adventure for a young Scot.

46. Period from 1811, when George III was declared unfit to reign, to 1820 when he finally died. During that decade his son, later George IV, was Regent.

Chapter 3

Papermaking As Profession

'I have two sons, of whom I wish to make Paper makers, the one about fourteen years old, the other a year & a half older.' Alexander Cowan's anxious concern in March of 1816 initiated a three-year quest for the right educational and vocational experience for his two oldest boys. His inquiry was addressed to John Morgan, a stationer on Ludgate Hill in London. 'We still look to the south as the cradle of all that is good in the art – I am anxious to give them the benefit of any knowledge that can be acquired there & to fix them in some mill in Kent or its neighbourhood where good writing papers are made, & where a regular & well conducted business is carried on.'

Massive changes were occurring in the manufacture of paper and Scotland was in the vanguard of innovation in its production. The accelerating industrialisation of the country was initiated by family-owned businesses dependent on the entrepreneurial skills and the technical mastery of new science. Paper manufacturing became one of the most significant industries in Scotland and the Cowans played a major role in its expansion. Charles' next three years would be spent learning the trade and his father set out to provide him the best possible initiation. As Charles approached the year of his majority, the family and its fortunes were experiencing fresh challenges.

Shortly after Charles' twenty-first birthday, the Cowans resumed life at Penicuik.

'Some of the small mills,' Charles' father continued in his exploratory inquiry to John Morgan, 'would for my purpose be preferable to the more extensive ones. I would wish them to be constantly employed in the Mill & to be made as useful to their master as possible, but at the same time not to be worked beyond their strength. As to terms, I should not like the total expenses for each of them to exceed from £100 to £150 per annum – and I would propose that they should continue two or three years.'[1]

It took time for Morgan to find an appropriate apprenticeship. By April the following year, he had written back with a suggestion. 'I am very much obliged by your letter,' Alexander Cowan responded, '& I am happy to find that I shall likely find a situation for my Boys....' Then he drew back: 'From what you say, I think now, that I ought not to send them until they are almost 16, by which time they will be able to do a day's work well, & regularly, at a day stool and when they will be more useful to their master & more able to derive benefit to themselves.'[2] The day stool was the perch from which a paper-maker worker operated and the reference demonstrated their ability to do a man's work.

Significant changes were indeed occurring in the manufacture of paper. For centuries, paper had been prepared by hand through a labour-intensive process. But in 1799, a Frenchman, Nicholas Robert, invented a machine that allowed paper to be manufactured continuously, quickly, and with flexibility in its size. France was in political and economic turmoil after the Revolution and the Napoleonic takeover. So the invention was taken to London stationers Sealy and Henry Fourdrinnier, who agreed to finance it. Patent 2487 was registered in 1801. John Hall (no relation to Alexander's brother-in-law) set up the first Fourdrinnier machine at his mill in Dartford England the next year.

The first Scottish mill to use the new invention was licensed on 1 July 1807, one of eleven patents granted that day. It took a while to

1. AC to John Morgan, stationer, Ludgate Hill, London 12 March 1816, NAS GD 311/2/37. 26.

2. AC to John Morgan, 4 April 1817. NAS, GD 311/2/37. 28

catch on: when Alexander Cowan reopened Valleyfield Mill in 1821 he became one of the earliest to install a Fourdrinnier, and four years later, one was acquired at Melville. The capital outlay involved in setting up such a machine was extensive: the Fourdrinnier brothers paid out £60,000 for the first continuous paper maker, and they were soon forced to declare bankruptcy, never having profited financially from the invention. Times were indeed tough for the struggling paper industry. As Alexander wrote in 1816, 'The trade is so bad that we intend shutting down 3 or 4 bats for some time ... we have proposed to our Men a reduction of wages of 3/- p week to which I think they will agree but even that will do us little good.'[3]

However, papermaking soon became more profitable – thanks largely to the new invention, lower costs, and greater demand. The Fourdrinnier machine came just in time, not only to rescue the business but also to provide cheap paper, and this had tremendous societal implications, as it fed a growing thirst for knowledge. 'The late Mr Alexander Cowan,' the *Scotsman* noted in a 1868 article on the manufacture of paper in Scotland, 'was among the first in Britain to appreciate the value of the paper-making machine and to introduce it into the trade; and both he and his successors have shown a readiness to seek out and adopt whatever appliances or arrangements have promise of improving or facilitating the manufacture of paper.'[4] Charles and his brother George were sent on a reconnoitring excursion to England in September 1818, and at a mill in Tunbridge, Charles saw a Fourdrinnier machine for the first time.[5] Sixty years later, he would state categorically: 'I regard the paper-machine, in displacing an enormous amount of severe, costly, and tedious labour, as one of the most invaluable inventions of the present century, so prolific of wonderful achievements for lightening toil and expense, and increasing the comforts and happiness of society.'[6]

---

3. AC to John Hall, 'paper mould maker,' Dartford Kent 11 April 1816. NAS, GD 311/2/37. 27.

4. *Scotsman*, 5 October 1868. 6.

5. 'With which I was surprised and delighted.' *Reminiscences*, 66.

6. *Reminiscences*, 67.

'Charles returned home about a month ago, much improved we think, by having spent a year at Geneva,'[7] his father wrote to his brother-in-law John Hall, then a self-employed trader in Cadiz with some business connections with Alexander. With a grandiloquent flourish on the first page, on 7 June 1818 Charles started a 'Journal or Diary showing how much business is being done by Charles Cowan Esquire, Melville.' He set goals for himself: rising early and being at the mill at six for two hours of papermaking before breakfast – 20 reams a week was his target. After a half hour each for breakfast and his Bible reading (eight chapters a week), he returned to the mill at nine for a further two hours. At eleven, he bathed and dressed and then spent a further hour before dinner at one o'clock, doing French studies. In the afternoon, he focussed on drawing and botany with the goal of becoming familiar with twenty genera (which would make up a family of common species).

At the end of each week, he would evaluate himself and how far he had fallen short of these goals, counting up his hours of sleep (85 in all) and determining whether the week had been well spent. Elaborate mathematical charts, in columns, toted up the progress he was making over the months of 1818. July that year was particularly difficult: the first week was idle 'except for French and drawing,' the second 'only tolerable,' the third (with a day at Bank Mill) again 'only tolerable,' with the notation 'warm weather.' It certainly was a hot summer as his father wrote his cousin Charles Vertue,[8] a shipbroker in London, which 'burned up with heat, the thermometer was in the shade yesterday at 79, and for the last 3 or 4 weeks it has often been as high as 74 and oppressive both night and day.'[9] In mid-August Charles spent a fortnight in Dumfriesshire with his father's sister Marjory Bell and her two oldest children, George and Marion, who were a little older than Charles and already both married. 'Had the honour of laying hold and killing a fine salmon of about 8 lbs. Weight,' he recorded.

7. AC to John Hall, Cadiz, 26 June 1818. NAS, GD 311/2/37. 51.

8. Son of AC's sister Margaret (1765-1816) who died without issue.

9. AC to Charles Vertue, London, 13 June 1818. NAS, GD 311/2/37. 49.

And so the work went on, continuing right into December and Hogmanay morning,[10] which Charles spent stocktaking at the mill. Then, as 1819 approached, Charles attended a local dance with his parents. For the New Year, he signed a solemn covenant, attested to by his brother George and his father: 'Charles Cowan to execute in the course of ensuing year 1819: Make himself Master of Finishing of most branches of Papermaking tolerably, perfectly. Read Hume's H[istory] of England, Shakespeare, Milton's Paradise Lost and other English. Read close printed volumes in German. Improve in flute blowing. Maintain a French correspondence, read some good French.'

Alexander Cowan's sons took diary writing very seriously. Charles' younger brother George also kept one. Charles' diary was passed down through the Wilsons and ended up in the archives of the London School of Economics.[11] George's was handed on through his brother John and is still in their family. Comparisons between the two provide interesting insights into the differences between them. George's so-called 'report book' dates from 30 May to 27 November 1819.[12] Who was he reporting to – presumably his father, the ever-watchful Alexander? Each week has a page with two columns 'Proposed' and 'Performed'. It is very self-reproachful and has references to being 'Very idle for various reasons, bad ones.' One week was 'good except in Rising' as he had trouble getting up in the morning. Towards the end of that period, berating himself for procrastinating, he started to concentrate on his German in preparation for his departure to study on the continent. Perhaps some of his self-reproach may have been due to what turned out to be his precarious health, but there is little evidence of intellectual curiosity or the intense and introspective faith of his brother. In four years he was dead.

*****

10. Scottish New Years Eve celebration which took precedence over Christmas in Scotland.

11. Presented in 1944 by Gertrude Lenwood, Charlotte's youngest child. Her niece, Margaret, daughter of Oliver Wilson, married in 1933 to Nobel laureate James Meade, taught at at LSE.

12. George Cowan *Report book/Diary 30 May 1819–27 Nov 1819*, in the possession of Elizabeth and Jane Errington, Elie, Fifeshire, Scotland, and used by kind permission.

'Charles would have no objection to engage for two years,' his father wrote to John Morgan in October 1819 after the stationer proposed a position for Charles at the mill of one Samuel Lay,[13] '& he thinks he could have no difficulty to do a man's work at finishing after having a month's trial.... I shall be much obliged to you for your opinion of Mr. Lay both as a man and as a Papermaker, & as soon as I receive it, I think Charles may probably go up to London again, and fix for himself.'[14] By the end of November the arrangement with Samuel Lay had been made. Charles ('now just 17') was to go to Kent the next spring. 'I trust you will find him, an agreeable Inmate in your Family, & very anxious to make himself useful in the Mill.' In the meantime Charles was to spend time 'improving himself.'

On 27 April 1819 Charles Cowan set sail from Scotland to study papermaking for six months with Samuel and Martha Lay at St Mary Cray, now a part of the borough of Bromley in London, then thirteen miles out of the city. The Lays had located their mill by the Cray River, 'a beautiful stream of clear water' with 'a constant levee of splendid trout in the tail-race below the water wheel,' as Charles remembered it.[15] The previous summer, they had lost a twenty-eight-year-old daughter and a thirty-one-year-old son,[16] so Charles' presence in the home must have been particularly poignant and his help at the mill very timely. Not that Samuel Lay was at the mill very often: Cowan recalled that he came only three or four times, presumably remaining at his other mill in Sittingbourne, Kent, as he was avoiding the bailiff. 'I hope that you find Charles, a pleasant member of your family,' Alexander Cowan wrote, 'I am happy to hear that you think him attentive, & I have no doubt it will be his own

13. AC to Samuel Lay, St Mary Cray, Kent, 28 November 1818. NAS, GD 311/2/37. 57.

14. AC to John Morgan 20 October 1818. NAS, GD 311/2/37. 56.

15. *Reminiscences*, 71.

16. Inscription in the St Mary Cray Parish Churchyard: 'An altar. In the memory of Catharine Lay, daughter of Samuel and Martha Lay, late of Sittingbourne, Kent, died 18 June 1818 aged 28. Also Samuel Lay son of the above died 18.8.1818 aged 31.' No further details are known. http://www.kentarchaeology.org.uk/Research/Libr/MIs/MIsStMaryCray/MIsStMaryCray.htm. Accessed 13 August 2012.

fault, if he does not derive considerable advantage from being at St Mary Cray.'[17]

'Your father is much pleased with your industry,' his mother wrote in early July, '& we hope you are gaining much information about Papermaking, & habits of application which will stick to you thro life, & which are of immense consequence to a man of Business.'[18] More maternal advice followed: 'I have always neglected to mention, in one of your letters you say the Lays do nothing to amuse you, now my dear Chas. a young man like you should never *expect anyone* to amuse you but do all in your power to amuse, & be obliging to those around you. What makes me the more anxious to *inculcate* this now is that I fear your failings in this respect are partly my fault.' She worried about his devotional life: '[I]n your letter you spoke with too little respect of your Clergyman, whatever his sermons may be, you may reap some benefit from then. I hope you are attentive in going to Church, & in reading your Grandfather's Bible, which I sent you. I rather think you left your French Prayer book at Mr Vertues, if so get it from him, & read it regularly.'

The local incumbent was the Revd. William Townley.[19] Cowan's mother's comment about Charles' critical attitude towards his preaching may well indicate more than the customary disdain of the Scots for English homileticians. Townley, a Cambridge graduate, seems to have had some difficulty qualifying for ordination, and had only recently been instituted as vicar. He was described on his death in 1847 (he served the church for thirty-one years) as 'a great miser'. Similarities to Thomas Coulston, the Penicuik parish minister, must have resonated for Charles. We are left in the dark as to when he

17. AC to Samuel Lay, St Mary Cray, 11 July 1819. NAS, GD 311/2/37. 65.

18. CathC to AC, 6 July 1819. Letter in possession of Judith Alison MacLeod, author's spouse.

19. William Townley (1773–1847), probably from London, BA Trinity College Cambridge 1792. One of the 'ten year men' whose special qualifications for ordination were not obtained in the usual manner. Townley was ordained a deacon in 1810 by the Bishop of Salisbury (*Gentleman's Magazine*, vol 182. 662). His wife predeceased him but though he had children his property was escheated to the crown for want of an heir and only finally claimed by a distant relative. The description 'great miser' is in Usher, James. *History of the Lawrence-Townley and Chase-Townley estates in England*. 5 of 9 pp. Thanks to Debra Buchanan, Sydney, Australia, for this information.

experienced Christian conversion, though it is clear that at this time for a young man he had strong convictions, an earnest faith, and a disciplined devotional life. In common with Evangelicals of the period, he held the clergy up to a high standard. The vicar of St Mary Cray did not meet his criteria.

Charles' time at the mill was spent learning the trade. He followed the entire process through to the final production of paper: first watching the paper engines as the pulp was prepared, then making the paper at the vat into single sheets (at St Mary Cray there were only two vats), couching the paper on a frame – an activity that required the work of two men and a boy for half an hour. Manufacturing paper was a skill that required considerable training and experience, and the demand for skilled paper workers was great. Couching the paper was physically demanding, and men at fifty who had spent their adult lives working twelve-hour shifts, six days a week, in the paper mills were often aged beyond their years. The women who worked for a very modest wage preparing rags to be made into paper were even more stooped and crone-like. Their salaries often represented little more than voluntary slavery.

In July 1819 Alexander Cowan sent £95 to Samuel Lay but indicated that because of his own financial challenges, he was going to have to reduce his son's time at St Mary Cray, breaking his contract with him. This suited Charles, who was not happy with the boarding arrangements.[20] His father cited the present economic downturn in the printing business and resulting difficulty in meeting Lay's fees. Things were not going well in the business, he told Charles: he had 'shut down one mill at Melville,' only two were going at Low Mill,

20. In his *Reminiscences* Charles gets the date of his departure to London wrong ('The end of May' 67) actually 25 April 1819. He never refers to the Lays by name but calls the woman who kept house a 'sister' of the owner describing her as a 'staid, grave lady' (72) and that she was very limited; asking for instance 'Is Scotland a country?' Martha Lay, then around 60 judging from the ages of her children, comes across as an astute woman of business. In a 4 December 1819 letter to Buttenshaw at Hampton Mills in Sevenoaks Kent negotiating on behalf of son George AC refers to problems at St Mary Cray (NAS GD 311/2/37 82.) At this point in the *Reminiscences* the narrative moves from the chronologically ordered to the anecdotal. The letters all suggest that he was boarding with Samuel and Martha Lay and working in the mill, going into London Sundays to visit his aunt and uncle, Erskine and Charles Vertue.

and there was 'no prospect of things mending soon.'[21] So he wrote John Lay: 'As I have altered my mind with regard to my son George whom I intended to have sent to you in November but whom I now find it more convenient to keep at home, I should wish the agreement between us to be at an end for the present, when Charles leaves you at the end of the month.'[22]

'I am most anxious to hear from you,' Alexander then wrote to his son, 'what you determine to do during the winter, whatever that is I suppose it will not prevent you spending a week in London about the end of this month, to try whether you can sell any paper, and for this purpose I will send a fine sample ream.'[23] Alexander suggested that Charles call on the papermaker John Dickinson, being sure to inquire tactfully about his wife's health.[24] Dickinson had acquired two mills at Apsley, Hemel Hempstead, and was the inventor of two new paper-manufacturing processes, one a rival to the Fourdrinnier. The English and Scottish papermaking fraternity was a close one.

*****

The Valleyfield paper mill in Penicuik remained empty after the last prisoners of war were sent home in September 1814. It deteriorated rapidly through disuse, as the government seemed unable to decide what to do with the buildings. Each time Alexander would bid on the property, he brought the figure down until finally, in the autumn of 1817, he made a final offer of £2200 to 'His Majesty's Victually Office.'[25] A series of conditions between the Clerks as the local landed gentry, Alexander Cowan personally, and the company were negotiated over a two year period, conducted through the lawyer

21. AC to CC, 22 July 1819 GD, 311/2/37. 66-7.

22. AC to Samuel Lay, 11 October 1819, copied to CC. Original letter in possession of Judith Alison MacLeod, author's spouse. The copy is entered as NAS GD 311/2/37. 72.

23. AC to CC, 11 October 1819. Original letter in possession of Judith Alison MacLeod, author's spouse. The copy is entered as NAS GD 311/2/37. 72.

24. AC to CC, 22 October 1819. Original letter in possession of Judith Alison MacLeod, author's spouse.

25. AC to Charles Vertue, 11 October 1817 NAS, GD 311/2/37., 65.

Alexander Naismith.[26] The Cowans finally obtained a lease for twenty-one years dating from Whitsun 1821.

In the completed arrangement water rights were clearly specified. The lease document stated emphatically that 'Alexander Cowan has a right to them'. The Clerk family were to lease the buildings, grounds, the Valleyfield house and seven acres Scotch measure, as well as the water course, the ponds, and the reservoir, including the spring of water in the upper reservoirs. With water rights came responsibilities: nine conditions were imposed on Alexander himself, and the last one was 'not to permit any of the water to be diverted from the lead of the Bankmill except so much as may be required, to drive one Hogwheel for the Bankmill.' Six conditions were to be met by the company, the fourth of which was 'not to divert any of the water from the Mile head'. Water rights and responsibilities were at the heart of the negotiation: the future of the mill depended on their security and availability.

*****

On his return to Scotland in late 1819, Charles Cowan found himself, at the age of eighteen, in charge of the mill at Melville. His father had moved with the family to Moray House in Edinburgh when his brother Duncan had vacated the property. In addition to his negotiations about the Valleyfield mills, Alexander had been trying to secure a more permanent lease for the Melville Mill, citing the amount he had paid for improvements since 1814 (£2,210 17).[27] Dealing with his landlord there, Lord Melville, proved every bit as difficult as coming to an agreement with the government. He made an offer 'on behalf of him and his brother £300 for a lease of this mill & lands for fourteen years,' the answer to be in Alexander's hands by 1 May.[28] That offer was withdrawn by the end of 1818, but a year later, Alexander wrote Lord Melville that he was 'more agreeable to your Lordship that the lease of Melville Mill should still go on, and altho' I had made arrangement for giving it up, it is no material inconvenience to continue.'[29]

26. AC to Alexander Naismith 24 Nov 1819 NAS, GD 311/2/37. 80–81.

27. GD, 311/2/37. 53.

28. AC to Lord Melville, 17 January 1818. GD 31/2/37. 41.

29. AC to Lord Melville 20 Dec 1819. GD 31/2/37. 85.

In spite of this openness it appears that there was no resolution and the Cowans left the Melville operation. But the financial position there appears to have altered and negotiations resumed in 1821, as bankruptcy for the current owners seemed to be inevitable. 'I suppose that the Collector will not long delay taking steps for bringing the property at Melville to a sale,' Alexander wrote the financially stressed owner, 'and when that takes place I suppose the sale of the household furniture is also unavoidable. But if so I shall have much pleasure in becoming the purchaser, if your venerable Uncle and Aunt will continue in the house for another year or as long as may be agreeable to them. I feel sincerely for them, and would gladly do any thing in my power to soften their misfortune.'[30]

Alexander finally bought that mill at sale on 24 May 1822 and therefore was unable to advance Archibald Constable (who was a regular customer) a loan of £1000, needed by the impecunious and speculative publisher whose subsequent bankruptcy would bring both him and Sir Walter Scott to an early death.[31] The Cowans maintained the Melville Mill until 1840, but it was too small to be economically viable. The company concentrated its manufacturing at the three mills in Penicuik: Valleyfield, Bank and Low Mills. In the 1830s they acquired Kate's Mill in Slateford where James, Charles' brother would live after his marriage in 1842. Following the company's loss in a civil suit in 1867 (ch. 15), a mill in Musselburgh was purchased so that effluent from esparto grass, used in the manufacture of paper, could be sent immediately out to sea. Proximity to the North Sea also proved decisive in the locating of a rag-sorting operation in the port of Leith. Most rags were imported from the Baltic.

*****

30. AC to Alex Naismith Melville 11 May 1822. NAS, GD 311/2/41. 425.

31. AC to Archibald Constable. NAS, GD 311/2/41. 442. 'I have changed sides, and from being a lender, am now become a borrower. I have just paid for articles sold by the Excise at Melville about £1000 and it is out of my power to turn over the bills you allude to at the present moment. Had you given me a little more notice I would have attempted it, but all I can now do is to say, that in a month hence, I may be able to advance you £300 or £400 for a month or so. I now perceive I shall be in difficulties myself, owing to Melville Mill etc.' Son Thomas (1812-1881) married Alexander's daughter Lucy (1818–1901) in 1837.

Other changes were occurring in the family. On 30 November 1819 Marjory Cowan (née Fidler), died at the age of eighty-five. Two years previously, Swedish Prince John Rocherstadt of the Stuart line, had come to dine at Melville, and after the meal Alexander Cowan had taken him to his mother, who knelt before him in tears. To the end, she would ask 'if there was any hope of the Charlies coming back again.' She had lived in Regent House, part of Moray House, since her husband had died fourteen years earlier.

That final summer of her life, Thomas Chalmers came to visit, wishing to set his mind at rest that she was prepared to die. 'Dr Chalmers has spent a good deal of his time with your grandmother,' Charles' mother wrote to him in Kent on 23 June 1819, 'conversing and praying with her & went frequently to see poor John Pearson [Alexander's sister Charlotte married a Pearson] & prayed with him – he is a very worthy man & so zealous in his profession to do good, that it improves ones heart to see & hear him. He enquired for you affectionately & hopes you are improving your precious time.'[32] Chalmers, for all his growing fame, never lost the common touch and a deep pastoral conscience.

*****

Early in 1820, Alexander, full of plans, wrote once more to John Morgan, the London stationer, saying that he had recently gained a long-term lease on the mills at Valleyfield. Formerly, he explained, there had been six vats, and he wanted to fit them up again 'that they may not continue unproductive.' He then announced that he was going to England for a month or two to check out recent advances, particularly a process to facilitate copper-plate printing and transference of papers in 'a process similar to veneering in cabinet-maker's work.'

The family gathered that summer of 1820 for a holiday in Moffat, a spa town seventy-three kilometres (or forty-five miles) south-southwest of Edinburgh in Dumfrieshire that was known for its sulphur springs. Another vacationer who observed them at the time

32. ElizaC to CC, 23 June 1819. *The Cowan Letters*. 11.

commented that they were 'the happiest, best, and most intelligent people imaginable.' She was particularly struck by Alexander: 'a man possessed of much general information, derived from a more extensive library than one usually finds in the possession of a private individual: his wife shares mentally in the treasures of her husband's knowledge, though personally devoted to the care and education of eleven promising and well-trained children.'[33]

Valleyfield Mill came on stream for the business at the right time. In November 1821 a desperate plea from Archibald Constable the publisher to make their requirements a priority for the delivery of paper explained that 'we have a strong demand just now, & I wish you could delay sending the 50 reams to London for another week – the reason is this – we want about 100 reams of Post very much we cannot have it a day too soon, & wish you to send it as fast as you can make it to Ballantynes 20 or 30 reams will even do us good – we are short to complete the *Pirate*.'[34] Sir Walter Scott's latest novel *The Pirate* had been delayed. Sent to the printer the last half of October, the book was finally released on 22 December. The story was about John Gow, a buccaneer who had retreated to the Orkneys as a respectable 'Mr Smith' but was sent to the gallows after an unsuccessful raid in order to secure funds to marry his new true love. The novel was based on a true story, and the John Gow to which Scott refers was the maternal grandfather of the first Charles Cowan.

*****

Alexander's large family had on-going health concerns. Susanna, the last of his children by his first wife, was born in March 1820, only to live for twenty months. It would appear that Elizabeth Hall, Alexander's wife, was physically worn out by eleven pregnancies over a twenty-year period. Three sons (Charles, John, and James)

33. From *Letters of Mrs Grant of Luggan*, letter ccxxxiii, 26 July 1820. Found in Boog Watson *Appendix to Alexander Cowan*. 72.

34. Robert Caddel to Alexander Cowan, 29 November 1821. Walter Scott papers. E MS 791. 428. Www.british-fiction.cf.ac.uk/publishing/pira22-68. Accessed 22 November 2011.

and four daughters (Helen, Marjory, Elizabeth, and Lucy Anne) would fill out their allotted span. Another son Duncan was sickly from an early age, never married, and left a memorial (as we will see) in the Penicuik Free Church school. The two other sons, the gifted Alexander, nicknamed Sandie to avoid confusion, and George, became a major health concern in the early 1820s as each seemed to have inherited weak lungs, reminiscent of the deaths earlier of so many of their father's siblings.

The family was reunited that summer of 1821 after Sandie (Alexander), aged seventeen, and George, a year older, had returned home from studying German in Lunenburg. Sandie's health was a matter of concern. In late August that year, against family forebodings and to prove a point, Sandie walked sixty miles from Penicuik to Woodhouselees, Dumfriesshire, to visit the Bells, a family connection through his grandfather's sister Marjorie.[35] The ever-solicitous father wrote, 'Your legs appear to have done their duty to you and I think you appear to have done yours.' But then he warned: 'I beg you will not walk too much in one day.'[36] Alexander wrote to the healthy and robust Charles: 'You ought carefully to avoid great fatigue or great heat, if in consequence of anything of this kind you should ever be attacked with pain in your side or any other symptom of inflammation, immediate recourse to prompt medical advice & bleeding & blistering immediately had would very likely save your life.'[37]

Meanwhile, George was sent to London as an agent for the company. His father wrote just the week before Christmas 1822: 'I am not in any hurry [to sell some paper reams] as Melville Mills, in place of falling into my hands has fallen into the Court of Session, where it may probably remain [for] years.'[38] George was obviously homesick, as he wrote his two younger brothers, aged six and eight, 'They do not keep Hogmanay here, but they keep Christmas day,

35. Marjorie Bell (1769–1855) whose husband James (1758–1832) was a tenant in Woodhouselees. Their unmarried daughter Rebecca (1800–1861) ('very handsome') was a farmer and horse-breeder there.

36. AC to Sandie Cowan, 30 August 1822. *Letters*, 12.

37. AC to CC, 22 July 1819. NAS, GD 311/2/37. 66-7.

38. AC to George Cowan, 17 December 1822. NAS, GD311/2/40. 151-2.

they go to Church on Christmas Day.'[39] And just as he was prone to do with his son Charles, Alexander sent some stern, fatherly advice to George: 'As you have given up theorizing devote yourself to mechanics as you proposed doing some time ago. By so doing you may assist us and enable us by & by in the machine way to get a head of our English brethren.'[40]

George came home a few months later to die. His mother wrote to her niece in Liverpool on Christmas Day 1823, that her daughters 'are delighted with attending dear George in turn.... He is a very charming dear fellow fondly beloved by us all – everything in character & feeling, what we could wish – cheerful, free of pain. Oh Helen, what would we have him spared to us, but I try to submit to our Almighty God.'[41] On 21 April 1824 George Cowan died at the age of twenty-one. His mother never fully recovered from the crushing loss.

Alexander's reaction, as family deaths multiplied, was to become even more compassionate to the disadvantaged. In this concern, he was deeply influenced by his cousin Thomas Chalmers. Chalmers attempted to improve poor relief in Scotland by creating a new church in Glasgow that would rely on its members, not an impersonal agent, to care for its indigent members, thus encouraging self-respect and self-responsibility. The concern Chalmers and Cowan showed for the poor can be illustrated by the help they provided for Renton Schoof, the natural son of a man who been in India sixteen years and whose grandfather had been a Penicuik surgeon.

The correspondence between Alexander Cowan and Thomas Chalmers provides a window on their interdependent and practical concern for the poor. Renton Schoof had come back from India alone at the age of sixteen. His grandfather, the surgeon, in whose care he had been committed, had become mentally unstable. Alexander explained the situation to Chalmers in Glasgow: 'The old gentleman requested me some time ago, to endeavour, to obtain a situation for the youth, as a Millwright Apprentice. Glasgow is an excellent place

39. GC to brothers Duncan, John and James. December 1821. 12. *Letters*, 12.

40. AC to George Cowan, 18 January 1823. NAS, GD311/2/40, 223.

41. ElizaC to Helen McCorquodale, Liverpool, 25 December 1823. *Letters*, 12-13.

for the purpose & I have now to request that you will apply to one of your mechanical friends.'[42]

The correspondence continued throughout the autumn of 1821. 'I am much indebted to you for the information you sent me,' Alexander wrote Chalmers two months later. 'You mention that the wages are 3/6 per week for the first year going on progressively to 8/ or 9/ during the last two years. I presume therefore that besides providing him in clothes and tools, his friends must for three or four years at least pay his board in part and also any schooling fees, if he is allowed to attend any evening school.' Towards the end of 1821, Alexander wrote again: 'I got matters arranged ... with many thanks to you.'[43] The 'friends' and 'uncles' Cowan cites were probably Alexander himself, increasingly well known for anonymous charity. A note to Chalmers he sent with the boy, and dated 3 January 1822, enclosed two five pound notes. 'You may put these in the hands of the good man who is to receive some degree of inspection over him and when they are expended, I will apply again to his friends.'[44]

As Alexander and Elizabeth's firstborn approached his majority at twenty-one, the ever impulsive and mercurial Charles was demonstrating greater emotional resilience, an encouragement to his anxious parents. 'Charles is getting steady,' his mother wrote to his fifteen-year-old sister Elizabeth, 'and attentive to superintend all the different things at the Mill – I am often very much pleased to think of him having been made a Papermaker, & partner with your Father.'[45] Charles Cowan's apprenticeship was over. He had run the Melville Mill on his own and proved adequate to the task. A third generation of Cowans was set to continue the family's enterprise.

Alistair Thomson in his *The Paper Industry in Scotland* finds significance in its family nature. He cites the Cowans, along with the Collins of Kelvindale and the Davidsons of Mugiemoss, as families that provided stability in a rapidly expanding enterprise in the early

42. AC to TC, Glasgow, 4 September 1821. NAS, GD311/2/39 261.

43. AC to TC, Glasgow, 17 December 1821. NAS, GD311/2/39 310.

44. AC to TC, Glasgow, 25 December 1821 sent by post 3 January 1822. NAS, GD311/2/39 315.

45. ElizaC to Elizabeth Cowan, January 1825. *Letters*, 13.

nineteenth century.[46] Stability was something that did not come naturally to the young Charles Cowan. His youthful exuberance and high spirits had only begun to be tamed. Now, everyone agreed, it was time to settle down and establish a home and put down roots. The question was: who would he find to marry? His choice of a partner, for once outside the immediate family circle, would prove decisive for his restless personality and focus his interests as he continued the work of his father.

46. Thomson, A. G. *The Paper Industry in Scotland*. Edinburgh: Scottish Academic Press, 1974. 193.

Chapter 4

Lanark, Love and Losses

Three days after Christmas 1822, Charles Cowan's life took a dramatic turn. Robert Menzies, a former classmate from the Royal High School, invited him to spend a week at his parents' home, Lanark Manse. Robert's father, the redoubtable Rev. William Menzies, had been minister in Lanark, a mill town thirty miles south southwest of Edinburgh since 1793. His son was at the time tutor to two boys, Robert and Thomas Trotter, and was living at the Trotter family estate, the Adams mansion Bush House, three miles north of Penicuik. As young bachelors in a small town, Robert twenty-three years of age and Charles twenty-two, they became fast friends. Robert invited him to spend the holidays at his home in Lanark. 'On arriving at the Manse,' Charles later recalled, 'I was shown into the dining room, and a young lady soon entered, Miss Catharine Menzies, the second daughter of the minister of the parish. There was no one to introduce us, nor in fact was it necessary.'[1] In less than two years, they were married.

Rev. William Menzies came originally from Fife, which gave the families similar roots. His father had been a shipbuilder in Kinghorn,

1. *Reminiscences*, 93.

near the northern end of what is now the Forth Bridge, not far from Kirkcaldy. At the age of seventeen, William had been appointed to the Stamp Office in Edinburgh, 'acquiring habits of regularity,' his daughter and family chronicler Elizabeth Bailie Menzies later wrote, 'and attention to business, which proved most valuable to him in after life.' His theological training was largely non-academic, though when given a rigorous examination in theology, church history, and the original languages of the Bible by the Presbytery, he passed without difficulty.[2] He was inducted into the parish church of Lanark, St Nicholas', on 27 December 1793 and served until his death on 8 May 1848. Theologically, William Menzies was an evangelical. On his gravestone, against the wall of St Nicholas' Church, these words are inscribed: 'He preached the doctrine of the cross with an earnestness of a heart that felt their power.' Given his theological convictions, he had a strong sense of calling and personal responsibility to and for the community.

Lanark is best known today for the New Lanark mills two kilometres out of town. Now a major tourist attraction and a World Heritage site, the mills were constructed in 1786 by Glaswegian David Dale, a devout man who brought the poor from Glasgow and Edinburgh, as well as Gaelic-speaking Highlanders, to work there. In 1779 Robert Owen married Dale's daughter and, with other partners, bought him out. The site, with over 2000 residents, became a great egalitarian social experiment. It was Owen who coined the word 'socialism' in 1836. Karl Marx and the Communist Manifesto are often cited as heritors of the Owen legacy.

In 1816, inspired by Owen, the firm built a school originally called the 'Institute for the Foundation of Christian Character' at

2. Menzies, E. B. *The Lanark Manse Family*. 3. Her family memoir was written in 1854/5 and published, with notes by Thomas Reid of Lanark, by her great nephew William John Menzies (see footnote 10, chapter 4), in 1901. 105. 'Proceeded and in their presence, and appointed the said Mr Menzies an exegesis, 'An spiritus sanctus sit verus deus'; an Exercise and Addition, Rom. vii.13 – 'Was then that which is good made death unto me?' a lecture from I Cor. 1.13 from the beginning; and a popular Sermon from the 13th verse, same chapter; to answer the chronological questions on the sixth century; to read the 16th Psalm in Hebrew, and the Greek Testament. These trials were satisfactorily passed. Extract from the *Minutes of the Presbytery of Lanark*, 1 November, 1793, as quoted in footnote 1, Menzies, E. B. *The Lanark Manse Family*. 6.

New Lanark. For Owen, however, 'Christian' was a misnomer: his business partners were alarmed that he was becoming increasingly anti-religious. Misgivings were also expressed in the community about what was being taught – or more specifically, what was not being taught – in the New Lanark school. Because education was at the time a matter for ecclesiastical supervision, the regional Presbytery of Lanark inevitably became involved. William Menzies, as Presbytery clerk, was at the centre of the conflict.[3]

In the usual Owen narrative,[4] Menzies appears as an *éminence grise* who, according to one recent account, 'felt slighted by Owen's patronage of dissenting clergy,'[5] and took issue with his 1816 speech at the opening of the Institute for the Formation of Character, calling it treasonous. Owen had stated that 'men have hitherto been directed by their inventive faculties, and have almost entirely disregarded the only guide that can lead to true knowledge on any subject – experience.'[6] He continued, in words that must have appeared ominous to Menzies: 'I therefore determined to form arrangements preparatory to the introduction of truths, the knowledge of which should dissipate the errors and evils of all the existing political and religious systems.'

Menzies did not see that approach as particularly Christian, or supportive of the State Church as by law established. As Owen's theories, articulated in his *Science of Circumstances*, were applied to the New Lanark school, their implications for education became more

3. *Reminiscences*, 99.

4. This narrative had a shock of reality when Michael Fry took issue with a Scottish Parliament motion to place Owen's picture on Scottish banknotes exposing his racism (Michael Fry: 'History has been unduly kind to the founder of New Lanark' *Scotsman* 2 June 2010.) A recent description of Owen in Indiana states 'Robert Owen was not that progressive. While still at New Lanark, he disagreed with abolitionists. He insisted that slave owners were benevolent because it was obviously in their own self-interest.' (Pitzer; Donald *New Harmony Now and Then* Evansville, IN: Indiana University Press, 2012. 71).

5. Donnachie, Ian and Hewitt, George. *Historic New Lanark* Edinburgh: Edinburgh University Press, 1993. 133.

6. Owen, Robert. 'An Address to the Inhabitants of New Lanark, 1 January 1816' http://www.infed.org/archives/e-texts/owen_new_lanark.htm. Accessed 23 February 2013.

apparent and challenging. Rumours circulated about Owen's atheism and the lack of religious instruction in his schools, particularly the absence of daily instruction in the Shorter Catechism and the Bible, then a part of every Scottish primary school curriculum.

The 1822 General Assembly of the Church of Scotland asked the Presbytery of Lanark to make further inquiries. Menzies was one of three who were charged 'to visit and report upon the religious instruction given to the New Lanark children.' On 28 October 1822 they went to New Lanark and ascertained that catechetical instruction was allowed only on the Sabbath, and the Bible was read only two days a week. There was some confusion about Owen's instructions as he had departed hastily on a trip to London. While there, Owen – never a diplomat – was quoted as having expressed some unfavourable views about current training of the young in Scottish schools and about church interference.

A special meeting of Presbytery was called for 14 August 1823, by Menzies as Clerk, 'to consider the propriety of taking notice of the calumnious accusations brought against their characters and conduct by Robert Owen, Esq., at a meeting held in the City of London Tavern.' Menzies' report to Presbytery maintained, on the basis of the witness of a teacher, 'that the entire exclusion of the Scriptures from the schools of New Lanark was ardently wished and positively ordered by Mr Owen,' and that the only reason they had been reinstated was because of public pressure. At the meeting particular umbrage was taken at the letter by Owen's son recently published in the Edinburgh *Star*. As he was merely 'a stripling thoroughly initiated in the *Science of Circumstances*' it was dismissed as not meriting a response. An unfavourable contrast was drawn between Owen and his father-in-law, 'the late excellent Mr David Dale.' The Presbytery urged, successfully it would appear, the reinstatement of catechetical and Biblical instruction in Owen's schools.

In one account of that so-called 'emergency meeting' (the actual technical term used was *pro re nata,* literally a meeting specifically devoted to a single issue that has arisen) it is claimed that the Presbytery's reaction was 'without proof' which seems disingenuous considering all the investigatory trips, the report of at least one teacher, and the solicitation of evidence that Menzies had assembled.[7] It has been too easy to caricature Menzies as the dour enforcer of Presbyterian orthodoxy, who tried to stamp out Owen's enlightened and innovative educational and communitarian theories, many of which are today accepted as givens. A further Presbytery attempt in April 1824 to visit New Lanark – which was their legal responsibility – was rebuffed in an exchange of letters between Menzies and 'the Robert Owen & Co.' A final letter to Menzies dated 29 April 1824, this time signed by William Owen, Robert's son, closed the matter: 'I shall be sorry if the Presbytery of Lanark still persist in their determination to inspect the private schools of New Lanark, as I shall, in that case, be under the disagreeable necessity of a refusal, having received expressed orders to that effect.'[8]

Just before Charles' wedding there was an incident that illustrated the interconnectedness of his circle of family and friends. On 1 August 1824 Thomas Chalmers came to Lanark for an interdenominational Bible Society Sunday.[9] After breakfasting at the home of the local laird with William Menzies and two local dissenting ministers (so much for the canard that Menzies was not on good terms with them), they visited New Lanark where Owen briefed Chalmers on 'the coming great moral revolution'. The party had no time to attend a special music and dancing performance. They hurried on to high tea at the Lanark Manse and at six o'clock Chalmers addressed three thousand people.

Charles Cowan brought his father over to Lanark shortly before his wedding so Alexander could meet the Menzies family. One day during their visit father and son ventured out to New Lanark, met Robert Owen, and were shown the mill site. They were impressed by the schoolroom: 'the healthy and happy appearance of the young people, contrasting so strongly with the too frequently repelling aspect of ill-aired, ill-lighted, dirty dens under the appellation of

7. Donnachie, Ian and Hewitt, George. *Historic New Lanark* Edinburgh: Edinburgh University Press, 1993. 133.

8. See Menzies, E. B. *Lanark Manse Family* (Lanark: D. A. V. Thomson, 1901 50.

9. The account of the visit is to be found in Hanna, Wm. *Memoirs of the Life and Writings of Thomas Chalmers* Vol iii. (Edinburgh: A Fullarton and Co., 1853). 43.

parochial schools.' While in the classroom Alexander Cowan turned to Owen and remarked: 'Mr. Owen, I would like to live twenty years, just that I might see what is to be the upshot of all your plans.' 'Twenty years,' Owen replied. 'if you live two years more you will see my system in operation throughout the whole of Europe.'[10] Subsequently, according to a 1904 family account, 'Mr Owen's interest in communistic questions began to be diverted from New Lanark to other socialistic schemes, especially that of New Harmony on the Wabash River in the State of Ohio [*sic*], America.'[11] That narrative charitably omitted mention of another factor that may have led to his abrupt departure: the outbreak of typhoid at New Lanark which belied the claim that the community was uniquely 'hygienic'.

Charles Cowan had a further final encounter in 1832 with Owen over dinner in London. After the meal, he recalled, 'we were treated to a dissertation upon the duty and great advantages of Co-operation.'[12] The hour-long lecture by Owen was illustrated by a transparency of his model village lit with gas lamps as a small servant boy pointed out with a wand its various features. Cowan worried that the child was as close to the gas fire 'as a joint on the spit', and subjected to great heat. The boy did survive but was 'destitute of either *Cooperation or sympathy* in the fiery trial which he had to undergo.' Both Cowan's humour and his humanity also emerged intact from the incident.

*****

Cowan or Owen: the two approaches to ameliorating the social and economic consequences of the Industrial Revolution had both similarities and marked differences. At Penicuik and at New Lanark the Cowan and Owen mills sought to be examples of responsible industrialization, compassionate employee relations and good management skills. Both appeared paternalistic and without much employee participation in determining work conditions. Each tried to redress the harsh realities of child labour by providing schools on

10. *Reminiscences*, 97.
11. Menzies, E. B. *The Lanark Manse Family*. 51.
12. *Reminiscences*, 99.

the site of their factories. In New Lanark the classrooms became a centrepiece of the village. In Penicuik one of the buildings returned by the government in 1821 had already become a schoolhouse where children of Cowan employees could receive a rudimentary education and learn basic skills. The Cowans also provided a doctor for their staff and their families. As the century progressed more and more amenities were provided. Cowan employees were loyal, committed, and generally grateful for the family's personal interest in their welfare.

But there were differences. 'The Cowans appear to have believed in progress through market, rather than social mechanisms such as Owen's, as a way of promoting welfare,' one recent analysis by Peter Smail suggests.[13] These polarising ideologies have a very contemporary ring. The contrast between an authoritarian reliance on regulation and trust in a developing economy remains controversial. Later, after fifty years in business, Charles Cowan was still bullish about market momentum and looked back in retrospect on 'the wondrous advance in knowledge and discovery which has marked the course of the nineteenth century.' He cited James Watt and his tea-kettle, Rowland Hill with his penny postage, but particularly Adam Smith on the sands of Kirkcaldy writing his *Wealth of Nations*. Smith maintained that a so-called 'invisible hand' would protect society from the worst excesses of capitalism because it was in everyone's self-interest – investor, employer, entrepreneur, and labourer alike. Charles Cowan's confidence in free market forces, even if moderated by a strong commitment to Christian business ethics and societal justice, seems naive. Owen's theories appeared to his critics idealistic, unrealistic and authoritarian and likewise innocent. Charles Cowan and Robert Owen were early participants in an unresolved debate that has continued for a century and a half.

Ultimately it was in matters of faith that Robert Owen and Charles Cowan parted company. As a sceptic, Robert Owen had little use for organized religion. While full of praise for Owen's

---

13. See Smail, Peter. 'A Study of Economic and Social History in 19th Century Scotland: Comparison of the Philosophies of Cowan vs. Owen' *The Quarterly* No. 53 (January 2005) 1-5.

'thoroughly benevolent desire to promote the happiness of his numerous workpeople,' Charles Cowan reflected that he 'had no foundation on which he could rear a solid and permanent structure tending to bless society. He and his followers could not or would not believe that man was a fallen creature, or that the sorrow and misery in the lower world were the result and consequence of the primeval curse; they believe in the power of the fallen creature, by reason alone, to subdue all evil passions and advance the perfectness of the race.'[14]

*****

Catharine Menzies and Charles Cowan were married in the Lanark Manse on 19 October 1824. They took up residency in Melville. Charles' mother seemed pleased, writing to her daughter Elizabeth shortly after the wedding: 'We had a visit from Charles & Catharine, they seemed very happy with each other. I hope she will make him very happy. She seems a superior young Woman & already a favourite with us all.'[15]

Catharine brought to the marriage the example of a loving and caring Christian home life, which she exemplified in all their years together. 'She always spoke of her parents with great tenderness & veneration,' a daughter remarked, 'and in writing to one of her children in 1860 she says, "if there be any spark of good in me or in my guiding of you and the others it is all the work with God's blessing of my dear parents".'[16] Thomas Chalmers, when once consulted by a friend about ideal home economy, replied: 'You should see Mrs. Charles Cowan's house, it is a real example of what housekeeping should be.'[17] She had been brought up in a home where careful management and thrift were essential, and Alexander Cowan could be pleased that his son had certainly not married wealth. William Menzies at first

14. *Reminiscences*, 96.

15. Eliza to Bissie Cowan, Liverpool, January 1825. *Letters*, 13.

16. Untitled life of Catharine Menzies, mss written by Margaret Cowan, and in possession of Judith Alison MacLeod, page 1.

17. Boog-Watson, 'Charles Cowan, Esq., M.P.' in *Alexander Cowan of Moray House and Valleyfield*. Perth: D. Leslie, 1915. 6.

received a salary of £90 a year, and it never exceeded £190. On that, a descendant proudly stated, he raised a family of eleven 'in which the sons all entered the learned professions.'[18]

By marrying into the Menzies family Charles Cowan brought together two families: the Menzies-Cowan connection developed into a complex set of intermarriages, close friendships, and business and professional partnerships with many future consequences. Of William Menzies' eleven children, five had issue. His oldest, William, became minister at Keir in 1824, remaining there until his death in 1869. His fourth child Robert, Charles' initial contact with the Menzies, went on to become minister in Hoddam, Dumfrieshire, where he served for forty-three years. Hoddam was near Ecclefechan, home of Thomas Carlyle, who became a friend. Shortly after Robert's arrival there, with his usual insightful wit, Carlyle remarked: 'What a cub is Menzies! Wrapt so joyfully in his Hoddam stipend, in a coat of oily health, glad pepticity, potato-culture and limited self-sufficement: there let him rest, and bless Heaven.'[19] Allan Menzies, the sixth son and Charles Cowan's close friend, married his sister Helen. He was the first professor of conveyancing at the law school of the University of Edinburgh. It was his son, the lawyer and investor William John Menzies, who became an important member of Charles Cowan's inner circle, a favourite nephew and kindred spirit. The youngest daughter, Margaret, wed John Coldstream, a doctor, a founder of the Edinburgh Medical Missionary Society and its first secretary.

*****

In later years the family would brush over an early incident in the life of the just-married couple. Court records show it in an interesting light, and some discussion of it is essential for a rounded view of Charles Cowan. The records provide only the barest of details but they demonstrate the newlywed's exuberance, inexperience, and

18. Menzies, E. B. *The Lanark Manse Family*. 2.

19. Thomas Carlyle to John A. Carlyle, 2 October 1839; DOI: 10.1215/lt-18391002-TC-JAC-01; *Carlyle Letters, vol* 11: 196-200. http://carlyleletters.dukejournals.org/cgi/content/full/11/1/lt-18391002-TC-JAC-01

lack of wisdom. It had to do with two Lanark families: the Lambs and a Thomas Moffat. James Menzies, Catharine's younger brother, the seventh in the family, a sickly lad, had come home to work as a secretary to a Mr Lamb. It would appear that the Menzies and the Lambs were on friendly terms and when Catharine and Charles visited the family in Lanark they also called on 'the Misses Lambs in Lanark'. At some point Charles while at their home allegedly libelled one Thomas Moffat, an offence Catharine uttered twice more at the home of John Lamb, presumably the brother for whom her brother was working. The libel was that Moffat 'had failed in his circumstances and became Bankrupt'.[20]

The Lambs must have quoted the hapless couple to Thomas Moffat who in turn sued them for defamation. On 20 February 1827, a jury court awarded him £2000 in damages, a huge sum in those days. In an era of debtor's prisons, bankruptcy was a serious charge which could destroy a person's livelihood or reputation. In impoverished and gritty Lanark, the son of a prosperous paper manufacturer who had married the daughter of the local parson, was an easy target. Nothing further was said about this youthful indiscretion but the incident reveals their innocence at that juncture, and particularly Charles' volatility and volubility.

That punitive award could not have come at a worse time. A speculative frenzy had erupted in the stock market in 1825, followed by the collapse of several banks. Sir Walter Scott was caught in the middle of the crisis. The publishers Archibald Constable and Company, as we saw earlier, had been in shaky financial condition, along with the printer James Ballantyne. Not only were Scott's best-selling novels published by them, he had a strong financial interest in the companies. The Cowans had an emotional tie with Walter Scott, as did most Scots, but they were also bound by trade interests, supplying much of the paper for his popular novels.

In January 1826, Charles (who was made a partner in the business the year of his marriage) was sent to London as the family firm's representative just at the time that Archibald Constable & Co. was

20. Thomas Moffat vs. Catharine and Charles Cowan NAS (West Record House), CS311/875.

forced to declare bankruptcy, leaving an indebtedness of £250,000. The Cowan Co. did not do a great deal of business in London at the time, but owing to the interdependency of several firms in the paper and publishing business, they could also have been forced into insolvency. But James Bell, the husband of Alexander's sister Marjory, who was a director of the British Linen Co., rendered 'wise and generous help' and disaster was avoided. On 26 January 1826, creditors of Sir Walter Scott unanimously agreed to a private trust, and several weeks later it was announced that 'Mr [Alexander] Cowan, a good and able man, is chosen trustee in Constable's affairs, with full powers. In doing so, they not only chose prudently for their own interests, but gave confidence of justice and consideration to the bankruptcy, and smoothed the way for dealing with the complicated relations of the firm with that of James Ballantyne & Co.'[21]

Thomas Constable would later remember those days and what Alexander Cowan had meant to his father. 'His tender sympathy with my father, Archibald Constable, in the arrangements consequent on bankruptcy, to which his office as trustee made him a necessary witness, was brotherly; and I have been told by members of my family who were present on the occasion, that they never saw our father so deeply moved as when Mr. Cowan, on hearing that my elder brother and I, who had been sent to Germany for education, were to be at once recalled, insisted that my father should alter that decision and allow him to undertake the pecuniary responsibility therein involved, adding in his own simple, yet commanding way, "Let it be repaid by our children's children." The debt remains uncancelled, and the generous donor crowned the obligation ten years later by the gift of a daughter as my wife, so that their children's children owe each other naught but love.'[22] Archibald Constable, crushed by the experience, died in the arms of his sons on 27 July 1827. Thomas, then in his mid-teens, eventually reorganized the firm and took it to new heights. A decade later, in a real love match, he would marry Lucy Cowan. Lucy, nicknamed 'Puss', was Charles' youngest surviving full sibling and was a family favourite.

---

21. As quoted in Boog-Watson, C. B. *Alexander Cowan His Kinsfolk and Connections.* Perth: D. Leslie, 1915. 19.

22. Boog-Watson, Charles 'Charles Cowan, Esq., M.P.' in *Alexander Cowan of Moray House and Valleyfield.* Perth: D. Leslie, 1915. 15.

On 3 August 1827, Alexander Cowan co-signed 'Lord Newton's [promissory] Note' on behalf of Sir Walter Scott, assuming personal responsibility for some, if not all, of the writer's debts. At about the same time, Charles Cowan returned to London for a fortnight to offer Scott's manuscripts at sale as part of the bankrupt's assets, but they garnered only £317 at the bankruptcy auction by Hodgson of Fleet Street. Alexander was allowed to keep the manuscript of *The Heart of Midlothian* as an expression of the thanks of the creditors.[23]

While Charles was staying at St Paul's Coffee House in London, Catharine wrote to him about domestic life at Melville.[24] Their firstborn, Jean,[25] was two years old ('Jeanie is very well indeed, rosy and good-humoured but I think she misses your songs'), and Elizabeth had just been born the day before.[26] But Catharine seems to have been much more preoccupied with a drunken rat catcher who had spilled poison at the mill door, and as a result, two cocks, three hens, and a duck had died, and two sick hens had been fed castor oil. The previous day's birth passed with barely a mention.

*****

It was out of frustration with the ministrations of Thomas Coulston in the Penicuik Parish Church that Charles became actively involved in 1827 in the establishment of a *quoad sacra* parish in nearby Roslin. The *quoad sacra* parish did not have legal or civic functions, nor was it supported by teinds (the Scottish word for the tithes assessed for support of the clergy). The bans of marriage could not be read in a *quoad* sacra church. It had, as its name suggests, a purely spiritual function. As such it was a way for evangelicals to respond to the explosive growth of urban Scotland at the time, adding congregations that did not weaken

23. It was left to his son John and remained at Beeslack until his death when it passed on to a daughter. It is now in the National Library of Scotland.

24. CathC to CC, London, 5 April 1827. *Letters*, 14.

25. Jean (née Cowan) Chalmers (1825–1864), married Thomas Chalmers (the nephew) in 1847 and died at Charles Cowan's Edinburgh residence in 1864 leaving six children.

26. Elizabeth (née Cowan) Lundie (1827–1921) married Rev R H Lundie in 1854, a Liverpool Presbyterian minister and twice moderator of the Presbyterian Church of England.

the financial and political functions of existing parishes and therefore were not a threat to the establishment. Chalmers was in favour of *quoad sacra* churches across Scotland and Roslin was an ideal place for such an experiment, a place where there was an obvious need for a church.

'It was impossible for me to attend the services in the parish of Penicuik,' Cowan declared.[27] So for the final three years of Coulston's ministry he made the four mile trip to Roslin. Roslin was known as the seat of the Sinclairs who had maintained their Roman Catholic faith until the eighteenth century. The Sinclairs were buried in the family crypt in Rosslyn Chapel, a mediaeval architectural jewel. The Chapel, contrary to Dan Brown's *The Da Vinci Code*, was not built by the Knights Templar nor does it have a Star of David, but it had provided a place of worship for the village until the Reformation.[28]

Without a Church of Scotland in the community, Charles saw an opportunity for a congregation with which he could identify. He enlisted Thomas Chalmers to inaugurate the new *quoad sacra* church. Church extension had irresistible appeal to Chalmers so it was an easy sell.[29] Negotiations for Chalmers' visit to Roslin started in early 1827.[30] The organizing minister in Cockpen was to invite him to preach. By early summer the date was set: Thomas Chalmers was to come to Roslin on 5 August, according to Charles' brother Sandie. He added, '[W]e cannot expect a very long visit I fear, from your numerous avocations.'[31]

Charles sent a further letter three weeks later: 'Should you for any reason prefer any other later day, I shall feel obliged by your informing at your earliest conveniency. If I do not hear from you, we shall expect to have the pleasure of seeing you and if it will suit your other arrangements it will give Mrs. Cowan & myself much

27. *Reminiscences*, 282.

28. The Sinclairs re-established Rosslyn Chapel as an Episcopalian church in 1861. It is now a major tourist attraction.

29. Roslin was recognised as a *quoad sacra* church by the 1834 General Assembly of the Church of Scotland. It is now linked with Glencorse Parish Church and the minister lives in Roslin.

30. AC to TC, 14 February 1827 New College archives, CHA 4.71.17.

31. AC2 to TC, 16 June 1827.New College archives, CHA 4.71.24 16.

pleasure to see you in our house here.'[32] Chalmers did turn up at the service and after the all-too-short visit, Alexander wrote in regards to a possible further engagement at Roslin: 'We all regret your not being able to come to us at present. We are unwilling to tease you with invitations which you might be unable to accept. But remember your visits in your own time and manner always give us pleasure. I am going from home tomorrow with two of my daughters, and my son Alexander, on account of the health of the latter.'[33]

So the *quoad sacra* church at Roslin was established, and for the final three years of Coulston's ministry Charles and his family made the three-and-a-half mile trek from Melville (or just over four miles from Penicuik when they were there) by pony-cart to Roslin on Sundays. How many other Cowans joined them is not known.

*****

Chalmers could not give the church at Roslin much attention, as he was in the process of disentangling himself from the university politics and petty jealousies of St Andrew's that year. He had been invited by Lord Brougham to move to the new University of London, but Alexander Cowan did all that he could to make Edinburgh a more attractive option. On 24 October 1827, he wrote: 'I dare say you don't yet know whether you are to be our professor of Divinity or not. God bless you all. Your affectionate friend of yore, Alex[r] Cowan.'[34] The appointment was announced in early November and, as classes had already started, Chalmers had a year to settle in Edinburgh, the chief drawback being a completely inadequate salary.

The Cowans were eager to help, and Alexander pummelled him with suggestions for making the transition easier. 'I write you now to say that if Mrs Chalmers has no particular friend or one she would prefer, that she will be most welcome to my eldest daughter to assist her in her arrangements for passing the winter in Edinburgh and that

32. CC, then at Penicuik, to AC, 8 July 1827, New College archives CHA 4.71.26.

33. AC to TC, 19 August [1827] New College archives CHA 4.71.19.

34. AC to TC 24 October 1827 New College archives CHA 4.71.21.

for two or three weeks or longer if she can be of use.'[35] 'If you have not yet fixed on a house in Edinburgh I wish before you do, you would allow me to shew you one in St John Street. You perhaps remember one there in which I resided some years, and from the back ground of which I had a door into my brother [Duncan]'s garden. You are perhaps aware that I am never to occupy the Canongate house and Garden as my brother does not return to them, but on the contrary prefers a situation nearer the Sea.... But if Mrs Chalmers and all your regiment of Womankind chose to take up their residence in the Canongate with you, you would find abundant accommodation as the house is fully furnished and nobody in it except my oldest daughter and the boys who are attending the High School. Your affectionate coz, A Cowan.'[36] Thomas Chalmers settled into Edinburgh that summer and delivered his inaugural lecture on 10 November 1828, but there is no indication that he took up his cousin's offer.

*****

Sometimes Charles' travel led to unusual encounters that stimulated his ever curious mind. On a business trip en route to London, writing from Derby in May of 1829, Charles described to Catharine a journey he'd had with Thomas De Quincy.[37] De Quincy, a neighbour at nearby Lasswade, had secured his reputation in 1821 with the publication of *Confessions of an English Opium-Eater*. Taking a coach from Keswick to Kendal, 'I had for a companion for some time as I discovered from Kendal Mr. De Quincy whose dose of opium per day he assured me sometimes amounts to 700 drops. A most extraordinary scene occurred at Kendal.' He continued, describing an encounter with a drug-crazed De Quincy and a 'great tall Yorkshire man, a little in the Quaker cut,' who seemed a little worse for wear 'and who did not know the difference between opium and coffee'. Eventually, Charles managed to disentangle himself, but

35. AC to TC, undated [late 1827] New College archives CHA 4.71.23.

36. AC to TC, 13 May 1828 New College archives CHA 4.92.13.

37. CC to CathC and AC, 2 May 1829. Original letter in possession of Judith Alison MacLeod, author's spouse.

the incident was a reminder of the hazards of business travel by coach in that era.

*****

As the 1820s came to an end, the entire Cowan family was preoccupied with health concerns. Charles' mother was becoming increasingly feeble and was being cared for at Moray House (where she and Alexander had finally settled late in 1828) by his sisters Marjory[38] and Elisabeth.[39] She died on 21 March 1829.

A year later (on 15 August), Sandie was the one chosen to write to Chalmers: 'My father desires me to communicate to you his approaching marriage with Miss [Helen] Brodie – He is himself much occupied at present. The marriage will take place in eight or ten days, and is entered into with the satisfaction of all parties. The lady is well known to us all and is already one of the family and I trust that as his children are one by one leaving his roof, he is to have a repetition of the happiness he enjoyed with my dear Mother.'[40] Helen Brodie was indeed known to the family: her sister Janet was married to Alexander's older brother Duncan Cowan. The wedding took place 23 August 1830. She was to give fifty-five-year-old Alexander nine children, the first (Janet) the following June, with eight more over the next eight years,[41] adding to the eleven he already had.

38. Marjorie (née Cowan) Simpson (1808–1891), married Henry Simpson in 1833, and had ten children.

39. Elizabeth (née Cowan) Thompson (1810–1887), married Alexander Thompson in 1831. They had no children. Alexander was brother to Jane who married Alexander Cowan, w.s.

40. AC2 to TC, 15 August 1830, New College archives CHA 4.136.47. Some of Alexander's first family were not at all enthusiastic. 'The poor thing has been brooding over it ever since only telling of it to Johnnie and considering it a terrible thing for them. Pussie says she is always quite happy when Papa speaks with her about it–but John says he is very glad he is not to be at home this winter.' (Elizabeth to Alex Thompson, her future husband, 14 August 1830. *Letters*, 21.)

41. Janet (1831–1867) married Robert Boog Watson; George (1832–1885); Isabella (1833); Alexander Oswald (1834–1882); Jane Thompson (1836–1841); Mary Wood [McVean] (1837–1868); Josephine (1839); Susannah [MacKenzie] (1840–1861) Charlotte (1842–1872). Also listed in the geneology table on page 12.

Meanwhile, Sandie was causing a great deal of concern to the family. In many ways the most gifted of Alexander's children, he had shown early promise at Lasswade Parish school when the family was living at Melville. There he was privileged to have been a pupil of the popular poet William Tennant,[42] who mentored him in bardic and poetic lore. After his two years in Lunenburg, Germany, his tuberculosis was an increasing threat and in the Spring of 1825 he and his father went to the Low Countries for a two month recuperative tour. His poem 'The Rhine' was written that September and was published in *Blackwood's* the following February. Meanwhile he was articling with relatives James & Charles Nairne, W.S., and qualified that same year.

Sandie Cowan's verse was increasingly finding an audience; 'The First of May' appeared that June, again in *Blackwoods*. His literary interests were strengthened during the time in 1827 when he served as editor for Walter Scott's *Life of Napoleon*. The biography appeared in 1827, an impressive nine volumes written under great emotional pressure for Scott with the stress both of bankruptcy and the death of his wife. Sandie, as his editor and research assistant, helped in a project intended to restore Scott's fortunes. It was too late: Scott died the next year.

Sandie Cowan fell in love at that time and his frequent visits to the Lake District and his poetic reflections on the poet Robert Southey further honed his creative gifts. He was married on 1 September 1829 to Janet Annesley Thompson in Crossthwaite Parish Church, Keswick, Cumberland. They set off immediately for France, for the sake of his health – and hers, for it soon became evident that she had also contracted tuberculosis. Returning the following summer not improved, Sandie desperately wrote to Chalmers: 'The health of my wife makes a residence in Italy during the ensuing winter incumbent upon me. My purse is scarcely adequate to this necessity, and as I think I can do some good to

42. William Tennant (1784–1848) a native of Anstruther who came to Lasswade School in 1816, went on to Dollar Academy and was appointed professor of Oriental languages at St Andrew's in 1834. He wrote *Anst'er Fair* in 1812 which assured his reputation.

others by it, I mean to advertise for a pupil to accompany me.'[43] They went to join his three younger brothers in Bonn, but his wife, not yet twenty-one, died the following February 1831 and he succumbed that December.

It was a shattering blow to the family. Though they were accustomed to the spectre of death, the loss of Sandie was different from all the other losses they had experienced previously. Thomas Chalmers wrote that 'It gives me and my family sincere concern to hear of poor Alexander's death – an event which though long expected cannot fail greatly to affect and solemnize the minds of his relatives. May you and yours experience in this touching concern much of that comfort which He who can both inflict the wound, and who can find a sweetening and sanctifying balm into that cup of discipline Himself administered. He afflicts not willingly and though often dark and mysterious is His dealings with the children of men, there is wisdom in all His ways and friendship in all His visitations. Give our best regards and our warmest sympathies to all the members of your bereaved and mourning family and believe me, My dear Sir, Yours most truly, Thomas Chalmers.'[44]

For Charles, Sandie's death was a turning point. Though the second son, Sandie had always been the favoured one, combining considerable intellectual powers with excellent relational skills. He was naturally articulate, poised, steady, predictable and disciplined: qualities his older brother needed to develop. Trained as a lawyer his library, listed in his bequests, was substantial and weighty. Sandie Cowan was certainly the most literary and probably the most intellectual member of his family.

On Christmas Eve 1839 Alexander Cowan presented to Charles a beautifully bound copy of his brother Sandie's collected writings, his so-called 'remains'. Inscribed 'from his affectionate father' it was a reminder that eight years further on, the death of a favoured son was still an open wound. Sandie's demise represented a challenge to an older brother with different gifts to show that he was of a similar

43. AC to TC, 5 August 1830. New College archives CHA 4.136.46.

44. TC to AC, 22 December 1831. New College archives, CHA 3:14:14. In the New College Chalmers papers there is a bound volume of TC's condolence letters, which says much of his pastoral concern and wide circle of close friends.

mettle. First in the family business, then in ecclesiastical affairs, and finally in politics, Charles Cowan would ensure in the years ahead that he was every bit as much a credit to the family name as his dead brother. The first step towards success in business was the change in the excise duty on paper in 1836. It is to that we now turn.

Chapter 5

Exorcising Half an Excise

The dramatic financial improvement of the family's fortunes that came with the halving of the excise tax in 1836 has to be placed in the context of political events in Scotland and in the United Kingdom. In Europe the 1830s opened with revolts against despotism that were successful in Belgium and unsuccessful in Poland.

For Charles Cowan, and other paper manufacturers, the exorbitant tax on their product was a particular irritant. From the time of the Union of 1707 on, the levying of taxes, such as those on salt and malt, had angered the Scots. In his *Reminiscences* Charles Cowan quotes approvingly Samuel Johnson's definition of 'the excisemen' as 'wretches hired by men to levy a hateful tax'.[1] The seething anger of the middle class, most of them like the Cowans (and unlike Thomas Chalmers) identified with the Whigs, was becoming a major factor in political unrest in Scotland. But the rising Scottish middle class had no voice for change in London. Scottish paper manufacturers in particular were enraged but powerless.

Scotland had long seethed under the domination of a Tory hegemony, typified by the Tory Henry Dundas, described by irate Scots

1. *Reminiscences*, 127.

as King Harry the Ninth, 'The Uncrowned King of Scotland' or the 'Grand Manager of Scotland.' From 1774 for the next thirty-five years Dundas was MP for Midlothian. Under the patronage and friendship of the Prime Minister William Pitt the Younger he held various cabinet positions and successfully blocked the abolition of the slave trade in 1792. He maintained his grip on power through the generous use of patronage and his carefully cultivated network of cronies.[2]

The degree of control that Dundas exercised was a direct consequence of the unique electoral system that Scotland inherited from the Union of 1707. That constituency settlement meant that there were only 4,000 eligible voters in the entire Scottish electorate. When electoral reform was first mooted in 1831, ironically but predictably because they were so unrepresentative, it was the Scottish members of Parliament who were most opposed to electoral reform. The Welsh and English were evenly divided, the Irish by a small minority were in favour, but the Scottish MPs were obdurate. However, because of clamor, that was to change the next year: the first reading of the legislation titled Representation of the People (Scotland) Act 1832 (2 & 3 Wm. IV, c. 65), all but ignored by the rest of the Commons, went through in a single hour in a late night session.

This was in contrast to the extensive debate that occurred with the legislation for the other three countries of the realm. Changes to the electoral system in Scotland proved the most substantial though stability was the goal. The franchise was extended to £10 householders, growing the Scottish electorate to 65,000. The number of Scottish MPs increased by eight to fifty-three. A voting system was introduced, assuring a greater degree of individual choice without outside influence or coercion. In the burghs there were no longer meetings to choose a representative that had been easily manipulated. The total number of burghs increased from 15 to 23. Edinburgh and Glasgow were each allowed two members, a move with profound implications for Charles Cowan's future.

---

2. Dundas' friendship with John Graves Simcoe, Lt-Governor of Upper Canada (1791-6), means that Ontario today is reminded of his existence through the generous use of his name throughout the province.

Surprisingly stability was cited as the goal for these changes, particularly outside the burghs. In the rural areas both £10 owners, or holders of fifty-seven year leases in the same amount, were given the vote. 'Reform legislation,' one recent writer observes[3], 'was designed to strengthen the rule of an enlightened propertied oligarchy.' Cowan's local Member of Parliament, Sir George Clerk, who had served the Midlothian constituency for twenty-one years, saw the changes as strengthening his position within the new electorate. 'The Scotch Representation,' he is quoted as saying at the time, '[was] not likely to be led astray by popular influences as the members for the English counties, who were dependent for their seats upon the manufacturing interest. The body of Scotch Representations ... was most useful ... as a check upon the increasing democratic influence.'[4] By separating the rural constituencies from the influence of the urban burghs, Clerk and his ilk thought that there would be less future challenge to their political dominance of the countryside. How wrong that proved to be: Tory Sir George Clerk was voted out in the next election.[5]

On 7 June 1832, the third and final draft of the great Reform Act was approved by Parliament. The response in Scotland was ecstatic. Henry Cockburn to whom, as Solicitor General for Scotland at the time, much of the credit for its passage is due, wrote: 'it is impossible to exaggerate the ecstasy of Scotland, where to be sure it is like liberty given to slaves: we are to be brought out of the house of bondage, out of the land of Egypt.'[6] Subsequent events were to moderate that opinion, but at the time it was widespread.

The Reform Act received Royal Assent and the next day Charles Cowan presided over a tumultuous victory celebration in the *grande*

3. Devine, T. M. *The Scottish Nation 1700 – 2000* (London: Allen Lane, 1999) 275.

4. *Hansard* 7:549 as quoted by Dyer, Michael. *Men of Property and Intelligence: The Scottish Electoral System prior to 1884*. Aberdeen: Scottish Cultural Press, 1996. 24.

5. Clerk (1787-1867) was returned in 1835 but was defeated in 1837 by William Gibson-Craig. Clerk represented English constituencies from 1838 to 1852, when he left Parliament after 42 years.

6. Cockburn, Henry. *Journal of Henry Cockburn; being a continuation of the memorials of his time, 1831-1854* Vol 1. Edinburgh: Edmonston & Douglas, 1874. 5. Quoted by Dyer, Michael. *Men of Property and Intelligence: The Scottish Electoral System prior to 1884* (Aberdeen: Scottish Cultural Press, 1996) 23.

salle of the Valleyfield Mills. *The Scotsman*, a Whig newspaper, reported the event, noting that the 'Chairman ably alluded to the dangers of confiding the interest of reform to the avowed enemies of the measure and the necessity of returning a parliament favourable to Earl Grey and his Majesty's Ministers.'[7] A Whig electoral alliance was forged that evening: among the toasts there was one to Sir James Gibson-Craig who became MP for Midlothian five years later, when he defeated Sir George Clerk Bt.[8] In the 1847 election Gibson-Craig was again victor.

On 8 June 1882, the Midlothian Liberal Association gathered to mark the golden jubilee of the celebration in the same *grande salle*. Only two who had attended the original event were present fifty years later: Charles Cowan and Alexander Mitchell, Provost of Dalkeith. 'Both were engaged in the memorable contest which resulted in the passage of the Reform Bill,' Charles' brother John, chair of the Association's executive committee, noted. With the mention of 'their esteemed and distinguished friend, Mr. Charles Cowan,' there was applause.[9]

Cowan spoke to the assembled supporters with a recollection from 1832: 'A week or two after that banquet, [I] had the privilege of showing a woman of high rank and her daughters over the mills at Valleyfield. The ladies were intelligent and desirous of information, but the only remark their mother made – and which, he presumed, was the measure of her thanks – was, 'Well, what a deal of mischief paper has done in the world.' That gave one an idea of the conception some of the better class of that day had of the results of science and industry. That lady, if she could, would have prohibited the manufacture of paper altogether.'

*****

7. *Scotsman* , 4 August 1832. 2.

8. Sir William Gibson-Craig Bt (1797–1878) whose father James, first baronet, founded the prestigious Edinburgh law firm Gibson-Craig, Dalziel and Brodie. Unusual for his class, he was a Whig and served as Junior Lord of the Treasury in Lord John Russell's cabinet from 1846–52.

9. *Scotsman* 8 June 1882, 3.

It was a sense of outrage against a feeling of entitlement that fired the political ambition of Charles Cowan. His anger was originally ignited by the excise tax on 'home produced paper'. Tagged by its opponents as 'the tax on knowledge,' it had been the bane of paper manufacturers (and journalists and publishers) since 1711, when it had first been introduced. In his *Reminiscences*, Cowan describes his sense of powerlessness in the presence of collectors administering a completely arbitrary tax. These men were a sorry lot, castoffs from the aristocracy, 'butlers, coachmen, or footmen,' petty, unpredictable, and power-hungry. The labelling system, then required, gave them great scope. The trader or his surrogates were obliged to write the estimated weight on each ream or parcel based on numbers each quarter that could go into the five figures. The collector wrote his name and the date and then stamped the item, indicating the duty charged. A departure stamp was also required because forty-eight hours had to elapse before the item could be shipped, and this interval gave the inspector the opportunity to return, re-weigh, and haggle. The whole process provided endless scope for litigation, fines, and even confiscation and was very costly.[10]

In Parliament there were numerous calls for relief. In February of 1824, a Commission of Revenue Inquiry, originally set up to investigate trade with Ireland, was given broader powers,[11] allowing it to investigate customs duties. That November the Cowans made a submission.[12] 'We beg leave to inform you that we have been long in business as papermakers, and that it appears to us, that further means might be employed for preventing evasions of the duties of Excise upon Papers. In our opinion the label ought as formerly to be pasted over the knot of the string employed to tie up the ream. The

10. In his otherwise helpful chapter 3 'The Excise' in his *The Paper Industry in Scotland* Alistair Thomson appears to shrug off many of the concerns of the paper manufacturers as unjustified and makes a case for the government which seems somewhat unbalanced. The grievances of the industry were real and justified if one is to take the Cowan family correspondence and diaries as a source. (*The Paper Industry in Scotland*. Edinburgh: Scottish Academic Press, 1974. 62-83.)

11. *Hansard* HC Deb 25 February 1824 vol. 10 cc449-50.

12. 'To the Parliamentary Commission of Revenue Inquiry 4 Nov 1824' NAS, GD311/2/41. 310.

paper in the hands of Stationers, Printers, etc., as well as the carte or vessels bringing paper to towns ought to be frequently examined by the officers, and where any fraud is discovered, the penalties ought to be levied. It has long been our opinion that much benefit would result, if the attention of one or two intelligent Superior officers, well acquainted with the trade, were devoted exclusively to the survey of the Papermills.'[13] Civil servant bureaucrats and political hacks were continuing irritants to enterprising young men such as Cowan.

These frustrations with Excisemen continued to fire Cowan's sense of injustice and motivated his political activism. One case stands out and is worth examining in detail. On 30 March 1830, the Excise seized a large shipment of Cowan paper for some imagined infraction. Alexander prided himself on a peerless reputation for honesty. In high dudgeon and to defend his father (and the firm) from such patent injustice, Charles set off to London, seeking redress, and delivered in person a strongly worded appeal:

'... [W]e detailed to your Honour the particulars of this transaction; We offered to submit to you the evidence in our Books and our servants employed in our Manufacture which had you granted us an opportunity of producing we could have satisfactorily proved that the informality which has arisen was on our part wholly unintentional. It is extremely painful to have this business still remaining unresolved, that our Mr Charles Cowan at considerable personal inconvenience has come to London for the purpose of urging to completion. We therefore hope that your Honour will with as little delay as possible decide which course you mean to adopt.'[14]

Before leaving, Charles had prepared his case thoroughly. He wrote anxiously to the Chalmers family: 'I am very anxious to obtain

---

13. 'We beg leave to state to you that arrangements of the Port office at Edinburgh, with regard to this place do not appear to us to be so favourable as they might be. The mail from Edinburgh to Penicuik is dispatched at half past 6 AM but the bags are made up at 10 PM the preceding evening. In consequence of this when the London or Carlisle mails arrive at Edinburgh after ten o'clock, which has often happened, the Letters for Penicuik etc must remain upwards of a whole day in Edinburgh, and as the Glasgow mail arrives in Edinburgh after that hour, the letters thence are always delayed till the next day.' NAS, GD311/2/41. 310.

14. 'To the Honorable the Commissioners of His Majesty's Excise London 17 July 1833.' NAS, GD311/2/2.502.

a Certificate from Dr Chalmers as to what he knows of my Father's Character & how long he has known him, and mine, & if he wd express his confidence etc. in our integrity. Such a thing to lay before the Board would (I am told) from respectable friends have some weight. I am very reluctant to break in upon the Doctor, but it is a case of great importance to our happiness & character. I have no fear of the result tho' the delay & anxiety is very ill to hide.' He explained that he had spent the week at Fisherrow Harbour, Musselburgh, 'some of our vessels having arrived'.[15] Alexander, with brother-in-law and lawyer Allan Menzies in tow, broke the Sabbath to come out to Penicuik, 'to talk over Excise prosecution.'

On 2 May 1834, before embarking from Leith for London, Charles wrote to Chalmers again: 'I consider we have been exceedingly oppressed in the matter, a prosecution having been commenced against us in the Exchequer Courts, which has caused us great expense & most injurious delay. I stated to the Excise Board both in writing and verbally, my willingness, nay great desire, to produce every servant and every Book in our possession, & had no doubt of convincing them if they would institute a strict inquiry into the matter, that all our dealings in the matter referred to & everything else were honourable. I could get no answer either verbal or written except a written form from the Excise solicitor in Edinburgh six months after the alleged offence, that the matter was ordered into the Exchequer.' Chalmers offered to appeal to the good offices of an MP, Thomas Spring Rice.[16] Spring Rice was known to Chalmers – he had chaired a committee on poor relief which had summoned Chalmers as a witness.

Thus encouraged, on arrival in London Charles Cowan went directly to the House of Commons and met with Andrew Johnston,[17] MP for St Andrews burgh. The next week was a busy

15. *Diary*, 30 August 1833, Diary in the possession of Judith MacLeod, author's spouse.

16. Thomas Spring Rice (1790–1866), from 1839 First Baron Monteagle of Brandon. Monteagle was Chancellor of the Exchequer from 1835 to 1839, and Comptroller General from 1839 to 1865. He was MP for Limerick City (1820–1832) and from Cambridge (1832–1839).

17. Andrew Johnston (1798–1872), a Whig politician elected in 1831from the so-

one: Monday 12 May he was at the Excise office having 'the Paper weighed over'.[18] After meeting with family members and friends, they 'Had prayers etc. & [Charles] walked home to Camberwell' where he was staying. Tuesday he returned to Westminster and met with Henry Brooke Parnell, Whig MP for Dundee. He also had an appointment with 'Sir John D' – probably John Ponsonby, Viscount Duncannon,[19] the Commissioner of Works, soon promoted to Home Secretary. The case for the firm had been heard by several of the most influential Whig politicians of the day, and Charles was experiencing the rising power of the House of Commons. Cowan and Allan Menzies spent Wednesday at Somerset House with the Inland Revenue authorities 'with which [we] were very well pleased.' On Thursday he was at the Excise again to discuss problems with torn wrappers and setting terms for final adjudication the next day. Friday Charles wrote cryptically in his diary, indicating considerable progress, a triumphant 'Got 138 [reams] correct.' By Saturday morning, he had succeeded in getting 'all the Reams filled and left the place.' By the following Friday he was back home, his business completed and the company vindicated. But the root cause of all the injustice, the excise tax, had yet to be dealt with.

The matter did not rest there, however. The real problem, as Charles knew well, was not the irritation caused by the pettiness of the ways in which the Excise Tax was enforced, the basic issue was the tax itself. The following year, 25 October 1835, Charles spent a day preparing a plea for the reduction or elimination of the Excise at the request of Parnell. The response was a whole year in coming, but when the Enquiry released its finding, the Excise Duty was halved by government action. The Excise on first class paper was reduced from

---

called 'rotten borough' Anstruther Burgs eliminated by the Reform Act. The following year he was elected from St Andrews Burgs. He stood down at the 1837 election.

18. *Diary*, 12 May 1834. Diary in the possession of Judith MacLeod, author's spouse.

19. John Ponsonby, Viscount Duncannon, in 1844 the Fourth Earl of Bessborough (1781–1847) a scion of the Ponsonby family of Cumberland. He was first Commissioner of Works under Lord Melbourne at this time, served as Home Secretary from July to November 1834 and was subsequently (1835–1839) Lord Privy Seal. The Cowans appear to have had some Lake District connections and the Ponsonbys were a northern family with many Scottish connections.

3d. to 1½d. per pound. Charles recorded victoriously: 'A great charge of Paper today at Valleyfield first day of reduced Duty. Busy thereat and writing a great deal and at Stock etc.'[20]

The impact on papermaking in Scotland was dramatic: it was only seven years later that excise duties on paper exceeded the previous amount raised (in spite of the excise being halved), so great was the increase in paper manufacturing.[21] From the end of the Napoleonic Wars to the final withdrawal of the excise on paper in 1861, paper production in Scotland rose from five to fifty million pounds per annum. It was clear that the Cowan firm, as a leading paper manufacturer in the country, was riding a wave of economic expansion and prospering accordingly.

In his negotiations with Westminster over the excise, Charles Cowan had cut his political teeth. He was accused, during the election campaign of 1847, of being a political neophyte, a lightweight when it came to knowledge of the political process. In truth, he was anything but. His regular trips to London over the previous twenty-five years had equipped him well to navigate the halls of power. He was no stranger to the House of Commons and its ways.

*****

The journal that Charles Cowan kept during this period attests to an annual rhythm in his life. The year was punctuated by trips to London – generally one in the spring but also often (and increasingly) a second visit later in the year. Summers were devoted to family, with a house rented in the countryside. In 1833 they went fishing and shooting in the Trossachs. The following summer, while Thomas Chalmers holidayed with his wife and daughters at Valleyfield, they returned to ancestral roots along the Fife coast at Elie, and the next year was spent at Lundin nearby. Later his brother John would build a summer home in Elie, looking out across the Firth of Forth towards Leith and Edinburgh.

As the children grew, so did their numbers. In the custom at

20. *Diary*, 11 October 1836. Diary in the possession of Judith MacLeod, author's spouse.

21. Alistair Thomson *The Paper Industry in Scotland*. Edinburgh: Scottish Academic Press, 1974. 71.

the time, each of the females had two names, the males only one. Three girls and a boy had been born in the 1820s: Jean Menzies, born in 1825, was the first of the thirteen. She would marry Thomas Chalmers, named for his famous uncle. For the next twenty-one years Catharine continued to bear children with a daunting regularity. Like Charles' own mother the process was physically (and emotionally) exhausting, in spite of a large staff.

There were constant worries about the children's health. The second child was Elizabeth Hall (1827) robust and strong, with a definite religious bent. Then two arrived in quick succession: first Helen Hall (1828) who struggled with health issues and lived only to the age of seventeen. The following year, the first boy arrived, named Alex after his grandfather and uncle (though his name was shortened to 'Gander,' to avoid confusion). Gander was remarkable, as his mother would record in 1840: 'From his earliest time he was very engaging, at 6 months old he could when asked make his funny face, his manner was very docile but when excited his laugh was the merriest I ever heard.'[22] Another boy, named William, joined the family in 1831, but he lived for only eight months. All eyes were on Gander as the only male heir.

At the time of William's death, Catharine was expecting her sixth child. Born in 1832, Catharine was known as Kate to avoid confusion with her mother. Ten months later, Charlotte's birth on 11 August 1833 seemed almost incidental: '[A] little girl born early Sunday morning' is all her father could say of the event. Health of children was always an issue: the family, with its six survivors, almost lost Charlotte the following April.[23] Then death stalked the family and this time it took the only surviving male heir. For Charles, losing the boy who was his only son at the time was a particularly bitter blow.

On 13 February 1835 he set off on a business trip to Liverpool (where his cousin Lucia had settled following her 1803 marriage to Hugh McCorquodale) and then on to London. He later wrote of his departure: 'Bid all adieu about 12. All the children looking well except

22. Catharine Cowan, 'My dear girls,' 16 March 1840. Mss. notebook (33 pp) in possession of Judith MacLeod, author's spouse.

23. 'Very unwell in her Breast & Bowels & very uneasy about her. Gave up going to London in consequence on Saturday as I had intended.' *Diary*, 24 April 1834.

my beloved Boy who was coming in from a walk with his 2 younger sisters. Little thought I that should never see him again but in bed of Death.'[158] He arrived in London a week later worrying letters from home about Gander were awaiting him. Charles consulted London doctors about the descriptions he was receiving of Gander's symptoms, and as a result he was 'Very uneasy about my Boy'. A sermon at Camden Chapel about Christ's resignation in the presence of suffering brought some comfort. But the next day a letter came that 'exacted my worst apprehensions that I should not see my darling alive'. At eight that evening, his business completed and memos written, Charles caught the night coach out of London at the Bull and Mouth.[24] Letters followed him on the route north: between Darlington and Durham 'a letter was handed unto me which made me unspeakably happy that my Boy was considered better'. A further letter waiting for him at Berwick post office confirmed this word. But it was not to be so.

Two days later, Wednesday, the coach finally arrived in Edinburgh. As he alighted, Charles was met by his father and brother John, who immediately took him out to Penicuik. He was not allowed to see his son that night. The following day, he records: 'Up to Alexander's room about 12 but he did not know I was there. For more than a moment he pronounced "Papa" but wandered after something else. Friday he had hallucinations about a "Jew he had seen with a long beard"'. On Saturday, the end approached. The minister arrived for prayer, the doctor was attentive, but the child said little. Cowan recorded the last moment after his night vigil. 'Mostly in the Room till 5, when this much loved & only Boy resigned his spirit in peace.' He lay beside his afflicted wife, as Catharine kept to her bed all day. The family rallied in support, a funeral was held four days later, and Gander was laid in the Penicuik churchyard. The family gave all the support they could, and Charles' Christian faith, nurtured by his Calvinist confidence in divine providence, provided solace: 'Much reason for thankfulness in our support & comfort, & in the pleasing retrospect of the amiable and delightful character of this child now in glory.'[25]

---

24. The pub was taken down in 1831 and rebuilt as the Queens Hotel but the name continued in usage.

25. *Diary* entries, 13 Feb–22 March 1835.

Catharine, seven months pregnant with her next child, would always mark 16th March as a time to mourn Gander's passing. Sixteen years later, she said, 'I seem to feel Gander's death more than I used. This is I think feeling that all of you would have been the better of him as a friend and protector.'[26] It is a mistake to think that because the Victorians had so many children – in Catharine's case thirteen pregnancies – the death of one was quickly forgotten. It was Charles William, born ten weeks later, who was most affected by the death of his older brother. 'Charles' and 'William': the names freighted the child at birth with heavy expectations as the son of his father and a 'replacement' for a dead brother. Charles William's birth into a home in deep mourning seemed unnoteworthy: according to Charles' record, he only wrote in his diary that he had been out riding a new pony 'and on returning found the Boy was born about 8'.[27] Charles William, the first of Charles' sons to survive to manhood, entered the family business, was active in church and municipal concerns, but retired early to Dalhousie Castle, where he became known for his cultivation of daffodils.[28]

The final three children born to Catharine and Charles were Anna Thompson (born 27 December 1840), the sickly Margaret ('Maggie') Menzies, who nevertheless lived to the age of 82 (born 21 August 1842), and finally on 6 April 1846 John James, born in Torquay, where the family had started to winter in order to protect Catharine's health (and that year to protect the pregnancy). Because they were the youngest in a large family, several of whom had left the home before they were grown, Anna, Maggie and John James were

26. Margaret Menzies Cowan, 'Life of Catharine Menzies,' 38 pp untitled mss. in possession of Judith MacLeod, author's spouse.

27. *Diary*, 27 May 1835.

28. Charles William Cowan (1835–1920), received at the age of 19 a commission in the Edinburgh and Queens Light Infantry Militia, then occupying Edinburgh Castle during the Crimean War, It was a short assignment: twenty years later he joined a local regiment, the 2nd Midlothian and Peebles Rifle Volunteers. This fascination with military had a tragic consequence when three of his five grandsons, serving in the Royal Scots, died in the First World War. Charles William maintained an interest in Penicuik, serving for 32 years as Chief Magistrate and living in Valleyfield. He was also active in the Penicuik Free Church, ordained as elder in 1872 and representative elder at several General Assemblies.

regarded as a threesome, as their1863 life-size charcoal head-and-shoulders portrait by William Crawford suggests.[29]

*****

What kind of a man was Charles Cowan as he approached mid-life, both in his business connections, his intellectual and religious interests, and the friends to whom he was close? There are some fascinating insights culled from his diaries at the time.

As far as his commercial interests and business associations are concerned, we discover that Charles Cowan, naturally gregarious, had a wide range of associations and friendships centring in paper manufacturing. The company (and family) would always be identified with T. & A. Constable, described as the 'Prince of booksellers' by Sir Walter Scott, but there were other publishers for whom the firm provided paper stocks. William Collins, whom Thomas Chalmers had set up in business as a result of his split with the publisher John Smith in 1818, was one of these. There were also stationers with whom the firm dealt on a regular basis. In the autumn of 1833, while on a business trip to Glasgow, Charles Cowan recorded that he 'called for Orr, to whom sold a great deal.'[30] Andrew Orr, the same age as Charles, was busy growing his father Francis' stationery firm and shared many common business, religious, and philanthropic interests with Charles.

Alexander Cowan's papermaking business was prospering but there were always risks and dangers. On 27 October 1835, a winter gale pummelled the *Royal Victoria* steamer as she was sailing out of Leith for London. The boat came aground on Leith Bar. The crew threw overboard much of the cargo – mail coaches, two horses, and a large quantity of meat. Charles notes laconically, 'We had about

29. William Crawford ARSA (1795–1869) known for Scottish genre pictures bought by wealthy Americans such as. 'Highland Keeper's Daughter' (1866), 'Waiting for the Ferry,' 'Return from Maying,' and 'Too Late'.

30. *Diary*, 29 October 1833. Sir Andrew Orr (1801–1872) became Lord Provost of Glasgow in 1859. As Provost he was instrumental in bringing water to the city from Loch Katrine. He set apart Queen's Park in 1859 and was for 22 years chairman of the Glasgow and South-Western Railway Company. He maintained an interest in education and in the penitentiaries.

£260 of paper on board'[31] – a huge loss for the firm. By the spring of the next year, as the company recovered its losses from insurance and the Atlantic trade started up again, Charles remarked that he was 'Busy packing 32 Boxes & Bales today for Canada. Busy in Counting Room till past 9 making out Invoices.'[32]

*****

Charles Cowan's reading demonstrated a wide range of interests. Sunday afternoon was the time for religious literature. Biographies were a favourite: McCrie's *Life of John Knox*[33] appeared in 1811 but he only discovered it twenty-five years later. Thomas McCrie, a secessionist theological professor, used Knox to inspire Scotland with reminders of the sixteenth century and the Reformation. The book proved a powerful motivator for young men such as Cowan. Another inspirational biography he read was John Sargent's 1820 classic, *A Memoir of Rev Henry Martyn B.D.*, that had popularised the heroic missionary whose example helped birth the modern missionary movement.[34]

Other classics on Cowan's book list came from the seventeenth century and reflected an earlier piety that had gained new popularity as evangelicals sought their historic roots: Burnet's *History of the Reformation of the Church of England*,[35] written between 1679 and 1714, and Thomas Watson's *Body of Divinity*.[36] At a Bible Class for five or six young men that he taught on Sunday afternoon, Charles used Bishop Wilson's *Evidences of Christianity*.[37]

31. *Diary*, 20 February 1836.

32. *Diary*, 7 April.1836.

33. *Diary*, 25 November 1835.

34. Cf Stanley, Brian. 'Henry Martin and the Ardour Of Devotion' in Young, Richard Fox, Ed. *India and the Indianness of Christianity*. Grand Rapids, MI: Wm Eerdmans, 2009. 108-126.

35. *Diary*, 4 December 1836.

36. *Diary*, 26 April 1835.

37. *Diary*, 10 May 1835. The book, in two volumes, appeared in 1828 and 1830. Bishop Daniel Wilson (1778–1858) was the first (Anglican) metropolitan of India and Ceylon.

Charles also delved into speculative books, showing the range of his interests. He read the American psychiatrist Amariah Brigham's *Influence of Mental Cultivation on the Health* (which had been published in 1832).[38] The extraordinary autodidact geologist-cum-chemist, John Murray from Stranraer, had also piqued Charles' interest,[39] as he had read Murray's 1831 *The Truth of Revelation*, which attempted to prove the veracity of the Bible through archaeological and geological evidence. There is some light reading as well: Grace Kennedy's then popular 1825 novel, *Father Clement: A Roman Catholic Story*, a scatological anti-Catholic novel.[40] When it appeared in May 1833 he was quick to read Thomas Chalmers' demanding Bridgewater Treatises, *On the Power, Wisdom and Goodness of God as Manifested in the Adaptation of External Nature to the Moral and Intellectual Constitution of Man* – perhaps a gift from the author.[41]

His friendships at the time also show the breadth of his inquiring mind. James David Forbes, the seismologist and glaciologist, paid a visit to Valleyfield shortly after being appointed professor of Natural Philosophy at Edinburgh University in 1833.[42] Clergy visitors read like a Who's Who of the evangelical party in the Church of Scotland, often visiting Penicuik for the five-day annual communion season,[43] and finding hospitality at Valleyfield or at the Manse. The *quoad sacra* church in nearby Roslin also provided access to guest preachers.

Holidays and frequent business trips, particularly to London, meant worshipping at different churches and denominations, a broadening

---

38. *Diary*, 27 December 1835. Brigham (1798–1849) also published that year a second volume: *Influence of Religion upon the Health and Physical Welfare of Mankind*. He was against revivals which he thought contributed to mental instability and could cause insanity.

39. *Diary*, 10 January 1836. John Murray (1786?–1851) was an inventor, populariser of science and geology and a prolific writer. Much of his career was spent in Hull. He was disappointed in 1831 when he failed to win the chemistry chair at King's College London in spite of 100 recommendations from many eminent scientists of the day.

40. *Diary*, 29 January 1836.

41. *Diary*, 30 January 1833.

42. James David Forbes (1809–1868) taught at Edinburgh for 27 years until being appointed Principal at St Andrews in 1859.

43. Three days of preparation services Thursday, Friday, Saturday, the sacrament on Sunday, and a service of Thanksgiving on Monday.

experience keeping him abreast of the wider ecclesiastical scene. The Victorian pulpit was a significant contributor to the national dialogue and Cowan was an eager participant and learner. Sermons were not only heard but also were read: on a bitter wintry night on 18 January 1835, while visiting his in-laws in Lanark, he stayed home and read the latest offering in *The Scottish Pulpit*. The editor, John Mitchell, though a secessionist, printed sermons from across the contemporary Scottish denominational divides, providing a kind of evangelical ecumenicity.[44]

Nineteenth century sermons are increasingly being seen, to quote one recent analysis, as 'responses to moral, social, and political concerns generated by rapid industrialization, urbanization, rising secularism, and the perceived decline of Protestantism over the century.'[45] As such, preaching 'indicated a theological remit infused with transformational aspirations and a much freer discussion of social, cultural and political concerns.'[46]

Each service Charles Cowan attended when away from home was meticulously described in his diary with an impression (not always positive) about the sermonizer, the text chosen, and the response expected. That careful recording of sermons reflected the importance he attached to them. As he travelled widely in Scotland, and also in London and beyond, he was motivated, encouraged, and challenged by preachers he heard but also critical of those who failed to provide him with either an intellectual or a moral challenge.

During a holiday in Elie Charles Cowan was introduced to George Milligan, the patriarch of a dynasty of Scottish clergy, whose preaching he particularly enjoyed. One Sunday (8 June 1834) he heard him preach twice, noting the texts (Matthew 10:16, disciples of Jesus as sheep among wolves, and John 14:1, Jesus leaving peace for his followers) with satisfaction. Generally Cowan preferred practical and devotional themes, and did not appreciate

44. John Mitchell (1768–1844), minister of the United Secession Church from 1793 to his death and from 1825 to 1842 he was Professor of Biblical Literature at his denomination's theological academy.

45. J. N. Ian Dickson. *Studies in Evangelical History and Thought: Beyond Religious Discourse* Carlisle: Milton Keynes 2007. 243.

46. J. N. Ian Dickson *Studies in Evangelical History and Thought: Beyond Religious Discourse* Carlisle: Milton Keynes 2007. 242.

speculation. That evening he went on to the nearby Ferry Chapel for a third sermon on Ecclesiastes 8:11 (the perceived delay of God's judgment being an encouragement to do evil) by a less experienced preacher. His caustic comment: 'Long rambling discourse but one that pleased the people.'

Charles Cowan did not limit himself denominationally to Presbyterian and Reformed churches. On an 1846 trip south he visited the Maidstone Baptist congregation where he heard Eustace Carey,[47] nephew of William, returned from India because of ill health and then deputising for the Baptist Missionary Society, speak twice in aid of Baptist missions. Eustace's biography of his famous uncle, published 1836, had already become a missionary classic on both sides of the Atlantic. Carey's two sermons Cowan found 'very good' and 'very interesting'. Particularly telling for him was the evening message on Psalm 72 and the extension of the Kingdom of Christ.[48] Perhaps Cowan's lifelong interest in missions (see ch. 23) was stimulated, if not begun, by this encounter.

While in London on business he usually made a point of attending the National Scottish (or Scotch) Church. The church had recently erected on the southwest corner of Regent Square an imposing edifice, modelled after York Minster, to accommodate the crowds who came to hear the minister, the flamboyant Edward Irving, described as 'the first charismatic'. In 1832 Irving was expelled from the Church of Scotland for heresy and took with him seven hundred of his parishioners. The following year, at a midweek service on 10 July, Cowan attended the church as Chalmers gave 'a fine essay on [the] value and necessity of religious establishment'.[49] Irving had been Chalmers' assistant at St. John's Glasgow and theirs had been a close friendship. But Chalmers was strangely absent as Irving's case was heard the year before by the General Assembly. His so-called essay at the Scotch Church, so soon after Irving's expulsion, was significant in its argument that the establishment was a necessary

47. Eustace Carey (1791–1855) went out of India under the (English) Baptist Missionary Society and remained there ten years. http://www.edintone.com/blog/biography/baptists/eustace-carey/. Accessed 23 March 2012.

48. *Diary*, 22 Feb 1846. Edinburgh Central Library.

49. *Diary*, 6 July 1833.

safeguard against extremism and heresy. Ten years later it would come back to haunt him.

Irving's successor, the hapless Peter MacMorland, tried to pick up the pieces of the shattered congregation. On 2 August 1835 Charles Cowan records a sermon he heard MacMorland preach on the Samaritan woman's invitation: 'Come see a man who has told me all things whatever I did' (John 4:39).[50] He applied the text to the Bible 'which is applicable to all ranks & conditions of life.' Irving had been notorious for hob-nobbing with the rich and famous who, his critics alleged, had turned his head. It was MacMorland's courageous social commentary that particularly impressed Cowan.

In 1836 he was invited by the Regent Square Church, as a visiting ordained elder, to assist in the serving of communion. He noted that 250 were served, a far cry from the thousands who had attended when Irving's popularity was at its height. As Irving had shown, preaching can easily become manipulative and sensational, but Charles Cowan, true to his Calvinist roots, preferred expository preaching that was based on the Biblical text and avoided hyperemotional appeals. But important as the preaching of the Word was, the sacraments as they accompanied the Word, also greatly mattered to Cowan as a 'means of grace'. At the Lord's Table, throughout his life and to its very end, as we will see, he found in the Eucharist the emotional release that Irving had sought in so-called spiritual gifts and the excitement of an imminent Second Coming.

Cowan's close links with the congregation continued after he went up to the Commons and was a part-time resident in London. The National Scotch Church left the Church of Scotland at the time of the Disruption and became a part of the Presbyterian Church of England. On 20 March 1848, shortly after his electoral victory, Charles Cowan presented to Parliament a petition from the congregation titled, 'For Better Observance of the Lord's Day.'[51] By that time MacMorland[52] had long gone and the congregation

50. *Diary*, 2 August 1835.

51. *Hansard*, 20 March 1848.

52. Peter MacMorland, Ll.D. (1810-1881) was a minor Scottish Victorian religious poet.. Reflecting later on his ordination and call to Regent Square at the age of 23 he wrote: 'Edward Irving preceded me, James Hamilton came after me, and I always look

had stabilized, though its glory days with Irving were now only a memory.

*****

On 7 June 1836 Charles Cowan turned thirty-five. It was a time for celebration: 'The children had decorated the library with a bower and canopy for me,' he wrote in his diary, 'all very happy.' But the day also found him in a reflective mood. With life expectancy for Scottish males at the time pegged at forty-eight years, it was an opportunity for serious reflection. He wrote: '35 years old, *half* the time assigned by the Psalmist, a time calculated making one pause & think.' Questions abounded: did he want to be known as more than just another papermaker? Where else could invest his time and gifts? The next five years would mark out the course for the rest of his life.

---

upon my incumbency of four [*sic*] years as having been a short parenthesis of twilight between the two great lights – a short parenthesis of weakness between the two great strengths! Still, it was something to have stood, however unworthily, even within the shadow of the great figure of Edward Irving.' D.H. Edwards *Modern Scottish Poets*: Vol 6. Brechin: D H Edwards, 1883. 87. MacMorland started as a probationer in Paisley with Robert Burns, was at Regent Square from 1833 to 1839; went on to St Matthew's Glasgow, did not come out at the Disruption, served briefly at Inverkeithing, St Luke's Edinburgh; and finally for 17 years, N Berwick.

Chapter 6

Duty and Destiny

'God save the Queen!' Charles Cowan's voice boomed out as he announced the beginning of the Victorian era from a podium provided by a gallery of Westminster Abbey after eighteen year old Alexandrina Victoria was crowned on 28 June 1838. For him also a new age had dawned, new obligations were incurred, a new sporting organization established, and a serious midlife crisis brought on as he contemplated his future.

'Up to this time,' he wrote his daughters later that same day,[1] 'no distinct words had been uttered by any of her loyal subjects so I was determined to let her hear my voice, so I called out as loud as I could bawl above the noise of the cheering, "God save the Queen!" and I was followed immediately, repeating these words, by 1000 voices, which did not cease till she got out of the Western Gate into her robing room.' The ever-enterprising Charles Cowan had secured a ticket for admission by the early post that day. He left immediately for the Abbey, arriving at about eight that morning, pushing his way through the immense crowds, said to number over 400,000.

1. CC to Jean, Elizabeth, Catharine and Charlotte Cowan, 18 (*sic* presumably 28) June 1838, copied in *The Cowan Letters* Isabel Buckoke, Ed. Lymington, Herts: Published privately, 2000. 38-9.

'I wish you could have from me any idea of the splendour of this scene,' he continued. He watched as peers and peeresses of the realm, bedecked in mantles of crimson velvet with collars of ermine, entered through the West Door. 'The trains of the women could fill the whole dining room at Valleyfield,' he marvelled. Ambassadors ('some had beautiful wives with them') followed. His attention was particularly riveted by Nicolas Jean-de-Dieu Soult, whom he had heard speak a fortnight earlier at the Chamber of Peers in Paris. Marshal Soult, a veteran of the Napoleonic Peninsular Wars, was said to have been grabbed by Wellington at the event. 'I have you at last!' was his comment. Only the young Queen was received any better than the Duke. Cowan's location in the Abbey meant that Charles could not see the actual coronation, as he was not in the North Nave. The procession leading out was more magnificent than the entrance as it was continuous. 'The Queen had on her Crown which looked beautiful and there was a great deal of colour in her cheeks, for the same reason, I fancy, that some people have it after their calisthenics, for she had a great deal of work to go through.' It was at that point that Cowan, with his distinct Scottish brogue, let out his lusty 'God save the Queen'. He did not mind the long delay ('the Queen took a long time to get ready and there was such bustle of carriages and people') because he had a vantage point and enjoyed observing the scrum. His only regret, as he wrote to the family, 'I wish you could all have seen it for 5 minutes.'

Charles Cowan was indeed a family man. A year before his family had narrowly avoided a tragedy that seems to have brought them closer together. 'On Saturday afternoon, an alarming accident happened near Colinton,' the *Scotsman* reported on 19 August 1837 (a week after the fact), 'which most providentially was attended with no fatal consequences. Mr Charles Cowan of Penicuik and his family were descending a steep hill in their carriage, when a horse, drawing a heavy laden coal cart, which they had just passed, took fright, knocked down and passed over its driver, and descending the hill at a fearful rate, came in contact with and much damaged the carriage.'[2]

The story, as Charles recalled it forty years later, was rather different. The driver of the runaway cart and nine other carters had

2. *Scotsman* 19 August 1837, 3.

stopped at Hunter's Tryst, a local pub, to enjoy 'strong drink'. Charles was understandably worried that the other horses would break lose with their carts and further endanger the women and children, as Catharine and her sister Margaret Coldstream, together with several of their children, were still in the carriage. The shaft of the cart had penetrated the back part of the carriage just below where the ladies were seated: three inches higher and one of them would have been killed. Such were the dangers of coach travel at the time, a drinking and driving scenario with a difference: the driver inside the pub drunk, the neglected horse outside driving as if drunk. It was probably the worst of a series of travel mishaps over a lifetime that the much-travelled Cowan characterized in his *Reminiscences* as 'Repeated Preservations from Danger'. The collision in Penicuik ended with an investigation, during which it was discovered that the tavern was not on the direct route the carters were supposed to have taken. Their owner was later forced to pay Cowan £20 in damages.

At the time of the accident, the Cowans were en route to Kate's Mill on the Water of Leith, another Cowan operation, where Charles' brother John lived. Happy domestic summer outings like this were typical of the growing family. The *Scotsman* reported the birth of a daughter, Marjory Isabella (to be known as Mabel), to Mrs Charles Cowan, Valleyfield, on 25 February 1838. But once again, this joy was tinged with sorrow: another daughter, Jessie Ann, had died the previous month, having only just marked her first birthday. 'The baby had six leeches on Tuesday,' it was reported when she was five months old, but she never gained strength.[3]

*****

Charles Cowan was also a sportsman. The winter of 1838 was known throughout the British Isles as 'the Canadian winter' – bitterly cold but ideal for the game of curling. As a Scot, Charles Cowan had long enjoyed the country's favoured winter sport. 'He saw,' a later tribute would state, 'the beneficial moral effects of curling on the community, and became a keen curler, not so much because of any selfish delight

3. James Cowan to Elizabeth Cowan Thompson, 31 May 1837 (*The Cowan Letters*, 38).

to be had in it, but because it was social, manly, and healthy.'[4] As a skip, he revelled in a sport that depended not so much on youthful physical strength as the keen eye and tactical skill of an experienced curler. He was an active member of the Penicuik curling club, which drew together men of all classes and backgrounds in an egalitarian community that provided both physical and social outlets for the men of the whole town. Here employer and employee, professional and non-professional, mingled in friendly fraternity.

Curling had developed as a sport more or less on its own – without much organization, consolidation or rationalization. But this meant that there was little consistency from one group of curlers to the next. One Penicuik participant in the sport, a local physician John Renton (who was a friend of Charles), had been particularly frustrated by the fact that the rules, such as the amount and size of curling stones, and the number of players allowed in each rink, varied from club to club. 'Often previous to 1838 he conversed with me on the desirableness of having a grand central club, to which all local clubs should be affiliated,' Cowan recalled. In June 1838, an invitation went out in the *North British Advertiser* to all curling clubs to come together for an organizational meeting.

As a result, forty-four 'gentlemen' from thirty-four clubs attended a rendezvous at the Waterloo Hotel in Edinburgh on 25 July. The roster reveals a wide variety of social backgrounds, including not a few members of the aristocracy. Charles Cowan would later be cited as 'a member of the gallant band that formed the club'.[5] John Cairnie of Willowbank was in the chair, and Cowan's friend John Renton moved, heartily endorsed by all present, 'that this meeting do form itself into a club, composed of the different initiated clubs of Scotland, under the name of the "Grand Caledonian Curling Club"'. The organization of the newly founded club was left to a committee of ten, of whom only seven were active. The first named were the three from Penicuik: Dr Renton ('of this club he was one of the best friends and brightest ornaments for many years'), a Mr Gilbert ('of whom we have not heard much'), and Charles Cowan. 'Since that

4. Kerr, John. *History of Curling*. Edinburgh: David Douglas, 1890. 239.

5. Kerr, John. *History of Curling*. Edinburgh: David Douglas, 1890. 239.

time,' stated the fiftieth anniversary *Annual*, 'the Royal Club has had no more loyal or staunch member, and the rink which he skipped always held an honourable place in all Matches, National, Provincial, or those of local Bonspiels.'[6]

Cowan was creative and innovative in his approach to the sport. In 1847, for instance, he contributed an article to the club's *Annual* entitled 'The Prospective Advantages of Railways to Curlers,' in which he argued for 'the propriety of sheets of water being procured in juxtaposition with some one or more of our leading lines of railway.'[7] From this germinated the idea of curling rinks, an improvement over the unpredictability of using outdoor rivers and lochs.

The royal couple, though not Scottish, took considerable interest in curling. Prince Albert was an honourary member of the Merchiston Curling Club of Edinburgh, founded in 1809. While their majesties were visiting the Earl of Mansfield at the Castle of Scone in 1842, a demonstration of the sport was held on the oaken floor of a room in the castle specially set up as a rink. Victoria tried her luck throwing a stone, but it proved 'too heavy for her delicate hand'. A pair of stones, made from the finest Ailsa granite, quarried in Scotland, were presented to Victoria and Albert. The following year, a petition from the club was sent by Sir George Clerk of Penicuik, asking the Queen to allow them to use the word 'Royal' in the name – and permission was granted. From then on, the club was officially known as the Royal Grand Caledonian Curling Club. At the Great Exhibition of 1851 in Hyde Park, Charles Cowan presented Prince Albert with a pair of curling stones sent by the secretary of the club, Alexander Cassels, an Edinburgh lawyer and a curling legend. The English, he marvelled, apparently 'having no knowledge of our great national pastime, rushed to the conclusion that the stones were exhibited as models for cheeses.'[8]

Charles purchased the iconic nineteenth century Scottish painting of curling: *The Grand Match at Linlithgow, 1848* and hung it at Westerlea in Murrayfield, Edinburgh, which after 1869 became

---

6. *Annual of the Royal Caledonian Curling Club for 1884-85*. Edinburgh: Crawford & McCabe, 1884. viii.

7. As quoted in Kerr, John. *History of Curling*. Edinburgh: David Douglas, 1890. 273.

8. Annual *of the Royal Caledonian Curling Club for 1884-85*. Edinburgh: Crawford & McCabe, 1884 viii-ix.

the family's city home.[9] Forty-seven of Scottish curling's greats at the time, including Charles Cowan himself, are featured. Later it came into the possession of the Royal Caledonian Curling Club and, after considerable negotiation, plans are that it will be exhibited at the National Portrait Gallery of Scotland, on loan from the Club.

In proposing a toast to the Royal Caledonian Curling Club at the 1877 annual meeting, Cowan declared that he had never lost his 'liking for the game which placed peer and peasant for the time on a level.'[10] At that meeting, the club members also discussed an invitation that had been received from the branch in Ontario, Canada, 'asking a few rinks of Scottish curlers to play a friendly match in Canada next winter.' Charles' response was that he 'did not see any objection to a party of curlers going out to Canada, and having a friendly game. In fact,' he considered, 'it would be as wise a proceeding as sending marksmen to the other side of the Atlantic.' Applause followed. Curling was bringing Scots throughout the Empire together.

At the golden jubilee dinner of the club, held at the end of November 1888, a telegram of greetings from Charles Cowan, described as 'the venerable curler who had done so much for curling and for the Royal Club', was read out. Charles, 'the only survivor of the fifty that had founded the club,' sent his regrets. His daughter Maggie wrote on his behalf: 'Please assure the assembled company of my continued interest in the "roaring game".' Within four months, Charles was dead. Curling had been a great part of his life, helping him hone his leadership skills but also leveling and humanizing him.

*****

While Charles was in Paris and London on business that spring of 1838 when he witnessed the coronation, there were indications that he was becoming restless as a paper maker. Two years previously he had joined the Highland Agricultural Society of Scotland.[11] After

9. 'Mr Cowan also stated that he had purchased Lees great picture of 'Curling on Linlithgow Loch' merely for the purpose of preventing such a valuable historical work from going out of the country.' *Scotsman* 26 July 1877, 3.

10. *Scotsman*, 26 July 1877, 3.

11. *Scotsman*, 16 January 1836.

a summer two years earlier spent in the Trossachs he appeared to hanker after the life of a gentleman farmer. This would mean getting out of the business but he would need a cash buyout in order to be in a position to purchase an estate. As he approached forty, was Charles dreaming of freedom from the family enterprise and inependence from his father?

On 15 November 1839, Charles and Alexander Cowan had a long and (it would appear) emotional conversation. They seem to have discussed Charles' business relationship with his brothers James and John, thirteen and fifteen years younger, now getting involved in the family business. Initially, Alexander suggested that the other two might take over the Valleyfield mill. He was now proposing that Charles be bought out of the business altogether, for an amount of £35,000, payable in increments. In a follow-up letter after their discussion, Alexander wrote:

'I should have liked very well while I am in good health, to have seen the connexion betwixt yourself and your brothers secured for a period of years, but it is better that it should be delayed until you are all perfectly satisfied of the propriety of it, and until you have perfect confidence in each other. You have frequently hinted at giving up business and certainly, thanks to a good Providence, it is quite in your power to do so. You know however, as well as I do, that it is the Duty of every Christian man to do the most that may be in his power for the happiness and virtue of his fellow creatures: and I doubt your finding any other place in society, where you can more effectively promote these objects than you can in your present state.'[12]

Alexander then emphasized his concern for the business should Charles opt out, leaving its management to him in his old age along with two young and unproven sons: 'One condition of this however would be that you should continue your brothers 6 or 12 months, and do your best in that time to introduce some kind of system into the management of the business and to assist them in all other means in your power. This appears to me a proper time to say, that at my death it will be found that I have first provided for my daughters and for some other objects dictated to me by conscientious feelings, and that

12. AC to CC, 16 November 1839, NAS GD311.2.43.89.

considering you & John & James sufficiently provided for by the shares of the business you have had, you have little else to expect at my demise.'

Three months later, the conversation continued, and the intensity had ratcheted up several notches. Charles' father was trying to understand the next generation and where his son was coming from – his insecurities and sensitivities and the pressures he was feeling.

'Knowing as I do how you are situated in some respects at Penicuik, I am not surprised at the determination you have come to relinquish business. I think you are much too dependent upon other people for your happiness and I would strongly recommend to you a plan I have followed with great success for many years which is not to vex myself beyond measure about any body's sins but my own. In this I have perhaps been more successful from a degree of self-complacency and insensibility to my own failing but I am quite convinced that my rule is a good one and that no happiness can equal that which we can have in our prayers to God when they are offered up in Integrity of heart, and with love to him & forbearance to our fellow creatures. In fact, every Christian must feel when he thinks of it, that his happiness depends much on himself and little comparatively on others.'[13]

He then turned from what he called a 'digression' to business; outlining (after two months of consideration) what Charles could anticipate receiving should he bail out.

'You propose retiring at Octr, next or in 1841. I would prefer your doing it from 1 October last having as I said before £5000 or £6000 put to your credit at that time in lieu of profit to be realized during the remainder of the present Contract besides which you must have whatever sum appears reasonable for the proceeds still to be expected from the old Concern.'

Alexander then provided the rationale for his offer:

'My reasons for a settlement at present and without waiting the termination of the Contract are two. The first is that feeling the uncertainty of my life & feeling less capable of exertion of mind than formerly I wish to have all important matters settled immediately. My other reason is that it would be better to settle with you in the way

---

13. AC to CC, 31 January 1840. NAS, GD311.2.43. 124.

proposed than when the Contract ends to have discussions about the value of various articles and any chance of a necessity arising for calling in third parties to arrange matters betwixt us of any kind.'

The thought of terminating Charles' business relationship with his father and the two sons obviously gave Alexander great pain. He emphasized the finality of the transaction: 'I think you ought when matters are completed to advertise yourself out as a Partner, in such a way that you or your family would run no risk from any change that may happen.' And later, at the age of 65 and with a daughter just born and two more children yet to come, he wrote: 'I should like it to be understood amongst us all, that in the event of my death you should render to your brothers any assistance they may require, and also that if you Charles have a son who by & by is inclined to become a Papermaker that he should be admitted into the Business.' And then a final stab: 'I have always said that I would rather that my descendants were Papermakers than Lords, and I should be sorry to think that the connexion between the family and the good folks of Penicuik should terminate I am sure you and our dear Catharine [Charles' wife] would be sorry too if it did.'

It is not clear what intervened to persuade Charles to stay in the business. Perhaps it had to do with the fact that the three sons were made partners shortly thereafter, the company's name was changed to 'Alexander Cowan and Sons Co. Ltd.' and, as we will see, regular monthly partners' meetings were initiated. There were cautionary indications that James lacked the maturity to assume senior management, particularly given the general economic uncertainties of the time. It may also have been considered unwise to remove capital from a company that was just gaining momentum after the repeal of the paper excise tax. Charles opted to stay in the firm, but he would soon become involved in a much larger drama than papermaking provided. A struggle that was dividing the Church of Scotland, which drew him closer to Thomas Chalmers and distanced him from his father. It would be ecclesiastical events, not business matters, with which Charles Cowan would now be preoccupied.

Chapter 7

Campaigning Churchman

As he was negotiating with his father Charles Cowan had other distractions on his mind. He was increasingly being caught up in 'The Ten Years Conflict,' that decade from 1833 to 1843 which forever altered the religious and social landscape of Scotland. For the rest of his life he would be identified with the Free Church of Scotland which was birthed out of that struggle. His intense relationship with, and great respect for, Thomas Chalmers, left him no alternative. Chalmers was the driving force behind what transpired. Charles Cowan, as a young, prospering and committed layman, became an important ally and confidant in the struggle.

A year into that decisive decade Chalmers' leadership was seriously challenged by sudden debilitating illness. On 23 January 1834, he was felled by a stroke while returning home from a meeting of the Presbytery of Edinburgh. Walking along North Bridge that evening he caught up with his 'bosom friend' Patrick McDougall, professor of moral philosophy at the university. He'd started to describe what had happened at the meeting: a brilliant defence of Church establishment against its critics, the Voluntaries, who wished the end of state establishment. 'We had not gone many yards when he suddenly stopped short,' McDougall recalled, 'and said in a subdued but agitated voice, that "he felt very giddy" – a numbness down one side, and a tendency to fall in that direction.' McDougall called a carriage and took Chalmers home. Dr Begbie, Chalmers' personal physician, was summoned, and though his razor-sharp mind was not affected, the charismatic leader's speech was slurred, and the right side of his body – face, arm and leg were partially paralysed. At the peak of his powers, as the evangelicals had finally become the dominant party in the Church of Scotland, almost two years after he had been elected moderator of its General Assembly, Thomas Chalmers was struck down. He would never again have the same energy. At fifty-four, health had never previously been an issue for him, in spite of his reckless drive and large girth – but now he was discovering the limits of aging.

The pressures under which he had been working were intense. He was committed to the church establishment principle but his critique of the present spiritual condition of the Church of Scotland could be seen as encouraging attacks on its privileged legal position. The recently elected Edinburgh town council had challenged the fairness of the levying on the city of a six per cent annuity tax for the support of clergy in the eighteen Edinburgh Church of Scotland parishes. The Edinburgh annuity tax went back to 1661 that made it, along with Melrose, unique among the burghs of Scotland. The Edinburgh annuity tax would be a continuing issue for the next two generations. Chalmers' detractors complained that his criticism of the Church of Scotland would inevitably and irretrievably weaken it.

In April 1833 Presbytery appointed Chalmers to its committee for the preservation of Presbytery's endowments and income. By January of the next year the debate between the Established Church and dissenters had become heated. Edinburgh City Council decided on 20 January to abolish the annuity tax, which would seriously curtail the power of the Established Church, and would set up a free marketplace for each denomination to compete on a level playing field. Chalmers' vision of the godly commonwealth, with the state providing enough money so the poor could come to worship and not be subject to unaffordable pew rents, was under direct challenge. 'The Presbytery,' he had stated that fateful afternoon, 'will never consent to a reduction in their number, so long as the peculiar service of reclaiming these outcasts remains unaccomplished – a service of the utmost importance to the moral and Christian interest of the community, and which, under the present system of seat-letting is utterly impracticable.'[1]

The evening of Chalmers' stroke, Charles Cowan was playing chess with Henry Constable (of the publishing family) at Valleyfield. It would be two months before Charles actually visited Chalmers as he recovered from his painful and debilitating right-side paralysis. There must have been considerable political tension in a family where the Cowans were strongly Whig and supported the 1832 Reform Acts, unlike the Tory Chalmers. 'When our opinions differ,' Alexander Cowan had written to his cousin Thomas the previous November, 'I have much cause to distrust my own, and I know I am sometimes uncourteous in the manner of expressing it. If this has been the case lately I hope you can bear with me. I have often thought that little differences of opinion are intended as opportunities for the exercise of charity. And I am sure you must often have felt it to be a delightful exercise. I have always felt much esteem & affection and I am not only happy always to see you in this world, but anticipate doing so in the next.'[2]

As he signed off he described himself as 'Your friend & cousin.' Alexander Cowan sought to live peaceably with all men, in accord with Biblical dictates, though he differed politically from Chalmers. But their relationship was not always easy and several years later they parted company only to reconcile later, as we will see.

*****

It would be mid-February before Chalmers was able to return to teaching his classes, but only on 23 March was his strength such that Charles Cowan was able to meet with him. He paid a further visit on 3 May as he was about to set sail for Gravesend to do business

1. Hanna, Wm. *Memoir of the Life and Writings of Dr Chalmers*, volume III. Edinburgh: A Fullarton & Co., 1853. 422.

2. AC to TC, 30 Nov 1833. New College, CHA 4.202.66.

in London. One of the items of conversation, raised in a letter the previous week,[3] was the possibility that Chalmers might find the home in Valleyfield a conducive place for a summer of recuperation. Chalmers was unable to attend the 1834 General Assembly. The big issue was to be the right of a congregation to veto the selection of a minister made by a patron against the wishes of a majority of the congregation and safeguarding the right of the church to choose its own clergy.

That Assembly was the first of the next ten in which the Evangelicals clearly were in the majority but their leader was absent. The main item of business was the consideration of a Veto Act that would give congregations the power to void a ministerial appointment with which a majority did not concur. In Chalmers' absence the responsibility for moving the Veto Act motion and guiding the discussion devolved on to Sir James Wellwood Moncrieff. 'I cannot but remember,' Moncrieff began his speech, 'the manner in which this subject was presented to you in the last general assembly, by a man sufficient to adorn the annals of any age or church.'[4] He then spoke for an hour and a half making the case for the Veto Act. That morning ('a very hot day'), Charles stopped by to call on Chalmers, perhaps to console him about his being *hors de combat*. In the afternoon, he made his way to the Assembly and sat in the gallery. 'Very crowded,' he noted in his diary.[5] 'Heard Lord Moncrieff speak about the calls for 2 hours, very admirable one.' The Veto Act passed by a vote of 180 to 134.

The 1834 General Assembly made two decisions about creating new churches for a swelling population. The first was the Chapels Act, which finally granted legal status to the so-called *quoad sacra* congregations which had remained in ecclesiastical limbo. Their legality was now, it was hoped, assured – a victory for Chalmers

3. CC to TC, 28 April 1834, New College CHA 4.220.41. There was some talk with his cousin Charles Pearson of having CC's aunt, Charlotte Pearson, have the place for the summer but 'I said to him that I had already made offer of the House to you, but had not heard whether you were to come or not.'

4. Buchanan, Robert. *The Ten Years Conflict*, volume I. Glasgow: Blackie and Son, 1863. 217.

5. *Diary*, 25 May 1834.

and the Evangelicals who had been active in creating these new churches. The second action was to create a Church Accommodation Committee, to address overcrowding in parish churches. The Committee's new guidelines were to be implemented by Chalmers as convener of that committee.

As a direct result of these actions, Roslin congregation, which Charles Cowan had created in response to their local Moderate clergyman at Penicuik, was now granted legal status. Ironically however he was now happily ensconced back in the parish church in Penicuik where (following the death of Rev. Coulston and the settlement of the evangelical Rev. Moncrieff), he had been ordained an elder and was now serving on the Session. On 13 August Chalmers was strong enough to preach a communion sermon at the newly legalized Roslin church.

*****

Thomas Chalmers was able to preach at Roslin because he was already in Penicuik that summer, having accepted Charles' invitation to take his family to Valleyfield for rest and recuperation. He remained very involved. On 9 June he wrote from Valleyfield: 'I foresee that however influential one Committee may prove for the whole of Scotland, tenfold revenue may be gained for the cause, by each distinct association being made to feel its own individuality, and to concentrate its efforts on the object of providing for its own wants wherever these wants exist.'[6] The principle (and the experience) of raising money for church extension – and the principle of local involvement – would prove invaluable for Charles Cowan and his business friends as they set up the Sustentation Fund ten years later.

For three months that summer Chalmers, his wife and two daughters stayed at Valleyfield, occupying several rooms. Slowly, his health returned as he found strength in the beauty of the surrounding Pentland hills, which he loved. On Tuesday 1 July, at the conclusion

6. As quoted in Brown, S. J. *Thomas Chalmers and the Godly Commonwealth.* (New York: Oxford University Press, 1982), 237. It is rather misleading for Brown to describe Valleyfield as a 'cottage in the village of Penicuik' (233).

of the communion season in Penicuik, Thomas Chalmers, Charles, Charles' minister Scott Moncrieff, and Marcus Dods[7] climbed up Carnethy Hill (which is 573 feet above sea level) and compared its elevation, using a spirit level, with that of its East Sister. They went on to picnic near Loganhouse and then returned by the Martyr's Monument, a reminder of the so-called 'Killing Times' and the Covenanters of the seventeenth century. For Chalmers and his friends the monument evoked the memory of events one hundred and fifty years earlier, now very much in the minds of Evangelicals contending once again for what those Covenanters had called 'the crown rights of Jesus Christ'.

Robert Louis Stevenson, exiled in Samoa, remembered that obelisk with poetic license as the 'grey, recumbent tombs of the dead in desert places', and the peewees' call overhead was the only sight and sound he wished to recall when he lay dying in faraway Valima.[19] As for Stevenson in memory, so also for them: a magical and mystic moment. The four paused to sing a psalm and pray before they made their way home. From his description of the day it is clear that Charles was deeply moved by the experience.

*****

At the 1835 General Assembly of the Church of Scotland Chalmers brought in his first report as convener of the Church Accommodation Committee. £65,626 had been raised and four new churches erected. Chalmers' fundraising abilities were legendary: while in Valleyfield the previous summer, he had started to send out appeals to the rich and famous, many of them Tories (as he was). But it was the Whig middle class, whose wealth was increasing substantially in this period, that proved his most reliable source of funds. Among them, as we will see (ch. 16), none was more generous than Alexander Cowan.

Nowhere was the political venom of the time more evident than in the appointment of a Royal Commission to examine the

7. Marcus Dods (1786–1838), speaker at the summer 1834 Penicuik communion weekend, was the father of New Testament professor Marcus Dods, born that same year. The father and the son had widely divergent views over Biblical inspiration.

extent of 'religious destitution' in Scotland. The membership of the Commission, as appointed, was regarded by Chalmers as a thinly veiled Whig attempt not only to thwart church extension but also, it appeared, to disestablish the Church of Scotland. A great deal of nastiness and infighting ensued as Chalmers blocked the election of a nominee whose candidacy for moderator he disapproved of, thus consolidating his position as head of the Evangelicals.

Meanwhile, the older Whig Evangelicals were gradually being displaced. A delegation sent to London to meet, in March 1838, with Whig Prime Minister William Lamb, 2nd Viscount Melbourne, was composed entirely of Tories, and this didn't make sense to the Edinburgh Church Extension Committee or to some young urban Whig Evangelicals who, as most interested, had been snubbed. As Brown says in his biography of Chalmers: 'His hatred of Whigs became a consuming passion. He was blind to the fact that while his power within the Church was unrivalled, his dictatorial behaviour was in fact weakening his influence as well as that of the Church, in the nation as a whole.'[8] The day the committee arrived in London, Melbourne announced that Scottish cities would get no money for any new churches in spite of Scotland's recent urban population explosion. The Whig Prime Minister Melbourne showed every evidence of personal hatred towards the Tory Chalmers and refused even to acknowledge his presence when he came to Westminster.[9] Cowan, as a Whig but very much allied with Chalmers, was placed in an invidious position.

*****

8. Brown, S. J. *Thomas Chalmers and the Godly Commonwealth*, 268.

9. D. Close in his 'The formation of a two-party alignment in the house of commons between 1832 and 1841' *English Historical Review*, vol. 84 (1969), 257-277 says '... partisans on both sides saw enormous issues at stake in the party conflict. Reformers saw themselves as fighting to secure the relief of Dissenters' disabilities, the reform of municipal corporations, and the reform of the English and Irish churches. Conservatives saw themselves as fighting for safe, strong government, and for the integrity of the English and Irish churches and of all branches of the constitution.' He (characteristically for English historians at the time) leaves out Scotland which can be included in the Irish and English church agitation.

All eyes were on the 1838 General Assembly. Charles Cowan, increasingly engaged, wanted to be a part of the debate and to have a voice. But in the fractious mood of the hour, his nomination as an elder commissioner was blocked by the Presbytery of Lanark. This move took Cowan by surprise, and he appealed to Chalmers for help, family loyalty trumping political party allegiance. On 4 April 1838 he stopped by at Chalmers' home in Morningside, Edinburgh, but finding him not in he hastily penned a letter to him. 'I called here on my way out [to Penicuik] to ask what your movements were, also to ask if you would be so good as write [*sic*] on a sheet of letter paper 3 lines to say that *you know me*. The purpose I must tell you. I was last week voted the '*rejected*' of Lanark Presbytery, for which I expected to have come in without opposition. They have behaved exceedingly ill to Mr Menzies [Charles' father-in-law, the outspoken Evangelical minister in Lanark] but more anon.'[10] He went on to state that friends 'had made application to the Presbytery of North Isles in my behalf,' as the one chosen, a Mr Balfour, had died after his nomination. The nomination went through, and Charles Cowan attended the first of his forty general assemblies, generally as an elder representing the Orkney Islands, the Presbytery of North Isles as it was then known. It was the only way that that remote and impoverished presbytery could be assured lay representation at the national meetings and Cowan was glad to oblige.

The 1838 General Assembly is identified with the Auchterarder case: a schoolteacher probationer (i.e., candidate for ordination), Robert Young, was presented to the parish of Auchterarder by the patron but rejected by 287 male heads of families, with only three agreeing to sign the call. There was an appeal to law by the aggrieved candidate who stated that his rights had been violated, and, by a vote of eight to five, the [supreme] Court of Session ordered Robert Young to be inducted as minister in Auchterarder.

A defiant General Assembly, insisting that the church must be governed by its members, agreed on an appeal to the House of Lords as the highest legal authority in the land. As Robert Buchanan, minister of Chalmers' former congregation in Glasgow, stated emphatically: 'The union between Church and State was an

10. CC to TC, 4 April 1838. New College CHA 4-273-7.

alliance entered into between two co-ordinate powers.'[11] Though that issue dominated proceedings, there was also good news: Thomas Chalmers announced that thirty-two new churches had come into being during the previous year, bringing the total to 187. Having just returned from giving lectures (later published as *Lectures on the Establishment and Extension of National Churches*) in London to packed and rapt audiences, it was gratifying for him to see so many new churches being created in Scotland.

Immediately after the General Assembly, Chalmers left for Paris to deliver a paper before the Royal Institute of France. He had been made a corresponding member four years earlier, in recognition of his academic and intellectual achievements. Now it was time for him to appear before the Institute and demonstrate his erudition. Charles Cowan, fluently bilingual after his time in Geneva, had volunteered to serve as interpreter. They sailed from Granton, Edinburgh's dockland, arriving in London on 1 June and going on to France four days later. That Chalmers' attempts to speak French were excruciating is demonstrated by the reaction of a woman who turned out to be from Northumberland and who finally said, 'Dear sir, I wad understand ye far better if ye wad jeest speak in broad Scotch.'[12]

In Paris, Chalmers and Cowan found accommodation in the Hôtel Castellane in Faubourg St Germain. There they encountered an interesting collection of Scottish expatriates, one of whom was Erskine of Linlathen, a Scottish aristocrat, a layperson and theological autodidact, who had challenged the Calvinist doctrine of election in order to defend, as he saw it, the love of God. As a result, he had become a universalist. Their dinner conversation was not recorded, but it must have been interesting.

Erskine and Chalmers, with Cowan as translator, went to visit François Guizot, the chief architect and enabler of the 'citizen king,' Louis Philippe.[13] Guizot's two significant interests, aside from his substantial government responsibilities, were the Royal Institute and

11. Quoted in *The Scotsman*, 26 May 1838, 2.

12. *Reminiscences*, 177.

13. François Guizot (1787–1874) Minister of Education, Ambassador in London, Foreign Minister and finally for the last year of Louis Philippe's reign, Prince Minister of France.

the consistory of the Ėglise Reformėe in Paris where he worshipped. Chalmers gave lectures at both institutions: at the Royal Institute, he addressed the problem of a typhus epidemic that was sweeping Europe at the time, stressing the need for taxation for adequate medical facilities. At a service in Chapelle Taitbout (which many British expatriates attended), he preached 'a most powerful and eloquent sermon' for an hour and ten minutes on the theme of love, an appropriate topic if Erskine of Linlathen was in the congregation that day. However, as Cowan later observed, 'I fear that there were but few present, either English or French who were able to understand or appreciate the power and eloquence of the argument.'[14] The two returned home at the end of July to a warm welcome. There is nothing like international recognition to enhance local reputation.

*****

On 22 May 1839, the General Assembly engaged in a fourteen-hour debate that helped determine the future of the Church of Scotland. The lines had been drawn, party lines defined, issues clarified, and the path to eventual separation clearly marked out. George Cook, successor to Chalmers as professor of moral philosophy at St Andrews, led the Moderates, while the Evangelical Chalmers was the champion of the Non-intrusionists, who believed in maintaining the rights of the Church over the civil courts and now the House of Lords, and that no candidate could be *intruded* on a congregation without their consent.

The two motions had been placed on the table two days before. Cook's motion started by reviewing the Auchterarder case in the judiciary and concluded: 'Under these circumstances, it is moved, that the act on calls, commonly denominated the [V]eto [A]ct [passed by the 1834 General Assembly], having been thus declared by the supreme civil tribunals of the country to infringe on civil and patrimonial rights, with which the church has often and expressly required that its judicatories should not intermeddle, as being matters incompetent to them, and not within their jurisdiction, it be an instruction by the general assembly to all presbyteries that they

14. *Reminiscences*, 182.

proceed henceforth in the settlement of parishes according to the practice which prevailed previously to the passing of that act.'[15]

Essentially Cook (and his fellow Moderates) were seeking to return to the situation before the Veto Act, eliminate all the successes achieved by the Evangelicals, and rely on the State to assure their hegemony in the Church of Scotland by allowing the settlement only of those they (and/or their patrons) approved.

Chalmers' motion affirmed the priority of the church over the state in the governing of its own affairs. While supporting the rejected Auchterarder candidate Robert Young, saying that he had every legal right to the emoluments of the congregation, it went on to state emphatically that 'the principle of non-intrusion is one coeval with the reformed kirk of Scotland, and forms an integral part of its constitution, embodied in its standards and declared in various acts of assembly, the general assembly resolve that this principle cannot be abandoned, and that no presentee shall be forced upon any parish contrary to the will of the congregation.'[16]

The debate began at noon that day and continued on through the night. At two in the morning, the General Assembly adjourned, having taken the decisive vote. Dr Cook's motion was supported by 155 – of whom 100 were clergy and 55 were elders. Thomas Chalmers' motion was supported by 204 – of whom 90 were elders, a much more even division, signifying lay support for the Non-intrusionists. At the very end of the list of elders as it appeared a week later in the *Scotsman* was the name 'C. Cowan'.[17] It would appear that he had finally broken with his ever-cautious and non-confrontational father in favour of his father's cousin's defiant stand. Thomas Chalmers had trumped Alexander Cowan.

The number of elder commissioners voting with the Non-intrusionists and thus aligning themselves with Thomas Chalmers was highly significant. The Disruption was a revolt by Evangelical laity against the Moderate establishment, who were bent on keeping

15. Buchanan, Robert. *Ten Years Conflict.* volume I. Glasgow: Blackie and Son, 1863. 436.

16. Buchanan, Robert. *Ten Years Conflict.* volume I. Glasgow: Blackie and Son, 1863. 453.

17. *Scotsman*, 29 May 1839, 4.

the *status quo* and willing to grovel, it was claimed, before the civil authorities. The Non-intrusionists had fought for freedom for the kirk against what they regarded as tyrannical interference, particularly by those in London, most of whom had no understanding of Scottish sensitivities and Scotland's historical and religious development, nor were they particularly pious. The laity at General Assembly who voted with Chalmers were deeply committed Evangelicals, products of the revivals that were then sweeping the country, among whom was Charles Cowan.

Charles Cowan, *circa* 1795
Oil, attributed to Sir Henry Raeburn, RA, RSA
(1756-1823) SNPG

Alexander Cowan, *circa* 1840
Oil, Colvin Smith (1795-
1875) SNPG

Alexander Cowan and His Family at Moray House, 1830

Watercolour by Kenneth MacLeay, RSA (1802-1878)

In possession of Thomas Errington

Surety bond posted by Alexander Cowan on behalf of Sir Walter Scott 3 August 1827

(NAS GD311.7.66.7)

GD311/7/66

Copy Order on Note for A Cowan Esq

(7)

3d Augt 1827

The Arbiter has advised this Note and is willing to receive the proposed condescendence but as he means to leave town in a few days and may not return for a considerable time it is necessary that it should be lodged immediately. He therefore intimates that if it is not lodged by Thursday next, he will proceed to pronounce an interim decree in terms of the opinion signified in his last Note

(Signed) Alexr Irving

3 August 1827
Lord Newton's Note
A. Cowan Esq
v
Sir Wal. Scott Bart

Walter Dickson Esq
WS

Napoleonic prisoner-of-war monument, Penicuik, 1830

Cowan old and new well monument, High Street, Penicuik

Valleyfield Mills about 1860, from an Old Engraving.

Charles Cowan, *circa* 1835

Watercolour by Kenneth MacLeay, RSA (1802-1878)

Catharine Menzies Cowan, *circa* 1835

Watercolour by Kenneth MacLeay, RSA (1802-1878)

"The Three Graces" (John James, Anna Thompson, and Margaret Menzies Cowan) May 1863

Pastel by William Crawford, ARSA (1825 – 1869)
In possession of Judith A. MacLeod

We shall be with you in thought
on thursday both at the Chrystal
Palace,ˣ and before the Speaker.
Ever Your affectionate father
Rowan

29 April 1851

ˣ Opened 1st May 1851.

Charles Cowan, 1843.

Collotype by Octavius Hill (1802-1870)

James Cowan, 1855

Oil by Kenneth MacLeay, RSA (1802-1878)

Yours very truly
Chas Cowan

Sir John Cowan, Bt., 1890

Charles Cowan

Alexander Cowan

Bronze bas-relief by William Brodie, ARSA, RA, sculptor, (1815-81)

Office building, Alexander Cowan & Sons, 1864, West Register St., Edinburgh

George Beattie & Son, architects

Chapter 8

Stakes Staked Out

At the 1839 General Assembly the majority of commissioners, including Charles Cowan, had thrown down the gauntlet. By appealing to the House of Lords the Church of Scotland had greatly increased the stakes in this ecclesiastical poker game. If the appeal went against them, as later became apparent, there could be no turning back. Their truculence and the reaction of their opponents and particularly those in London who were growing impatient at those bothersome Scots, made compromise impossible. Alex Cheyne noted 'the general unwillingness of the participants to conciliate or mediate or concede anything'.[1] He characterised the attitude of both sides as a 'bellicosity' mirroring 'the confrontational attitudes of an entire society' and citing other equally divisive contemporary battles – Chartism, the Anti-Corn Law League, and Owenite Radicalism and now this debate within the Church of Scotland. They were part of the temper of the times.

As with all such movements, leadership was a determining factor. In Scotland Chalmers may have given the movement a voice but there were many others, young men, often with a fiery temperament,

1. Cheyne, Alexander *The Ten Years' Conflict and the Disruption* Scottish Academic Press, 1993. 117.

religiously zealous, harbouring as Scots a deep sense of resentment and marginalization. As the Disruption approached a whole new generation of elders, such as Charles Cowan, was galvanized into action by each new challenge from London to their congregations' autonomy and self-governing rights. Left to themselves, the so-called 'Fathers of the Disruption' could never have done what they did without the encouragement – and enthusiasm – of younger members of their Kirk Sessions. Should the traditional rights of the patron be denied, and should they give up the annuities, endowments, and teind levies that came with patronage, it would be they, and not the clergy who incited them, who would have to pay the bills.

Questioning the patronage system created a new set of issues about church support and stewardship to which the pew would have to respond. And ultimately the matter came down to the spiritual commitment of members, and their willingness to sacrifice financially in order to preserve the independence of the kirk. Just at that time, as a result largely of a surge in numbers of Evangelicals in pulpits across Scotland, and a remarkable spiritual awakening, the church was experiencing renewed vitality and a fresh sense of urgency for its mission. This was epitomised by the 1841 revival at St. Peter's in Dundee during the absence of its minister, the iconic Robert Murray McCheyne, who was away on a fact-finding exploratory visit to central Europe and Palestine. The clergy were sometimes running to keep up with the enthusiasms of a reenergized laity.

Each of the collisions between church and state in the 1830s had a geographic identity. Now the name Strathbogie was added to Auchterarder and Lethendy as scenes where a great national drama was being acted out, each case ratcheting up the intensity of feeling. The patron of the church in Marnoch, presbytery of Strathbogie, was the Earl of Fife. In 1838 he presented a forty-four-year-old schoolmaster, John Edwards, as his candidate for the living. Edwards had previously served the parish as an assistant and was thoroughly disliked as a Moderate – the only person (out of 300 male heads of families) to sign the call was the local tavern keeper. The 1838 General Assembly rejected Edwards, and the patron then produced a popular Evangelical minister who was strongly supported by the parish.

But John Edwards did not let the matter rest there, appealing to the Court of Session and it banned the popular candidate and instructed the presbytery of Strathbogie to take Edwards on trials for ordination and induction. Seven of the twelve ministers in the presbytery proceeded to do so: the direction of General Assembly being trumped by the state's judiciary. In December 1839 a commission of General Assembly suspended the compliant clergy and appointed others to provide worship in their parishes, now by necessity in the open air as the church buildings of the 'Strathbogie Seven' were state property. On 14 February 1840, the court banned any clergy from conducting services in the parishes pastored by the Strathbogie seven. This interdiction created a firestorm of protest.

In the midst of what was popularly known as the 'Bogie reel', Charles Cowan lobbed in a pamphlet to add to the many then being published. On 8 January 1840, his first literary offering, a response to the issues now raging in the Church of Scotland, appeared anonymously but it was soon attributed to him. It was freighted with a lengthy title: *The Analogy Which Subsists Between the British Constitution in its Three Estates of Queen, Lords, and Commons, and That of the Church of Scotland in the Mutual Relations of Patron, Presbytery, and People, Shortly Considered, Being a Letter Respectfully Addressed to the Scottish Representatives in Parliament by the Head of a Family in Communion with the Church of Scotland.*

Among the many tracts and pamphlets published at the time *The Analogy* is of interest for the light it sheds on Charles Cowan as representative of many young laymen caught up in the emotion of the hour and trying to make a case for their cause. Addressing his message to the Scottish members of the House of Commons and their constituents, he wrote: 'As far as Scotland is concerned, there can be no subject to equal in importance that to which I trust your deliberations will be speedily directed. I mean the unhappy collision which exists between the civil and ecclesiastical tribunals of our country, and which, I hope, you will anxiously consider in all its bearings, with a view to devise some means for restoring harmony between them.'[2]

2. *Analogy*, 3.

He affirmed the Veto Act of 1834. As a Whig, having been enfranchised (by the Great Reform Act of 1832) for the first time, his opinions about political matters mattered and had to be taken seriously by his Member of Parliament. He drew an analogy between Queen, Lords, and Commons on the one hand and Patron, Presbytery, and People on the other. Both sides, Queen and Patron alike, had the right of nomination to positions in State and Church. But just as the monarchy was limited, there were certain checks and balances over the patron's power of appointment. The Lords and the Presbytery also had an analogous position, as 'a permanent body of individuals who have been raised from out of the people to honourable office, in temporal and spiritual things respectively, and according as they possess the Christian dignity and grace of the high station assigned to them, and evince a concern for, and promote the welfare of the people under them, will their example and influence as mediators or otherwise be valuable among the civil and religious communities over which they preside.'[3] Here – in the governing bodies both of church and state – laypeople and clerics vote as one, without distinction or weight being given to their office or title.

Accountability he felt was the key issue. The third estate, the Commons, had been made more accountable when the Great Reform Act of 1832 extended the franchise. If, by extending the parliamentary franchise, the Legislature 'considered the people of Scotland to be sufficiently qualified to exercise a judgment upon civil and political matters, to which their attention had previously been but little directed, let it be remembered, that in matters of faith and doctrine it has been the business and advantage of the Scottish people to be long familiar, and that their qualification to judge of matters affecting their religious and moral interest from such subjects having been pressed upon their attention from their earliest education, is of an infinitely higher order.'

He asked the Legislature to restore 'this system of efficient checks now threatened to be altogether swept away, unless redress be granted to the Church and people of Scotland through [their]

3. *Analogy*, 5.

intervention.'[4] It was a direct appeal to the House of Lords to hear the Auchterarder case and give redress to the injustices of a repressive and unaccountable court system that no longer served the people justly.

He accused two of the leading advocates in the 1839 Assembly (Dr Cook and Lord Brougham) of capitulating to the unjust imposition of the judiciary and thus taking a 'despotic view'. He needled Cook (an historian) about going against the spirit of the Magna Carta, and took Lord Brougham to task (describing him as 'half a Scotchman'), someone who had advocated for the common man in the months leading up to the adoption of the Reform Act, and who should therefore have known better than to take such a dismissory view of the call system of the Church of Scotland.[5]

Cowan's democratic hackles were also raised by a comment made at the Assembly dismissing a congregation's calling of a minister as a convenient but essentially meaningless ceremony. The procedures for this calling, Cowan pointed out – preaching two Sundays, having an Edict read, and going through an appeal process – were safeguards to protect 'the voice or wishes of the people'.[6] He made reference to the committee, chaired by Chalmers, tasked to implement 'the fundamental principle of non-intrusion' and to investigate ways of restoring the privileges of ministers of the Church of Scotland, which had been 'invaded by the opinions expressed by the House of Lords'.

His closing argument reached back into the Church of Scotland's 'glorious past'. He cited acts of 1567, 1592, as well as those of ensuing years as 'the honoured instrument of generating a nation'. These had made Scots and Scotland 'honoured and esteemed throughout the world'. Five individuals were specifically noted as outstanding: Thomas Chalmers predictably led the list, followed by Alexander Duff the missionary to India, and Robert Gordon at St Giles,'

4. *Analogy*, 7.

5. Lord Brougham compared the insignificance of the calling of a minister to the part in the Coronation ceremony where a champion of the monarch comes in on horseback but no one would say that if the horse resisted the crowning was rendered invalid. Brown, Thomas. *Annals of the Disruption* vol 1. Edinburgh:Maclaren & MacNiven. 23—24.

6. *Analogy*, 15.

the High Church, Edinburgh. Significantly the other two were laypeople, both of them mentored by Chalmers while in Glasgow – the educator David Stow and the publisher William Collins. The principle, which these five personified, was their common prayer for Scotland: 'Long may she abide as the bulwark of religious and constitutional freedom, and of all that is valuable in our common Protestantism, for the promotion of "that righteousness which alone exalteth a nation"'.

It was a time when an unprecedented number of broadsheets were being published about the issue of non-intrusion and its wider ramifications. Charles Cowan's pamphlet was an attempt by an articulate layperson to demonstrate by reasoned argument the support of the pew for those clergy whose principles and rhetoric were about to lead to a fracturing of the kirk. We do not know what kind of a response Cowan received, but as a businessman he had gone on written record, publishing at his own expense his personal reasoned commitment to the cause. From then on he was a marked man. When the roster of elder commissioners for the momentous 1843 General Assembly was drawn up he was not among them. His position was too well known.

*****

Cowan's tract could not have appeared at a more opportune time. 1840 was a difficult year for Thomas Chalmers. In his capacity as chair of a Non-intrusion Committee set up by the 1839 General Assembly, he was engaged in secret negotiations with George Hamilton-Gordon, the Earl of Aberdeen, and Scots representative peer in the House of Lords. Aberdeen was trying to be a bridge builder, a person in high office who was both sympathetic and knowledgeable about the Church of Scotland. The negotiations broke down, there were mutual recriminations, and Chalmers (and those soon to go into the Free Church) lost the good will of Lord Aberdeen as honest broker.

A series of reverses occurred for Chalmers and his friends. On 14 February 1840 a legal opinion in response to an 'extended' edict of the Court of Session was announced. It was not in the church's favour. Chalmers responded ten days later with an ill-tempered (and intemperate) speech that alienated many of his friends. A bill that Aberdeen introduced in May failed to give presbyteries absolute power and was subsequently rejected by the General Assembly. Confidential correspondence between Chalmers and Aberdeen was then leaked because Aberdeen no longer felt Chalmers could be trusted. A personal setback for Chalmers occurred that year as well – he lost both the Principalship of Edinburgh University and a nomination to be Professor of Theology at Glasgow.

Chalmers was now over sixty-two, a voice from the past. The Non-Intrusionists, energized by young activists, sometimes appeared to be a youth movement. Clerics in its vanguard, such as William Cunningham[7] and Robert Candlish,[8] were in their mid-thirties. There was, however, a downside to their youth. While they brought great gifts, courage and conviction to their cause, compromise was difficult. The perspective of age and experience got lost in debate. The final (and tragic) irony of the Disruption was the reality that just as the Evangelicals had gained their long sought majority in the Church of Scotland they surrendered it, and it would never be regained.

At the 1841 General Assembly Cowan's voice was heard high above the commissioners who were about to adjourn. Robert Candlish, whom Cowan admired, and whose worship services at St George's Edinburgh he regularly attended, addressed them as the final session adjourned: a substantial debt that had been incurred,

---

7. William Cunningham (1805–1861) was called to Trinity College Church, Edinburgh, the same year as Candlish also moved to the city. His 1840 *Defence of the Rights of the Christian People* went far beyond the Veto Act and even Chalmers, arguing for the supremacy of the people in the choice of their minister. He was appointed to teach at New College in 1844 and became Moderator of the Free Church in 1859. His early death meant that little was published in his lifetime but his posthumous *Historical Theology* became a classic Reformed text.

8. Robert Smith Candlish (1806–1870) became minister of St George's Edinburgh, one of the more prestigious pulpits of the Church of Scotland, when only 28, and at 41 on Chalmers' death, became the leader of the Free Church. He was appointed Principal of New College in 1862. No stranger to death (his father died when he was a month old), Candlish lost two children: in February 1840: Walter, aged 6 months, followed the next month by Jane, a year and nine months old. He went on to lose two others. Infant mortality was a fact of life but the blow, coming in the height of the controversy just before the 1840 General Assembly, has to be taken into account.

he stated, most of which could be attributed to the legal costs of the various court cases in which the church had been involved. Candlish went on to say that '[i]f the struggle between the two sides of the Church was to be one as to the length of their purses, he was sure that his friends would go to the very depth of poverty before they would see the Church defeated.'[9] And then (as reported in the *Scotsman*), just before the commissioners were about to scatter, 'Mr Charles Cowan expressed a hope that his brethren of the eldership would not separate that night without an effort being made, on their part, to relieve the Church of her pecuniary difficulties. The debt was upwards of £2000. Now, suppose that 100 elders, whether members of the House or not, should subscribe £20 or £25 each, that would cancel the debt in a moment.'[10] The Assembly concluded with cheers for Cowan's suggestion.

In a speech to the January 1842 meeting of the Presbytery of Edinburgh, Candlish stated his convictions forthrightly. 'Is this to go on year after year?' he asked. 'The course of these events has shown that these negotiations are useless, that they lead to confusion and misunderstanding every day; and is not this an indication of the intention of God to shut up all other doors of escape, that the Church may look to that great and effectual door, the extinction of the right of Patronage altogether?'[11] Candlish had thus gone far beyond Chalmers on the path to a full endorsement of Voluntaryism, defined by *Chambers Encyclopaedia*, as the belief 'that all true worship ... must be the free expression of individual minds.... therefore, religion ought to be left by civil society to mould itself spontaneously according to its own' spiritual nature and institutions.'[12]

That 1842 General Assembly began with a tussle between the two delegations from Strathbogie – those who had proceeded to ordination and had been deposed by the Presbytery and those who

9. *Scotsman*, 2 June 1841. 3.

10. *Scotsman*, 2 June 1841. 3.

11. Wilson, William. *Memorials of Robert Smith Candlish, D.D.* Edinburgh: Adam and Charles Black, 1880. 177.

12. Watner, Carl. 'On the History of the Word 'Voluntaryism'' http://voluntaryist.com/forthcoming/historyofvoluntaryism.html#.UQKMlr9X1j4. Accessed 25 January 2013.

had obeyed the instructions of Assembly and defied the judiciary. Moderate George Cook moved that neither be recognized by the General Assembly, while elder Alexander Murray Dunlop, moved – in defiance of the legalities – that the ones who had been obedient to the Church over against the State, be seated.[13] The vote was a clear indication of the direction that the Assembly would take. Following a strong statement from Chalmers, Charles Cowan is recorded as having voted, along with 85 other elders, with Alex Dunlop and against George Cook.[14] The final tally was 215 to 85.

The 1842 General Assembly is best known for its adoption of a Claim of Right. Cowan's friend, the lawyer Alex Dunlop, the author of the draft five-thousand word Claim of Right, took the lead in a debate that finally endorsed an historic declaration of spiritual independence by the Church. 'They cannot in accordance with the Word of God, the authorized and ratified standards of this Church, and the dictates of their consciences, intrude ministers on reclaiming congregations, or carry on the government of Christ's Church, subject to the coercion attempted by the Court of Session... and, that, at the risk and hazard of suffering the loss of the secular benefits conferred by the State, and the public advantages of an Establishment, they must, as by God's grace they will, refuse so to do: for, highly as they estimate these, they cannot put them in competition with the inalienable liberties of a Church of Christ, which, alike by their duty and allegiance to their Head and King, and by their ordination vows, they are bound to maintain, "notwithstanding of whatsoever trouble or persecution may arise"'.[15] It was approved by a vote of 241 to 110, Cowan again voting with the majority.

It was brinkmanship to the extreme. Chalmers and his 'wild boys' (as they were called by some) had brought the Church of Scotland to the brink. Widespread consternation – and condemnation – greeted

---

13. Alexander Murray Dunlop, MP (1798–1870), an advocate, MP for Greenock (1852–1868) and legal adviser to the Free Church of Scotland. His daughter married T. M. Lindsay, from 1870 to 1914 professor at the Free Church College, Glasgow, and defender of William Robertson Smith.

14. *Scotsman*, 21 May 1842, 3.

15. Buchanan, Robert. *The Ten Years' Conflict*. Vol II. Glasgow: Blackie and Son, 1863. 361. Originally it was known as the Claim of *Rights*.

the Claim of Right. It was not only revolutionary to attack the government's ultimate authority over the church; it was also foolish. 'The proceedings of the General Assembly,' a special correspondent for the *Scotsman* sniffed from London, 'are greeted with astonishment in England. We think that the Kirk is committing suicide and nothing can save her from falling by her own hands. All parties abuse the non-intrusionists, and it is the general opinion that the government... will declare most strongly against the parties bringing in legislative relief.'[16] No further legal remedy could be expected from either political party. Sir Robert Peel, as Prime Minister, stood up in the House of Commons to announce that 'Her Majesty's government has abandoned all hope of settling the question in a satisfactory manner'.

In August, the House of Lords assessed, on behalf of the patron Lord Kinnoull and Robert Young (the rejected then reinstated candidate in Auchterarder), damages against the Church of £16,000. This move made untenable the position of those in the Established Church who were trying to maintain its spiritual independence. Separation became the only course. The Court of Session and the Lords – and, some would argue, the refusal on the part of the Evangelicals to compromise – were about to sever the Church of Scotland.

As the 1842 General Assembly adjourned, there was a palpable air of apprehension and even dread as to what loomed ahead for the Scottish church. Charles Cowan's diary for the period discloses a crescendo of excitement regarding the separation that seemed inevitable.[17] Cowan frequently stayed in town, worshipping at St George's to hear his favourite firebrand Robert Candlish preach. And his sermons sometimes took a bizarre turn, ratcheting up the

16. *Scotsman*, 8 June 1842, 2.

17. The donor was Charles Boog-Watson (1858–1947), daughter of Janet (Alexander Cowan's first child of his second marriage), an antiquarian and family genealogist. He writes to a Miss Balfour on 5 June 1944: 'I have gone through about one half of the Diary of Charles Cowan, later M.P. of Valleyfield, Penicuik, more, I must own, after the manner of a butterfly than of a mole or earth worm, and I fear that there is very little of public interest therein contained.' That was an extraordinary statement, given the material. He had originally received the Diary from Marion Cowan (1877–1951), John James' daughter.

emotion. On 11 December 1841 Candlish chose the thirteenth chapter of Revelation for his sermon, a passage that speaks of the beast coming out of the sea. The apocalyptic imagery was vivid and the application to the present crisis obvious, at least to his congregation. Cowan recorded the message: 'That beast apparently [represents] principalities and their powers attacking such important superstitions and Popery.... Very solemn address to be ready for the harvest [i.e., judgment] which seems at hand as in the close of the thirteenth chapter.'[18]

As the drama unfolded, Cowan was preoccupied by every twist and turn in the saga, always staying in close touch with his mentor and guide, Thomas Chalmers. Yet through it all he maintained the disciplines of a busy and pious man, concentrating on his business commitments, which demanded seven to ten hours a day, his reading, and never neglecting his devotional and philanthropic duties. At the age of forty he was a highly organized, deeply committed, and very time-conscious man. He was in the midst of a wrenching and distracting conflict, but he did not allow events swirling around him to reflect on his personal and religious priorities.

And still the Ten Years Conflict ground on, seemingly unstoppable as it approached the point of no return. 'From much personal intercourse with ministers from all parts of Scotland for many years previous to 1843 I had ample opportunity,' Charles Cowan later wrote, 'for being convinced how gladly and thankfully they would have hailed any measure, from whatever quarter it had been offered, that would have enabled them to continue their services as parish ministers to the people, and have saved them and their families from being turned out of house and home, in which they could only have continued by disobeying the law as declared by the House of Lords. To this most painful ordeal were they subjected, and nobly did they endure the fiery trial.'[19]

---

18. *Diary*, 11 December 1842. Edinburgh City Library.

19. *Reminiscences*. 302-3.

Chapter 9

Disruption Drama

'The Disruption of 1843, when 450 ministers broke away to form the Free Church of Scotland, proved so traumatic and divisive that it is still referred to as if it were a recent event,' an editorial in *The Herald* of Glasgow recently stated.[1] The lesson of the Disruption that it drew was simple: 'If the Church of Scotland is to be a national church, it needs to be a broad church.' *The Herald*, the longest running daily newspaper in the world, is entitled to take the long view, but Magnus Llewellin, its recently appointed editor, draws a conclusion with which neither Charles Cowan nor the rest of those who walked out of the 1843 General Assembly would have agreed. They left out of principle. Their sacrifice was based on strong convictions and clearly articulated beliefs. However, disagree as one might with *The Herald*'s conclusion, 18 May 1843 was indeed a watershed in Scottish history, still seen by many, particularly in Scotland, as a recent event.

The Drama Unfolds

In the months following the 1842 Assembly elaborate plans were laid for a unified response by evangelicals to unfolding

1. *The Herald*, 20 May 2013.

developments. A great Convocation of clergy was called for November 'to seek light and direction from on high,' as Cowan explained it, 'and consult together as to their duty.'[2] He was deeply involved in the strategizing. A week before the Convocation was due to gather he wrote: 'I went on to College, & had a talk with Dr Chalmers about church matters, Hetherington etc. with him.'[3] William Maxwell Hetherington was a key player: he became the Free Church's publicist, a prolific writer, and founder of the *Free Church Magazine*.[4]

The Sunday before the Convocation opened, at the second service at St George's, Hetherington preached a sermon that had Cowan's warm approval.[5] The revivalist William Burns of Kilsyth led in a prayer meeting.[6] The struggle was seen by the planners as a spiritual battle and the Disruption, when it came, would represent for them a revival of true religion. 'Very full attendance of the ministers, & also of the public,' Cowan observed.[7]

Chalmers opened the Convocation five days later, after having breakfasted with Charles Cowan. He chose as his text for the opening worship: 'Unto the upright there ariseth light in the darkness' (Ps. 112:4). Again the venue was St George's Church, but immediately after, the Convocation adjourned to Roxburgh Place Church – it was less accessible and ensured greater privacy. Their desire for seclusion proved to be wishful thinking: almost five hundred clergy showed up. Spontaneous discussion was allowed, and then representatives from each synod were allowed

---

2. *Reminiscences*, 303.

3. *Diary*, 9 November 1842.

4. William Maxwell Hetherington (1803–1865) became minister of Free St Andrew's Edinburgh at the Disruption and four years later Free St Paul's. In 1857 he was appointed Professor of Apologetics and Systematic Theology at the Free Church College, Glasgow.

5. 'A very good sermon,' *Diary*, 12 November 1842.

6. William Chalmers Burns (1815–1868) a *locum* for McCheyne in Dundee, in his absence when revival occurred, assisted his father at a communion in Kilsyth when again revival broke out. In 1849 he went to China as a missionary, saw revival near Amoy. He died at 53 of fever there becoming a missionary hero to the Free Church.

7. *Diary*, 12 November 1842.

to speak. Synods, as the intermediary or middle judicatory of the church between presbyteries and the General Assembly, provided a convenient larger but cohesive organizing of the grass roots geographically. Robert Murray McCheyne, minister of St Peter's Dundee, scene of a recent remarkable awakening, set the tone with a deeply moving and memorable prayer. Everyone spoke 'with the most unreserved freedom'.[8]

It was at that point that Chalmers unfolded the idea of a common fund to sustain the clergy when they left the Established Church. He faced the future with both realism and faith: 'I should like to demonstrate the grounds on which, should the worst come to the worst, I look for the stability of our present Church of Scotland in these lands, should the fostering care of the State be withdrawn from her, and should she be severed from all her present endowments and civil immunities by the hand of violence. The arithmetic on which, under God, I found the confidence, I feel, is soon told.... I am not looking for much that is remarkable in the way either of noble efforts or of noble sacrifices, nor yet is it on the impulse of strong but momentary feeling that I at all reckon.... Such is the character – of the premises with which I am now dealing; and the conclusion I draw from them, what I call my minimum of result, because the very least to which I aspire is a hundred thousand pounds in the year.'

Chalmers had four points about setting up what he called for the first time the Sustentation Fund. First, there should be a general fund for salaries for all clergy 'for the high patriotic object of supporting a ministry of the gospel throughout the whole of Scotland.' Second, the funds would be divided equally among all clergy 'both in the rich and in the poorer parishes, the liberality of the former will be stimulated, not by the near and narrow consideration of support for their own minister, but by the great and soul-expanding consideration that they are helping out a provision for the gospel in the most destitute localities of the land.' Third, each congregation could then be free to add to the general stipend for their minister. And finally, 'monies should be provided, in connection with it, for the extension of

8. *Ten Years Conflict,* Volume II. 393.

the church, for not only maintaining the existing ministry, but for increasing their numbers as occasion might require.'[9]

*****

At a closing rally a week later in Lady Glenorchy's church, the main body of the sanctuary was crammed with clergy and elders and the gallery was filled to capacity with onlookers. The audience heard stirring words from Robert Buchanan of Glasgow: 'It is up to you, the nation, not the Church – it is by you, the nation, that this solemn question is now to be entertained ... whether you will, in your province, in the disposal of your temporal resources, honour Christ by giving of these resources to Christ's Church in a free and unfettered condition, leaving her free to receive Christ alone.'[10]

'I thought,' Cowan later reflected on his feelings at that moment, 'that the time had come for the eldership to express their confidence in the ministers, and assure them of our warm support.' He invited a dozen elders to meet in his Edinburgh residence on Melville Street, where he was then living, at four one afternoon during the Convocation. Only three turned up: George Smyttan of the Bombay Presidency;[11] Archibald Bonar, Manager of the Edinburgh and Glasgow Bank and uncle of Horatius the hymn-writer and Andrew the biographer; and Alex Dunlop the lawyer. Dunlop was someone whose skill in drawing up documents and his eloquence would prove invaluable to the cause. The ever-impulsive Charles wanted to send an immediate motion of encouragement to the clergy. Dunlop restrained him, saying that they did not know what course the Convocation would finally take.

The four drew up a statement for later use, expressing solidarity in very practical terms: '[W]e earnestly trust and pray that the ministers of the Church may to the glory of God be kept in the path of duty, what loss and suffering so ever they may expose themselves to, that it is our duty likewise, so far as in our power, to lighten that

9. As quoted in Buchanan, R.'Finance of the Free Church of Scotland,' *Journal of the Statistical Society of London*, vol. 33, no 1 (March 1870). 85-87.

10. *Scotsman*, 26 November 1842. 3.

11. George Smyttan FSE (1789–1863), physician, from Dunkeld.

loss and diminish those sufferings, and to make worldly sacrifices on our part also, in order to support the maintenance in this land, in truth and purity, of the Church of our fathers, when deprived of the benefits of an establishment on account of adherence to those very principles in respect of which, and for the perpetuation of which, that establishment was ratified by Statutes of the Realm, and guaranteed by solemn treaty – Do hereby bind ourselves in the event above mentioned, to contribute the amount attached respectively to our signatures to a fund for the support of the ministers of the Church left in consequence without their present means of subsistence.'[12]

This document was held back as the Convocation adjourned and Charles Cowan would call a further meeting. This was an early December meeting in St George's specifically targeting interested laity. Thirty-two were present: 'a class of men in widely different pursuits or sphere of life.' Ten landed proprietors, eight lawyers, five bankers or in business, four in the East India Company, three doctors, and two tradesmen represented a cross-section of the rising Scottish middle class, along with some older landed gentry. Charles Cowan was one of the younger and outlived them all. 'By this time,' he recalled in his *Reminiscences* and his diary confirms, 'we were in close and most friendly communication with Dr Chalmers, whose labours were unceasing.'[13] As were Charles Cowan's. His diary entry for Friday, 16 December, attests to some of his activities: 'After breakfast to A. Bonars about Books for Financial schemes of Church and to send letters on various subjects.' The way to a Great Convocation in February 1843 had been prepared.

*****

Charles Cowan was appealing to the whole of Scotland but he did so with a strong local commitment. He was a member of Dalkeith Presbytery and with five other elders he started to organize regionally. The five other elders worked alongside him for the cause: his brother John, David Chalmers (Thomas's nephew), David Dickson,

12. Thus, for instance, a 15 December 1842 meeting with Chalmers and Hugh Miller.

13. *Reminiscences*, 308.

Chalmers' son-in-law and later biographer William Hanna, and Walter Paterson, the minister from Kirkund.[14] The six sponsored a series of public meetings throughout the district early in 1843.

Cowan also prepared a Protest for the local constituency described as 'an able declaration and protest, which appeared in the public prints'. Signed by seventeen elders of the Dalkeith Presbytery, five of whom were from Penicuik, it concluded: 'Being convinced, as we now are, that by longer remaining in connecting with the State, faithful ministers of this Church must either be instruments of oppressing the Christian people or be themselves oppressed in the conscientious discharge of their high and sacred functions, we hereby solemnly resolve, in the event of the Church and the people of Scotland being deprived of that national support to which by the Constitution, we must ever hold them to be entitled, to join with others in the adoption of such means as may be best fitted by the blessing of God, to secure a continuance of the benefits of a Free Presbyterian Church in this land to ourselves and to our children.'[15]

*****

A second great convocation was held on 1 February 1843, this time at St Luke's, a *quoad sacra* congregation established by Candlish out of St George's, and recently declared illegal by London. So quickly had momentum grown that nearly a thousand elders, coming from all parts of Scotland, attended. 'The most perfect harmony prevailed, and a hearty desire manifest to provide liberally for the outed ministers,' Cowan reported. One elder signed up for £1000 and then 'the infection was catching, and like some other epidemics, continues wide in its range.'[16] They had been galvanized by the government's curt refusal the previous month to accede

14. Walter Paterson (1790–1849) ordained 1837 was presented to his parish by Thomas Carmichael of Skirling, also Hanna's patron. In 1860 Hanna published a memoir of Carmichael's life.

15. Wilson, John J. *A Fifty Years Retrospect Being a Short History of the Free Church Congregation in Penicuik*. Glasgow: W Pollock Wylie, 1893. 4.

16. *Reminiscences*, 308–309.

to the Claim of Right or to repeal patronage. Concurrent with this blow, the Court of Session had declared on 20 January that *quoad sacra* churches were illegal. The Evangelicals, now denied a significant part of their support at the General Assembly by the disenfranchisement of those congregations, saw their majority threatened. The clergy and elder commissioners from these new congregations who had been denied were among the brightest and most progressive people in the Church of Scotland, and now that they would be absent, the Evangelicals feared that votes in the Assembly would be permanently skewed towards the Moderates. The break became inevitable.

Out of that large gathering, a Provisional Committee was established to prepare for a new denomination. Divided into three sections – Finance, Architecture, and Statistics – Charles Cowan immediately joined the Finance section, working closely with Chalmers. He would continue for many years as a member of the Finance Committee of the Free Church of Scotland, but at this early stage, Charles and other elders would fan out across the country establishing 'Associations' of people sympathetic to the cause in as many congregations as possible. 'In the summer and autumn of 1843,' John McCandlish (Cowan's associate and later antagonist in the insurance business) recalled, '[M]any deputations went forth to organize such Associations in different parts of the country, and the present writer had the privilege, along with a friend, of visiting every parish in one of our south-western counties on this errand, holding meetings in each, or twice speaking from a cart in the corner of a field.'

As the thousand elders met in February they set about to plot the financial future of what was soon to be the Free Church of Scotland. In so doing they were initiating a whole new attitude to church financing. In declaring their independence from state control and in resigning so much wealth and endowment, the new denomination established a new pattern of stewardship. In doing so, it limited its base to those who were prepared (and had the means) to provide sacrificially for the needs of the new church. The generosity of the nascent Free Church and the audacity of their fundraising efforts for new church buildings, new schools, and particularly clergy salaries, was amazing. It radiated out from a committed core of business and professional associates, among them Charles Cowan and his friends, who embarked on a course to ensure that the new enterprise was financially viable.

18 May 1843, Day of Drama

For Charles Cowan, Thursday morning, 18 May 1843, according to his diary, started with breakfast at his father's home on St John Street. One would like to have known what Alexander Cowan had to say by way of wisdom to his oldest child: advice, caution, or resignation? Leaving the house, Charles went along the street outside Moray House, known as the Royal Mile. He caught up with his mentor Robert Candlish. Again, one would like to known what they talked about. The two parted as Cowan went into St Giles. At the Assembly service he heard the incoming Moderator, Professor David Welsh, take as his text the final clause of Romans 14:5: 'Let every man be fully persuaded in his own mind.' 'Very able & most appropriate' was Cowan's verdict, though he recorded the wrong reference. As the worship concluded Cowan crossed over to Princes Street to Edinburgh's New Town, trudging up Hanover Street, and joining the scrum at St Andrew's Church. Crowds had been gathering outside along George Street since four o'clock that morning.

Cowan forced his way through the melee, experiencing 'great difficulty getting in.' Once inside he could see commissioners streaming in from St Giles and finding seats in the railed-off pews. The sanctuary was elliptically shaped, assuring a good view for all. The Moderator soon took his place in the chair behind the communion table. The Marquis of Bute, Queen Victoria's commissioner to Scotland's State Church, was announced as he entered with full military guard. Then it happened. Cowan records that defining moment in recent Scottish history: 'After prayer among the members, Dr Welsh read the Protest, & walked off, followed by the whole of the members on the left. Most impressive scene.' The break had come, a Disruption had occurred, and the religious life of Scotland altered irretrievably. 'I doubt if such a noble sacrifice of the world's possessions has ever been offered in any other country,' he reflected thirty-five years later.[17] That afternoon, 123 ministers, accompanied by 70 elders, left the Church of their birth forever. In so doing clergy abandoned their livelihoods, their homes, and a safe, comfortable, and predictable future. When the news was reported to journalist and jurist Lord Jeffrey later that day, he responded: 'I am proud of my country. There is not another country upon earth where such a deed could have been done.'[18] Similarly, lawyer Lord Cockburn said: 'I know no parallel to it. It is the most honourable fact for Scotland that its whole history supplies.'[19]

With the crush of people on either side, the departing delegates walked in single file. They proceeded on to George Street and then turned on to Hanover Street. 'I walked near the last, with the English and Irish Deputies,' Cowan continued in his diary account. 'Most striking scene outside. Great concourse of people who were in general in solemn silence; a sort of procession within the double line of the crowd all the way to Canonmills.' Tanfield Hall was their destination. 'The immense Hall filled most solemn prayers & able & affecting addresses from Chalmers and Welsh. Business not over until 6 ½, sat with John Bonar.' Charles Cowan would live and relive that day, as did many Scots, for his remaining forty-six years.

'I'll eat a' that come out,' an eccentric rural Lanarkshire minister had told Cowan before that day. Cowan passed the comment on to Chalmers, who laughed and asked Cowan to 'congratulate him on the prospect of a plentiful meal'. As Charles passed the Tron Church en route to Tanfield Hall, that same cleric was standing in the porch. Cowan passed on Chalmers' retort and got the response: 'Did I really say that? I dinna mind, but it's very like me. But I hope I am no bund to eat them a' in aince [once] I may surely have a mert [fattened bullock] or twa – But there is ane amongst them' (referring to one of the Disruption leaders) 'that I am sure I'll no can manage, he'll no keep still, and he's sure to come up again.'[20]

17. *Reminiscences*, 301.

18. Brown, Thomas. *Annals of the Disruption*. Edinburgh: McNiven and Wallace, 1893. 95.

19. Quoted by James Stalker in 'The Jubilee of the Church of Scotland Disruption,' *Northern Messenger* vol. xxviii, no 19 (18 August 1893) 1.

20. *Reminiscences*. 310.

Two hundred and three commissioners walked out of the Assembly that day. Octavius Hill would later bring together the Tanfield Hall delegates in a montage that was copied and sent throughout the Empire wherever religious Scots, particularly of the Free Church variety, could be found. Charles Cowan can be seen clearly to the right of the podium. The deed of demission, placed on the table before the assembled delegates, is being signed by 474 ministers, out of a total of 1203 clergy in the Church of Scotland. It was an impressive, determined, and earnest group – and gifted too. As Lord Balfour of Burleigh put it, 'The majority of the most zealous and active among both clergy and laity left the Church in 1843.' Young Norman MacLeod of the Barony (as he was later known), who stayed in the Established Church, admitted that the 'best portion of our people have gone.'[21]

The Drama Plays Itself Out

The Sunday after the Disruption, Charles Cowan set out to go to St George's but turned aside, 'fearing it would be full,' and instead went to Morningside Church, where he 'heard Walter Wood preach excellent sermon to the solemn occasion' from Psalm 68:18. This was a customary text for Ascension Sunday, but the picture of the reigning Lord giving gifts to his triumphant people seemed especially timely, given the circumstances. 'The church was crowded,' Charles wrote in his diary, 'and the elders' bench held 17 including a Mr Nesbit from London.'[22]

Mr Nesbit was not the only visitor from outside Scotland sent to witness the event. Across the Atlantic, there was warm support from American Presbyterians who had themselves divided six years earlier as 'Old School' and 'New School' for a cause they considered just and righteous. Six months prior to the Disruption, on 27 November Cowan was present when the Old School American Presbyterians' full-time liaison with Europe, Robert Baird, spoke at a special third service at St George's.[23] Earlier that year, the American connections

21. As quoted by J R Fleming in *A History of the Church in Scotland* Edinburgh: T & T Clark, 1927. 37-38.

22. *Diary*, entry for Sabbath 21 May 1843.

23. Robert Baird (1798 – 1863) PTS 1822; General Agent, American Sunday School Union (1829-1835) For the rest of his life he gave himself to the 'promotion of

had been reinforced when Princeton College conferred an honourary doctorate of divinity on Robert Candlish in recognition of his leadership in the Church of Scotland.[24] Some southerners of the Old School became less enthusiastic as they discovered how ardently the Free Church would oppose slavery.

Right after the Disruption the new church sent a blue ribbon delegation to the United States and British North America. The Canada Presbyterian Church, comprised of members sympathetic to the Free Church, split from the Church of Scotland in Lower and Upper Canada. Scottish issues had been presented to a British colony as the cause of separation in a place where most were irrelevant. In the United States there was keen interest in the debate in Scotland. The Cowans' American trade interests and family connections meant that they were more knowledgeable than many in Scotland at the time about North America. Charles took a keen interest in both business and religion in the United States.

*****

If, as has often been said, all politics are local, then church life is ultimately not much different. The heady experience of 18 May 1843 would be tested in local realities. The second Sunday after the Disruption, Charles remained in Penicuik. Instead of going to Edinburgh in his pony cart he arranged for it to bring the Rev. Andrew McKenzie to the village. McKenzie had been invited to preach the inaugural service for the new Free Church in Penicuik. He had been with the 'Auld Lichts,' the more Calvinistic of the Burgher and Anti-Burgher divisions of the Secession churches.[25]

---

the interests of evangelical religion in the various countries of Continental Europe' (*ad loc* in Nevin, Ed. *Encyclopaedia of the PC(USA)*Philadelphia; Presbyterian Publications, 1884). He was a key liaison between the Free Church of Scotland and the Presbyterian Church (USA) Old School.

24. Then the College of New Jersey.

25. In *Auld Licht Idylls* J. M. Barrie caricatures his mother's uncompromising Auld Licht faith: 'For forty years they have been dying out, but their cold, stiff pews still echo the Psalms of David, and, the Auld Licht kirk will remain open so long as it has one member and a minister.' (Barrie, J.M. *Auld Licht Idylls*. New York: H. M. Caldwell Co, 1900. 53) There was indeed, however, a narrowness to their faith.

Unlike many of his sect, McKenzie had exposure to a wider Christian community through his chaplaincy at the Blind Asylum, a work that had brought him into contact with the Cowans. The new denomination encouraged him, and many of the Secession, to feel that in the Free Church they would find a theologically congenial home. But it was a Trojan horse.

The Secession, most of whom merged in 1847 to become the United Presbyterian Church, was strongly Voluntary, a position which the Free Church, loyal to Chalmers, had not yet espoused. The 'UPs', as they became known, were the third force in the religious configuration of urban nineteenth century Scotland. They also influenced Charles Cowan, and others with him, to be more open to a Voluntaryist position. In spite of the Disruption, Thomas Chalmers longed for the day when a reunited and establishment church would help make Scotland his ideal of a Christian commonwealth.

Mr McKenzie made a great impression that first Sunday. 'Went to [the Gardener's] Lodge at ½ past 11,' Charles wrote in his diary, 'and found it well filled. Mr M[cKenzie] preached a most attractive sermon which gave great satisfaction from Luke 12 ch 32.'[26] The Gardener's Lodge was an early farmers' cooperative society that provided accommodation for community meetings. A second Sunday service was held at the earlier-than-usual hour of three o'clock in the afternoon and was also well attended, with Mr McKenzie preaching again. His presence that day represented an extraordinary degree of commitment: he had lost his youngest child to whooping cough the day before. After the services, he rushed back to his family in Edinburgh.

He received the call and on 24 August 1843 the Rev. Andrew McKenzie became the first minister of the fledgling Penicuik Free Church of Scotland. The induction took place on the grounds of Valleyfield, just a stone's throw from the parish church, in an out-of-doors service reminiscent of the ones held by the Covenanters. Thomas Guthrie, considered one of Scotland's ablest preachers at

26. Penicuik Thistle Lodge of Free Gardeners was a benevolent organization established in Penicuik in 1822 along the lines of the Masons. (www.scran.ac.uk/000-000-502-630-C. Accessed 12 October 2012.)

the time, minister of Free St John's Edinburgh, delivered the message. The Valleyfield grounds overflowed, thanks in part to Guthrie's reputation, even though the Established Church, featured as a counter-attraction, the Edinburgh sermonic spellbinder Archibald Binnie of Lady Yester's Church of Scotland. Binnie was no match for Guthrie: '[T]he scantily filled pews in that edifice gave evidence of the greater popularity of the distinguished divine from St John's and no little sympathy with the principles which he advocated.'[27] Charles Cowan presented the new minister with a cassock and gown. McKenzie remained until 1855 and set the new church on a clear course.

Charles was one of the first five elders (all from the parish church), and Charles' brother John was ordained an elder in 1850. Most of the congregation of the new church were employees of the Cowans, as Penicuik was a company town. Charles continued to teach his young men's Bible class until his duties elsewhere became too pressing and his absences from Penicuik too frequent. 'Confidence in his judgement and in that of his brother, Mr. John Cowan, and esteem for their personal character,' a member reflected at the time of the church's fiftieth anniversary, 'undoubtedly influenced many in Penicuik to throw in their lot with the Free Church at the Disruption who might otherwise have remained in the Establishment.'[28]

The new church grew rapidly – 153 communicants attended the first communion. They sought a place to build but Sir George Clerk, the local landholder, refused to allow any property to be sold to the congregation, and it was only through the good offices of Charles and his brother John that a cottage with a four-hundred-year lease was purchased. The lot was triangular, and a rather awkwardly shaped building (which still stands) was erected. When the church was dedicated on 24 October 1844, Charles wrote: 'To New Church soon after 11 o'clock. Well filled. Mr Pitcairn preached from Exodus. Collection about £ 47.10.8½. In afternoon Mr MacKenzie [preached] admirable sermon from 74th Ps 22v.'

27. Wilson, John J. *A Fifty Years Retrospect Being a Short History of the Free Church Congregation in Penicuik*. Glasgow: W Pollock Wylie, 1893. 5.

28. Wilson, John J. *A Fifty Years Retrospect Being a Short History of the Free Church Congregation in Penicuik*. Glasgow: W Pollock Wylie, 1893. 10.

Thomas Chalmers was a name to conjure with in Penicuik and so, to dedicate the new building, William Hanna his son-in-law (and later biographer), with close links to the Cowans, was asked to preach. 'Admirable sermon from Mr Hanna from Colossians 2 ch 15v. Audience of 600 persons, much gratified. Collection in the afternoon £ 23 18 11, and in the evening £35 14 6 which added to former collection & some from Presbytery, from Melrose, Dr Madsen & speakers in whole £ 160 12 5. Of this John & I gave each £ 50 but the contribution is truly wonderful.'[29] The Disruption had a profound impact on the religious life of Penicuik, as it did in many small towns across Scotland, bringing division and hard feeling as well as spiritual renewal.

*****

The event of 18 May 1843 not only fragmented the Church of Scotland; it also brought division in the Cowan and Menzies families. Neither father, William Menzies or Alexander Cowan, identified with the Free Church, nor did Catharine Cowan's two clergy brothers. William Menzies, who had served the Lanark parish church for fifty years, remained in the Established Church until he died four years later. His daughter described the agony he went through in making that decision. 'How hard a trial it was, few can know. My poor Father suffered deeply; those who went out were the party he had always sympathised with in their evangelical sentiments; yet he could not see that they were right in the rejection of all patronage, which he had held all along as the most advantageous system for keeping the parish minister in the position of independence so essential for the fitting discharge of duties to all ranks of his people.'[30]

William Scott-Moncrieff, parish minister in Penicuik, whose arrival thirteen years earlier had pleased Charles, also elected to stay in the Established Church, but only two of seven elders in that parish remained with him. He was 'a good and faithful minister, who, up to

29. *Diary*, entry for 24 October 1844.

30. Reid, Thomas. *The Lanark Manse Family–Narrative Found in the Repositories of the Late Miss Elizabeth Bailie Menzies of 31 Windsor Street Edinburgh*. Lanark: D. A. V. Thomason, 1901. 27-28

a certain point, had identified himself with the non-intrusion party,' Charles later recalled.[31] The pain of those staying with the Church of Scotland was compounded by the other side appearing to have taken the moral high ground: the implicit assumption was that those who stayed had sacrificed principle for privilege, choosing ease and comfort over uncertainty and insecurity.

*****

At the first General Assembly of the Free Church of Scotland, held in the autumn of 1843, Thomas Chalmers announced that 687 congregational associations had already been created for the express purpose of fundraising. Of these, 239 had sent in a total of £17,000 for the Sustentation Fund. In addition, £105,000 had been raised for new church buildings. A Sustentation Fund Committee was created and for the next thirty-four years Charles Cowan would serve, standing up in the General Assembly to move the adoption of its report or, increasingly, reminding a new generation of the history of the Fund.

At the 1844 General Assembly William Cunningham, in the absence of Dr Chalmers, who was ill, reported that £68,700 had been received. The amount did not include what had been raised for church buildings. Had the number of ministers stayed the same, there would have been enough to pay each of the 470 the original sum that Chalmers had aimed for, £150 per annum. But there were now another 110 new ordinands, so the annual salary had been kept at £105. 'This exhibits in a remarkable manner the wisdom and sagacity of Dr Chalmers [who] set the early part of our history, at which the estimate was firmed, on very imperfect data, and notwithstanding all the difficulties we have had to encounter,'[32] Cunningham told the Assembly.

To raise £61,000 to pay the stipends of 470 clergy, providing each with an allowance of £105, was a stupendous achievement. In being

31. Wilson, John J. *A Fifty Years Retrospect Being a Short History of the Free Church Congregation in Penicuik*. Glasgow: W. Pollock Wylie, 1893. 4.

32. *Proceedings of the Free Church of Scotland General Assembly (1844)*. 186.

asked to resign their livings, abandon their comfortable manses, and sometimes conduct worship in the open air, Free Church clergy set an example of high principle and a disdain for worldly emoluments, which galvanized their congregations into generosity and sacrifice. As well as generously providing for their ministers, Free Church congregants would be asked to build 470 churches and reconstruct a whole educational system previously operated by the Church of Scotland.

*****

Inevitably the question as to what it meant for the Free Church to be the Free Church of the whole of Scotland focussed on the Sustentation Fund. Questions were raised in the Committee as to the viability of some congregations in remote areas of the country, and whether subsidising them out of the common pool made sound business sense. As an initiator of the Committee, and a hard-headed businessman, Charles Cowan had a strategic role. 'Having been a member of the Sustentation Committee for many years, I have seen many cases pass the Committee as sanctioned charges which I consider ought to have been constituted preaching stations only in the meantime.'[33] But despite his reservations about the funding of such congregations, he continued to support the Fund on the basis of a common cause.

In a time of economic and social challenge, most adherents of the Free Church came primarily from two areas of Scotland: first, the Highlands – with its subsistence agriculture, ravaged by clearances, evictions, and now a potato famine and populated by an economically depressed and sometimes illiterate peasantry, and second, the increasingly affluent urban centres of the Lowlands with their rising artisan and middle class.[34] These two disparate groups of people were held together by a common conviction.

Financial demands placed on adherents and members of the

33. *Reminiscences*, 319-320.

34. In MacLaren, A. Allan; *Religion and Social Class: The Disruption Years in Aberdeen*. London: Routledge & Kegan Paul, 1974. 30.

Free Church led to a situation that exists to this day. Particularly in the Lowlands, the Free Church was dominated by skilled labourers and the middle-classes – and the new so-called 'shopocracy'. In the Highlands, theological concerns and spiritual loyalties kept even the poorest loyal to the principles of the Disruption. But further south, the working class in the large, increasingly industrialized urban centres was often alienated (in spite of Chalmers' earlier social concerns) from a cause that demanded more of them financially than they felt they were in a position to provide. The year after the Disruption, a Church of Scotland propaganda pamphlet stated 'Money! Money! With the "F. C." is everything.'[35] True or not, this perception may have contributed to the distancing from the church by the urban poor and the growing and pervasive secularization of the working class which existed and accelerated in Scotland to this very day.

*****

Charles Cowan was shaped by the events surrounding 18 May 1843. His Christian experience, as one reads his diaries of that period, was galvanized by the conflict and controversy swirling at the time. There was that profound sense of injustice he first experienced with the excise, a feeling of deep resentment of individuals who wielded power insensitively and, as he and his fellow Free Churchmen saw it, as an end in itself. As his life in the new Free Church of Scotland developed he became caught up in its operation, politics and financing. One can observe a subtle shift, a change in his religious orientation. He was becoming a churchman, a denominational loyalist, proud of the heritage and sacrifices of the Free Church of Scotland, and determined that it should never be forgotten.

In an 1838 letter to Chalmers, Cowan spoke of a sermon he had recently heard as being 'nearly entirely destitute of all adherence to

35. MacLaren, A. A. *Religion and Social Class: The Disruption Years in Aberdeen*. London and Boston: Routledge & Kegan Paul, 1974, 104. See also Brown, Callum. *Religion and Society in Scotland since 1707*. Edinburgh: Edinburgh University Press, 1997. 25 – 28 who suggests that 'The dependence on 'Free Church progress' was judged year by year on the volume of donations to central funds."

Gospel truths as it is possible to imagine.'[36] 'Adherence to gospel truths' was what Chalmers had taught him was the one thing that mattered. As he grew older other items crowded that list: success in business, reputation as a politician, intellectual respectability, being thought well of by his peers. For a brief moment in Scotland's history these were tangential to many. The clear teaching and preaching of the Bible was what mattered. Charles Cowan would go anywhere to hear a good sermon. The young men of the Bible class he taught most Sunday afternoons, the district he visited as an elder, his deep friendships with many clergy contemporaries, these were what sustained him. Was what changed over the years, both for the denomination he loved, as for Charles himself, a loss (like the church in Ephesus described in the book of Revelation in the Bible) a 'loss of the first love'? Could what happened to Charles over the next forty-five years have been true as well for others in the Free Church?

*****

For the rest of his life Charles Cowan was identified in the public mind as a Free Churchman. He became a lightning rod for the political, religious and social opinions then roiling and dividing Scotland's capital city. His entry into politics and his election to Parliament as a person closely identified in the public perception with the Free Church came at a decisive moment. Nothing demonstrates the developing and shifting allegiances better than the election of 1847. It is to that bellwether election that we now turn.

36. CC to TC, 28 April 1838. New College, CHA 4.273-9. The probationer, a Mr Smith, went on to become 'a most deserving young man. There has been a very marked change in his preaching since he first came to Penicuik, and he is to me & the people hereabouts generally just as acceptable & likely to be useful as a Preacher, as he was at first the reverse ... Several times since I have heard him with great pleasure, & I shall be inclined to think him well qualified to be an useful Parish minister.'

Chapter 10

Election Euphoria

On 31 May 1847, Thomas Chalmers died suddenly. The General Assembly of the Free Church of Scotland was in session and the news was greeted by the commissioners, one of whom was Charles Cowan, with consternation. Though shocking, his passing was predictable, given his age, history of ill health, the tireless energy that had possessed him since the Disruption, and the burdens he was carrying. Robert Candlish and Charles Cowan were allowed, while stopping at Chalmes' home in Morningside, to view 'the remains of the mighty dead, which were the embodiment of placid and majestic repose.'[1]

Charles Cowan was chosen by the family to be a pallbearer. Chalmers' funeral was one of the great events of Victorian Scotland: his son-in-law William Hanna wrote, 'Never before did we witness such a funeral; nay, never before, in at least the memory of man, did Scotland witness such a funeral.'[2] Over ten thousand people joined the cortege out to the newly opened Grange Cemetery. Chalmers was buried immediately across from the Cowan plot where Alexander himself would be interred twelve years later.

1. *Reminiscences*, 184.

2. Hanna *Memoirs of Dr Chalmers* (vol 4) Edinburgh: Fullerton, 1852, 608.

Chalmers' passing dealt a cruel blow not only to the nascent Free Church of Scotland but also to his family. Charles Cowan's oldest child, Jean, was engaged to marry Thomas' nephew, also named Thomas Chalmers. She was in England at the time, preparing for their wedding, and wrote home shortly after the death: 'All seemed to receive the tidings with much interest, and a general feeling that his death was a loss to the country at large.'[3] When the wedding took place the uncle of the groom, his namesake, who was to have performed the ceremony, was missing. The loss cast a shadow over what was to have been a happy occasion: Jean was the first of Charles and Catharine's children to marry. Her life was later to end in tragedy.

*****

Charles Cowan felt the loss keenly that summer. He was about to undertake the greatest challenge of his life so far: running for legislative office in opposition to the sitting Whig candidate, Thomas Babington Macaulay. And there was no Thomas Chalmers to guide him. If there was ever a David and Goliath situation, this was it. Macaulay, then one of the two sitting members for Edinburgh in the House of Commons in London, gave great lustre to a proud city. He was one of the best known and most erudite members of Parliament. Following his return from India in 1838 it was the publisher Adam Black who had approached him to stand for election as a Whig.[4] The following year he was returned unopposed. He was immediately appointed by the Prime Minister as Secretary for War, an office he filled until Melbourne's defeat two years later. In the summer of 1846 he became Paymaster-General under the new Prime Minister Lord John Russell. A year later he was up for re-election, which appeared to every pundit to be a no-brainer.

In spite of his reputation, however, Macaulay was not invulnerable. The previous year his friend the lawyer Lord Cockburn observed that 'The truth is that Macaulay, with all his admitted knowledge,

3. Jeanie Cowan to Elizabeth Cowan, 3 June 1847, in *Letters*.

4. Adam Black (1784-1874) whose statue is in the East Princes St Gardens, Edinburgh, bookseller, founder of A. & C. Black publishing company. He published the editions 7, 8 and 9 of the *Encyclopaedia Britannica*. He was MP for Edinburgh 1856 to 1865 and also Lord Provost.

talent, eloquence, and worth, is not popular. He cares more for his History than for all the jobs of his constituents, and answers letters irregularly, and with a brevity deemed contemptuous; and above all other defects, he suffers severely from the vice of over-talking, and consequently of under-listening. A deputation goes to London to enlighten their representative. They are full of their own matter, and their chairman has a statement bottled and ripe, which he is anxious to draw and decant; but, instead was listened to, they no sooner enter the audience chamber than they find themselves all superseded by the restless ability of their eloquent Member, who, besides mistaking speaking for hearing, has the indelicate candour not even to profess being struck by the importance of the affair.'[5]

Macaulay's vulnerability was exacerbated by two current issues. His lukewarm support for the repeal of the Corn Laws in 1846 was noted by the electorate, in spite of his ostentatious hand-shaking with Cobden, the leader of the Chartists, after the bill finally passed the Commons. There was also the matter of the government's decision to provide a subsidy for the Maynooth College in Ireland. The school was established in 1795 to prepare priests for Roman Catholic orders so that ordinands no longer had to go overseas. In 1845 Peel, as Prime Minister, had increased the annual grant from £9,000 to £26,000, and provided a capital grant of £30,000 for building extensions. A firestorm of protest, initiated by Protestant extremists, had created a serious clash, exacerbated by the strong feelings on both sides. Joining the newly constituted United Presbyterians (the two Secession churches having merged that summer), the Free Church represented a powerful lobby against the Maynooth grant that Macaulay showed every sign of dangerously discounting and disdaining.

One of the powerful United Presbyterian politicians was Duncan McLaren, a draper on the Royal Mile with a seat on the Town Council, and an eye for politics which gained him the sobriquet 'the snake.'[6] McLaren was a member of the radical section of the Whig party. In the

---

5. Trevelyan, G. O. *Life and Letters of George Trevelyan Macaulay*. 2nd Ed. Vol.2 . London: Thomas Nelson. 1876. 184-5.

6. McLaren (1800-1886) see obituary *Scotsman* 27 April 1886. Two biographies of McLaren: one by J. B. Mackie (two volumes), 1888; and Pickard, Willis *The Member for Scotland*. Edinburgh: Birlinn, 2011.

early summer of 1847 an election committee consisting of McLaren and his Whig coalition determined that of the two sitting members Macaulay could most easily be defeated, Sir William Gibson-Craig being too well connected in the city. One possible candidate, Sir Culling Eardley-Smith, English with an impeccable pedigree (Eton and Oriel College Oxford), was considered because he had been chair of the Anti-Maynooth Committee.[7] Eardley-Smith had campaigned vigorously against Maynooth and Macaulay in Edinburgh the previous year in a by-election necessitated by both Edinburgh MPs being appointed to the cabinet in Lord Russell's new government.

Now with a General Election looming a choice had to be made. Dissenters and United Presbyterians were uncomfortable with Roman Catholicism becoming the issue, identifying with the Roman Catholic sense of exclusion from the political process. This impacted Eardley-Smith as a strident anti-Catholic, but he was also denied a second attempt because, it was claimed, he opposed Sunday trains.[8] This would later prove ironic: Charles Cowan was to be a staunch defender of the Scottish Sabbath. Duncan McLaren was also a potential candidate but he denied interest in standing and he too was potentially divisive.[9] The lot fell on Charles Cowan, supported by former Provost and radical Whig politician Sir James Forrest.[10] Cowan was known mostly for his opposition to the excise on paper and thus presumably he was a free-trader and acceptable to the Chartists. Charles Cowan was selected as the least bad choice.

Thus Cowan entered the electoral lists in an almost accidental way. He had, he stated, no 'expectation of ever being called to occupy

7. Sir Culling Eardley-Smith (1805-1863) was grandson and heir through his mother of the Jewish financier Sampson Gideon. As a wealthy and prominent member of the Evangelical party of the Church of England he stood out against growing Anglo-Catholicism. He was Treasurer of the London Missionary Society (1844-1863).

8. Pickard, Willis. *The Member for Scotland, A Life of Duncan McLaren*. Edinburgh: Birlinn, 2011. 90.

9. Christopher Harvie's simplistic assertion that McLaren's 'domination of Scottish Liberal politics began with the Anti-Corn League in the 1840s', and for backsliding on this issue he had Macaulay ejected from his Edinburgh seat in 1847 'notwithstanding the charm of his oratory and his world-wide reputation as a man of letters." (*Scotland & Nationalism* 2nd Ed. London: Routlege. 1994.) is not borne out by the facts.

10. Sir James Forrest, B. (1780–1860) Lord Provost of Edinburgh 1837 – 1843, created a baronet 1838.

so prominent a position, and notwithstanding the support cordially tendered. My aim and object was simply to show to the Government that there would be a respectable minority by whom the oppressive treatment inflicted by the Excise on various classes of traders was keenly felt.'[11] He was also favoured because of his religious affiliation. Macaulay's agnosticism was suspected and poorly hidden. He was not regarded as either a sincere or devout believer; in fact, his scepticism was well known in certain circles: this in spite of (or perhaps because of) his father's membership in the Evangelical Clapham Sect.

At first, Charles didn't take his campaign seriously, and that led to a careless oversight. He failed to establish his eligibility to be a Member of Parliament. Because Alexander Cowan & Sons sold paper to the government, he had a clear conflict of interest as a legislator, which could potentially have barred him from taking his seat. The oversight came back later to haunt him, but at the time the prospect of his being elected was so unlikely that the subject was never raised.

There was one hurdle that Charles Cowan had to overcome before he could proceed. He met with the electoral committee and explained that he could not accept the nomination without sounding out his father and receiving his blessing. Charles duly consulted with Alexander, who, as Charles later wrote, 'Expressed himself, though not strongly, against my entertaining the proposal.' But then Alexander asked how he himself felt about running for Parliament. Charles provided an answer that seemed to come straight from Thomas Chalmers: 'I told him that it was part of my social creed that unless there were grave objections to such a course a citizen ought to place his services in any position where in the estimation of his fellow-men he might be useful.'[12] Alexander was not likely trying to be obstructionist. He was probably attempting to protect his son, knowing only too well the effects of living in the glare of publicity (which he had spent his life avoiding) and understanding the cost of public office.

******

11. *Reminiscences*, 212-3.

12. *Reminiscences*, 215.

The public attacks were not long in coming: when the rumour of Charles' candidacy reached the *Scotsman*, the paper was livid. '[Is] this not a hoax which some wag has palmed upon our contemporary?' Charles Cowan was a 'junior member of a respectable firm but as an individual, not one in a hundred of the electors of Edinburgh ever saw his face or probably heard his name.' 'Charles Cowan,' the article continued to pontificate, 'though he has spent his life here, never, so far as we know, delivered a speech, gave a toast, made or seconded a motion, at a public meeting in Edinburgh. Except among the members of the Free Church, to which he belongs, he is nearly as little known in this city as in Cork or Bristol.'[13]

Indeed, Charles Cowan was the Free Church response to all that had happened during the decade of conflict. Betrayed by their government's refusal to redress what they perceived to be wrongs in the Established Church of Scotland or to provide them with adequate financial assistance for new churches, Scottish Free Church voters were not pleased about aid for the Irish Roman Catholics. At one candidates' meeting, Macaulay came across as equivocating on the Maynooth grant and subsequently made an ill-timed comment (which was said to have cost him the election) about opposition to the grant being 'the bray of Exeter Hall' – the place in London where meetings of the Protestant Reformation Society were held.[14] William McCrie, son of John Knox's biographer, called out at a Cowan rally that 'the same animal that could bray could also kick'.

Not that the Cowans agreed with the crude anti-Roman Catholic rhetoric of the day. In 1844 Alexander had written to Bishop Andrew Carruthers, Roman Catholic Vicar Apostolic of the Eastern District of Scotland: 'My wife and I have frequently visited your School for Female Children at Milton House, and we have been much interest[ed] by the simple and artless manner of many of the children, but the judicious kindness and attention with which they are treated by the worthy ladies of that establishment – what would you and Bishop Gillis say

13. *Scotsman* 10 July 1847. 2.

14. *Scotsman* 28 July 1847. 3.

to our providing advantages of this kind for fifty of the present children of your communion at Milton House – my Friends and I engaging to pay for it.'[15] A subsequent follow-up letter to Bishop James Gillis,[16] offered to underwrite the education of local Roman Catholic girls and commended the nuns for their 'judicious kindness and attention' to those poverty-stricken children.[17] There is an interesting sidebar to this: at the same time George Edward Clerk, one of eight sons of Sir George, laird of Penicuik, a former Royal Navy sailor and sheep-farmer in Australia, converted to Roman Catholicism and became a strident advocate for his new faith as a journalist in Montreal.[18] Founding *The True Witness and Catholic Chronicle* he entered into the lists on behalf of Irish Catholics in Canada at the behest of Bishop Bourget, to the considerable embarrassment of his family and the incredulity of the town of Penicuik.

Cowan never succumbed to the rabid anti-Catholicism that the Maynooth grant debate aroused and that was so popular at the time. 'Nothing in my experience of Parliament pained me more,' he later wrote, 'than the annual Maynooth debate, or baiting, as it might well be termed, of the Irish Roman Catholic members. The bigotry, intolerance, and imputation of sinister motives and practices levelled against a large section of our fellow-subjects, was eminently fitted to

15. Andrew Carruthers (1770–1852) Vicar Apostolic of Eastern Scotland.

16. James Gillis (1802–1864), born in Montreal. At the time he was Coadjutor Vicar Apostolic of Eastern Scotland. He succeeded Carruthers on his death.

17. AC writes on 7 March 1845 to Bishop Gillis: 'Some friends and I were anxious about a year ago to give some assistance to our poorer Roman Catholic Brethren in educating their children ... [but I]... only received a verbal answer through Mr Malcolm informing me that you contemplated removing the Establishment from Milton House and that therefore nothing could be done at that time. I hope you will be able to establish a similar Institute in a more suitable locality. In the meantime I hope you will be pleased to learn that many persons are desirous of aiding in any good work of the kind proposed, and among others may I mention that Lord and Lady Ruthven have expressed an anxious desire to be useful. I think I may therefore say that with their assistance and that of other friends we shall be able to give one hundred pounds per annum to assist in the matter.' GD311/2/43 365 NAS 365. See also AC to Bishop Caruthers Greenhill College 12 January 1844 GD311/2/43 330.

18. George Edward Clerk (1815-1875) He appears to have been disinherited by the family.

produce that disaffection and hostility amongst our Irish brethren which has so often caused anxiety to the Government and danger to the unity of the empire, the continued existence of which is in a great degree traceable to the irritation produced.'[19]

Charles Cowan's electoral supporters were diverse, and one unsympathetic correspondent for the *Scotsman* reported after an election rally: 'We can tell whom he stands *against* – not what principle he stands *for*. Looking at those who appear as his supporters, we find every possible opinion on every possible subject represented among them, and often represented, too, by the most bitter and unreasonable of each party. The worst annals of electioneering do not present any combination so monstrous and motley as that which was represented by its leaders on Mr Cowan's platform on Monday evening. There were Tories, Whigs, and Radicals; Establishment men, Free Church men, and Voluntaries; Educationists and anti-Educationists; 'No-Popery' men and loud advocates of toleration; the agitators for Untaxed Whisky, and the President of the Total Abstinence Society; the declaimers against the 'licensing system,' and the ex-magistrate whose fame rests on a most absurd and tyrannical use of that system; the bitterest opponents of Sunday trains and their warmest friends – in short, every question, great and small, had every one of its sides and shades represented on that platform.' The editorial concluded: 'They agree in no one thing but in declaring that Mr Charles Cowan is the best possible representative for the city of Edinburgh.'

In a letter to the editor, 'A Reformer of the Old School' predicted 'defeat and mortification' for Cowan, who was 'the victim of the folly and killing kindness of our red-hot patriots.... He is the son of one of the worthiest and most respected of our townsmen, and he is himself an amiable and accomplished young man, and exemplary in all the relations of life ... the heaviest charge that can be brought against him is the temporary weakness that made him yield to their importunities against his own impressions and better judgment. He will return to the privacy of domestic and, if he will, civic life, which he is so well qualified to enjoy and adorn; and the reluctance

19. *Reminiscences*, 332-3.

he showed in entering the lists will soon make this episode in his history forgotten.'[20]

*****

The final ten days of July were ones of feverish activity for the candidate as he attended meetings of electors in the afternoons and stayed up late into the night interacting with the electorate and speaking in every part of Edinburgh, expounding his views and explaining why he had become a candidate. The Whig *Scotsman* was first dismissive in its reporting, and then angry, as his campaign gained momentum. One of the charges against him was that he would split the Liberal vote. He responded to this complaint in one speech, pointing to all the Conservatives who were on the platform who then 'joined loudly' in cheers, assuming that Cowan's candidacy would indeed divide the Liberals. Many Tories, it was anticipated, would give their second vote to Cowan as an avowed Voluntaryist.

The feisty Cowan effectively mocked journalists who claimed he was not known by more than a hundred, that he was 'very little thought of, because ... [he] had never made a speech, nor even proposed a toast.' Amid laughter and cheering, he added, 'Now, it did appear to me as one of the oldest qualifications possible in a member of Parliament – that of proposing toasts. It may be a very good qualification for a convivial club, but I am not aware that it is a qualification which has ever been set before any other constituency as necessary to enable its representative to make an appearance in the House of Commons.'[21]

On polling day, Friday, 30 July, Adam Black sat up with Macaulay in a room of the Merchants' Hall as the ballots were counted. 'At ten o'clock we were confounded to find that he was 150 below Cowan, but still had faint hopes that the next hour might turn the scale. The next hour came, and a darker prospect. At midnight he was 340 below Cowan. It was obvious now that the field was lost; but we were left from hour to hour under the torture of a sinking poll, till

20. *Scotsman*, 28 July 1847. 3.

21. *Scotsman*, 28 July 1847. 3.

at four o'clock it stood thus: Cowan, 2063; Craig, 1854; Macaulay, 1477; Blackburn, 980.'[22] Macaulay, bitter in defeat, attributed the result to electors who felt that 'the patronage of Edinburgh had been too exclusively distributed among a clique'.[23]

Psephology – from the Greek suggesting inspecting pebbles used in an election for an analysis of the electors – is helped in this case by a document published the following year: *List of Voters in the City of Edinburgh who voted for Mr Charles Cowan MP (1847)*. That it was published – the only such publication for Edinburgh in the nineteenth century – is an indication of just how controversial the outcome of the election really was.[24] Voting for Cowan on the first ballot, according to the survey, were 567 Free Churchmen, 492 United Presbyterians, and 160 from the Church of Scotland. The remaining electors were a mix, with Congregationalists the largest with 65 going down to 6 Roman Catholics and a similar number of Unitarians. 621 were listed as 'religion unknown'.

In a conversation with Queen Victoria, Lord John Russell described Macaulay's defeat as 'disgraceful'. He was also quoted as saying that 'the absence of any party contest, or of any great question has led to results of a very unfortunate character – the indulgence of caprice, ingratitude and injustice.'[25] The party structure after the election of 1847 was impacted by the repeal of the Corn Laws the previous year: the Tories fractured into pro and con while the radical Whigs, with their recent triumph, were now in the ascendency. Given his longstanding opposition to and hatred of the excise on paper, it was these radicals with whom Cowan was identified. The fluidity of party loyalties in the new Parliament presented a challenge to Lord John Russell as Prime Minister.

---

22. Trevelyan, G. O. *Life and Letters of George Trevelyan Macaulay*. 2nd Ed. Vol. II. London: Thomas Nelson. 1876. 190.

23. TBM to Hannah Macaulay 30 July 1847. Trevelyan, G. O. *Life and Letters of George Trevelyan Macaulay*. 2nd Ed. Vol. 2. London: Thomas Nelson. 1876. 191.

24. The two others specifically connected with electors were 'A political analysis of votes in the first municipal district of Edinburgh with their religious profession and police assessment' from 1840 and 'Street list of electors of the City of Edinburgh' (1854.). In neither case was the name of the one elected mentioned making this one unique.

25. As quoted in Prest, John *Lord John Russell* London: Macmillan. 1972. 262, and cited by Pickard, 93.

In Scotland the old Whigs were largely swept aside in favour of a new Radicalism. In Glasgow both Whigs were defeated and in Aberdeen the Free Church demonstrated its power as one of its members replaced the Church of Scotland incumbent. A new political alliance between the Free Church, flexing its political muscle, and the dissenters was being forged. And nowhere was the turmoil in the public arena more evident than in the election of Charles Cowan, the radical Whig and Free Churchman, in Edinburgh.

*****

Press reports indicate the level of consternation occasioned by the results. The *Times* commented that '[t]he most eloquent of Liberal politicians is rejected by a city that arrogates to itself no petty claims for its appreciation of Liberal politics and its love of literary amenities.' The Scottish papers were embarrassed. The Conservative *Fifeshire Journal* wrote, 'Mr Cowan beats Mr Macaulay by 586 votes; and the constituency of that city which Mr Macaulay deemed the most intellectual in the empire, may now fairly lay claim to the disgrace of being the most ignorant, besotted, and degraded, in the three kingdoms.' The *Morning Chronicle* complained that '[t]he defeat of Mr Macaulay at Edinburgh is, in every point of view, a disheartening circumstance. No explanation can place it in a light which does not throw discredit on the character of a great popular constituency.'[26]

Many, of course, blamed the result on the extension of the franchise to untutored and socially limited middle-class electors. And it is true that the Reform Act of 1832 and then the repeal of the Corn Laws in 1846 initiated a process, originally in borough constituencies, by which the social composition of the House of Commons shifted from landed gentry to the bourgeoisie.[27] However, Cowan's victory was attributed to many additional factors: the anger of the Free Church over the way the government and the courts had reacted during the Ten Years' Conflict; the 'Excise Reformers who have cut a figure in

26. *Scotsman*. 4 August 1847. 3.

27. See Hoppen, K. T. *The Mid-Victorian Generation 1846–1886*. Oxford: Clarendon Press, 1998. 28.

this election';[28] and not least the unpopularity, the unresponsiveness, and the unaccountability Macaulay had demonstrated as he devoted much of his time to completing his *History of England*.

Cowan's legitimacy as an MP was challenged immediately after the election, when the *Times* published a letter from the Comptroller of the Stationery Office, who had a paper goods contract with Alexander Cowan and Sons, raising the conflict of interest matter. Macaulay's name surfaced yet again. He wrote to Adam Black on 11 August 1847: 'If the facts are as I understand that Mr. Cowan admits them to be, there is no doubt that his election is void. Whether you will petition or not is a question which you will do well to consider carefully. It is one in which I have no interest. For under no circumstances will I ever again be a candidate for Edinburgh.'[29]

Charles put the issue in the hands of a lawyer. On 25 November, in a letter addressed to the Speaker, which he read to the House, he intimated that, because of the heavy fines involved, he did not intend to take his seat.[30] A new writ was issued and, without any challenge, he was finally allowed to sit as an MP on 3 February 1848.[31] Meanwhile, considerable razzing was taking place in Edinburgh with one humourist describing his biographical entry in *Dodd's Parliamentary Companion* ('perhaps we should say autobiography') as the shortest in the book. At this point, his entry did compare badly with that of the parliamentarian he had replaced. He would have to work hard to prove that the electors of Edinburgh had not made a grievous error.

His entry in the latest *Dod's Parliamentary Companion* provided an opportunity for a particularly snide attack 1 December 1847 in the *Scotsman*.[32] Charging him with plagiarism for having appeared to cite as his own an article on paper almost identical to one in the 1798 *Encyclopaedia Britannica*, it was a sarcastic lampoon of Cowan's presumed literary pretensions. To fill out his resume Cowan had

28. 7 August 1847.

29. TBM to Adam Black, 11 August 1847. *The Letters of Thomas Babbington Macaulay*. Thomas Pinney, Ed. Vol. 4. Cambridge: Cambridge University Press, 1977. 349.

30. *Hansard*, HC Deb 25 November 1847 vol. 95 cc209-10.

31. *Hansard*, HC Deb 03 February 1848 vol. 96 c2.

32. 'Literary Inquiries Regarded the Age of our New Member' *Scotsman* 1 December 1847.

referred to an article that he had written, or been asked to write, in the *Encyclopaedia Britannica*. Stating that Cowan now was claiming 'to be not only the political but the literary rival of his predecessor', it referred to 'a curious chronological fact'. 'We cannot presume that the author of so learned an inquiry was less than 25 years of age when he wrote it; and this brings us to about the year 1772 as the date of our member's birth, making his present age about 75. We are bound to say that he is a hale-looking man for his years.'

His father was right. The world of politics was indeed a nasty place. All eyes were on Charles Cowan: how would this untried Scottish manufacturer behave as an MP in England, the mother of parliaments? He was entering a new, and hitherto uncharted, world for which the first forty-five years of his life, and his family's wealth and respectability, had barely prepared him.

Chapter 11

Commoner in the Commons

All eyes were on the new Member of Parliament, Charles Cowan, as he took his seat in the House of Commons. Questions had been raised about his suitability as representative of the 'Athens of the North'. Could he possibly take the place of Thomas Babington Macaulay? Was it possible that a northern businessman in trade ('northern' and 'trade' being spoken in ill-disguised contempt) could ever rise to the challenge? Would he be a credit to his constituency or would the unflattering press reports about his election prove true? And, most seriously, would he expose the Free Church with which he was identified, to ridicule and reproach? Meanwhile Macaulay, with some reluctance, finally accepted the inevitable and resigned on 23 April 1848 when no other alternative eventuated, in spite of promises from his friends that they would ensure that he remained in the Commons.

His fame as an orator aside, Macaulay's reputation as a parliamentarian was not actually that impressive. Five years earlier Lord John Russell as Leader of the Opposition had reproved him for his frequent absences from the front bench. The criticism was valid, since Macaulay was not fond of the dull routine of attendance and participation when there was no glory involved. For him, the House of Commons provided a stage: when he could not draw attention to his powerful gifts of rhetoric, the democratic process held no allure for him.

*****

On 17 May 1848, Charles Cowan rose in the House of Commons to make his maiden speech – during the debate on a bill titled Places of Worship (Scotland). The legislation had been drafted to ensure that seceding Free Church of Scotland congregations would be given the opportunity to own property in order to erect new places of worship. Some churches had been blocked by local gentry from purchasing property for this purpose. Even in Penicuik, the Clerk family had prevented such a transaction from taking place. The opposition was fierce and Cowan was anxious, in an overheated atmosphere, to vindicate the Free Church and particularly Thomas Chalmers.

So far, the parliamentary rhetoric had been inflammatory and not necessarily based on a familiarity with the issue at hand. One purveyor of such opposition was Thomas Alexander Mitchell, the honourable member from Bridport, Dorset, who was a London merchant and a Liberal, with scant understanding of or concern for Scotland and its unique religious culture. Immediately before Cowan's speech, he had stated that 'a more mischievous, a more arrogant Bill had never been introduced to that House. Hon. Members seemed to forget the history of the Free Church of Scotland; that it was a Church nurtured in revolution; and that it sprang into existence with the Reform Bill and the French Revolution of 1830. Nothing was more arrogant and presumptuous than its pretensions. They had refused every compromise.'[1]

Cowan defended 'the late Dr. Chalmers' against Mitchell's calumnies: 'he should not have supported the measure if there had been any other mode of obtaining the desired object. Public opinion had been brought to bear upon the site refusers; yet there was not, after all, the slightest indications of the Free Church congregations obtaining that right to which both by the laws of God and man

1. *Hansard*, HC Deb 17 May 1848 vol. 98 cc1149.

they were justly entitled.'[2] The bill was subsequently approved and received royal assent. Charles had passed his first test as a parliamentarian.

As a Scottish MP, he soon found himself busy forwarding petitions from his constituents to the House. Among them were pleas from various Free Church entities, from Scottish Royal Burghs (there were seventy at the time, their origin going back to the Middle Ages), and from business and commercial interests north of the Tweed.[3] By Cowan's time the Scottish Royal Boroughs were beginning to be an anomaly in their assumption of special privileges, particularly at the Court of Exchequer.

Throughout his time in the Commons, and for the rest of his life, a long-standing family friendship supported him. As William Ewart Gladstone used to say, there was not a drop of his blood that was not Scottish. His grandfather, Thomas Gladstones, had moved into Leith from Biggar in Lanarkshire ten years before the first Charles Cowan arrived in Leith. Like him he was a merchant, though he dealt in corn, not paper. In 1781 his son John, now called Gladstone, moved to Liverpool to improve his prospects. His second wife was Anne, a Highlander from Dingwall on the east-coast of Ross-shire. It is through her that their son William received his first religious training. Swept into Parliament on the tidal wave of the Great Reform Act of 1832, when only just past his majority, Gladstone had already been in the Commons for fifteen years when Cowan was elected. It was to be a lifetime's friendship that included all three Cowan brothers and influenced the future course of their lives.

Among issues of concern to many who had elected him was Sunday observance,[4] representation at 'the court of Rome',[5] opposition to the relief of Roman Catholic electoral disabilities,[6] and estate duties on charitable benefactions.[7] The status of *quoad sacra* churches and the

2. *Hansard*, HC Deb 17 May 1848 vol. 98 cc1165-7.
3. *Hansard*, HC Deb 20 July 1848 vol. 100 c583.
4. *Hansard*, HC Deb 20 March 1848 vol. 97 c769.
5. *Hansard*, HC Deb 10 July 1848 vol. 100 c306.
6. *Hansard*, HC Deb 13 March 1848 vol. 97 cc457.
7. *Hansard*, HC Deb 09 June 1848 vol. 99 c573.

repeal of the excise laws were also of particular interest,[8] as well as a petition from the city of Edinburgh against the elimination of sugar duties.[9]

The much-hated Edinburgh Annuity Tax was of continuing concern to the Edinburgh electorate. In 1849 Lord Russell sent Sir John George Shaw-Lefevre, a lawyer and civil servant, to meet with the Edinburgh city council and the Anti-Annuity Tax League, set up to fight the levy. He proposed, as an alternative, a parliamentary annuity for a reduced number of Edinburgh Established Church clergy at a lower rate than before. Action was still being taken against conscientious non-payers of the Annuity Tax: Shaw-Lefevre was concerned about the possibility of an insurrection. A committee of the House of Commons was appointed and heard twenty-three witnesses. Duncan McLaren, the former Edinburgh city Treasurer who brought the city out of bankruptcy and sat on council (later Lord Provost and subsequently MP for sixteen years) provided testimony based on extensive research. McLaren's recent biographer, Willis Pickard, notes that 'the city's MPs, though well intentioned, did not have much clout' and adds 'Charles Cowan in particular was a lightweight'.[10] In Cowan's defense there must initially have been some ambivalence on his part in further weakening the Established Church in Edinburgh by depriving it of an income that helped secure the kirk as a positive presence in urban society.

On 16 April 1850, Charles Cowan made one of his more memorable first-term Commons appearances, seconding a motion by Thomas Milner Gibson, Whig MP for Manchester, seeking to eliminate completely the excise tax, now generally referred to as the 'tax on knowledge'. Milner Gibson, a polished Cambridge graduate and member of the landed gentry, was in his element during the cut and thrust of debate. He spoke from the second bench on the ministerial side, and below him at the lower end of the Treasury bench sat Charles Cowan. In a two-hour speech, Milner Gibson made the case well, raising issues of the newspaper stamp, the

8. *Hansard*, HC Deb 18 May 1848 vol. 98 c1172.

9. *Hansard*, HC Deb 10 July 1848 vol. 100 c306.

10. Pickard, Willis. *The Member for Scotland*. Edinburgh: Birlinn, 2011. 102.

advertisement duty, and the duty on foreign books. The session was described as 'instructive and lively'.

'Being new in Parliament,' a report for the *Scotsman* noted of Charles' seconding speech, 'he has not acquired a House of Commons style, and he has a somewhat strong northern vernacular, which fastidious Englishmen are rather prejudiced against. Though there was at first some deficiency in the externals of manner, the House gradually began to pay him attention when they perceived that, as a practical man, he was addressing himself to the motion in a business-like way; and some amusement, as well as interest, was excited.' Cowan was on strong ground as he spoke from personal experience: 'Perhaps the House would allow him to explain the peculiar restrictions which oppressed the manufacture of paper as distinguished from other excisable productions.'[11]

Cowan then cited his frustration as a member of several delegations to London in the 1830s that the government had ignored. He spoke of American book pirates who defied copyright. He went on to demonstrate the international impact of free trade, with British paper being at a distinct disadvantage in relation to French and Italian manufacturers. In closing, he graciously mentioned that Macaulay was not in the House 'to aid the cause with his splendid eloquence, and intimated that he almost regretted to have been the instrument by which he had been excluded from the Legislature.'[12] Benjamin Disraeli, along with others, rose to support the motion, but it failed to pass. Both the excise and the annuity tax controversies seemed to be endless irritants without any final resolution.

On 17 February 1851, Cowan rose again in the House to speak on another tax issue, this time income tax and the way it was levied. Armed with petitions from the Lord Provost and Town Council of Edinburgh, the Merchants' Company, and the Chamber of Commerce, he railed against the way the tax 'offered a premium to evasion and dishonesty'.[13]

11. *Hansard*, HC Deb 16 April 1850 vol. 110 cc387-396.

12. *Scotsman*, 20 April 1850. 2.

13. *Hansard*, HC Deb 17 February 1851 vol 114 cc750.

Cowan's speech about the Universities (Scotland) Bill made on 25 June that same year, was included in his *Reminiscences* as one of his more memorable of his years in the Commons.[14] Its inclusion there as the Robertson Smith case was brewing is possibly because of its relevance to the whole matter of creedal subscription for university professors. The Universities (Scotland) Bill sought to eliminate the test for admission to the faculties of Scottish universities. These tests had recently been used by the Established Church to exclude Free Churchmen from academic positions. Cowan started by explaining to the English MPs that there was 'scarcely any similarity between the constitutions of the Scotch and English universities.'[15] In response to an Oxford University MP, who had claimed that there was no religion in Scotland outside the Established Church of Scotland, Cowan responded defiantly: 'As evidence of the efforts made by the Free Church to diffuse education and religion,' as later reported, 'he begged to state, without wishing to boast of the efforts of the body to which he had the honour to belong, that in the year ending March last there were no fewer than 1,671 Sabbath schools, 8,506 teachers, and 99,019 scholars, in connexion with that body, which, in the eight years ending March, had expended in various enterprises abroad and at home, £2,475,616.'

Urging that his fellow parliamentarians support the elimination of all religious tests for entry into faculties in the Scottish universities, he cited the case of the Free Churchman David Ewing, Principal of one of the St Andrews Colleges. After the Disruption, the Established Church Presbytery sought to depose him because he had gone over to the Free Church and was thus unable to pass the required test. Ewing's application had been even more vehemently rejected because he had also dismissed the Confession of Faith that those appointed were asked to affirm. As Cowan explained it, 'The fact was, that the Confession of Faith, which the parties signed, was a large volume which, he believed, not one in fifty of them had ever read – a volume, indeed, of dogmatic theology, containing many abstruse points with which none but accomplished theologians could well be expected

14. *Reminiscences*, 474-497.

15. *Hansard*, HC Deb 25 June 1851 vol. 117 cc1210-21.

to grapple and yet the mere putting of their name to this volume was held to be a security against the intrusion of improper and unfit persons into the university chairs!'[16]

As later events would prove, the Free Church, in seeking to provide freedom for its members, loosened many of the traditional bonds that had maintained religious orthodoxy in Scotland. This reality would come back to haunt them in later years. The MP for Lanarkshire, William Lockhart, who was a member of the Established Church and was at the time dean of the faculties at Glasgow University, expressed his astonishment. Cowan's speech was in 'direct opposition to the principles and practices of the Church of which he is a distinguished member. The late Dr. Chalmers, and the other leaders of the Free Church, were at all times, and under all circumstances, the zealous supporters of those tests. As long as they remained in the Church, they advocated them, and when they seceded from it and founded a college of their own, they consistently provided that its Principal and Professors should conform to their opinions; but the hon. Member, in the whole course of his speech, has never alluded to that college.'

Lockhart went on to state that, given the current religious ferment, this was no time to remove a test that ensured some degree of intellectual and theological order, if not conformity. 'The Bill of the hon. Gentleman, although it excludes the Theological faculties, offers no sufficient safeguards even as to them; and it is obvious that with regard to patronage, and in other respects, they must be injuriously affected. Under the existing system the Universities of Scotland have ever been an honour to their country; and it may with safety be asserted that religious dissensions have never penetrated within their walls.'[17]

*****

During his first term in the House of Commons a family scandal was brewing that could have had damaging implications for Charles. His brother James had been an on-going problem. Naturally boisterous

16. *Reminiscences*, 482.

17. *Hansard*, HC Deb 25 June 1851 vol. 117 cc1221-21.

and highly-strung, he challenged the family's Victorian proprieties. James was lots of fun and children loved him, but he had a streak of irresponsibility. He was a prankster, and the story went around in family lore that one day, as a cousin, George McCorquodale, was bringing cash from the bank in Edinburgh to pay the mill employees at Valleyfield, he was set upon in a lonely spot of the road in a dark wood by two men who sprang out on him, jabbed a pistol in his face, and said, 'Your money or your life!' He surrendered the funds, and in a terrible state of shock, arrived at the mill and described what had happened. Suddenly, James and John burst in, 'carrying the money-bag and delighted with the successful escapade.'[18] The probability is that it was James, and not John, who initiated the incident.

In the mid-1830s, while still in his teens, James was sent to London to learn the business and develop some maturity. But much to Charles' annoyance, he made a muddle of inventory and was responsible for several costly mistakes. 'In consequence of what you write and of what I have seen myself and heard from others,' Alexander wrote Charles, 'I have decided that James shall not again remain in London, until he has passed a year or two at home.' The arrangement was that he would come home and work at the mill under Charles' supervision, 'employed in such a manner as you may find useful.'

Instead of reprimanding James, whom he said had 'acquiesced with such readiness and cheerfulness as is very creditable to him,' Alexander set about to admonish Charles. 'I am sorry that you feel oppressed with business. Opinion as you already know is that you don't take sufficient assistance. I think that business is a delightful employment, when we can say that it is well managed, and when we feel that it is not carried on for personal exaltation but for the advancement of human virtue and happiness. When in fact we are Fellow workers with God.'[19] In this exchange there is a variant in the parable of the prodigal son: the father here appears to have set about remonstrating the responsible stay-at-home old brother.

---

18. Forsyth, Mary. *The Cowans at Moray House*. Edinburgh: T & A Constable, 1932.14.

19. AC to CC, 7 July 1836. *The Cowan Letters*, 37.

Nonetheless, there were limits to Alexander's patience. A decade later, he wrote to James, then in London: 'We don't appear to understand each other and are not likely to do so until we meet and have a conversation on the subject. You appear to have taken offence at something in some of my letters. I beg you may send me copies of them (I have kept none) and if you will point out anything that requires explanation I shall be ready to give. You allow that you took Cash from Cowan and Coy and applied it to your own purposes without previously getting permission from your partners to do so. If you allow that this was a Breach of confidence you ought surely to acknowledge it and make some apology. I have never supposed otherwise than that you did it inadvertently, and don't have the slightest evil intention, but still the act must bear the epithet that I have applied to it. If you don't allow this consult Allan or any honourable lawyer on this subject and see who is right. We all love you very much for your frank amiable manners and your unbounded kindness to others, and I believe we scarcely love your dear Charlotte less, and I shall bitterly lament for the rest of my life any interruption to the harmony that has hitherto prevailed among us. P. S. I have just learned that Charles is to be in London. At all events you ought to meet with him there or at Torquay before you return. If as appears to be the case, you think you have not been to blame, why delay meeting with him?'[20]

In 1841 James had married the Charlotte to whom the letter refers.[21] She was also a Cowan – the youngest child of his uncle Duncan and therefore his first cousin. James distanced himself from the family, moved from Slateford (where he had been living at Kate's

20. AC to James Cowan, 17 November 1845, NAS, GD311/2/43, 384. Alexander frequently bailed James out. In a letter to Henry Bruce of Kenleith Mill, written two years later, he writes about another business transaction: 'In my opinion you and my son have been very foolish in making an offer of what was not in his power and you of taking advantage of it. The greatest blessing I know is to repent of our sins and the next is to confess them to each other. I advise you then to give up all your claims upon James and pay your agents accounts yourself. If you will do this I am willing immediately to pay £1000 to some of our public charities in your name and James' conjointly or £500 for each. As it is the proceeds of folly, I would suggest the Lunatic Asylum as a proper object for it.' NAS, GD311/2/43, 435.

21. Charlotte (1822-1892). They had no children.

Mill, a Cowan establishment) to Portobello. He was a partner in 'Alexander Cowan and Sons', and the four men, father and three sons, met monthly. There must have been some interesting dynamics in their caucus, masked as they are by the politely worded company partners' minutes. But by 15 January 1848, even these could not conceal the fact that James was in deep trouble financially and was required to assume responsibility for some of his riskier ventures.[22]

On 29 June 1849, he declared bankruptcy, and his property was sequestered. The case involved five 'obligations' he had undertaken as a director of the Edinburgh, Perth and Dundee Railway Co.[23] On 4 September 1850, James settled for five shillings on the pound, and Alexander Cowan, together with his other two sons as fellow partners in the firm, were described as 'cautioners' (a Scottish legal term describing individuals who have co-signed on obligations). The case between James Cowan and John Balfour of Balbirnie, Markinch, Fifeshire came before the Outer House on 30 August 1852 (in Scotland the Outer House is the first court of the two parts of the Court of Session, the supreme civil court of the realm).[24] The case was eventually settled, apparently to the satisfaction of both parties. Because of his affable manner, it was difficult to remain an enemy of James Cowan.

For Charles Cowan as MP, James' bankruptcy was an especially unpleasant situation, particularly as Charles was dealing frequently with railway amalgamations and James had lost his money in railway speculation. But for Alexander, who safeguarded his privacy and his honour, the situation was particularly galling. The case came to court again on 30 August 1852, and one presumes a settlement was made, perhaps with father's money. We hear no more about James. He resurfaced fifteen years later over the water wars the family waged.

---

22. *Minute*, 15 January 1848, partners meeting. NAS, GD 69/7/69/4.

23. Originally Edinburgh and Northern Railway when incorporated in 1845 by Parliament. It operated out of Burntisland on the north side of the Firth of Forth. Two years later it amalgamated with the Edinburgh, Leith and Granton Railway, and in 1850 operated the first railway ferry, from Granton to Burntisland. It amalgamated with British Northern in 1862.

24. 'Summons of Relief J Balfour Esq. against James Cowan and cautioners' West Record House, NAS, CS228/B/20/8.

James went on to become Lord Provost of Edinburgh for just over a year and MP for eight. On his death in 1895, he was described as 'a well known and respected citizen of Edinburgh'.[25] Yes, there is a second chance even for repentant debtors and scofflaws.[26]

*****

Cowan's first term at Westminster had been unspectacular and uneven. He had not disgraced himself, as many had expected, but had also not distinguished himself. He had proved to be a faithful representative of his constituents' interests and a defender of Scotland's uniqueness in a body known for English obtuseness, and he had established a reputation as a defender both of Scotland and of its Free Church. While he started by defending his mentor Thomas Chalmers from a charge of creating anarchy, by the end of the five years in Parliament he was defending a kind of ecclesiastical state of *laissez-faire*. This had considerable appeal to his constituency: the practical, no-nonsense approach of his shop-keeping, artisan and middle-class supporters. But he had singularly failed in the one thing that had energized him to stand for election: the total repeal of the excise on paper. It would be another nine years, ironically soon after he finally retired from the Commons, before that would happen. In that instance Whig free-traders would ultimately trump Conservative protectionists. In the meantime the constituency needed to determine whether Charles Cowan had earned the right to a second term.

25. *Scotsman*, 25 November 1895.

26. John Balfour and James Cowan are both listed together as Fellows of the Society of Antiquaries of Scotland the year of James' death.

Chapter 12

Radical in Retreat

The General Election of 1852 has often been called a watershed. As a result of the repeal of the Corn Laws in 1846 party structure had become fluid. The Conservatives divided over the Corn Laws into protectionist and non-protectionist (or 'Peelites' after Sir Robert Peel, the Tory prime minister). The Whigs were also fragmented and hyphenated into Radicals and non-Radicals. The non-protectionists claimed that the repeal of the Corn Laws had brought unprecedented prosperity to the country after a period of economic stringency in the mid-1840s. The Crystal Palace exposition of 1851, a harbinger of a new confidence, was churlishly denounced by protectionists as encouraging the entry of foreign products. As the election results demonstrated, the country was almost evenly divided, with the Tories gaining more seats, the Liberals more votes.

It was thus a polarized electorate in Edinburgh as the election of 1852 approached. There were three Whig electoral committees. The first, the Aggregate Committee, sponsored the return of Thomas Macaulay. His earlier violent assertions about Edinburgh needing to sit on the cutty stool seemed forgotten, thanks to the ministrations of his friend Adam Smith.[1] The Liberal Independent Committee, which had sponsored Charles Cowan five years previously, was now divided, the uneasy alliance between Dissenters and Free Churchmen had fallen apart. Sir William Gibson-Craig, the other Edinburgh MP, was retiring, having inherited his father's estate and title two years earlier. He conspired to try to ensure Charles Cowan would not be returned to Parliament. The alternative, the new Edinburgh Provost Duncan McLaren, who (as we have seen) had not been nicknamed 'The Snake' for no reason, was also unacceptable to Gibson-Craig. A third grouping, basically the Free Church faction, thought they could offer two of their own: Alexander Campbell of Monzie (formerly a Tory MP for Argyll but an ardent member of the Free Church) and Charles Cowan.

It became clear that, after the debacle of 1847, electing Macaulay was the only way of righting that perceived wrong. Duncan McLaren was entering the lists as an alternate Radical candidate, sponsored by Dissenters who now dominated the Liberal-Independent Committee. It narrowed down to a contest between Duncan McLaren, the United Presbyterian dissenter, and Charles Cowan, the Free Churchman. Here the second vote phenomenon came into play: if McLaren alienated too many of the Cowan contingent they would not give him their second vote. McLaren chose as his issue opposition to the annuity tax and, as a recent biography stated, sought to position himself on that burning issue between 'the distant Macaulay and the ineffectual Cowan.'[2]

Cowan's supporters fought back. With the election just a fortnight away they called a nominating committee. On Monday, 28 June 1852, in Edinburgh's Music Hall, Charles Cowan rose to defend his stewardship as MP. 'The hall was well filled, and towards the close became crowded,' the *Scotsman* reported.[3] It was the speech of his life and demonstrated how far he had come since 1847. There was strong representation from the Free Church crowd, and

1. The cutty stool was the three-legged milking stool that adulterers were to sit on in full view of the congregation as penance after being reprimanded by the minister for their breach of the seventh commandment.

2. Pickard, Willis. *The Member for Scotland*. Edinburgh: Birlinn, 2011. 110.

3. *Scotsman* 30 June 1852.

a prominent Free Church man, Sir William Johnston of Kirkhill, McLaren's immediate predecessor as Lord Provost, was in the chair.[4] Fighting for his political future, Charles Cowan addressed his critics head-on. Fortunately he was among supportive friends, whose continued bursts of applause during an hour's speech must have been encouraging. Amid cheers he said, 'It is my duty, as is it will be my pleasure, to afford to you all every explanation which you can desire of the motives which have actuated me in my public conduct.'

He began by referring to a 'very absurd report' that at a Free Church General Assembly he had stated that he was the member for the Free Church. Though slightly equivocating on the veracity of the rumor, he responded with passion: 'allow me to say that, with all the attachment which I feel for those principles which have made the Free Church an accomplished fact throughout Christendom, I should despise myself if I place myself before you on such narrow and sectarian grounds for none hold more strongly than I do that the being attached to any religious denomination is neither a recommendation nor a disqualification for a civil office.' That said, he denied any responsibility for the breakup of the Liberal Independent Committee, an accusation made against him. Having cleared the air, he defended two controversial positions he had taken: the income tax, which he favoured only as a short-term relief for current government indebtedness, and voting by ballot where he urged considerable caution and took an equivocating stand. Neither response was popular with the radicals.

Cowan went on to address the thorny issue of the Maynooth grant. Three weeks earlier, on 7 June, he had presented a petition to the Commons against it from the General Assembly of the Free Church of Scotland. Now he identified himself with their position, not because of anti-Catholicism but on the basis of the separation of church and state, walking a fine line between that principle and capitulating to virulent Rome-rants then proliferating. 'They must be insensible to all that is going on in the various Roman Catholic countries in the world

4. Sir William Johnston of Kirkhill, (1802 – 1888) Lord Provost of Edinburgh 1848-51, devout Free Churchman, partner with in the W & A K Johnston mapmaking company.

when they calmly propose, not merely the payment of the education of Roman Catholic priests, but the establishment and the supremacy of the Roman Catholic Church in Ireland.' Macaulay, writing to his sister Frances at the time,[5] said that Edinburgh was Maynooth-mad and refused, in an exchange of letters between him and the Scottish Reformation Society published in the *Scotsman*, to be drawn on the issue: 'I have a great respect for the gentlemen in whose name you write, but I have nothing to ask of them, I am not a candidate for their suffrages; I have no desire to sit again in Parliament.'[6]

Cowan concluded on a personal note as he reflected on the possibility of re-election: '[B]e assured of this, that there is no man, perhaps, who is now a candidate for your suffrages, who so little values for its own sake the high and honourable distinction of being the representative even of such a constituency as this. I have felt it often to be a great sacrifice that I made. I have been removed for a long period from those most near and dear to me; but I considered it to be my duty again to place my services at your disposal ... there is no one who feels more strongly than I do that amid the turmoils of political life, and the engrossing duties that devolve upon a representative in Parliament, there is no little danger of the attention being withdrawn from matters of far graver and more permanent importance.'

A question period followed. The items raised by constituents are of interest as reflecting some of the work he had done in the Commons and issues soon to be raised in the new session. When the university tests came up, Cowan affirmed that he 'would do all he could to aid the movement in favour of general education.' The incomplete nature of the Reform Act of 1832 and the need for an extension of the franchise was also raised. There was a loaded question about the Free Church taking £13,000 from the public purse 'for the purpose of teaching religion along with the other branches of education.' Cowan replied that he would be sorry to see religion, or religious instruction, banished from the schools, to which there was applause. Questions increasingly became more pointed, the meeting more uproarious,

5. TBM to Frances Macaulay, 16 June 1852, *The Letters of Thomas Babbington Macaulay*. Thomas Pinney, Ed. Vol.5. Cambridge: Cambridge University Press, 1981. 34.

6. *Scotsman*, 30 June 1852.

and one person stated that having voted for Cowan once he would not make the same mistake again.

From the chair James Balfour drew the question time to a close by placing Cowan's name in nomination. '[W]hen I recollect the circumstances under which Mr. Cowan came forward at the last election – when I recollect that on that occasion the opinions and principles which he then stated were so largely in consonance with the feeling of the electors that, by a large majority, they placed him at the top of the poll; and when I see that, since then, he has in Parliament uniformly acted in consistency with the opinions he avowed before his election, I am very confident that the electors are now prepared to show their consistency by again assigning to him the same distinguished place at the poll he had upon the last occasion.' He went on to speak of 'his great attention to the interests of this city, combined with his remarkably humble disposition, and the urbanity of his demeanour – (applause) have secured for him a large portion of the esteem of the electors.' It was a good summary of the strengths Cowan brought to his tenure.

Curiously when the resolution was put to the meeting not more than a third voted in favour, but subsequently those opposed numbered only six. '[T]he great majority, the report in the *Scotsman* noted,[7] 'not expressing an opinion one way or another.' The chairman commented on 'the unanimity of the meeting'. 'Away with the aristocrats, fox-hunting, fighting men, that were now the Majority in that House, and let us have plain men that belong to our country, and our town, that know what economy is – then we shall have reform.' There was laughter and cheers. Though there were shouts in the background for another possible candidate, Alexander Campbell of Monzie and Inverawe, Charles Cowan seemed unfazed as he expressed the accustomed thanks.

The election on 13 July 1852 was described as 'the most exciting ever known in Edinburgh'.[8] The big news when it was over was 'The triumphant return of Mr. Macaulay' at the top of the poll with 1872 votes. As Adam Black crowed at the end of the day, 'The honour

7. *Scotsman*, 20 June 1852.

8. *Scotsman*, 14 July 1852. That *Scotsman* account of the 1852 election is very extensive and full of fascinating detail.

of the city had been retrieved in the eyes of the country.' Between McLaren and Cowan it had been a close run thing: Bruce, the Tory candidate, was always far behind, though he encouraged his electors to cast a second ballot for Cowan. Somewhere around noon, McLaren claimed later, the Tories met with Cowan's men in a secret cabal, and by one o'clock Cowan pulled ahead of McLaren. As the polls closed at four he was the clear second choice. McLaren was further embittered by the fact that none of the Free Church group appeared to give him their second vote. '[W]e have had the hostility of the Free Church,' he told his supporters at the end of the day, adding that 'The fact that 1546 of the stanch [*sic*] friends of civil and religious liberty having recorded their votes in my favour ... is a matter of triumph. (Cheers)'

As a victor, Charles Cowan could afford to be magnanimous, but that was his nature. 'I beg leave to be allowed to return my best thanks to my 1754 supporters at the poll.... The contest has been one involving principles of no ordinary importance, and has been carried on with unexampled keenness ... the kindness which I have this day received will be an additional stimulus to me to devote all the energies I possess to promote the good of the city and all its inhabitants.' With that he dismissed his supporters and went home.

What was it all about? The differences between McLaren and Cowan provide interesting insights into two mid-nineteenth-century Edinburgh politicians. Both were radical Whigs, both originally part of the Liberal-Independent Committee, and the contrast between them seemed more of style than substance. McLaren was, as his later career showed, much more in his element as a parliamentarian. He had a quick grasp of facts, saw the wider picture, was good at figures and financing, and was generally sharper in mind. Cowan was slower, less opinionated, and as a result less polarising, and was not as quick on his feet, though he had improved his style with stump speeches. Relationally he was much more gracious and accommodating than McLaren, at least as McLaren was at the time. Cowan was more shaped by religious conviction. Not that he was dogmatic: he was increasingly tolerant and prepared to see the other side of an issue. McLaren's time would come. In 1865, at the age of 65, he launched into a sixteen-year career in the House of Commons which made him famous as 'The Member for Scotland'.

*****

One cause that brought McLaren and Cowan together was the National Association for the Vindication of Scottish Rights which made its debut at this time. Both their names headed the initial 1853 subscription list. The previous year Cowan had been one of three initiators of the Association, the other two being the romantic novelist James Grant, a second cousin of Walter Scott, and Lord Montgomerie, the Earl of Eglinton, appointed Lord Lieutenant of Ireland that year. It was a diverse trio, reflecting the different groups to whom the organization appealed. James Grant, an Edinburgh antiquarian and author of historical fiction, had published a newspaper article with the provocative title, 'Justice for Scotland.' He claimed that England had broken the terms of the Union of 1707. Eton-educated Eglinton, a Tory politician best known for the large stud he maintained, provided social cachet. And Charles Cowan as MP gave the cause parliamentary legitimacy. In response to a complaint from Grant about 'centralization' in London he promised, prior to the election, 'to shower Scotland in gold.'[9] Twenty-four grievances, stretching back to the Union Riots of 1706, were cited by the Association. Its specific concern was the need to appoint a Secretary of State for Scotland, a position that had expired in 1746.

At the first public meeting of the National Association for the Vindication of Scottish Rights a letter was read from Cowan who was unable to attend. He wrote about the apathy of the government in regards to Scotland, particularly with professorial endowments and religious tests in the Scottish universities. Graeme Duncan has made a meticulous study of the connection between Cowan's supporters and the constituency of the Association.[10] The poll books for the 1852 election indicate that the Association had negligible effect on voting though there is some evidence for a tie-in between the Free

9. Morton, Graeme. *Unionist Nationalism* East Linton: Tuckwell Press, 1999. 136.

10. Morton, Graeme. *Unionist Nationalism* East Linton: Tuckwell Press, 1999. 137-8.

Church, those who voted for Cowan in 1847, and membership in the Association.[11]

The National Association for the Vindication of Scottish Rights has been described as 'the first effective nationalist movement' in Scotland during its short lifetime.[12] Strong passions were aroused, as today, over Scottish nationalism. The *Scotsman* said caustically of the membership that it had 'found a good many more foolish people in Scotland than we suspected of.'[13] It spoofed the whole enterprise, parodying its concern: 'Arise ye Goths, and glut your ire.'[14] The only visible reminder of its patriotic enthusiasm is to be seen in Stirling's Wallace Monument, erected in 1869. Three years after its formation the Association disappeared in the patriotic and thus unifying fervour of the Crimean War. Twenty years later Charles Cowan failed to give the Association a mention in his *Reminiscences*. His major contribution in Parliament during his years as an MP was to assert a proud Scottish identity, at no small cost to his reputation in some quarters, particularly among readers of the *Scotsman*.

*****

On his return to Westminster Charles Cowan found a divided house. Though the Tories had won the election of 1852 they lacked the affirmation of a majority of the popular vote and were defeated in December that year. The Whigs, now largely Liberalized, would dominate the political scene under the long shadow of Lord Palmerston. The 1850s were a time of shifting political and personal allegiances among politicians and it was only on 6 June 1859 that the Liberal party was officially established and the old Whig-dom finally buried.

Issues of Scottish national identity continued to dominate Cowan's time in Parliament. The National Association for the Vindication

11. Morton, Graeme. *Unionist Nationalism* East Linton: Tuckwell Press, 1999. 137.

12. Hanham, H. J. *Scottish Nationalism*. Cambridge, MA: Harvard University Press, 1969. 77.

13. *Scotsman*, 24 May 1854. 1.

14. *Scotsman*, 24 May 1854. 1.

of Scottish Rights, with its insistence on the appointment of a Secretary of State for Scotland, was but one manifestation of this. In May, Cowan spoke in favour of a private members' bill proposing modernisation of the Scottish sheriff courts. Mostly anecdotal, occasionally humorous, and always deferential, at one point he even spoke as an old radical: 'He did not wonder at the feeling of disappointment and vexation, and the demand for reform, that existed in Scotland. The people there had had a great deal to bear; they had been very patient under it. The matter was one of national concern and importance, and it behaved [*sic*] them to do everything in their power to remove whatever was injurious to the social character or prevented harmony or good feeling in the community and to replace that with something which was of substantial benefit.'[15] The bill passed.

Scottish education was the matter that most dominated Cowan's interest as an MP. Since the Reformation and the reforms of John Knox, it had been the pride of Scotland. The school and the kirk had been bound together, though in places like Penicuik (as we have seen) the partnership had been abused: it could be argued that the rise of Moderatism had had an adverse effect not only on the church but also the quality of instruction. The Disruption had dramatically impacted education: 400 teachers had been thrown out of the schools of the Established Church. The Church of Scotland had, it was claimed, engaged in open warfare against the Free Church whose new schools threatened their monopoly of educational authority.

In setting up their alternative and parallel school system, the challenges were immense. Salaries and buildings had to be provided by the Free Church. In Penicuik the Cowans supported a new school (in addition to the one on their site) but in other communities raising the necessary funds for church, clergy salaries and education proved a heavy burden. In 1847 the government responded with grants-in-aid if the school passed muster. By 1851, 712 new schools, with attendance at 62,000, had been established by the Free Church, and teachers' colleges had been founded in Glasgow and Edinburgh – the latter having been located in Moray House which the Cowans now vacated.

15. *Hansard* C Deb 1853 vol 127 cc 151.

But the Free Church now wanted a complete systemic change in the way education was administered in Scotland: a national system that would be non-sectarian but would make provision for moral and religious education. The National Education Association was set up to achieve a transformation in Scottish education. In late January 1854 a meeting was called, under the chairmanship of Fox Maule (who two years earlier had become the second Lord Panmure),to discuss five radical resolutions to overhaul Scottish education. MPs Charles Cowan, Alex Dunlop and E. H. J. Craufurd (whose motivation was more secular than religious) headed the list of sponsors, followed by notable Scots clergy, among them United Presbyterian ministers John Brown and John Cairns, and Free Church luminaries such as Guthrie, Cunningham, and Candlish. Educational reformer and preacher Thomas Guthrie's *Plea for Ragged Schools* had appeared seven years earlier. There was some diversity: the Liberal publisher Adam Black, soon to join Cowan as an MP (and a customer of his firm), was among the signatories.

'Scotland is now ripe for a Bill embodying the principles of a non-sectarian system of education,' was its categorical affirmation. 'A good general system, by which every child in the kingdom may receive a sufficient Education, is of essential importance to the well-being of the country.' The management of schools, then legally vested in the heritors and presbyteries of the Established Church, should instead be entrusted to 'committees elected by the heritors, and other contributors and parents having children at the school,' the petition declared. Duncan McLaren's brother in law, in a letter to the *Scotsman*, fulminated against it, calling it as an 'outrage against the Voluntary principle,'[16] presumably because it still allowed for a role in education for the Church of Scotland. Rallies in the Music Hall in Edinburgh (25 January) and the Merchants' Hall Glasgow (9 February) were well attended. A petition was approved, and sent on to Macaulay as an MP not already committed.

Charles Cowan was in the forefront of the series of Commons debates over the legislation titled Education (Scotland) that began in March 1855.The legislation was a response to the petition and

16. *Scotsman*, 26 April 1854.

ended the unilateral power of the Established Church of Scotland in favour of a more representative authority. 'The Free Church had done a vast deal for education, having built 500 or 600 schools,' Cowan asserted, as he addressed the tricky question of government subsidies for religious education, which the heckler during the1852 election had demonstrated.[17] One possible way to make subsidies fair and equitable, he suggested, was to provide funds based on the majority denomination in each county. 'In sixteen counties in Scotland the plan proposed ... would place the whole education of those counties in the hands of the Free Church alone, and there were only two counties in which the Established Church was in an absolute majority.'

In a subsequent speech he maintained that 'the [present] variety of denominational schools was a strength not a weakness: He would be guilty of an injustice if he did not say that the schools of the Established Church were in a state of great efficiency. The competition which had occurred during the last fifteen years had created a great deal of energy in that quarter.'[18] It was a not so subtle dig at the Church of Scotland's 250-year stewardship of Scottish education.

Religious instruction was, of course, the big issue if the schools were no longer to be church sponsored. In spite of denominational diversity in Scotland, Cowan could still speak of a general consensus: 'In Scotland nine-tenths, or, at all events, seven-eighths of the population were agreed in creed,' and, he continued, 'he knew the people of Scotland to be a religious people, and that the thing they had most deeply at heart was the religious education of their children.' He concluded his speech, which raised more questions than it answered, 'that, because Scotland would not have secular education; it would only have education with religious instruction at the same time.' Cowan recommended a recognition of the 'attachment of the people of Scotland to the use of the Holy Scriptures in the schools, and then to have a provision that certain hours should be set apart for religious instruction in the schools, and that no one should be bound to attend at those hours against his will.'

17. *Hansard* HC Deb 23 March 1855 vol 137 cc991-2.

18. *Hansard* HC Deb 18 May 1855 vol 138 cc792.

The debate continued on into the summer of 1855. Charles Cowan seemed to have a knack of irritating those opposed to the bill by holding up the Free Church's generosity.[19] The final vote came on 13 July, 1855. It was pointed out that the proportion of children to the entire population of Scotland was presently one in seven, a total of 600,000 children. With one schoolmaster responsible for a hundred children, the bill would require 6000 schools, an increase of 760 over the present figure. 'The eyes of the people of England would now be open to the true character of the bill,' an MP from south of the Tweed averred as he spoke in opposition. By a majority of fifteen (130 to 115) the bill finally passed. Even weakened by amendments the final result was a tribute to the tenacity and moral suasion of the Free Church with articulate MPs such as Alexander Dunlop speaking well, and Charles Cowan in support, if not always tactfully. The legislation was a first step in freeing Scotland from the domination of the Established Church for good or ill, and broadening the availability of education for a wider and more diverse constituency. The unintended consequence was that the long march toward secularization in Scotland had begun.

*****

When an allied expeditionary force landed at Calamita Bay on the coast of Crimea in September 1854 MPs in London were caught up in war-related concerns. For Charles Cowan this raised the issue that Scottish homes were required to accept billets of soldiers without compensation. Cowan was asked by the Edinburgh Police Commissioner to see whether this obligation, causing considerable irritation, could be changed. He had been in touch with his friend Fox Maule, Lord Panmure, in March but no response had been made. In Dalkeith required billeting had become a particular vexation. Drunkenness and blasphemy had been brought into private homes along with vermin and disease. There was a growing danger of resistence if the situation did not improve. The response from Fox

19. Thus on 22 May 1855 Cowan is quoted as saying, at the end of his remarks, that 'The Free Church had by its exertions, raised 500 schools.' (*Scotsman* 23 May 1855.)

Maule's undersecretary was that an encampment would be made in Scotland (as well as Ireland and England) and 'they would soon have a good and permanent army'.[20]

The capture of Kars and 11,000 Turkish soldiers (commanded by a British general) by the Russians on 26 November 1855 was a military disaster. The Opposition was quick to criticize the way the Tories were prosecuting the war. Charles Cowan jumped into the fray but Disraeli hit back during a debate in wounding and personal attack. 'The hon. Gentleman is, no doubt, entitled to notice, because he is the successor, and I believe, the successful rival, of one of the greatest ornaments of British literature, and formerly one of the greatest ornaments of this House – Mr. Macaulay. He declares all this discussion to be vain and worthless, and says it is only an assault on the Treasury bench.'

Questions followed in rapid fire: 'Does he mean to say that there is in the city of Edinburgh, which, by some strange anomaly, he represents, such a total want of sympathy with all that has happened at Kars.... Does he represent faithfully the feeling of his constituents when he says that any discussion on this subject is vain, futile, and selfish? Sir, I have a higher opinion of the educated, intelligent, and accomplished inhabitants of the modern Athens. I do not believe that the hon. Member on this point faithfully represents his constituents: I am sure that our discussion of this subject will be read in that city with the deepest interest, and will be judged with the severest criticism.'[21]

Contrary to Disraeli's assertions, the *Scotsman* observed later, Edinburgh was unimpressed and 'there is something rotten in the state of Disraelism'. Disraeli's real concern was not the fall of Kars but the fall of the government.[22]

*****

20. *Hansard* HC Deb 06 July 1855 vol 139 cc540.

21. *Hansard* HC Deb 01 May 1856 vol 141 cc1855.

22. *Scotsman* 7 May 1856. Renton was brother to McLaren's second wife Christina who died in 1841.

It was not long in coming. The election in the spring of 1857 gave the Whigs a resounding victory. The Independent Liberal Committee, formed to elect Cowan a decade earlier, now directed their fire against him. That Committee was almost devoid of Free Churchmen and Cowan 'was now accused of having struck a bargain with the Whigs.'[23] But the Committee was unable to get another candidate, and, as *The Scottish Press* reported, 'nothing more grotesque in the annals of electioneering ever took place.'[24] Macaulay, who had made but a single speech during the previous term, had retired from the Commons and his place was taken by his friend and agent Adam Black. Cowan and Black were uncontested.

Cowan was clearly wearying of public office. On 31 January 1857, in company with a delegation from Edinburgh, he made a visit to the Lord Advocate regarding electoral reform. Three days later he wrote a candid letter to one of the group, Free Church minister James Begg, asking that it be treated as confidential. Begg broke that trust: two days later readers of the *Scotsman* learned of Charles Cowan's frustration as he wrote Begg: 'I care little for the low and vulgar abuse which I am from time to time assailed in certain quarters, and which every public man must expect to meet in greater or smaller measure.'[25] Their relationship never recovered and the animosity would do the Free Church no good as relations between the two became increasingly rancorous. The Free Church, like most families, was close-knit but when there were slights and hurts they were not always quickly forgotten and forgiven.

Before leaving the Commons Charles Cowan made a final attempt to provide once and for all a solution to the Annuity Tax, a constant irritant to the Free Church and Dissenting constituency. It was however Adam Black, the junior member for Edinburgh, and not Cowan who took the initiative for its elimination, a move which was initially successful only in the Commons but not the Lords. In the debate Cowan spoke of 'a spirit of self-reliance' among the churches.

23. I. G. C. Hutchison *A Political History of Scotland, 1832-1924*. Edinburgh: John Donald, 1986. 81.

24. *Scottish Press*. 24 March 1857. As quoted in I. G. C. Hutchison *A Political History of Scotland, 1832-1924*. Edinburgh: John Donald, 1986. 82.

25. *Scotsman*, 7 February 1857.

The Disruption, never mentioned by name, had made a considerable impact on the charitable instinct of churchgoers in Scotland. He cited figures to show a dramatic increase over the past thirty years in donations. 'No man, he was sure, was more anxious to assist in removing that spirit of rancor which at present existed on account of this tax.' The next year the tax was partially dropped. A decade later it was finally eliminated, to the considerable improvement of relations among the churches.

On 8 April, as Parliament was about to be prorogued, Charles Cowan spoke emotionally in favour of honouring a constituent's son, a Bengal Sapper named Grierson, who had given his life to ignite explosives that blew open the Kashmir Gate in Delhi two years earlier and thus had assured victory in the Indian Mutiny. In addressing the Commons he stated that 'No one wished more than he did that they should continue in the prosecution of the various branches of legislation in which they had been so honourably and successfully engaged, and, in addressing the last words which probably he should ever utter in that House, he could assure them that it was his most earnest wish that the new Parliament should apply themselves to the promotion of such objects both at home and abroad as would conduce to the honour and prosperity of the country.'[26]

Priscilla McLaren, Duncan's wife and an astute observer of politics, best described the political journey Charles Cowan took during his twelve years in the House of Commons. She wrote to her stepdaughters in 1853 that 'he has fairly sold himself to the Whigs'.[27] As the sister of John Bright, the personification of the radical movement, she spoke from personal knowledge. From the hotheaded disciple of Thomas Chalmers, religiously committed and eager to redress the wrongs London had inflicted on the Free Church, redressing the inequities of the excise tax on paper, he had settled into the faith and politics of compromise, of accommodation to the realities of mid-Victorian Britain. No longer the great campaigner,

---

26. *Hansard* HC Deb 08 April 1859 vol 153 cc1592. See also *Scotsman,* 26 November 1857.

27. Edinburgh City Archives McLaren papers Box 1 Duncan McLaren to Priscilla in Blackpool, 27 July 1853. (Pickard, Willis. *The Member for Scotland* Edinburgh, Birlinn, 2011. 146 and footnote 26. 287.)

increasing prosperity, late middle age, and the weight of directing the family business now that his father was gone, weighed upon him. Between his arrival in Westminster in the autumn of 1847 and his departure in the spring of 1859 life had changed. Earlier certainties, both in politics and religion, were becoming more ambiguous, more blurred. He had retreated from being a radical.

Chapter 13

Life after the Limelight

The year 1859 marked a turning point in the life of Charles Cowan thanks to two significant events: on 13 February his father died at the age of eighty-four and then three months later he stood down from his seat in the Commons.

From the time he left the business that perpetuated his name Alexander Cowan had made the most of his nine remaining years, showing no signs of diminished mental acuity. In the summer of 1855 sixty-three of his family, children and their spouses, grandchildren and great-grandchildren, gathered at Auchindarroch on the west coast of Scotland to celebrate the twenty-fifth anniversary of his marriage to Helen Brodie. As the family acknowledged, 'what we owe to you – to your training, and precept, and example; above all how much we have reason to thank you for that pattern of benevolence and universal love, by which you have shown to us the true source of domestic bliss, and of happiness in all the relations of life.'[1] Particular tribute was paid to Alexander's second wife for her 'unwearied attention to [Alexander's] welfare and happiness.'[2]

1. 'Address Presented to Alexander Cowan.' Broadsheet in possession of Judith A. MacLeod. It is also to be found in *Reminiscences*, 455 and 'Alexander Cowan' 13-14.

2. 'Alexander Cowan' 13-14.

A breathless, fulsome and very Victorian ode with six stanzas titled 'August Twenty-third MDCCCLV' was composed in his honour.

For Alexander Cowan, his employees were his major concern as his life came to its conclusion. During the summer of 1857, while at Penicuik, he wrote: 'I have now gone over all our workpeople at their own houses, and I do not anticipate continuing such visits.'[3] The following year, he wrote: 'I have had a very happy life and I feel truly thankful for it'; and later that same summer, he added: 'I know nothing more productive of happiness, than a disposition to do all that is in our power to make worthy servants comfortable in their old age.'[4]

'His long and extensive connection in business in Edinburgh,' the *Scotsman* noted in an obituary the day after his death, 'his great but unostentatious munificence in ecclesiastical and charitable affairs, and the prominence of the firm of which he was the head, rendered his name very conspicuous in our city, and it was not more conspicuous than respected.'[5] He was laid to rest in the Grange cemetery along a wall with a sculptured bust of him positioned as though he was looking for the grave nearby of his cousin Thomas Chalmers.[6]

Charles Cowan's last several months as an MP were uneasy, filled as they were with criticism and complaints. There was soon to be a compensation for all his efforts to eliminate the excise tax. It did not come without a fight. The tax was a highly lucrative way for the government to raise money. The revenue the tax generated increased each year. In 1857, it was £1,244,652, of which sum Scotland contributed £263,786. Three years later, the total amount had risen to £1,397,349. W. E. Gladstone, Chancellor of the Exchequer, took the lead. On 8 May 1860, the bill to repeal the excise on paper passed its third reading in the Commons by a narrow majority of nine, only to be defeated in the House of Lords a fortnight later by a majority of eighty-nine. Gladstone was outraged: 'Their action in so doing was contrary to use and custom.' He called it 'one of the most gigantic and dangerous encroachments on constitutional usage which had

3. 'Alexander Cowan' 8.

4. 'Alexander Cowan' 9.

5. *Scotsman,* 14 February 1859, 2.

6. With the inscription 'Leaving his descendants who bless his memory.'

been made in modern times.'[7] During the next few months, owing to a treaty with France which lowered the import tax on paper not only from that country but from others as well, British paper makers were placed at an unfair disadvantage, which was compounded by an export duty on rags brought into the country by British paper manufacturers. They were successful in their agitation: on 15 April 1861 Gladstone announced that new legislation had finally abolished the excise tax on paper.

The effect on British papermaking was dramatic, production increasing by a third in the next seven years. Alexander Cowan and Sons shared in the growth and a newspaper report described the Valleyfield mill as 'vast'.[8] The original Greenlaw barracks, a two-storey building stretching a hundred yards in length that had been used to house French prisoners during the Napoleonic Wars, was now piled high with rags. Charles Cowan, no longer in the Commons and head of a successful business enterprise, was now involved directly in the mill, establishing a routine that continued for the next sixteen years.

There was a definite rhythm to the manufacture of paper. It started as women sorted the rags, cutting off fasteners and buttons. The rags were then taken to the boiling house and put into several large cauldrons where they were steamed and boiled. They were then sent on to a washing-engine, a long trough revolving 120 times a minute, and after two hours in this machine, they became 'half-stuff.' At this point, they were placed in bleaching vats filled with chloride of lime, which twenty-four hours later turned them completely white. With the help of a hydraulic press, the bleaching liquor was removed, and after an hour in another washing-engine, which further separated the fibres, the material was placed in a beating engine for five hours in order to be completely pulped.

Now that the fibres were reduced to a sixtieth of an inch, the former rags were ready for the five machines that occupied several large buildings. These machines, described as 'some of the largest and finest in Britain', could turn out 2,500 square yards of paper in an

7. Morley *Gladstone*, vol 2, 26.

8. 'The Manufacture of Paper' concluded *Scotsman* 5 October 1868, 6, from which this is derived.

hour. The mass was put through a sieve called a 'knotter'. The water was drawn off and the fibres interfaced. The result was paper, which was then passed under a wire roller, which produced a watermark. The web then passed through two felt-covered rollers, which extracted moisture, and the paper was then sent on to five large drying cylinders to be heated by steam. Once it had passed over various steam-heated cylinders, the drying was nearly complete. In the final stage, the paper passed through another, two-hundred-foot, drying machine, and a finishing glaze was added. The whole distance from pulp-vat to cutting machine was almost a mile. The paper was then cut, finished, and packed into quires and reams and removed to the warehouse.

*****

The Cowan operation turned out two to three thousand tons of paper a year. The firm employed six hundred people. It was very much a family with Charles and his brothers, soon to be joined by other partners, being deeply committed to employee wellbeing. Since 1823 the company had arranged for the education of employees' children and in 1849 an attractive school was built near the mills. By 1868 120 children were enrolled and additionally 80 young people (male and female) who worked in the mills were given the opportunity of attending free evening classes during three months in the winter.

The Factory Acts, particularly those of 1847 and 1850, and the agitation of Charles' friend Lord Shaftesbury, had resulted in restraints being imposed on the exploitation of women and children by capitalists. But all the provisions in this legislation had already been anticipated by the Cowans. They had adopted three binding regulations for their own operations: first, no child under thirteen would be employed; second, no young person would be employed before they were able to read, write, and figure, and in the case of girls, to sew; third, wives would not be employed because they were to be 'keepers at home' for the sake of husband and children.

By 1868, 250 members were on the roll of a society established thirty years earlier by the Cowans and now with assets of £380 for the benefit of female workers and providing help to those over sixty-five. All Cowan employees were made to join a medical club and, thus, for a small payment health assistance was provided for themselves and their families. The total payroll was £1,300 a month: salaries varied from mechanics, who received 25 or 26 shillings a week, to millworkers ('men and lads'), who were paid 18 to 19 shillings, and women, who received 8 to 10 shillings.

*****

No longer an MP, Charles Cowan now had time to provide leadership in two trade organisations: the Merchant Company and the Scottish Trade Protection Society. Each of these roles represented Cowan's on-going commitment to the life and commerce of Edinburgh. The summer he left the Commons, Cowan agreed to stand for office in the Merchant Company as Assistant, a first step to becoming Master. The Merchant Company had a long history, growing out of friction between the guild of merchants and the guild of craftsmen. It had been officially established in 1681 'to protect the trading rights of the city of Edinburgh'. During the next century, the Company set up a network of schools quartered in hospitals. By a series of acts after 1833, the status of the Scottish royal burghs was altered, and the monopoly of the Merchant Company was taken away. As a result, the Company's focus shifted increasingly to such issues of local interest as 'the city's water supply, smuggling, taxation, Sabbath observance and postal services.'[9] The Company was looking for a new identity, and Charles Cowan would help them find it.

When Cowan was nominated as Master the mover mentioned in his nominating speech that '[h]e did not require to inform the members of the Co[mpany] of the claims which Mr Cowan had on their esteem. He had been upwards of thirty years a member of the Co[mpany]; and it had rather surprised him that Mr Cowan had not been an Assistant before now, considering his eminence as a merchant and a citizen, and his many amiable qualities.'[10] Cowan

9. See 'The Merchant Co of Edinburgh' http://www.mcoe.org.uk/webpages/companytoday.htm

10. *Scotsman* 24 June 1849. 2.

was unanimously elected. Four months later, he became Master by acclamation and was greeted with a tribute: 'Mr Cowan, as they were all aware, stood high in the mercantile body of Edinburgh, being, indeed, one of the first merchants amongst them. He had recently succeeded to be the head of one of the principal houses in this city by reason of the death of his ever-to-be-lamented father, Mr Alexander Cowan, a man of such munificent benevolence (hear, hear) – as must be a recommendation to any member of his family who might come before them. (Applause) Mr Cowan had also, till a very recent period, represented the city of Edinburgh in Parliament, having been one of its members for a period of eleven years; and he had recently retired with the undivided esteem, and regard, and gratitude of his fellow-citizens. (Applause)' The seconder added that there was 'nothing more likely to confirm the stability and influence of the company than the energy, talent, and popularity of its Masters,' and he thought that 'under [Cowan's] auspices, it would not be too much to expect that the affairs of this company would continue to flourish, and that the company would continue to flourish.'[11]

Cowan had helped found the Scottish Trade Protection Society in 1852 (with a membership after its first year of 293), and he was now in a position to give more of his energies to that organisation. He explained that it was more than a trade protection society, 'as they were daily receiving and accumulating information, tending to inform the mind of the Mercantile community as to the precise status of their customers and thereby to strengthen the credit of the respectable Merchant.' By the eighth (1860) annual general meeting, the Society had over a thousand members and had become very effective as what today would be called a lobby.

To protect the trade interests of its members, help collect bad debts, and assure the fulfilment of contractual arrangements, involved extensive legal counsel. In the words of the Lord Advocate for Scotland, the organisation was working on 'general principles which sought to regulate legal reform and the true relation of systematic jurisprudence to judicial administration.' The Society reported in 1861 that of the £26,555 claims submitted, £9,500 had been

11. *Scotsman* 6 Sept 1859. 4.

collected, in addition to £3,500 in legal costs, which the Society was seeking to avoid by emphasizing negotiation. In 1862, there had been 3,037 inquiries (compared to 2,815 during the previous year) and, increasingly, there was concern about small debts. Charles Cowan, as president, told the tenth annual meeting that 'Trade Protection Societies are now acknowledged to be essential requisites for the safe conduct and prudent extension of Commercial Enterprises and that the Mercantile Community has derived great advantage, both directly and indirectly, from the Scottish Trade Protection Society.' Meetings were held to discuss bankruptcy laws, and one occasion a *conversazione* was held with the remarkable polymath Robert Chambers about 'The Assimilation of English and Scottish Law.'[12] Under Cowan's leadership, the Society also effectively improved existing trade legislation by petition and education.

The Society's eleventh annual meeting was held at the height of the American Civil War. Cowan spoke of the prosperity of the Society, which 'presented one of the most satisfactory and gratifying evidences of the value of co-operation which had ever attended any undertaking of the same magnitude.' However, the times were dire: nearly half a million individuals had been 'deprived of bread' in consequence of the bloody war in America and the elimination of the British cotton inventory. In spite of this, they had assurance from the revenue tables for the last quarter that trade revenue had exceeded that of the previous year. Members could observe for themselves a vast number of their fellow-countrymen bearing hardship, reduced from a state of comparative affluence to absolute penury without the slightest murmur or complaint. He thought that 'the support of the country would be such as to render it unnecessary for their having recourse to Parliament to supply in the shape of a tax that which was being so generously contributed by all grades of society.' Without unemployment insurance, or any kind of safety net, it was

12. Robert Chambers (1802-1871) publisher, author. *Chambers Encyclopaedia* bears his name. In introducing him Cowan referred to his 'long-continued and successful endeavours to popularize literature in a healthful, useful, and improving character; and his more recent exertions in connection with others to advance the greatly needed improvement of the dwellings of the working-classes in this city. (Applause).' *Scotsman* 4 February 1862.

left to the Christian compassionate generosity of men like Cowan to ensure that those out of work were treated with dignity and justice. Whether those who were experiencing such deprivation were really doing so 'without the slightest murmur or complaint' is open to some question.

*****

Charles' retirement from Parliament also gave him the opportunity to travel extensively, and he made two lengthy trips overseas in the 1860s. The year after he left the Commons, he travelled to Russia with his daughter Mabel. The company depended increasingly on the quantity of rags available only in southern Russia. They sailed from Hull up the Baltic to St Petersburg – taking the same route Charles had travelled two years earlier on a trip to Norway to collect on a debt. They then took the twenty-hour express to Moscow, where Charles was the guest of a Mr Hopper, originally from Penicuik, who had not seen a Scotsman since he had migrated there seventeen years earlier. While in Russia, he also visited a government factory that manufactured bank notes from paper made from flax. The mill had nineteen vats, and the output was enormous: in Russia there were few coins at the time, notes being used for even the smallest amounts.

*****

His children were scattering. In 1858 his daughter Catharine, known to the family as Kate, was the third to marry.[13] Her husband, Charles William Wahab, came from an Ulster family well known to the Cowans. He served in India with the Bombay Staff Army and went up through the ranks to be a major general. He and Kate returned to Edinburgh in the 1880s and she died shortly after, her husband living until 1913. As a civil engineer he proved invaluable to the Cowan enterprises, particularly in regards to drainage projects. Charles Wahab shared an informed and active interest in charities such as the Edinburgh Medical Mission. They had no children.

13. On 15 September 1858.

A year later, on 23 November 1859, Charlotte married a devout Quaker, Henry Joseph Wilson. The Wilsons and the Cowans both wintered in Torquay, and the families had become acquainted there. The newlyweds returned to Henry's farm in Nottinghamshire, but he was not a gentleman farmer for long, as he was asked to take over the failing family business in Sheffield. That smelting company soon became a thriving success. Charlotte and Henry, of all the family, came closest to following in Charles' footsteps: Henry, later an MP, and Charlotte an early feminist, were a remarkable couple and their progeny proved to be high achievers.[14] One subsequent incident in their early married life is particularly telling. In 1868 their firstborn, Charles' seven-year-old granddaughter Katie, contracted scarlet fever and died two days later. The ever-practical Charles stormed down from Edinburgh, diagnosed the source of the problem as drains, and ordered the grieving and incapacitated father to move the family immediately from their home in Rotherdean to a furnished house in Sheffield, which he rented for them.[15] Charles' tender heart for his family was balanced by robust common sense.

In 1861, there were two family weddings. On 8 August, twenty-three-year-old Mabel married Hugh Francis Clarke Cleghorn, the Co-Chief Conservator of Forests and later Inspector-General of Forests in India. He had gone out to Madras at the age of twenty-one after training as a doctor at Edinburgh and St Andrews. Childless, he and Marjory returned from India in 1869, and he took up the life of a country gentleman in Stravithie, Fifeshire, 'although he never ceased to do all in his power for the promotion of arboriculture and botany in this country.'[16] On 15 September, twenty-three-year-old Charles William and Margaret Dick Craig were wed. Margaret was the daughter of paper miller Robert Craig and had three brothers who

14. The grandson of Charlotte's son Alexander Cowan Wilson (1866–1955) is the epidemiologist Thomas Wilson Meade (1936-), winner of the Balzan Prize in 1997. His father, married to Elizabeth Margaret Wilson (1908–2008), was the 1977 Nobel Laureate James Edward Meade (1907–1995).

15. Fowler, W. S. *A Study in Radicalism and Dissent: The Life and Times of Henry Joseph Wilson, 1833–1914*. London: Epworth Press, 1961. 13-14.

16. Obituary: Hugh F. C. Cleghorn, M. D., LL. D., F. R. S. E. *The Geographical Journal* Vol. 6, No. 1 (July 1895), 83.

joined the family firm when it was located in Newbattle, Edinburgh. The firm subsequently moved to Moffat.

In 1864 tragedy struck. Jean Menzies, Charles and Catharine's oldest surviving child, was married to the papermaker Thomas Chalmers, namesake of his uncle.[17] She brought her six children to live briefly with her parents in Edinburgh while repairs were being made to their home in Penicuik. Jean caught an infection and died suddenly on 8 May that year, leaving her husband and parents devastated and the six children (aged fourteen months to ten years) motherless. Thomas never remarried, giving himself to raising his children. In addition to his trade as a paper maker, he was actively committed as an elder in the Penicuik Free Church. On his death, it was said that '[m]any still speak gratefully and lovingly of his well-known habit of house-to-house [shut-in] visitation on Sabbath mornings.'[18]

It is not clear whether the proximity of the Glencorse military barracks had anything to do with two of Charles' daughters marrying into the military, but on 13 July 1865 Anna Thompson was married at Valleyfield to Lieutenant Edward George Newnham of the Seventeenth Bengal Cavalry. The son of a Bath vicar, he had been in India since 1859. For the wedding he was granted a six-month leave 'without pay'.[19] Two months later, a pregnant Anna sailed with him to the subcontinent where she would spend much of the next twenty-one years. Their four children were sent back to be raised in the Wilson home in Sheffield.

---

17. Thomas Chalmers learned his trade as a papermaker with the Cowans and then went to Loch Mill, Linlithgow, which he managed. He lost substantially in City of Glasgow Bank failure.

18. Wilson, John J. *A Fifty year Retrospect.* Glasgow: W. Pollock Wylie, 1893. 10-11.

19. 'Record of the Services of Lt. Col. Edward George Newnham' Bengal Book Form, 1 February 1881, in the possession of Judith A. MacLeod. Newnham died in 1887, leaving an estate of £10. Anna lived in Auchindinny House, near Penicuik, until her 1909 death. She was caregiver to her invalid sister Maggie, who lived until 1934, subsequently attended by Anna's daughter Edith Margaret Newnham.

Chapter 14

Inspired Investing

On his retirement in 1850 Alexander Cowan had been anxious to ensure a well-planned transition so the future of the business would not be threatened. 'I intimated to my sons two years ago,' he wrote that summer, 'that it was my intention to retire from business and to advertise myself out about the first of October next, and this I still wish to do unless it can be shewn that my continuance would be for the advantage of other parties. I don't want the profits and as I don't wish to be richer than I am I would probably give them away.'[1] There was, as we have seen, a single caveat: 'James would not again become my Partner until he had paid his debts in full.' James was unfinished business for the company and an exception to the family's reputation for shrewd investment, fiscal probity, and financial integrity.

The elimination of the excise tax, the expansion of the business to Australia, and possibly even to Canada, meant that the Cowans by the mid-1850s were prospering. Based on total income deposited in the family's bank, the British Linen Bank, for a nine month period in 1853 of £42,310 or a ten month period the following year of

1. AC to Professor Allan Menzies (son-in-law) 20 August 1850. *The Cowan Letters*, 41.

£51,408,[2] the business was becoming very profitable and provided excess capital for investment elsewhere.

Scottish economic historian Clive Lee notes 'Many of the best investment opportunities open to Victorian financiers lay overseas, in the establishment of the infrastructure of the growing international economy.... In contrast, there were fewer, and less attractive, opportunities open in Scotland for accumulated capital that was seeking profitable investment outlets.'[3] Though they had made their money in paper manufacturing, by the 1840s the Cowans were investing shrewdly in some of the growing business enterprises of the time. As venture capitalists, they focussed primarily at the time on railways and insurance.

The 1840s were a time of prodigious railway expansion in Britain. At its beginning only a few small, isolated lines had been built, but by the end of the decade there was a national network bringing all the major cities and towns together and greatly speeding transportation and communication across the realm. Vast sums were needed to capitalize the venture, and the Cowans were very much at the forefront of such speculation. During that period Charles, first as a private speculator, but after 1847 as an MP, had a ringside seat that provided him a detailed knowledge of the legislation and regulation of the growing railway system.

The first inter-city rail line in the world was opened between Liverpool and Manchester in 1830 with George Stephenson as engineer in charge. Plans were being made at that time for the first railway, the Edinburgh and Glasgow line, to be constructed in Scotland but it took eight years before Parliament allowed the project to go ahead. Charles was an early shareholder and subsequently a director of this enterprise. On Friday, 18 January 1842, the line was finally opened. Shareholders' tickets for the event never reached Charles and John, so they had to sit out the event, although (as

2. NAS, GD311/7/69/1. Mrs Ying Yong Ding in her so far unpublished Ph. D. thesis, University of the West of Scotland, estimates the annualized sales figure to be £60,000 based on these figures (page 78, used by kind permission).

3. Lee, C. H. 'Scotland, 1860-1939: growth and prosperity' in Floud, R. and Johnson P. *The Cambridge Economic History of Modern Britain* Volume2: *Economic Maturity, 1860-1939*. Cambridge: Cambridge University Press, 2004. 441.

Charles records regretfully in his diary) it was a very beautiful day. 'The opening went off admirably, excepting that the Rope over the Glasgow Station was found cut ... through, which caused the arrival of the Trains to be so late as 12 o'clock at night.'[4]

In 1845, capitalization of the Caledonian Railway was approved by the Commons. When Charles arrived at Westminster, he used his expertise to explain to the Commons not only the geography of the area where the line would run, but also to point out some lack of foresight as railways expanded in Scotland. The Caledonian Railway was a case in point: the engineers had 'constructed a line from Edinburgh to Carlisle through a district noted for bleakness and sterility, but was in addition exposed to the competition of two nearly parallel lines, one on each side of it.'[5] The original stock had sold for £50 but had gone down to £14 and was now worthless. The two railways needed to amalgamate.

In March 1850, Charles Cowan seconded a motion to join the two railways but drew heavy fire from friends and fellow MPs such as William Ewart Gladstone, Fox Maule (later the Earl of Dalhousie and one of the few aristocrats with a strong commitment to the Free Church), and the President of the Board of Trade at the time, Henry Labouchere. He withdrew the bill, but the next year, legislation to relieve the Caledonian Railway of its heavy obligations was approved by a large majority. After the second reading was carried, one Scottish investor told a London broker to buy a ween of stock. Cowan remembered that the Englishman was totally mystified and thought the order was for fifty. 'Hoots man, ye may buy me a thousand!' responded the Scot, annoyed at the man's ignorance of Scots dialect.[6]

Another railway venture which Cowan sponsored, and in which he invested, was the 1852 Hawick–Carlisle line. A spur of thirty-nine miles, it joined the North British Railway terminus at Hawick to the Caledonian station in Carlisle, linking southern Scotland's most productive agricultural land with the lucrative English urban

4. *Diary*, 18 January 1842 (Edinburgh City Library archives).

5. Caledonian and Edinburgh and Glasgow Railways Amalgamation Bill. *Hansard*, HC Deb 18 March 1850 vol. 109 cc1050.

6. *Reminiscences*, note 1, 220-221.

markets. Capitalization called for £360,000, with shares priced at £10 each. The line was opened in 1862 and was later absorbed by North British, as was the Edinburgh to Glasgow line three years later.

In the aftermath of the railway scrambles of the 1840s, Cowan, as an MP, was generally in favour of railway reorganization, as evidenced by a speech he made in the Commons in 1853, stating that 'he was convinced that many amalgamations, if properly carried out, would prove of great public advantage.'[7] There was a danger here for members of Parliament, now increasingly middle-class businessmen. As Herbert Spencer stated in his 1846 *Edinburgh Review* article (reprinted as *Railway Morals & Railway Policy*), they needed to take great care lest those who 'administer railway affairs should be guilty of indirectly enriching themselves at the expense of their constituents.'[8] There was also great risk involved in investing in railways – as demonstrated by the Panic of 1857 caused by speculation and under-capitalization.

Cowan's last railway venture was the construction of a single-track line linking the Hawthornden station of the Peebles Railway with Penicuik by way of Roslin. This route was particularly advantageous for the Cowans, as it provided transport to their Bank Mill paperworks, which were immediately adjacent to the Penicuik station. On 1 April 1870, a bill to incorporate the Penicuik Railway with a capitalization of £36,000 came before the Ways and Means Committee of the House of Commons.[9] It was then approved and received royal assent. Construction of the line proved slow and arduous, and, as one of the eight directors, Charles Cowan was called on at every half-yearly meeting to reassure stockholders. In one such presentation, he claimed that 'in the course of a short time, the line would prove an excellent investment.' 'We hope,' he went on, 'that what of the stock remained unappropriated would soon be then taken up by persons in the district. The object of the directors had not been to

7. *Hansard*, HC Deb 06 December 1852 vol. 123 cc1049.

8. Spencer, Herbert. *Railway Morals & Railway Policy*. London: Longman, Brown, Green & Longmans, 1855. 4.

9. *Scotsman*, 1 April 1870, 3.

push the railway to the general market, but to have it held as much as possible by people in the neighbourhood.'[10] The terminus at Penicuik was duly opened in 1872, and the railway was amalgamated with North British, so that four years later stockholders were reimbursed with their purchase price.[11]

Charles Cowan always demonstrated great concern about the rights and protection of railway stockholders – particularly small investors. At a meeting of the Edinburgh Chamber of Commerce on 9 February 1870, for instance, he initiated a discussion on 'wasteful expenditures ruinous to railway shareholders.' Cowan got up on his feet and decried the profligacy of the North British line running trains with only one or two passengers to preserve the company's traffic rights. Millions of pounds had been wasted, Cowan claimed, and he blamed company directors, rather than Parliament. North British stock had been adversely affected, but the situation with the Caledonian Railway appeared catastrophic, with stock declining in value by 50 per cent and shareholders being saddled with yet heavier burdens. Investors became increasingly nervous about railway stock bubbles, particularly on the Continent, and their fears were confirmed on 'Black Friday' (9 May 1873) on the Vienna Stock Exchange. Cowan's words at stockholders meetings, often reported in the press, were a beacon of sanity and probity in a market overinflated by ruinous speculation.

Cowan told many stories of his adventures with railways. Some of them had to do with narrow escapes – including a derailment in 1855, when he was taking the express to London with his daughter Mabel and the carriages ahead of him went off the track because of heavy frost on the rails. Two years later, when he was travelling between Darlington and Leamside in the Northeast of England, the points misfired, but as the train went off the tracks, it was stopped by coal everywhere, and the carriages divided into four sections thus minimising the impact. After that accident, Cowan was asked to provide evidence in a litigation case for an injured passenger. But the 1877 train was likely the most spectacular accident that affected Charles. He was not on the train himself, but his son Charles William

10. *Scotsman*, 25 April 1872, 2.

11. *Scotsman*, 17 October 1872, 30 April 1875, 28 October, 1875, 13 April 1876.

was – and the event prompted him to send a letter to the *Times*.[12] It included an attachment containing Charles William's descriptions of his attempts, having crawled out of a destroyed carriage himself, to come to the aid of the dead, the dying, and the seriously wounded. Charles regarded the event as 'my son's miraculous preservation.'

Travelling by rail, as well as investing in railways, were both unpredictable. Fortunes were made and lost in the scramble to reap rewards from an expanding market. Railway stock did not make Charles Cowan a wealthy man: it was the paper trade that was the basis of his fortune. In spite of his failure to amass riches from railway expansion as other capitalists at the time had succeeded in doing, he remained fascinated by the innovations that rail transport made possible. It would be American railways that proved in the end to be more lucrative and rewarding.

*****

Insurance was another financial interest of the Cowans. On the eve of Charles' marriage in 1824, his father insisted that he take out a policy with the Scottish Widows Fund Life Assurance Company, Scotland's first mutual life assurance company. Alexander, who was an 'ordinary director' was one of those who met in 1815 in the Royal Exchange Coffee Rooms in Edinburgh, to consider setting up 'a general fund for securing provisions to widows, sisters and other females.'13 Fifty-two years later, as one of the oldest surviving annuitants and having paid out just under £3000, he reckoned his estate would receive twice that amount. Apparently, Alexander had promised that he would pay the premiums for the first ten years of his son's marriage, 'but never did so.' As Charles put it: 'I never required to remind him of his promise which probably he regarded as conditional only.'[14]

Charles championed both the thrift of the Scots in their banking habits and also the 'great prosperity, usefulness, and soundness of the

12. *Times*, 29 March 1877, quoted in *Reminiscences*, 367-9.

13. See http://www.scottishwidows.co.uk/about_us/who_we_are/our_history.html. Accessed 21 March 2011.

14. Reminiscences, 244.

Scottish Life offices, evincing the high appreciation in which they are held by the people of the South as well as of North Britain, due to the skill and uprightness in the management of those valuable institutions.'[15] As an MP he expressed pride over the growth of the insurance business in Scotland. On 6 April 1853, in a debate over legislation titled the Probates of Wills and Grants of Administration Bill, he rose to speak. The legislation was to ensure that Scottish wills had equal validity in England. Fourteen Scottish insurance companies had approached him to gain his support for the legislation. The firms represented a total liability of £33,000,000. Speaking of 'the hardship and expense to which many persons connected with them, whether as share-holders or having their lives insured, were subjected in consequence of the present law,'[16] he vigorously supported the new legislation as endorsed by the Lord Advocate for Scotland, Free Churchman James Moncrieff. The Bill finally passed into law.

*****

Cowan had long experience with insurance companies when he came to Parliament and he would continue to be involved for all of his working life with the insurance companies of Scotland. Some of this experience was negative: in March 1839, he was appointed an extraordinary director of the new Forth Marine Insurance Co. The capitalization was to have been £100,000, but only £74,669 was raised, and by 1843, the company's creditors had gone to law.[17] A year and a half later, at a partners' meeting, the Cowans were clearly worried. It appears that they had thirty shares in the company, valued at between £10 and £15, and by the annual meeting in June 1845, they were talking about dissolution of the company and trying to '[g]et out positively. But on as good terms as possible.'[18]

15. *Reminiscences*, 243.

16. *Hansard*, HC Deb 06 April 1853 vol. 125 cc664.

17. Dunbar, W. H.; Campbell, James; Heriot, Maitland. *Reports of Cases Decided in the Supreme Courts of Scotland.* Volume XVII. Edinburgh: M Anderson, 1845. 234.

18. Meetings 6 May and 3 June 1845 NAS, GD69/7/2-4.

In light of this debacle, it is surprising that in 1848, Charles Cowan, flush from his electoral triumph, agreed to become an 'Ordinary Director' of the Scottish National Insurance Co., founded seven years earlier. At the annual meeting on 18 October 1850, he was elected deputy chairman. It was to be a long relationship, going on for thirty years, until in 1878 the Scottish National joined with the Scottish Union to form the Scottish Union and National Insurance Co. In the minutes of the company (now deposited in Norwich, East Anglia, because of subsequent corporate mergers), there is evidence of Cowan's diligence. For instance, in 1852, in spite of commitments at Westminster, he attended a total of twenty-seven meetings of the directors. The chairing of meetings appears to have been shared around and he is regularly recorded as 'Preses' (the presiding director). The business of the directors was divided into three sections that met separately once a quarter: fire, life and investments ('Company funds'). There were generally six directors in attendance and twenty or more at the annual meeting.

The directors faced interesting moral dilemmas. On 6 December 1850 Charles Cowan and the other directors present were asked to adjudicate on a claim by a widow whose husband was a confirmed drunkard and had for two or more days of the week been carried home from the public house. He died of what was delicately described as intemperance. The directors said that they had been 'grossly deceived' but 'The Committee is extremely unwilling that a question that should be raised about the validity of any of the Company's Policies, or that the facts should be brought forward to hurt the feeling of the widow and family,' so they agreed to pay up.[19]

Another complication was Charles' brother. A particularly vexing matter for Charles as a director occurred when his brother James declared bankruptcy.[20] A loan of £20,000 had been given him by Scottish National, with collateral in the form of stock in the Stirling and Dunfermline railway as well as (it turned out) the Edinburgh and Perth railway, with his brothers as guarantors ('cautioners').

19. SNIC Minutes, first volume, 154 (6 Dec 1852).

20. Three meetings of the directors dealt with James' difficulties: 6 August 1852 (*SNIC Minutes*, 305-6), 13 August 1852 (*SNIC Minutes*, 306-7) and 5 November 1854 (*SNIC Minutes*, 401).

The Stirling and Dunfermline shares had declined in value and now were worth a fraction of their original cost. With their solicitor present, the directors decided to sell the shares. A week later it was announced that they had received notification from Gibson Clark's law firm that all was in order.[21] The other lawyer involved was Charles' brother-in-law, so tight were the interconnections, and so great the embarrassment to the family. Two years later legal costs were assessed against the Cowans.

Charles Cowan was compensated well for his involvement in the insurance business. In 1852 dividends were pegged at six per cent. The company was competently managed. The only potential conflict of interest was their granting of loans to railways and other businesses with which Charles Cowan had links through sitting in the House of Commons. But he apparently did not see the need of recusing himself.

*****

Risk hardly seemed the word to describe the manufacture of paper, a sure and steady source of income for Charles Cowan and the family. All seemed secure at Penicuik. But a challenge to the family's prosperity, looming since 1842, four years later would threaten their very livelihood. The whole paper-manufacturing enterprise in Scotland was under threat. Would the landed aristocracy eliminate a whole industry in the interest of their fishing rights? Or was there a legitimate concern that the longterm effects of pollution needed to be faced and dealt with. It is to the greatest challenge Alexander Cowan and Sons had faced so far that we now turn.

21. 'The letter contained a request that the Coy should take steps to preserve its claims against Mr James Cowan and the sureties for his Composition before the time declared by the 120th section of the Bankrupt Act as being allowed in such cases for lodging claims should expire which it would do. The Secretary was requested to intimate to Messrs Gibson-Craig & Co that the Scottish Union have taken such steps as they think necessary to presume their claim against the Messrs Cowan.' (*SNIC Minutes*, 307)

Chapter 15

Pollution Perils

'An abundant supply of fine water is very essential to produce paper of fine quality,' Cowan wrote in his *Encyclopaedia Britannica* article on the subject of papermaking. True to this observation, many of Scotland's paper-manufacturing operations were nestled along the banks of the River Esk, where they had access to good quantities of water. The need for water figured largely in Alexander Cowan's negotiating to keep the water rights when the Valleyfield mill was expropriated during the Napoleonic Wars. By retaining those rights, Alexander had made sure that the mill would be of dubious value when it came to a resale. Eleven years later, he triumphantly returned to Valleyfield, with his company's water rights still intact.

In 1866, however, water rights became a matter of litigation. To protect their fishing privileges downstream, three aristocrats – the Duke of Buccleuch, Lord Melville, and Sir James Williams Drummond – sued the owners of six Esk River paper mills for damages. The case, dealing with pollution of waterways, came to a jury trial, with the Lord Justice Clerk presiding, and was one of the earliest of its kind.

The suggestion was made that all six mills along the River Esk should be relocated to the edge of the sea. Called as a witness,

Charles' brother John was aghast. 'It would be very difficult indeed to remove the establishment for making half-stuff [paper pulp ready for the beater] to the sea-side. I don't know any place we could go to where we would find water and the necessary accommodation. That is not a suggestion which any man practically acquainted with the subject would make.'[1]

*****

The trial was described in the press as 'one of the most important which has for many years been before the Courts of this country' because of the 'grave public interests which are involved'.[2] The case, which went back twenty-five years, alleged that the pursuers 'had not only been deprived of the benefit which they formerly enjoyed in the use of the water, and of the amenity which it added to their properties, but that the river had been converted into an intolerable nuisance by certain proprietors of paper-mills on its banks, who polluted the water by disgorging into it the dirty and noxious refuse of the materials employed at their works. They asked the Court to declare that they had a right 'to have the water of the North Esk so far as it flows through, or by their properties, transmitted in a state fit for the use and enjoyment of man and beast'; and that 'the defenders had no right to pollute the said water, or to use it, or the channels of the stream, so as to render the water noxious or unwholesome, or unfit for all its natural primary purposes to the pursuers or in any way to destroy the amenity of the said stream.'[3]

The case had been a long time in coming. In 1841 a complaint had been made by the Duke of Buccleuch, Robert Viscount Melville, and Sir James Williams Drummond of Hawthornden, along with two others who had subsequently withdrawn from the suit: Wardlaw Ramsay of Whitehill and Mr. Brown of Firth. The court appointed

1. *Report of Jury Trial–The Duke Buccleuch, Lord Melville, and Sir James Drummond, Pursuers, against Alexander Cowan & Sons, Wm Somerville & Son, James Brown & Co., Archibald Fullerton Sommerville, and Wm Tod & Son Defenders*. Edinburgh: R. Clark, 1866. 1.

2. *Scotsman*, 28 July 1866, 8.

3. *Scotsman*, 28 July 1866, 8.

as experts the highly regarded Dr. Robert Christison[4] (later knighted by the Queen) and Dr. Henry Madden,[5] who was married to a first cousin of Charles and had strong Penicuik links. They came up with seven regulations that John Cowan testified had been faithfully observed when he made his 1866 testimony as defence witness. These regulations included commitments that rag-waste would not be thrown into the Esk but collected apart, that spent chloride of lime would either be reclaimed or sent down the river in a time of flood, and that alkaline liquor would be placed in pits for twelve or fourteen years, presumably before being dumped into the river. Two years previously, Charles and a foreman had applied for patents for a washer that kept back rag fibre from the stream, and Christison and Madden, it was reported, had 'approved very highly of them.'[6]

The suit lay dormant for another twenty-two years but was revived in 1863. In the intervening years, many changes had taken place, not the least of them being the vast expansion of the mills, particularly at Valleyfield, as the paper trade had expanded. Penicuik was also growing, thanks to the Cowans' prosperity. The litigants had also changed, as two (Melville and Drummond) had been replaced by their heirs in the suit. Originally, there were seven defendants, but now there were only three, and the primary defendants were the Cowans

4. Sir Robert Christison, Bt. (1797–1882) physician and toxicologist and a personal physician to Queen Victoria, professor of medicine and therapeutics at the University of Edinburgh (1832-1877). He was a frequent witness in cases requiring medical or toxicological expertise. As the Justice Clerk stated in his summation: 'Dr Christison is a man of great skill and ability in matters of this kind, and Dr Madden had the advantage of being a pupil of Dr Christison, and his assistant for a considerable number of years.' *Scotsman*, 11 August 1866, 8.

5. Henry Ridewood Madden, MD (1818–1884) married to Duncan Cowan's seventh child, Helen (1817–1858). They had ten children, four of whom had issue. He is described as 'another of our Disruption Fathers,' 'the only member of the medical profession who has ever held office in the Free Church in Penicuik. He was a good man and a trusted physician, and is spoken of in terms of the greatest respect by old residenters (*sic*) in our parish. These were days when identification with Free Church principles sometimes cost professional and business men not a little, by the withdrawal of the favours of those who thought otherwise. But Dr Madden was not one who would sell his conscience for his interest and I believe he never regretted the stand he made in those who exiled themselves from the Establishment.' (Wilson, John J. *A Fifty Years Retrospect*. Glasgow, Pollock Wylie, 1893. 10.)

6. *Report of the Jury Trial* ... 222.

at Penicuik. Alexander had dropped out in 1853 when the firm was reorganized, so Charles, John, and James were in the dock, along with two new partners: Charles William, Charles' older surviving son, and George, the second child of Alexander's second marriage.[7] The second accused was William Sommerville, non-resident partner of Dalmore Mills, and his son Archibald Fullerton Sommerville. The proprietors of Polton Mill, Alexander Annandale father and son, were the third defendants. The mills at Auchindinny (which had burned down) and Springfield (no longer a paper mill) were not now at issue. Two new defendants had been added: James Brown of the Esk Mill, Penicuik, and William Tod and Son, of St Leonard's Mill, Lasswade. Legal challenges as to the combinations and permutations of the defendants proceeded, as did the position on the Esk of the various mills and how far some, up river, were implicated in the pollution further downstream.

The case had serious implications for the Cowans, as they were the first cited as 'defenders', had the largest mill, and also had the most to lose in terms of their capital investment. But the concern was not just financial: as professing Christians, the Cowans' moral interest lay in the welfare of the community and of the environment, and they took these duties very seriously. As John Cowan stated at the trial: 'We have given constant and very great attention to the best means of preventing the matter going into the water. All our operations may be looked on as experiments. Within the last seven years we have spent about £1100 in experimenting and in practical operations for that object. I know of no measure taken to prevent impurities at any other mills in England which we have not adopted. We have tried everything that other people have suggested.'[8] And there had been real progress at the Valleyfield Mill: 'Our work has been steadily increasing since 1843 ... the discharge of fibre into the river is very much less now than it was before 1843.'

The presence of fibre in the river was hardly surprising, as prior to the introduction of patent washers in 1839, all rag-waste and

7. George Cowan (1832–1885) Married to Mary Forbes, they had three children. While visiting Madeira in 1870 his address was given as Valleyfield. He was described as 'the most enthusiastic Scot of the family.' (http://www.penicuikcdt.org.uk/Helen_Bannerman.html. Accessed 12 February 2011.

8. *Report of the Jury Trial ...* 223.

boiler-ley, along with spent chloride of lime, were dumped into the river. The washers had made a difference, and improvements had resulted from following the recommendations of Christison and Madden, but a significant change occurred after 1861 when three conical save-alls were introduced, following specifications suggested by Dr. Stevenson Macadam and a Mr. Adie to deal with any toxic waste.[9] This innovation occurred just in the nick of time, as rags were becoming scarcer and paper manufacturers now relied increasingly on esparto grass, which created what was described as 'very nasty brown liquor'.[10] Esparto grass effluent made the river browner and yellower than it had appeared before.

Cross-examination of John Cowan was then directed toward the impact of the Cowan mills on the local community. In 1835, he noted, the firm had paid wages of between £2000 and £2500. Thirty years later, that amount had increased to £12,000, so to shut down the establishment would cause great dislocation within the community. Charles William Cowan later testified that he had taken samples of the water three times a day, placed them in labelled bottles, put them in a clothes-basket, and retrieved them only a month ago when they were sent to the chemical laboratory at the university. By then, the labels had apparently been destroyed and were of no use. His testimony lasted only a few minutes and was quickly terminated.[11]

*****

The trial lasted for two weeks and caused no little stir in Edinburgh. The Lord Justice Clerk, John Inglis, later Lord Glencorse, was the second most senior judge in Scotland and had held the office since 1858.[12] His closing address lasted two hours and twenty minutes

---

9. Stevenson Macadam (1829–1901), son of the road paver, was Professor of Chemistry at the University of Edinburgh.

10. *Report of the Jury Trial* ... 223.

11. *Report of the Jury Trial* ... 252-3.

12. John Inglis, Lord Glencorse (1810–1891) as Solicitor-General in Lord Derby's first cabinet in 1852, would have been well known to Charles Cowan. He was Lord President of the Court of Session the year after the trial (a recognition of his skill there) until his death. His father of the same name (1762-1834), minister of old Greyfriars,

and was a masterful statement of jurisprudence. 'I do not remember in the course of my experience a case in which so large a number of witnesses have been examined, or in which the subject of inquiry has extended over such a variety of topics.' Amid all the testimony, he attempted to clarify what the case was really all about. The pursuers seemed to be seeking the 'power to require the defenders to make such improvements upon their works as might be considered necessary or desirable for the purification of the river without the necessity of obtaining the necessary formal judgment of the Court following upon the verdict. On the other hand, it seemed to be represented on the part of the defenders that the effect of a verdict in favour of the pursuers would be, as they expressed it, to put down these mills, and to stop the paper manufacture altogether upon the river Esk, and to annihilate the sources of its prosperity. Neither of these views is accurate.'

The case was therefore unique. A verdict would not be stated as 'out and out in favour of one party or another.' He then went on to argue the difference between a public and a private water. 'It is vested for public uses, and chiefly for the uses of navigation; and to these public uses all private rights are subordinated. No man who has property upon the banks of such a stream as that can set up any claim or right for himself which shall interfere with the public uses. The property of the river is in the crown....'[13] Inglis was clearly establishing a new social order in Scotland where the aristocracy could not lord it over public property used for the common good. In a curious way, this pollution case was allowing some pollution if it was in the public good. A hundred and fifty years later, polluters are generally portrayed as greedy, domineering capitalists who are careless of the public good – a dramatic power shift.

The Lord Justice Clerk went on to single out the Cowans for the efforts they had made to stop polluting the river Esk. 'I think also some of these defenders – and it is not invidious, I hope, to say more especially the Messrs Cowan – have devoted a great deal of attention to the devising of means for abating, as far as they possibly can, the nuisance complained of.' And a few minutes later, after citing expert

was described contradictorily as either a Moderate or 'Evangelical Erastian.'

13. *Scotsman*, 11 August 1866, 8.

witnesses at the trial called by the defence, Drs. Letheby, Madden, Audley and Hoffmann, the Lord Justice Clerk went on to say: 'The effect of their evidence was generally favourable, particularly to Messrs. Cowan, whose mills were situated farther up the river, their unanimous conclusion being that the matter discharged from their works was not likely to travel four-and-a-half miles, which was the distance between the Penicuik Mills and Hawthorden,' the location where the pursuers wanted to fish.[14] Inglis then covered the evidence from the witnesses called by the pursuers, including academics such as Professors Miller, Franklin, Penny and Maclagan, and noted 'a very considerable variance of opinion among the scientific witnesses on either side, and, what is not so easily accounted for, a considerable variance in matters of fact.'

In advising the jury, he concluded, 'You have the evidence before you and you can judge. If you find that the pollution from Messrs.' Cowan's mill does not find its way to Hawthornden, then you will return a verdict for the Messrs. Cowan.' There was some back and forth at the conclusion of his speech between himself and the Dean of the Faculty of Law at the University. The Dean claimed that he had written down *verbatim* a statement from the Lord Justice Clerk instructing the jury to determine that '[t]he water of the river must be sent down undiminished by any except by its natural and primary uses.' In a flash of anger, the Lord Justice-Clerk interrupted: 'No, no; that I think is downright nonsense.'[15] There followed a debate between the two as to what the Lord-Justice Clerk had actually said. Finally an addition to the statement was agreed on, as the Lord Justice said he would write out his instructions, adding the words 'that there should be no unnecessary or artificial operations by the upper heritors which should diminish or impair the purity of the water as sent down to the lower heritors.' It was a bitter exchange.

The court was crowded as the summation was given that Friday morning. The jury went out shortly after noon. Most of those present in the room remained to hear their decision. Three hours later, the jury bell rang, and the few vacant seats were hurriedly occupied.

14. *Scotsman*, 11 August 1866, 8.

15. *Scotsman*, 11 August 1866, 8.

The verdict was announced: by a nine to three vote, they had found for the pursuers on all the issues. A few cheered, but most of those present hissed. 'This unusual demonstration was at once put down by the macers,' the *Scotsman* reported the next day.[16]

A weekend intervened, and on Monday, the *Scotsman* was back at it, with an editorial that cautioned on drawing any quick conclusions about the result of the trial. 'What has been decided is merely a matter of fact, and a matter of fact so very obvious that, to the non-legal mind, it seems wonderful that there should have been any contention, much less nine days' witnessing, about it. On the one side, there was no denial of the fact that the paper manufactories pollute the water; on the other side, there was no denial that the water is polluted also by other causes.' It went on to recognize the populist dimensions of the argument: industrialization and full employment vs the privileges of a few. 'As there are more paper-makers than there are dukes, the majority of people are apt, in such a case as the Esk one, to give their sympathies to those who seem to represent industry rather than to those who are made to seem as if they represented only "amenities".'[17]

Indeed, it became clear from the hisses as the verdict was announced that the public stood squarely behind the Cowans and the other paper makers and against the Duke of Buccleuch, Lord Melville (whose carpet factory was polluting the Esk as well, it was noted in the trial), and Sir James Williams Drummond. And according to the *Scotsman*, one of the original litigants from twenty years before, Wardlaw Ramsay, had distanced himself from the other litigants. In an 1847 letter to Drummond he had stated: 'It is manifestly unjust to continue an action against mill owners who in every way have attended to, and still continue to attend to, the wishes of the proprietors.'

*****

Meanwhile, Charles and his partners were engaged in what today would be called damage control. The year after the trial, an article

16. *Scotsman*, 11 August 1866, 8.

17. *Scotsman*, 13 August 1866, 2.

appeared in the *Scotsman*, ostensibly about all the paper manufacturers, but focusing on the Cowan operation. 'About 600 workpeople are employed in the various departments, and these are treated with great consideration and liberality by Messrs. Cowan. The wives and daughters of the partners have always taken a special interest in the sick, and since 1823 managed a school for the education of the children of the workpeople.'[18] The article went on to reassure the public that 'Messrs.' Cowan have, though at great inconvenience, got rid of the most offensive of the polluting elements by having their rags cut at the subsidiary establishments at Musselburgh and Leith.' It was an example of nineteenth-century public relations.

The trial was an indication of how far the Cowans' Christian principles, consistent philanthropic activities and compassionate engagement with the community had created loyalties and a positive environment for their business interests. Unlike the hunting and fishing aristocracy, the Cowans were seen as protectors of the poor and the marginalised. In fact, working-class people throughout Britain were rising up against the forces of privilege and power, and the Cowans (and the other mill owners) were profiting from the temper of the times. Six weeks before the trial, through the conniving of Benjamin Disraeli (who was Chancellor of the Exchequer at the time), Earl Russell's Liberal government had been defeated over a proposed second Reform Act. The final bill, which received royal assent the next year, was even more sweeping in its scope, enfranchising all male householders and extending the electorate from one million to five million.

In such an atmosphere, it is not surprising that, despite the jury's decision in favour of the gentry downstream, the Cowans were not required to shut down their mills and were allowed to continue to add pollution-controlling technology at their own pace.

18. 'The Manufacture of Paper Concluded' *Scotsman*, 5 October 1868, 6.

Chapter 16

American Adventure

In July 1867 as four British colonies in North America joined to become the Dominion of Canada, and the United States was emerging from the trauma of the Civil War, Charles Cowan set off across the Atlantic to see for himself the New World. He was accompanied by his youngest child, twenty-one year old John James, and John James' friend and schoolmate William Blaikie. Their trip was proposed by Charles' oldest nephew, William John Menzies.[1] Menzies had visited the United States three years earlier, as the Civil War was still raging, and was now bullish about the opportunities that the country presented to the shrewd and careful investor. There was, however, a note of caution: 'I was once offered the bonds of a railway company in course of construction, which were recommended to me on the ground that the railway commenced nowhere and ended nowhere, and therefore was not bound to carry through traffic at unpaying rates!'[2]

---

1. Sir William John Menzies, Kt. Bach., W.S., (1834–1905), the oldest son of Allan, William's sixth child, married to Helen Cowan, and thus Charles' nephew. He was married three times, and had ten children. A daughter Frances married Charles Cowan's grandson Charles Menzies Cowan.

2. Menzies, Wm John *America as a Field for Investment A Lecture Delivered to the Chartered Accountants Students Society*. Edinburgh: Wm Blackwood and Sons, 1892.3.

There was, Menzies insisted, no substitute for thorough investigation and on-site examination by the would-be financier.

The travellers set off from Liverpool on the Cunarder *Cuba*, docking first at Halifax after a hazardous trip through icebergs and chilling temperatures. They lingered for a couple of days in Boston, seeing the usual tourist sights and hearing a lecture by Ralph Waldo Emerson at Harvard University. Travelling on to New York City, the four checked into the Clarendon Hotel at Fourth Avenue and Eighteenth Street, frequented at the time by European visitors. It is not recorded whether Charles went with his son, who admitted years later that while he was in New York City he had gone secretly to a theatre to enjoy a controversial Irish play.[3]

They crossed the Hudson River one day to visit the Passaic Paper mill at Patterson, New Jersey. Operated since 1837 by Henry V. Butler, the well-known paper maker, it was described in American understatement as 'one of the most extensive, beautiful, and complete establishments in the world.'[4] Two Fourdrinnier machines at that mill ran off 35,000 pounds of the finest quality paper every week. Of the 135 employees, two brothers were from Penicuik, sons of a former mill manager there. John James would recall being shocked that one of them, a machine man and recently a captain in the Northern Army, greeted them in his shirtsleeves. Sixty-five years later, John James would say revealingly that 'This prepared me for not being surprised in the Great War to see working-men promoted to acting as temporary gentlemen.'[5]

Journeying on to Washington, the men left their cards at the White House. But the unfortunate President Andrew Johnson, caught up at that moment in the dismissal of his Secretary of War Edwin Stanton (which would lead to his impeachment by the House

3. Cowan, John James. *From 1846 to 1932*. Edinburgh: Pillans and Wilson, 1933. 37.

4. See http://patersonhistory.com/industry/ivanhoe.html

5. The play featured an English beadle as the butt of the entertainment. Appearing just a year after the second Fenian raid on Canada from the United States and the battle of Ridgeway, the play included a quip that the Scottish John James remembered well: 'Ireland would not be happy until the American eagle was its flag and the British lion was cowering at its feet.' Cowan, John James. *From 1846 to 1932*. Edinburgh: Pillans and Wilson, 1933. 37.

of Representatives), had other things on his mind than Scottish visitors. Charles Cowan did attend the civil trial in Washington of John Surratt, 'a gentlemanly young man,'[6] who had been charged with being a co-conspirator in Abraham Lincoln's assassination. Surratt was freed on 10 August.

Charles and his travelling companions then made their way back to Philadelphia, where for three days they were the guests of George H. Stuart, an Irish businessman whose family firm in Liverpool had long business associations with the Cowans. Stuart, born in County Mayo, Ireland, came to Philadelphia in 1831 at the age of twenty-five and had prospered in the insurance and banking business. Excommunicated from his Reformed Presbyterian ('Covenanter') denomination for abandoning exclusive psalmody in worship, he abhorred sectarianism and played a prominent role in reuniting the Old and the New School Presbyterians three months later in Philadelphia. Among Stuart's many charities, he was best known for the Christian Commission that raised over six million dollars to provide comforts and alleviate the suffering of the Union Army. Later associations with Cowan interests would not be as fortunate: Stuart went into bankruptcy with the collapse of the City of Glasgow Bank in 1879. As a generous philanthropist Stuart was a model for Charles Cowan.

So was John Stewart Kennedy of New York, whom they visited next. Kennedy was a Glaswegian who had come to the United States at the age of twenty. He had just concluded a profitable partnership with Morris Ketchum Jessup, investing in railroads, and was about to set up his own company. He would become American Agent for the Scottish American Investment Company. The partnership between the impetuous and blustering William John Menzies and the cautious and canny John Stewart Kennedy would bring out the best in both. In the wake of the collapse of the City of Glasgow Bank Kennedy brilliantly retrieved its fortunes by parlaying devalued railway stocks into valuable assets. When Kennedy died in 1909, he left thirty million dollars to various American and New York charities, many of them Presbyterian.

6. *Reminiscences*, 414.

Cowan made a side trip to the paper manufacturing centre of South Hadley Falls, near Springfield, Massachusetts. Here he was hosted by the Carew family, whose company had just declared a 100 per cent dividend and were busy adding on to their extensive plant. The situation was ideal for the industry, and Charles must have been envious of their steady supply of water. The dam across the Connecticut River was a quarter of a mile long, and the fall, almost fifteen feet. 'The paper mills,' he noted, 'were of admirable construction, and of great power.'

*****

After returning to New York, on 1 August, they took a 'floating palace' up the Hudson to Albany with a band playing sentimental Civil War songs such as 'Just before the battle, mother.' Going along the Erie Canal route to Rochester and Niagara Falls, they spent three days on the American side, staying at the Mounteagle House Hotel, a favoured tourist honeymoon hideaway at the time. They took the mandatory visit under the Falls. 'For some time I was unable to realise the immensity of the features of the scene, but these were gradually made manifest from the American as well as the British territory.'[7] From there the men crossed the border into what had been Upper Canada but was now, as of the month before, the province of Ontario in the Dominion of Canada. They made their way to the largely Scottish town of Hamilton.

In Hamilton, they stayed at Bleak House, the home of George Hamilton Gillespie.[8] Gillespie had married his cousin, Charles' niece

7. *Reminiscences*, 417.

8. George Hamilton Gillespie (1827–1900) was the fourth of seven children of George and Helen Hamilton Gillespie and husband of his cousin Elizabeth Agnes Gillespie (1827–1890). Robert Campbell in his *History of the Scotch Presbyterian Church, St Gabriel St. Congregation* (Montreal, 1887) says of his father 'He was a gentleman of high honour and integrity, and helped to give a fine tone to the commercial sentiment of the period of his stay in this city.' His uncle Alexander Gillespie (1782–1846) married Catharine Cowan's older sister Jane, who died in 1839 giving birth to twins, one of whom survived. They were her twelfth and thirteenth children, born over a period of twenty years. Their second child, Jean Menzies Gillespie (1820–1854), was the first wife of Charles' brother John. She died giving birth to their fourth child.

Elizabeth Agnes – her sister Jean Menzies Gillespie had been until her death in childbirth his sister-in-law, John Cowan's first wife. John James had a love interest: two years later he would marry Sophia Margaret Gillespie, born in Montreal, the daughter of George's older brother Alexander. Her grandfather George Gillespie arrived in Montreal in 1790 at the age of eighteen. He was a fur trader in Mackinaw Island with the Northwest Company, and subsequently made a fortune and returned to Scotland as a country squire in Biggar. A great-grandson, Alastair Gillespie, was a well-known Canadian politician and cabinet member under Pierre Elliott Trudeau in the 1970s.[9]

While John James and his friend stayed on to become better acquainted with the Gillespies, Charles and William Menzies journeyed on to Chicago, which Menzies described as 'the type of western cities' which 'controls the commerce from the west and north-west'. For the next quarter-century he would plot its phenomenal growth. At the time of their visit Chicago was a city of 100,000. In 1891 its population had grown to a million and a quarter. As a railway hub Chicago would be a centre for their investments.

Two men took the Gillespie route of the *coureurs de bois* travelling to Green Bay, Wisconsin, on the just completed Chicago and Northwestern railway. They then took a steamer across Lake Michigan to Sault-Ste-Marie and on to Mackinaw Island. From there they went by steamer across Lake Huron to Sarnia Ontario and back by rail to Hamilton where they picked up John James and his friend. He added that 'we stopped at Toronto for two hours, and greatly admired the public buildings, wide streets, and the architecture of the churches and other buildings.' They apparently did not connect with the thriving Free Church community there. Indeed there is surprisingly little interest in Canada, which provided rich opportunities for investors. Then on to Ottawa, the capital of the

9. Alastair Gillespie (1922-), a son of Erroll Pilkington Gillespie and Catherine Gilllespie. In 1968 he was returned as MP for Etobicoke/Toronto, but was defeated in the 1979 election. In his *Made in Canada: A Businessman's Adventures in Politics*. Montreal: Robin Brass Studio, 2009, 15, he mentions hospitality received as a schoolboy in the 1930s while in Edinburgh at Loretto from the family of his great-aunt Sophie and John James Cowan.

new Dominion, then briefly in Montreal but again with no reference to the strong Free Church mercantile and business community there.

Neither is there any record of a visit to nearby Valleyfield. In 1833 four men from the area around Penicuik set up a paper mill in Portneuf, Quebec.[10] Their leader, Angus McDonald, who hailed from Roslin, moved on to Quebec City but William Miller (another local boy) set up a mill which he called Valleyfield to evoke memories of home. The town, presently called Valleyfield de Salaberry, maintains links with Penicuik, though the actual paper mill was demolished in 1900. The Cowan party proceeded to Quebec city by steamer, saw the Montmorency Falls, and cruised up the Saguenay River, comparing it unfavourably with Norwegian fjords and finally, on 31 August, they boarded the Allan steamer *Hibernian* out of Quebec.

*****

On the trip home, they had interesting travelling companions: six Anglican bishops travelling to the first Lambeth conference.[11] Charles' son-in-law Robert Lundie, minister of Fairfield Presbyterian Church, Liverpool, joined them in Montreal. He had been in the United States researching facilities for female inmates of prisons. 'If anyone,' Lundie reported to the Fairfield Literary Institute on his return, 'had cold or unkindly feeling towards the United States,' many in Lancashire having sided with the Confederacy during the American Civil War, 'the best thing that could be done to cure him was to send him to these institutions, and let him find, if he could, in the wide world, institutions so beneficent in their management, so wide in their range, and so wise in their conduct.'[12] Lundie stayed

10. William Miller (1807–1875) and Angus McDonald (1807–1887). McDonald is misidentified in the *Dictionary of Canadian Biography* as coming from Aberdeen.

11. The first Lambeth was convened by Charles Longley, Archbishop of Canterbury, at the request of John Travers Lewis, Bishop of Ontario, as a means of trying to stitch together the Church of England after the Colenso affair had threatened its unity. John William Colenso, (1814–1883) first (Anglican) Bishop of Natal, wrote *The Pentateuch and the Book of Joshua Critically Examined* (1862) anticipating the later views of Robertson Smith. The other South African bishops sought to depose him (on the basis of his heterodoxy) but the Privy Council ruled that they had no power to do so.

12. 'Rev. R. H. Lundie on American Institutions' unknown newspaper clipping

with the *Hibernian*, disembarking at Liverpool, but the Scottish contingent left the boat at Londonderry and made their way home by land and the Irish ferry through to Edinburgh, arriving on 11 September.

*****

On 14 March 1873, William John Menzies summoned nine business colleagues to his office at 22 Hill Street to share an idea that had been seeded by the visit he and Charles Cowan made to North America six years earlier. Fifteen days later, The Scottish American Investment Company was birthed. The prospectus stated that 'The growth of America in population, resources and wealth, is too well known to require any statement.' What Menzies and Cowan had witnessed on their journey – 'large and important Cities,' 'the wonderful fertility of the virgin soil, the multitude and variety of its production and manufactures, the rapid development of its railroad system' and 'the enormous immigration taking place' – all meant that this was a time for wise investment in America and Canada.

With William Menzies as Managing Director, his brother Charles as Secretary, and John Cowan as a Director for its first ten years, 'Saints' as it became known, was very much a continuation of the family's success in investing in North America and a pillar of their prosperity. They were also fortunate in their American advisers: John Stewart Kennedy was appointed the American agent for the Scottish American Investment Company and, as William Menzies stated six months later, 'the best thing we ever did was to appoint Kennedy our agent.' The two men enlisted three other significant New York businessmen: John Stewart (from the Isle of Lewis), James Roosevelt, and Thomas Denny, head of United States Trust Company.

Of William John Menzies it was said: 'He was splendidly versed in the history and ways of the Church of Scotland, but his leanings were towards finance ... Menzies was an optimist. He took a broad view of things, but he failed in detail. Through his kindheartedness,

dated 21 December 1867, Lundie file, United Reformed Church archives, Westminster College, Cambridge, UK.

his judgement was often swayed, the pendulum turning the wrong way to help some friend.' And then John Clay, who worked for the Company, gave the ultimate tribute: 'I lay this garland on his grave – that he had a heart of gold.'[13]

Originally investing in railway bonds, the Scottish American Investment Company soon included shares in industrial, public utility, and commercial companies. It stood in the vanguard of the financial innovation in the expansion of the Scottish economy that began in the 1870s and continued until the First World War. In *The Anatomy of Scottish Capital* reference is made to the impact of the Cowan family: '[t]he overlapping membership of the financial syndicates, reflected in interlocking directorships, [which] became a prominent feature of the growing investment sector in Scotland.'[14]

Much of this was set in motion by the visit to North America of William Menzies and Charles Cowan during the summer of 1867. But they observed more than the acquisition of unbelievable wealth on their North American foray. George H. Stuart and John Stewart Kennedy, both Scots and committed churchmen, exemplified a generosity with their prosperity that set a high standard for philanthropy. In the gilded age that was about to dawn, it often appeared that acquiring ostentatious wealth was the sole objective. By their charitable generosity, modeled on Christian principles and commitment, Stuart and Kennedy exemplified a radically different approach. Charles Cowan learned much from his trip to North America in 1867.

13. Weir, R. B. *A History of The Scottish American Investment Co. Ltd.* Edinburgh, SAIC, 1973. 8.

14. Scott, John and Hughes, Michael. *The Anatomy of Scottish Capital.* London: Croom Helm, 1980. 26.

Chapter 17

Committed Churchman

For forty years, from his first General Assembly of the Church of Scotland in 1838 to his final farewell at the 1877 Assembly of the Free Church of Scotland, Charles Cowan never missed his church's annual national gathering. His presence each year was reassuring. Disagree with him as you might, Charles Cowan could be counted on, his a voice umafraid to be heard. For four decades he provided both perspective and experience.

General Assembly (never The General Assembly as a mark of respect) has historically been a part of the Scottish psyche. The Scots, having in 1707 lost their Parliament to Westminster, looked to the annual national Established Church forum not only for debates about religious issues, but also for broader discussions about matters that affected their Scottish identity. For twelve of Cowan's forty years at assemblies, he was also an MP and so was able to bridge the secular and the sacred. As a Member of Parliament for Edinburgh, elected by a largely Free Church constituency, Charles Cowan provided reassurance to his fellow churchmen that they would be heard and their presence taken into account. He was the Free Church of Scotland man in London.

In order to attend the 1850 General Assembly, Charles had to hurry home from London, and he had gratifying news for the gathering. Two days before, he and Lord Anthony Ashley-Cooper, soon to be the seventh Earl of Shaftesbury, had moved a bill to curtail Sunday labour in the post office. Rowland Hill had introduced penny post a decade earlier, and the postal system was now expanding. Ashley Cooper, the social reformer honoured in Piccadilly Square London by the statue 'The Angel of Christian Charity' (misnamed 'Eros'), was asserting a Christian commitment to working people by endorsing a strict sabbatarianism. Ashley knew that the latter would particularly appeal north of the Tweed where a single petition had garnered 253,157 signatures.

In moving that post offices be closed throughout the country on Sunday and that a study be made to determine how mail transmission that day might be curtailed, Lord Ashley said that he was speaking to 'the deep and extensive interest which had been manifested' and the 'intense sentiment in the public mind. This feeling had been evinced in public meetings, by memorials and deputations to the Government, and by petitions to Parliament.'[1] 'Without entering into any theological argument, this might at least be said,' he continued, 'that all who received either Testament, or both – the Jew, the Roman Catholic, the Church of England, all the reformed churches of the Continent, the Wesleyans, the Protestant Dissenters – all recognised the divine institution of the Sabbath, and carried into practice, as well as confessed, the litigation of the observance of one day in seven for the purpose of worship and repose.'[2]

Lord Ashley approached Charles Cowan to second his motion, which extended the closing of the London Post Office to those of the provincial towns, and also called for an 'inquiry as to how far, without injury to the public service, the transmission of the Mails on the Lord's Day might be diminished, or entirely suspended.' The irony of the approach cannot have been lost on Cowan, given the lukewarmness of a Free Church Commission in 1846 commending Ashley-Cooper 'without expressing any opinion on the Factory Bills

1. *Hansard* C Deb 30 May 1850 vol 111 cc466.
2. *Hansard* C Deb 30 May 1850 vol 111 cc472.

which have been before Parliament'.[3] The Post Office Bill of 1851 passed 'by some freak of nature' as one of Shaftesbury's biographers railed,[4] by a vote of 93 to 68 in a half empty House. The division came early in the evening, between seven and eight, taking everyone by surprise. About eighty members, expecting the vote at the more customary hour of ten, were still attending a social event. In fact, the division bell had even taken Cowan by surprise. He had gone out of the chamber 'for some refreshment', and the speech that he intended to give was never delivered.

Following the division, Cowan reported to the General Assembly, as the minutes read, 'an honourable friend, a county representative, had come up to him, and complained about his role in getting the legislation passed, asking if he meant to force Presbyterianism on the people of England – (laughter) – and expressing regret that he had not been in his place to make a speech against this tyranny.'[5] Good-natured banter followed. Cowan then spoke about the importance of participatory democracy, and asked that, in future, petitions to the House of Commons be sent with legible signatures. His speech was interrupted by laughter and applause on several occasions. He was among friends.

England was not amused: Ashley-Cooper was widely denounced for his role in getting the legislation passed. Mill owners who had been angered by his factory legislation were now joined by the aristocracy who would not 'have their gossip in the country on Sunday morning.'[6] Three weeks after the Post Office Bill passed, Ashley wrote that '[t]he Factory Bill and the postal resolution taken together have brought on me a variety, universality, and bitterness of attack quite original.'[7]

3. Quoted by Fleming, J. R. *The Church of Scotland 1843 – 1875*. Edinburgh: T & T Clark, 1927. 99.

4. Battiscombe, Georgina. *Shaftesbury The Great Reformer (1801-1885)* Boston: Houghton Mifflin, 1975. 216. Battiscombe, an eminent biographer of Victorians, had no appreciation of Shaftesbury's evangelical faith and shows little objectivity about his religious commitments.

5. *PDGAFCS*, 1850, 253-4.

6. Battiscombe, Georgina. *Shaftesbury The Great Reformer (1801-1885)* Boston: Houghton Mifflin, 1975. 217.

7. Battiscombe, Georgina. *Shaftesbury The Great Reformer (1801-1885)* Boston: Houghton Mifflin, 1975. 217.

Implementation of the legislation lasted for only three weeks: then the government restored Sunday post. In Scotland, however, and specifically in the Free Church, Cowan's partnership with the future Earl of Shaftesbury won him nothing but gratitude for what was generally regarded as a heroic stand.

*****

Thirteen years later, Charles Cowan's views about the Sabbath had become more flexible. In a sharp exchange at the 1863 General Assembly, he argued for the opening of the Edinburgh Botanical Gardens on a Sunday afternoon.[8] Noting 'the alarm that seemed to have pervaded the minds of a large portion of the constituency,' he 'could not conceive that this was to be regarded as sinful as had been stated in this house.'[9] He pointed out that he had even gone, one Sunday afternoon, to Grange Cemetery, where his father, Thomas Chalmers, and many Free Church worthies were buried. He continued: 'There was a kind of crushing of the working classes, as if they were denying them a breath of fresh air. (Cries of "No. No.").' Then he spoke with feeling of 'the working man, with his wife and family, enjoying the open air, in the fields, or on the highways,' while going on a Sunday stroll. Cowan was addressing the reality that, at least in the Lowlands, the Free Church was becoming increasingly bourgeois and out of touch with the common man. More than most industrialists, Cowan had a heart for his employees and they loved him for it.

The exchange continued. 'Bailie Blackadder felt convinced that this was a great evil and that persons who were now advocating the opening of these gardens were the very same persons who were advocating the opening of museums. Not only the museums, but the theatres would be open.' To this, Cowan uttered a spontaneous 'No, no.' Then the bailie cut to the quick: 'Mr Cowan has been much abroad. He has been for a time in the south, where the seventh is

8. In Boyd, Kenneth. *Scottish Church Attitudes to Sex, Marriage and the Family, 1850-1914*. Edinburgh: John Donald Publishers, 1980. 314 n55. Boyd quotes Cowan as having addressed the 1879 General Assembly. Cowan's final General Assembly was the year before. (273-4)

9. *PDGAFCS*, 1863, 327-8

not only a day of work, but a day of amusement. The theatres are all open' – a statement Cowan promptly denied. Blackadder, nothing deterred, replied, 'I am afraid that will be the case in Scotland.' Bailie Blackadder had already become a byword for religious fanaticism. In press reports and in the popular imagination, his religious affiliation was always emphasized.

It was left to William Nixon, an earnest but humourless minister in Montrose, to have the final word: 'If Mr. Cowan's suggestions were carried out, the floodgates of evil would be opened and overflow the land and soon submerge everything dear to them.' 'The respect which [we] all had for Mr. Cowan,' he concluded, 'great as it is, would scarcely measure the feelings of deep and distressing opposition which [we] experienced to the sentiments which he had just expressed.'[10]

*****

Many of Charles Cowan's contributions in his forty years as a commissioner to the General Assembly were in response to the annual report of the Sustentation Fund. As an initiator, and then a member, of the committee, he took a vital interest in its affairs. Originally, the Sustentation Committee as set up had been divided into two subcommittees: an Ingathering Committee, under the chairmanship of Thomas Chalmers, and a Distribution Committee, chaired by Alexander Dunlop.[11] Dunlop, who had been Cowan's early partner in establishing a lay response to the need for funding should there be a Disruption, was described by Cowan as 'a gentleman of the most unselfish and self-sacrificing spirit'.[12] On 18 July 1844 forty-six-year-old Dunlop married Eliza Esher, heiress of a West Indian fortune. As Lord Cockburn, a friend of Dunlop's, said at the time of the wedding: 'The father and daughter are Free as he is, and it is a harmonious cell – on the voluntary principle I rejoice in his well-

10. *PDGAFCS*, 1863, 329.

11. Alexander Murray Dunlop, MP, LL.D., (1798–1870), advocate. W. Garden Blaikie in his *After Fifty Years* (Edinburgh: Thomas Nelson, 1893, 140) describes him 'to the Free Church what Johnston of Warriston was to the Covenanters.' He became MP for Greenock.

12. *Reminiscences*, 305.

deserved independence.'[13] The timing was fortuitous for the Free Church: it enabled Dunlop to be a major financial backer. In 1844, the two subcommittees were joined into 'The Committee for the Sustentation of the Ministry,' and the new committee was chaired by W. K. Tweedie, the minister of Tolbooth Church in Edinburgh. But Tweedie's real interest turned out to be foreign missions, and his brief tenure gave Thomas Chalmers an opportunity to ask Robert Buchanan, a successor of his in Glasgow, to become chair. Buchanan accepted the post the same week as Chalmers died and remained in that position until his own death in 1875.

As we have seen, Charles Cowan was a member of the committee – officially known as the Sustentation Fund Committee of the General Assembly of the Free Church of Scotland – from its formation. It was a large and unwieldy body: in 1851, it had fifty-five members, though the number was pared back to thirty-nine in 1864. The clergy-to-laity ratio in 1851 was 26 to 29, but by 1864 the proportion favoured clergy, 39 to 30, and among those ministers, there was a wide range of age and geographical location. The youngest on the 1864 roster appears to have been A. B. Bruce, then minister at Cardross, Dumbartonshire, at 33. He would later make a name for himself as an academic – one of the so-called 'advanced' thinkers of the Free Church. There was also the redoubtable Alexander Beith of Stirling, then in his sixties. Predictably, the ubiquitous James Begg was also on the committee, as was the legalist, Sir Henry Wellwood Moncrieff, Bart., Principal Clerk of the General Assembly. In 1864, Hugh Handyside, W.S., a lawyer who worked for the Free Church, was listed as secretary. He was succeeded that year by George Meldrum, C.A., whom Cowan described as 'most able and devoted ... admirably endowed with the qualities needful for perhaps the most important permanent office in the church.'[14] Meldrum died in 1876, just as Cowan's more than thirty years on the Sustentation Committee were coming to an end.

Meldrum was described as 'a quiet successful businessman, and a useful office-bearer in Free St George's [Edinburgh]' until called

13. Bell, Alan, Ed *Lord Cockburn: Selected Letters* Edinburgh: John Donald, 2005. 188.

14. *Reminiscences*, 328.

from obscurity to serve as deputy clerk of the General Assembly and secretary of the Committee. 'Of Mr. Meldrum's services as a church Official,' the *Scotsman* noted on his death, 'those who were associated with him speak highly, dwelling on his prompt business habits, his sound judgment, and his conciliatory manner.' He was, it would appear from this description, the sort of man like Charles Cowan who ensured that the Free Church was operated in a business-like manner, with professional skill, and careful money management. The middle-class Scottish Victorian ethos, combined with a strong Calvinist work ethic, informed the culture of the Free Church.

The Sustentation Fund Committee met several times a year, its main tasks being to set the actual amount payable to clergy during that particular year, to monitor the funds as they were paid by the local churches to the central office, and to provide a full financial statement and report to the General Assembly each year. Administrative costs were kept to a minimum: at the Jubilee of the Free Church, it was noted that they had totalled £9,800 – that is, only 1.5 per cent of all funds received and disbursed, a remarkable record and the envy of charities today. That figure prompted John McCandlish, the Financial Agent of the Free Church at the time, to observe that 'the Free Church has all along been singularly fortunate in her paid officials, and that at the present time she enjoys services of an amount and character which no secular institution could hope to procure of itself except at a greatly higher cost.'[15]

The original goal of paying each minister £150 *per annum* was still a long way off, and in 1854, a call went out asking that all members increase their contribution by a quarter. The response was dramatic: the Fund increased by over £13,000, and the dividend was raised from £119, to which it had fallen, to £140. But with the increased pressure to give, opposition arose. In the General Assembly of 1855, Cowan rose to defend what had been called the equal dividend, an equal remuneration for all clergy, one of the founding principles of the Sustentation Fund.

Three months earlier, at the February meeting of the Presbytery of Edinburgh, William Hanna, Thomas Chalmers' son-in-law

15. McCandlish, John M. in Ryley, Buchanan & McCandlish. John M. in *Scotland's Free Church: Progress and Finance* London: Constable, 1893. 332-3.

(whom the Cowans regarded as a member of the family) argued for changing the way the Fund was distributed.[16] Hanna's overture to the Assembly passed by a large majority, making it apparent that the Lowland urban congregations were chaffing under the equal dividend principle, their ministers being entitled to larger salaries because of the prestige of their pulpits and their greater expenses. The supplements – amounts paid over and above the equal dividend – were not sufficient, they argued, to ensure a ministry that was appropriate for city congregations.

The debate at the Assembly that year was intense and long. Cowan made an impassioned speech in favour of the equal dividend. 'He felt very strongly,' the minutes read, 'that the Sustentation Fund was originally framed on the principle of an equal dividend, and he should never consent, as a basis for negotiation as to the settlement of this question, to the existing rights of any minister of the Free Church being in the slightest degree invaded.' His friend Alexander Dunlop had proposed a 'Committee consisting mainly, if not almost exclusively, of the eldership of the Church, to take a fair and business-like consideration of the position in which they were now placed.' The amendment did not carry, but it demonstrated again the commitment of the Free Church eldership to taking a strong lead in the matter of clergy remuneration. And Charles Cowan was always consistently and personally generous to the ministers of his own church in Penicuik. He had a personal stake as well: his own daughter Elizabeth had recently married a minister.

As the debate about the nature (and future) of the Fund raged, Cowan's concluding comments were, as always in his contributions at the Assembly, an attempt to bring together what he called 'both sides of the house'. 'They had all one object at heart, – to secure the growth, security, and prominence of the Sustentation Fund, which had justly been called the sheet-anchor of the Church, in order that the remuneration for ministerial labour should be somewhat in keeping with the inducements offered to young men in all other professions.'

16. Wilson, William. *Memoir of Robert Smith Candlish, D. D.* Edinburgh: Robert and Charles Black, 1880. 492.

That the Sustentation Fund continued along the lines originally proposed by Thomas Chalmers owed much to the wisdom, political skills, organizational ability, and hard work of Robert Buchanan in his almost thirty-year stewardship of the Sustentation Fund. As a Glasgow minister, it is difficult to know how close his relationship with Cowan really was. The only indication of what must have been some collaboration is a quote in the *Reminiscences*. There Buchanan is included with Chalmers, Cunningham, and Candlish, as well as Guthrie, Welsh, Gordon, Macfarlan, and James Buchanan of Greenock 'and a host of other ministers too numerous to name, who sacrificed all worldly possessions on the altar of duty' and who 'will long survive in the hearts and memories of Scotland'.[17] The Sustentation Fund was the laity's response to the great renunciation of 18 May 1843, and as long as that memory endured, the money would be there.

*****

The equal dividend was again under attack at the General Assembly of 1863. This time, because of the difficulty in raising the funds required during a time of economic downturn, Sir Hugh Moncrieff was proposing a point at which the equal dividend paid by the Sustentation Fund could cease. James Begg, as a member of the committee, disclosed that there had been prior debate in the committee, bringing 'back old discussions from which we had departed'. In response, Cowan reviewed events just before the Disruption, beginning with the time when 'in his own house he convened a small number of friends' and going on to speak of the St Luke's convocation of 1 February 1843, saying 'It had always been his conviction that the Sustentation Fund from its origin, was founded on the principle of the equal dividend; and he thought the Church at large had a kind of vested interest in its being continued upon that footing.'[18]

In 1867, givings to the Sustentation Fund took a dramatic turn for the better, and a Surplus Fund was set up. Robert Buchanan

17. *Reminiscences*, 339.

18. *PDGAFCS*, 1863, 114.

proposed that the Church be asked to provide each minister with £150 a year and to provide an overplus for division among those ministers whose congregations gave at a certain specified rate *per member*.[19] The response was immediate. The Fund increased by £10,000, and by the mid-1870s, when Cowan left the committee, the dividend had grown to £157, paid to 774 ministers, with additional grants of either £36 or £18 paid out of the Surplus Fund. The total amount raised had increased from an initial £68,000 in 1844 to £166,000 in 1876.

At the 1873 General Assembly, Charles Cowan moved the adoption of the report of the Sustentation Committee, rising to reflect on 'the immense success which by the grace of God had attended the efforts of Dr Buchanan and his committee.' He again quoted Chalmers, describing the Fund as 'the sheet-anchor of the Church', and continued: 'Let that sentiment be impressed upon all office bearers, ministers, and elders, and through them let it be known to their people, that they never could maintain the position which they ought to occupy as a Church unless the fund was maintained upon a sure basis; for this was the only means they had of securing the regular supply of gospel influences and the promotion of vital Christianity throughout the land.'[20]

*****

Charles Cowan was also involved with Robert Buchannan, chair of the Sustentation Fund, in another cause important to both of them. As convener of the Church Union Committee, Robert Buchanan had been deeply committed, for a decade, to union negotiations with the United Presbyterian Church. This denomination, which as we have seen brought together various strands of eighteenth century secessions from the Church of Scotland, had much in common with the Free Church. However, the original sticking point was the Voluntary question. That is, they had left the Church of Scotland

19. Walker, Norman. *Robert Buchanan, DD An Ecclesiastical Biography* London: Thomas Nelson and Sons, 1877. 275.

20. *PDGAFCS*, 1873, 101.

because they were opposed to the political control of the state implicit in being a national or established church. For the Free Church to join the United Presbyterians meant giving up any claim of later rejoining the State Church with all the advantages (and disadvantages) that involved.

Charles Cowan had a clear position on the Voluntary question. While his father's cousin, Thomas Chalmers, had been a late and reluctant convert to Voluntaryism, Cowan regarded the state's interference in ecclesiastical affairs as an unmitigated disaster. In his *Reminiscences*, he noted that 'Voluntary' had become a word of reproach in Scotland. 'It is easy to give a dog a bad name; and it is not much to be wondered at that in the Free Church, which depends wholly, under providence, upon the free-will offerings of the people, there are a few, and happily but few, who, having formerly been ministers, and possibly still expectants of parishes, retain a hankering for regaining the compulsory power possessed by the presbyteries and ministers of the Established Church for providing for the ministrations of religion.'[21]

Cowan had great affection for the various Secession churches that had come together in 1847 as the United Presbyterian Church.[22] 'I can testify,' he wrote, 'that the better-conducted portion of our numerous workpeople at the mills have been generally connected with that body.'[23] So when negotiations with the United Presbyterians began in 1862, he was a strong advocate of reunion. The sticking point, initially, was the Voluntary question. As negotiations progressed, and as opposition intensified, questions were raised about the subscription formula of the United Presbyterians as an indication of possible laxer doctrinal commitment and more tolerant confessional identity. How committed were the United Presbyterians to the Westminster Confession of Faith, and the Shorter and Longer Catechisms, the bed-rock of Presbyterian belief and the standard of the Free Church of Scotland?

---

21. *Reminiscences*, 334.

22. The Burgher Meetinghouse at Bridgend, near Penicuik, and the Anti-burgher congregation at Howtown.

23. *Reminiscences*, 8.

The anti-unionists found a champion in James Begg, a feisty opponent of innovation, a strong conservative, and a wily ecclesiastical politician. Cowan had tangled with Begg many times on the Sustentation Committee and on the floor of the Assembly, and Begg appeared to be ubiquitous at each General Assembly, rising to speak on almost every question and operating the levers of power with consummate skill. Cowan's visceral dislike of the man – he appears always to have voted opposite to Begg as a matter of principle – may also have had to do with a latent anticlericalism on the part of some Free Church elders. In Cowan's case, this attitude was likely based on his experience with Rev. Thomas Coulston, the incumbent at St Mungo's Parish Church in Penicuik in Cowan's youth. The whole Cowan–Begg imbroglio came to a head at the Assembly of 1867 during discussions about a motion to proceed with union negotiations.

It started innocuously enough, with Robert Buchanan reading a trans-Atlantic telegram, just received, announcing that the New and Old School factions of the American Presbyterian Church had negotiated a basis of union 'almost certain to be approved of.' There was wide applause. Then the irrepressible Charles Cowan said, 'I beg to propose that a copy of that communication be sent to our friends, Dr. Gibson and Dr. Begg.' There was laughter and then an objection from the floor and a rebuke from the chair, Robert Candlish, who was serving that year as moderator.[24]

There the matter might well have rested, but two days later, a Sabbath intervening, Charles Cowan rose to his feet and grovelled: 'It was a breach of propriety, and it would have been a most undignified course for this House to adopt whatever the impulse of the moment I proposed.' He continued: 'However much I deplore the division upon the union question, I never had the slightest doubt as to the thorough honesty, and as little as to the manliness of the course, which these reverend gentlemen chose to take.... I am quite sure that they have acted from a regard to the best interests of the Church.'

James Begg was absent, indisposed because of illness, but Gibson accepted the apology, 'with thanks to Mr Cowan for the frank way in

24. *Reminiscences*, 8.

which he has made it. (Hear. Hear.)' There the matter was dropped, as were union negotiations in 1873. The cost of dividing the Free Church was too great, it was decided, for the majority in favour to press those opposed into schism to advance a union. But Cowan had been humiliated, and he never regained quite the same panache with which he had earlier addressed the General Assembly.

*****

The polarities between Cowan and Begg metastasized and they again found themselves at loggerheads over the question of education. The Argyll Commission on Scottish schooling had confirmed that the 1855 legislation had been only partially effective. 93,000 children were said to be without schooling. At the 1867 Assembly, Cowan, in responding to the report of the Education Committee, referred to Canada and held out the success of Lord Elgin ('whom he had the honour of escorting into this House on one occasion') in providing a system of universal education in spite of the twin divides of a Catholic majority in Lower Canada and a Protestant plurality in Upper Canada. This was the system 'the people of Scotland were entitled to, and which was so greatly needed in this country.'[25]

In a biting 1870 editorial in the *Scotsman* it was noted that in twenty years James Begg and Robert Candlish had reversed roles over the education question. James Begg, once 'an almost illimitable Liberal in educational matters', a signatory of the Manifesto of 1853 (along with Charles Cowan and James Craufurd) as members of the National Church Association was now 'the leader of a section which is extremely illiberal and we fear not extremely small.' Robert Candlish had now reversed himself, 'saying sweet things of a national or all-embracing system of education.'

Charles Cowan had certainly not changed his position and for the next two years, as one of seven members of the Scottish National Education Association acting committee, he was an active advocate for the legislation that was finally passed in August 1872. It represented a triumph of reason and eliminated the divide

25. *PDGAFCS*, 1867, 238.

between denominational and secular schools that characterises the English system. It involved a great deal of sacrifice on the part of both the Free and the Established churches. Nowhere was that more evident than in Penicuik where a brass plaque, taken from the old Free Church school, which is now on view at the local Historical Society testifies to the sacrifice involved. Describing the erection of the school by the church in 1845 and its extension in 1861 'by the liberality of Duncan Cowan,'[26] it concludes: 'After the passing of the Education (Scotland) Act 1872, the property was gifted with all the educational furnishings by the congregation to the Penicuik School Board, Whitsunday, 1873.' It was a noble gesture, repeated all over Scotland.

*****

Throughout his forty years as a member of the highest ecclesiastical court in the Free Church, Charles Cowan played the role of an informed and committed layperson. Over the years his reported speeches became less pious and principled and more political and pragmatic. His was a powerful voice, however, and a generous one. That generosity depended on the success of the family business and the success of his investments. To that we shall now turn.

26. Duncan Cowan (1812–1869), brother of Charles, John and James who never appears to have fully developed.

Chapter 18

Compassionate Charity

'His warmth of charity' were words used to eulogize Alexander Cowan on his death in 1859. 'While gathering with one hand, he profusely scattered with the other, and this, with so modest, though discriminating a spirit, that few save those who were more immediately benefited, knew the full extent of his benevolence.'[1] That obituary in the *Caledonian Mercury* highlighted a characteristic of the father that was passed from father to son. There were few Edinburgh charities to which Charles Cowan would not lend his name, as well as his money. He was exercised over questions of poverty. The variety of his charitable commitments provides a window into the scope and sweep of Free Church philanthropic interests.

The first Charles Cowan, as we have seen (p. 25), just before he left Fife to make his fortune in the city, gave money for the poor fund of the local parish. Indeed, since the Reformation the poor in Scotland had been a charge on the Kirk and the main source of relief was church collection. The Calvinism of the Scottish Reformation, affirmed by the Free Church, embraced the biblical principle of

1. *Caledonian Mercury* 13 February 1859. The obituary was written by Rev Dr Robert Menzies, Hoddam, Charles Cowan's brother-in-law. (Quoted in *Reminiscences*, xxix.)

stewardship, acknowledging that all that the believer possessed was God's and that, in Jesus' own words, 'to whom much was given much would be required.'[2] Free Churchman J. M. E. Ross called this 'the solemn Principle of divine judgment'.[3]

This Reformed emphasis obligated those more fortunate to serve the poor, the fatherless and the widow. The calling of the Christian was to identify with the poor as Jesus did. No one was predestinated to poverty nor were their economic condition and status immutable.[4] The Cowans provided educational opportunity for all the children of their employees and sought to encourage those with ability to advance. Once again we see the profound influence of Thomas Chalmers. His experiment with poor relief at St John's Glasgow in 1819 was an attempt to make the church more responsive to a rapidly evolving and urban industrial society by increasing the awareness of the parish to the poor within its bounds. His passionate concern for the disadvantaged was an integral part of his evangelicalism with its broad commitment to make Scotland a godly commonwealth. This ideal was based on the Old Testament ideal of a covenanted nation where, in the words of Professor Stewart Brown, the preaching of the Word gathered a people 'practicing benevolence toward the sick and indigent poor, and cultivating their spiritual and intellectual natures in the service of God.'[5]

Chalmers' vision was both practical and personal: in partnership with Alexander Cowan in 1822 he had helped Renton Schoof, the biracial, illegitimate and penniless immigrant grandson of a Penicuik

---

2. Luke 12:48.

3. Ross, J. M. E. *The Gospel According to St Luke,* Vol 2, 55. John Murdo Ebenerzer Ross (1870-1925), son and biographer of Wm Ross of Cowcaddens, served both in Free Church and Presbyterian Church of England.

4. It is astonishing to read in her *Philanthropy in Victorian Scotland* (the classic book on the subject) Olive Checkland affirming that the Calvinist doctrine of predestination, which she wrongly equates with determinism, meant that each individual was locked into a predetermined future from birth. 'The doctrine of pre-destination (*sic*) repudiated with theocratic authority any attempts to make the lives of the poor, or anyone else, easier.' (Checkland, Olive. *Philanthropy in Victorian Scotland*. Edinburgh: John Donald, 1980. 31.)

5. Brown, Stewart J. *Thomas Chalmers and the Godly Commonwealth.* Oxford: Oxford University Press, 1984. xvi.

doctor afflicted with dementia (ch. 3). Indeed, as Olive Checkland has pointed out, for three hundred years philanthropy in Scotland was always personal and direct, 'a social bond philosophy.'[6] It was only in the 1870s that 'a scientific base' was sought for charitable giving. By the turn of the twentieth century, with the rise of Fabian socialism, a third phase began as the state started to take over new areas of social need then becoming apparent.

Thomas Chalmers has been severely criticized, both in his day and ours, as 'wrong-headed'[7] and failing to recognize that industrialization and urbanization had created an entirely new set of circumstances. Chalmers' near contemporary, William Pulteney Alison, Professor of the Institutes of Medicine at the University of Edinburgh, examined the St John's experiment and found it lacking because, he affirmed, poverty was the result of social factors, not sin and sloth. It was thus essential to ameliorate the environment, eliminating overcrowding and lack of sanitation in order to avoid both disease and dysfunction.[8]

In response to Alison's concerns, the dire economic situation, and an overture from the Presbytery of Paisley, on 18 November 1842 the Church of Scotland commission (which met between Assemblies to transact emergent business) considered the state of the poor, regretting (as one speaker stated) that this urgent matter had been 'huddled into a corner' because the General Assembly that year had other matters on its mind. The comment was made that 'The church had only half the machinery necessary for doing her duty to the poor in proportion to the population.'[9] Patronage also provided an excuse. Charles Cowan is reported to have said 'a few words' on the subject but they are, alas, unrecorded. His friend Alex

6. Checkland, Olive. *Philanthropy in Victorian Scotland*. Edinburgh: John Donald, 1980. 3-4.

7. Checkland, Olive. *Philanthropy in Victorian Scotland*. Edinburgh: John Donald, 1980. 3.

8. William Pulteney Alison (1790 – 1859) Professor of the Institutes of Medicine (1822-42) and Professor of the Theory of Physic (1842-56) University of Edinburgh. *Observations on the management of the poor in Scotland and its effect on the health in the great towns* (1840) was his classic.

9. *Scotsman*, 19 November 1842.

Dunlop, lawyer and later MP, then rose and moved that the church had 'a duty of making every necessary inquiry into the condition of the poor in their respective localities, and to adopt such steps as may be necessary for their relief.' This was agreed and the Commission then adjourned.

A Royal Commission was set up by Parliament on 26 January 1843 and the result, following one of the most thorough investigations of the working class in the nineteenth century in Britain and expounded in six volumes, was the Poor Law Amendment Act of 1845. The legislation reflected the views of both Chalmers and Alison.[10] Alison may have been disappointed that the Act did not go far enough, but Chalmers represented the best of a long tradition going back to John Knox and the Scottish Reformation in its commitment to the whole of society.

Chalmers' influence can also be seen in the practical approach that his cousin and his cousin's son followed: their emphasis in their charity on the family unit, the importance of locality and creating a supportive community such as Penicuik for poor relief, and particularly the vigilance of district elders (which Charles Cowan modelled) and deacons in the local parish. Charles' faithfulness as a diligent elder in his district, visiting each of his assigned families, and the interest he took in young men through his Sunday afternoon Bible Class, were examples of his compassionate commitment to the poor, the young and the marginalized. The Sabbath was for Charles Cowan, as his diaries attest, a time of active engagement with the needs of his community: the adolescent and the aging, the widow and orphan, those about to emigrate and those who had strayed outside the law. He embraced them all.

A published tribute to Alexander Cowan shortly after his death opens with James 1:27: 'Pure religion and undefiled before God and the Father, is this: To visit the fatherless and widows in their affliction, and to keep himself unspotted from the world.' Making allowance for the fact that it represents hagiography not biography, the pamphlet (by an unnamed author) makes it apparent that Alexander Cowan's

10. See Checkland, Olive. 'Chalmers and William Pulteney Alison' in Cheyne, A. C. *The Practical and the Pious*. Edinburgh: St Andrew Press, 1985. 135-136.

sense of stewardship of his wealth was impressive: 'His liberality was really unbounded... he had no prejudices, no sectarian views, his gifts so kindly bestowed on churches and schools of many denominations... he was ever ready to respond to every call, and zealous in devising schemes of usefulness.'[11]

Two examples of Alexander Cowan's charity are cited: during the cholera epidemic of 1832, in his Edinburgh neighbourhood of Canongate, he lay down beside a patient to show the disease was not contagious.[12] One cold day, walking down the Canongate, he was struck by the number of windows that were cracked, broken, patched or stuffed with paper and rags He ordered his glazier to repair all the broken windows between Castlehill and Holyrood at a cost of over £500. When told of the expense, Alexander Cowan 'was more amused than disturbed'.[13]

His major monetary contribution to the city of Edinburgh, however, was his generosity to the Royal Infirmary. Founded in 1729, its Royal Charter, given seven years later, established a Court of Contributors to whom its managers were accountable at an annual meeting to be held the first Monday of each New Year. In 1840, in the interest of greater public participation (and contributions), the Court was given further powers of nominating representatives on the Board of the Infirmary. Charles, and later his brother James, were annual participants and played an active role.

The Cowans were also generous in their financial support. In 1850 Alexander contributed £4000 towards the construction of a new Surgical Hospital. Opened in 1853, that same year he donated an additional £2000. Three years later, when six medical and nine surgical wards had to be closed 'as a precautionary measure' because of financial stringencies,[14] Alexander donated a further £4000. Just prior to his death he made a final donation of an additional £4000, representing almost half the annual budget of the Royal Infirmary.

---

11. Author not named. *Alexander Cowan*. Published privately, 1859. 11.

12. Author not named. *Alexander Cowan*. Published privately, 1859. 19.

13. Charles Boog Watson, *Alexander Cowan His Kinsfolk and Connections*. Perth: D Leslie, 1915. 18.

14. Turner, A. Logan. *Story of a Great Hospital: The Royal Infirmary of Edinburgh, 1729 – 1929*. Edinburgh: Oliver and Boyd, 1937. 177.

Additionally he contributed £1000 each to the Lunatic Asylum, the Deaf and Dumb Institution, the Blind Asylum, and Leith Hospital.

*****

Alexander Cowan also shared Alison's concern about the impact of environment on the poor. He wanted every home in Penicuik to have access to good clean water. An 1864 monument on the High Street reminds present residents that water from Silverburn was brought into the village 'at the expense and the desire of the late Alexander Cowan'. It was a commitment that dominated the final two decades of his life, standing in sharp contrast to the foot-dragging of the local gentry. In 1839 Alexander wrote to John Irving, the Edinburgh agent of Sir George Clerk:

'An object I have in view in bringing in the Silverburn is to supply the villages of Penicuik and Kirkhill with Spring water. My sons as well as myself are most anxious to do all in our power to improve the habits and domestic economy of our servants and of the working classes in our neighbourhood generally, and it would give us great pleasure to cooperate with Sir Geo Clerk in any way for these purposes.'[15] He concluded by offering to bring water 'for supplying the villages on the most favourable terms.' There was no response.

Ten years later, conscious of his own mortality, Alexander appealed directly to Clerk: 'My sons and I being very anxious to improve the dwelling houses of our servants at Penicuik ... having been so long connected with the village, I am anxious to do anything I can for the benefit of it, and therefore, if you will allow me, I am willing to place £300 at the disposal of yourself or of any persons you may appoint, for the purpose of bringing in a supply of water solely for the benefit of the village, and for effecting a proper system of draining upon it. If the water were to be brought from such a level as to rise to the upper flats of the houses, I think you will agree with me, that this with good drainage would tend much to raise the moral status of the population, and I cannot doubt that is a matter as dear to your feelings as to my own. My plan would be, to lay a main

15. AC to John Irving Edinburgh, 9 Dec 1839 NAS, GD311/2/43, 107.

pipe through all the streets of Penicuik and to put it in the power of Proprietors or Tenants to lay branch pipes for themselves at their own expense, on their agreeing to pay a small sum for each house say 5/ or 7/6 per annum, which should be applied in keeping up the fountainhead, main pipe etc. and in paying a Lordship to you or Rent to you and your successors.'[16] It would appear that this time Clerk, perhaps reluctantly, agreed. The project was started before his death but only completed afterwards.

About that time Charles and John (who was a director) were involved in the relocation of the Edinburgh Association for the Reformation of Juvenile Offenders from Edinburgh to a site near Penicuik. Renamed the Wellington Reform School (the site had been the Wellington Inn), with the help of architect Frederick Thomas Pilkington, they transformed the buildings into a facility for juvenile offenders. The boys were taken out of Edinburgh and given a rural environment free of distractions where they could learn to read and write, acquire work skills, and have a healthy life doing farm chores. The purchase of the Wellington Inn was secured by a fundraising effort throughout Peeblesshire and the city of Edinburgh.

By a stroke of genius, the Association appointed John Craster as director. Craster came with previous experience in reformatory work in Newcastle and Inverness, and was recommended as 'a most efficient superintendent, likely to exercise a powerful moral influence over the boys, and to train them to habits of industry, as well as to impart secular instruction and imbue their minds with religious truth.'[17] That testimony was eminently borne out over the next thirty years. John Craster set his mark on the reformatory, establishing himself as a pioneer in prison reform in close partnership with John and Charles Cowan, both of whom supported him generously. On his death, the year after Charles Cowan, he was compared to the renowned headmaster of Rugby School: 'With much of Dr Arnold's repugnance to physical punishment, he had also much of his success in dealing with the most refractory boys.'[18]

16. AC to George Clerk, 27 April [1849], NAS, GD311/2/43, 429.

17. *Scotsman*, 15 March 1860. 2.

18. *Scotsman*, 3 July 1890. 3.

As he aged (and, one suspects, hardened), Charles Cowan became increasingly impatient with the way in which poor relief had developed as a result of the Poor Law (Scotland) legislation of 1845. In 1869 he expressed scepticism about its ultimate impact, claiming that it 'put a premium upon improvidence and intemperance'.[19] In a speech on the poor he gave that year he singled out three causes for their predicament: wretched housing, whisky-drinking, and ecclesiastical interference which had meant poor educational opportunities ('He had great respect for the clergy if they would just keep to their own province'). Yet in spite of misgivings he remained for years an active member of the St Cuthbert's Parochial Board, the historic distributor of poor relief in his part of Edinburgh.

At the 1869 annual general meeting of the Edinburgh Association for Improving the Condition of the Poor, Charles Cowan was appointed to the Committee of Management.[20] William Hanna, Chalmers' biographer and son-in-law, became Treasurer. At the June 1870 meeting Cowan spoke again on poverty in Edinburgh.[21] He was introduced by the chair, Dr. Alexander Wood: 'Mr. Cowan and his ancestors had shown their thorough appreciation of the duty of employer to employed long before the present movement for the improvement of the working-classes began, and that there was evidence in Edinburgh and elsewhere of the great benefits which that gentleman and his father had conferred upon the city and upon the working-classes in general.' Wood, the inventor of the hypodermic syringe, went on to vindicate Thomas Chalmers: 'Every attempt that had been successful in dealing with the poor had proceeded upon the principles that were enunciated by Dr. Chalmers.' He trashed the 1845 Poor Law, claiming that it was 'utterly inefficacious for doing what it was intended to do', and instead had actually increased pauperism and degraded 'the working-classes below the level at which it found them'.

Charles Cowan had been asked to speak on his recent visit to Elberfeld,[22] a rapidly growing industrial centre in Rhenish Prussia

19. *Scotsman*, 23 November 1869.

20. *Scotsman*, 23 November 1869

21. *Scotsman*, 17 June 1870.

22. Since 1930 Wuppertal.

facing similar challenges to Scotland at the time. Elberfeld's solution to poor relief had been commended by Norman Macleod, minister of The Barony Church of Scotland, Glasgow, in the first issue of his popular (and influential) periodical *Good Works*.[23] That article again showed the influence of Chalmers: Elberfeld is held up as a way of achieving Chalmers' godly commonwealth through an 'efficient communal charity operation'.[24] Part of the attraction to Cowan (and other Free Churchmen) was the fact that the response to the poor grew out of the religious revivalism of Pietism which regarded a Biblical response to poverty as of the essence of real religion. To Cowan, steeped in the rhetoric of Thomas Chalmers, that concept had a profound appeal.

In his speech Cowan stated that the Elberfeld plan addressed the root causes of 'pauperism'. Chalmers had always distinguished between pauperism, caused by laziness and an unwillingness to work, and 'poverty', the result of factors beyond the remedy of the individual on their own. The city, when Cowan visited, had been divided into 364 precincts, each fourteen of which made a district. Every precinct had an almoner, and there were fortnightly meetings in which the amount of aid was agreed on. Imaginative ways of restoring the dignity of the unemployed were utilized, such as the distribution of tools. The whole was placed under the control of a well-connected banker and businessman Daniel von Heyd who inspired Cowan's confidence. The adoption in Scotland of the Elberfeld plan would mean less institutionalizing of poor relief while at the same time using qualified volunteers to make regular house calls and provide individual attention to the root causes of the person's poverty. There was an encouraging response to Cowan's lecture, consciousness of

23. Thus, for instance, Hibbs, Rev Richard. *Prussia and the poor; or, Observations upon the systematized relief of the poor at Elberfeld. In contrast with that of England. Founded on a visit and personal inquiry*. London and Edinburgh: Williams & Norgate, 1876. See also 'Poor Relief and Welfare in Germany from the Reformation to World War I' Downloaded from EHNet http://eh.net/book_reviews/poor-relief-and-welfare-germany-reformation-world-war-i. (Accessed 3 September 2012.)

24. Brown, Stewart J. 'Thomas Chalmers and the communal ideal in Victorian Scotland' in Smout, T. C. Ed., *Victorian Values: A Joint Symposium of the Royal Society of Edinburgh and the British Academy, December 1990*. Oxford: Oxford University Press, 1992. 76.

the problem was increased, and his Elberfeld visit helped focus both on the problem and a possible solution. But the Elberfeld plan was never replicated outside of Germany.

Occasionally, however, the approach to poverty could appear stop-gap, *ad hoc*, and even patronizing. The marriage of the Prince of Wales on 10 March 1863, for instance, provided an opportunity to celebrate by feeding 'the deserving poor' and Cowan was one of the subscribers.[25] There were also more creative solutions: in 1869 he sponsored, with a start-up gift of £500, an appeal for the salary of a visiting nurse for the sick poor in Fountainbridge, a gritty area of west central Edinburgh, where new working class tenements were dominated by a recently constructed McEwan brewery.[26]

At a public meeting just before Christmas that year Charles Cowan moved 'That steps be taken to provide a free dinner daily for the destitute of the children of the city.'[27] The response was overwhelming. Four months later it was noted that 75,168 meals had been provided not only for children, 'most of who were poor sickly objects.' The extent of those receiving these meals provides a chronicle of social disaster – children of widows and widowers, children with both parents in jail, children of deserted wives or whose husbands were drunkards who did not live with them nor assist, fathers hospitalized or at home too sick to work. There were 523 in all being given a good meal a day. Addressing issues of housing for the poor, Charles Cowan was also involved in the Edinburgh Association for Improving the Lodging Houses of the Poor.

*****

Edinburgh was a pioneer in the education of deaf children. It was assumed that because they could not hear they could not speak, hence the designation of them as 'deaf and dumb'. Thomas Braidwood opened a private academy in Edinburgh for the deaf in

25. *Scotsman*. 9 March 1863.

26. *Scotsman*. 1 December 1869.

27. *Scotsman*. 15 December 1869, compare *Scotsman* 19 April 1870.

1760 and continued his work until, discouraged by a lack of support, he moved to London in 1783. Twenty-seven years passed before Alexander Cowan and others, led by the Duke of Buccleuch and the Lord Provost, reorganized the Edinburgh Institution for the Education of the Deaf and Dumb. As we have seen, he continued to give generously until just before he died. In 1843 son Charles became a Director.[28] Charles' particular contribution was to serve as President of a fundraising effort to secure a place of worship for the deaf, as well as a hall where a benevolent society could hold their meetings, providing a social outlet for those isolated by their disability. He stated that the 150 deaf and dumb in the city were like 'stray sheep and provision for the spiritual welfare of those above the age of 14 had scarcely been made'.[29] In addition to his interest in the deaf, Charles also maintained his father's generosity to the School for the Blind, on George Street, which had 35 students at the end of 1865.[30]

*****

As he was about to die, Alexander Cowan doubled a previous generous gift to the Edinburgh Lunatic Asylum. The mentally ill had been seriously neglected during the eighteenth century. It was some years after the towns of Montrose and Aberdeen had created theirs, that the Edinburgh Lunatic Asylum was established. In 1813 a building was erected in Morningside. The Asylum was not a popular fundraising cause, and it was chronically short of finances which the Cowans always seemed to be called on to provide. Queen Victoria gave the Edinburgh Lunatic Asylum royal patronage in 1840, a remarkably generous gesture, given the general opprobrium (and complete ignorance) of mental illness at the time.

*****

28. *Scotsman*. 12 July 1843.

29. *Scotsman*. 20 December 1876.

30. *Scotsman*, 17 March 1866. On 12 March 1874 he apologizes for not being at the annual meeting (*Scotsman*, 12 March 1874).

Later in life, possibly because of the influence of his daughter Charlotte in Sheffield, Charles Cowan took up the cause of women in the sex trade. Prostitution was a matter of intense social concern, particularly in the upper classes, in Victorian Britain. Gladstone visited brothels frequently as a matter of his Christian social concern. Upon leaving the Commons, Cowan launched an appeal for a new site for the Edinburgh Industrial Home for Fallen Women, moving it from Corstorphine to Alnwick Hill. In April 1863 the assistant matron accompanied a group to Toronto. On her return she reported that all were engaged as domestic servants after only a short time in Toronto.[31] The 1869 annual report disclosed that thirty-three prostitutes had been admitted to the Edinburgh Home, eleven of whom stayed only a short time. One resident had returned to life on the streets, another was dismissed 'for bad conduct'. But there were positives: £1087 had been raised and the debt on the facility had been reduced. Cowan's interest in the Home continued into old age: as an octogenarian he attended an 1883 Christmas party held in the laundry (ordinarily a major source of income for the Home) decorated with greens and the evening spent in 'instructive and interesting games.'[32]

There is something poignant about an old man enjoying Christmas festivities with a group of rescued women of the night who were beneficiaries of his generosity and compassion. Their redemption (and the repeal of the Contagious Disease Acts) was a cause that his daughter Charlotte Wilson (with Josephine Butler) was now pursuing in England. Thus across three generations of Cowans an active social conscience manifested itself. This conscientious commitment involved not only compassion for the poor, but (as we will now see) an active commitment to community needs. And there was no greater need at the end of the 1860s than the availability of safe and sufficient drinking water for the growing city of Edinburgh.

31. *Scotsman*, 5 February 1863.

32. *Scotsman*, 6 January 1883.

Chapter 19

Reservoir Rage

Nothing placed Charles Cowan more in the public eye in the early 1870s than his campaign over the proposed expansion of the Edinburgh waterworks. It was a part of his broader commitment to the welfare of the city of Edinburgh as a public benefactor and as a Christian. But it also put him in a compromised position.[1] Since 1842, some of Edinburgh's water came from his grouse-shooting property high in the Pentlands. And as a paper manufacturer, as we saw in chapter 15, he had recently been in the courts with the others whose mills polluted the River Esk, in a bruising legal fight against the local landed gentry. Now a second fight would work itself out in the local press with Charles Cowan a prominent player.

'Since the celebrated Disruption of the Church of Scotland in 1843,' one combatant noted later,[2] 'party feeling had never run so high nor was it so embittered, as in this great water struggle.

1. This great Edinburgh reservoir controversy appears to have almost completely eluded historians. Other than contemporary newspaper accounts and David Lewis' 1908 book, cited in this chapter, there has been little written about it. Charles Cowan makes no mention of it in his *Reminiscences* in spite of the fact that for three years it was a major preoccupation

2. Colston, James *The Edinburgh and District Water Supply* Edinburgh: Colston Printers 1890. 135.

Indeed, personal friendships were in danger of giving way to private animosities.' Private (and public) animosities there were in spades. Alliances were formed and broken, friendships came and went, and always there were the press further complicating relationships. The confrontation pitted progressive radicals against complacent middle class Whigs and Tories. Charles Cowan teamed up in a law suit with Colin MacKenzie, WS, the testy St Leonard's Ward city councilor.[3] Taking the opposite view was his erstwhile friend Dr. Alexander Wood, who (as we saw in the previous chapter) spoke well of Charles Cowan when he introduced him in July 1870. The following June the relationship was fraying. In a salvo written to the Editor of the *Scotsman*, Wood took issue with the person he still called 'my esteemed friend Mr. Cowan' on virtually every point Charles Cowan was making against the new reservoir proposal.[4]

The papers were filled with articles on both sides. Propaganda citing dubious scientific evidence was shamelessly used to influence people. Dr. Alexander Wood turned out to be the anonymous author of the 'Working Man's Catechism,' published on a Sunday, an appropriate day for catechetical instruction, though some were not impressed. It was pitched to the working class with questions such as 'Who are the sufferers from lack of water?' with the response 'The working men' and the next question: 'Who are the chief sufferers?' and the inevitable answer: 'The working men's wives and children, who like beasts of burden have to carry water down closes, and up long flights of stairs.' The so-called Catechism ended by describing the other side as 'Cowardly Rats.'[5]

That other side proved more effective in its publicity. Throughout Edinburgh large pictures of *Daphnia pulex* appeared, posted on walls and found in at least two newspapers. *Daphnia pulex* was the flea who, it was claimed, inhabited the waters of St Mary Loch and would surely do terrible things to the inhabitants of Edinburgh if that water was brought into the city. Quotes from a German entomologist were

3. 'Cowan & MacKenzie vs Law etc.' *Cases decided in the Court of Session, Teind Court*, Volume 10. Case 104. 578 – 610.

4. *Scotsman* 9 June 1871.

5. Colston, James. *The Edinburgh and District Water Supply*. Edinburgh: Colston Printers 1890-. 138-9.

added, providing graphic details of the gnat's capacity to do harm. *Daphnia pulex* proved a great friend of the opposition.

Water availability had long been an emotional issue in Edinburgh. As early as 1621, the Scottish Parliament had passed legislation that allowed water to be brought from Coniston Springs, a move that the citizens welcomed, provided no taxation was involved. Given the political turmoil at the time, it is not surprising that it took fifty years and much anger and recrimination before water from Coniston Springs finally flowed into the city. In the eighteenth century, water increasingly came from springs in the Pentland Hills, south of the city, conveyed by wooden pipes, which were later replaced by cast iron ones. The first years of the nineteenth century were marked by climate change and drought, creating severe water shortages. To help find a solution to this problem, the Edinburgh Joint Water Company was formed in 1819, and its immediate response was to create Glencorse Reservoir, a project that cost £200,000 and took nine years to complete.

The area around the reservoir was well known to Charles Cowan. At the age of twenty, he began to shoot in the Pentland Hills on land owned by a Nairne family connection.[6] After thirty years of grouse hunting, Charles Cowan bought the land for £31,000. He now had a property and would be known henceforth as 'Charles Cowan of Logan House'. Logan Burn runs through the property, connecting what today is the Loganlea Reservoir with Glencorse Reservoir and flowing into Glencorse Burn. A log between Loganlea Reservoir and Glencorse Reservoir regulated the amount of water that could flow into the Edinburgh water system. Charles Cowan's positioning of that log raised the level of Glencorse Reservoir and secured a larger flow of water, providing security for the city's supply. On 12 June 1860, he voluntarily 'became bound to convey to the Water Company, in perpetuity, as much of his land as might be required for the purpose of storing the additional quantity of water intercepted by the log.'[7] Thanks to Charles' generosity, shares in the Water Company went up immediately, and each year thereafter,

6. Alexander Cowan's first wife was Elizabeth Nairne. His father's nephew George had married a Nairne.

7. *Scotsman* 10 October 1873.

the contract was renewed, with the City paying him a nominal ten guineas *per annum*.

Edinburgh continued to grow, and agitation against the Water Company became more vocal as demand for water continued to outstrip the supply. In 1869, the Company was dissolved, and a new one, the Edinburgh and District Water Trust, was constituted, with representatives from Edinburgh, Leith, and Portobello. To relieve the shortage, the following year the Trustees brought in legislation that would make St Mary's Loch a new reservoir. St Mary's Loch was forty-five miles from Edinburgh in the Tweedsmuir Hills and the water would have to be piped in at considerable expense. Then the fight began, a fight unlike anything Edinburgh had seen. As the battle lines were drawn, Charles Cowan occupied centre stage. From the very outset of the discussion, at an 1869 meeting of the Chamber of Commerce he had addressed, he had expressed his opposition to the proposal. Pitted against Charles Cowan was Baillie David Lewis, chair of the city's works committee from 1868 to 1872.[8]

David Lewis was one of four Baillies serving under Edinburgh's mayor, the Lord Provost. Born in West Linton, a small town to the west of Penicuik and south of Edinburgh, Lewis went to Edinburgh after apprenticing as a shoemaker. He was a pioneer in selling ready-made shoes, setting up shop first in Bank Street, and, when it succeeded, on the prestigious High Street. He went on to open stores in Leith, Kirkcaldy and Aberdeen. When Lewis was elected to city Council in 1863 he became part of the 'shopocracy' that dominated Edinburgh municipal politics at the time: young Radicals out to make a difference, anxious to run the city as an efficient business, and opposed to Tory and Whig cronyism. Lewis was respected but not popular. Early in life he had taken 'the Pledge' to be a teetotaller for life. He wrote widely on the subject of temperance, did the research that assisted the passage of the Forbes MacKenzie Act in 1853, regulating the sale of alcoholic beverages, and helped build a case for prohibition in, of all places, the state of Maine in America. An Evangelical dissenter, identified with the revivalist Haldane brothers sect, to some he came across as a sanctimonious prig. There is a claim

8. David Lewis (1823–1909) see obituary *Scotsman* 14 April 1909.

that Thomas Stevenson found him so annoying that he called his son Robert *Louis*, instead of Robert Lewis, taking 'a Frenchified turn for fear the two families should be thought in any way connected'.[9]

Forty years after, at the age of eighty-six but with a firm hand, David Lewis wrote and published as a last survivor a 510 page account of the 'great water struggle'.[10] He died a year later, having left a final unapologetic *apologia*, irenic, fair, but also disclosing a lot of personal hurt and pain. 'In the capacity of exponent of the St Mary's Loch scheme,' he said speaking in the third person of himself, 'it was his fate to win for himself from a section of his fellow-citizens a measure of public contumely and abuse which, it may be hoped, rarely falls to the lot of the citizen whose public service – whatever may be its worth – is animated only by a sense of the public good and a desire personally to contribute thereto.'[11]

Cowan vs. Lewis: the names of the two chief protagonists became notorious to the public as the *persona* of the controversy, their names seldom appearing far apart in press reports. One such exchange was typical of many. Cowan had just proposed, as a less expensive alternative, making Farley Hope (nearby his property in the Pentlands) the new reservoir. In response, Lewis stated at a February 1871 meeting of the Edinburgh Town Council that he was not there 'to impute motive'. However, 'as one who knew the geography of the country, there was an idea he could not get rid of in connection with that proposal by Mr. Cowan [there would be] two benefits [to him], with 20 feet to Farley Hope: waste land on his estate would be utilized and doubling the quantity of water in Farley Hope which went in, not below, but above Mr. Cowan's paper mills.'[12]

On 24 April 1871 a committee of the Commons began hearings in London and by 12 May the St Mary's Loch proposal had been

---

9. Simpson, Blantyre *Robert Louis Stevenson's Edinburgh Days* London: Hodder & Stoughton, 1914. 15. A pained Lewis dismissed this claim, when it was first made, as 'a grotesque absurdity.' Lewis, David *Edinburgh Water Supply* Edinburgh: Andrew Elliot, 1908. 376.

10. My copy, from the University of British Columbia Library, is inscribed by Lewis to a Rev Stewart.

11. Lewis, David *Edinburgh Water Supply* Edinburgh: Andrew Elliot, 1908. 375.

12. *Scotsman*, 22 February 1871.

approved. The Sunday before the hearing opened, representatives from both sides had gone to the Metropolitan Tabernacle in London and heard the famed Baptist preacher Charles Haddon Spurgeon speak on the text, 'They could not drink of the waters of Mara for they were bitter' (Exodus 15:23). 'You may go fumbling over the Scriptures long before you get the true word,' Spurgeon had said, 'but when the Lord shows it to you, when it comes with power to the soul, when the heart can grasp it, and cry, "Ay, that is the word, my Master; indeed and of a truth that is the precious truth which can sweeten my sad discomforts," oh, what a bliss it is!'[13] Fortunately at least David Lewis saw both the appropriateness of the message and its humour.

The arguments became more heated preparatory to the case going to the Lords. By May 1871 Cowan had allowed himself to be called 'Chairman of the opposition' ('to the surprise of many of his friends,' David Lewis would later write[14]) and was chair of a meeting held in the Music Hall on 19 May 1871. There he characterised the Water Trustees as 'a packed body [who had] established a kind of dictatorship in the city' and were prepared to enter into contracts for £700,000, 'a millstone hanging round their necks for all time coming.' *Daphnia pulex* made her appearance, courtesy of Dr. Charles Bell of the Royal Maternity Hospital, as an 'animal of a most deleterious character.' Cowan had two policemen eject a town councilor (Romans) who did not agree with the meeting's tenor. It was all highly emotional and irrational, hardly Cowan's finest hour, nor indeed that of the opposition generally.

In the Leith Town Council, one councillor named Adam stated that '[h]e did not say Charles Cowan was a Red; but a man who could tell the ratepayers of Edinburgh and Leith that it was not part of the duty of the Water Trustees to ... take the ratepayers' money to execute works at the Pentlands to provide water for Messrs.' Cowan & Co and other manufacturers on the North Esk. [Cowan] was a man so eaten up with selfishness that what he might either say

13. Spurgeon, C. H. 'Marah; or, The Bitter Waters Sweetened Delivered on Lord's-day Morning, April 23rd, 1871.' http://www.spurgeon.org/sermons/0987.htm. Accessed 14 March 2012.

14. Lewis, David *Edinburgh Water Supply* Edinburgh: Andrew Elliot, 1908. 254.

or write on the water question would have no effect on the public mind.'[15]

Charles Cowan was by now over seventy years of age and still vigorous, but his brother and surrogate James, younger by fourteen years, was just reaching his stride, attending ward meetings, endorsing candidates, and getting into controversies with the old Water Trustees.[16] In that summer of 1871 water had been severely cut back, the Glencorse Reservoir was down almost fifteen feet, and Charles Cowan had made it be known that he would not restore the log unless he had parliamentary approval.[17] The situation was only regularised by legislation five years later.

The Lords considered the proposal at the end of June. Charles Cowan journeyed to London to make his case. On 7 July they brought down their verdict: 'They hold that with better use and regulation as regards waste, and with increased storage for the utilisation of the water drawn from present sources of supply, Edinburgh can obtain all that it required for their needs; and they hold, further, that they cannot sanction so large an expenditure of money, which appears not to be required at present.'[18] Cowan returned home jubilant, but Lewis was deeply depressed. As with the Disruption, the Lords had trumped the claims of Radicals and, for him, the people's interest.

Immediately prior to the municipal elections of 1 November 1871, Charles Cowan wrote to the *Scotsman* a letter in favour of creating two different water systems.[19] He had defended the Ratepayers'

15. *Scotsman*, 7 June 1871.

16. For instance, in a meeting to the Calton Ward, James Cowan had said that the chair and several flag wavers at a rally of 1400 in Queen's Park in support of St Mary's Loch were paid by the Water Trustees. This was later qualified as a misquotation by Wormald. (*Scotsman* 2 November 1871).

17. *Scotsman* 2 November 1871.

18. Colston, James. *The Edinburgh and District Water Supply* Edinburgh: Colston Printers 1890-. 145-6.

19. Detaching the lower-lying burghs of Leith, Portobello, Dalkeith, and Musselburgh, from Edinburgh. Cowan wrote: 'So confident am I that a bill embodying the necessary provisions for this would meet the approval of the Legislature that it will greatly conduce to the well-being of the various burghs, that the large supply will tend greatly to promote the prosperity and extension of manufactures and of the shipping, that it is calculated to heal any surviving animosities, and conduce to the general weal, that I for

Committee and launched and won a legal appeal, an interdict, to stop the Trustees from proceeding with their St Mary's Loch plans. The municipal election returned a whole new slate, with a majority opposed to the St Mary's Loch proposal, and all the former Water Trustees thrown out. With the defeat of their bill, the previous city councilors were held to be liable for the expenses incurred in the failed legislation, amounting to £19,000. The costs of the ratepayers opposed, £9000, had been underwritten by the Cowans and they assumed that cost.

Among those elected was James Cowan, the erstwhile scapegrace son. James' reinstatement, after all his youthful follies, indiscretions, and the bankruptcy, was now complete. James was beloved by all who knew him. As his niece Helen Menzies McFarlan, said, 'Uncle Jamie was the wonderful friend and fairy uncle of our childhood.'[20] Married for over fifty years, he and Charlotte (née Cowan) had no children. James was said to suffer from chronic depression, which was relieved only when a niece provided musical entertainment from operas, particularly Mozart's *Don Giovanni*. The question might be raised as to whether undiagnosed mental illness might have provided an explanation for this erratic behavior.[21]

*****

At a meeting of the Edinburgh Town Council held on 12 March 1872 James Cowan rose to state that he had 'read public opinion to the effect that the city was sick of the struggle which had been going on, and would gladly listen to any honourable compromise. He thought they must all agree that the question of the interdict had turned out unfortunate. It was gone into at a period of profound excitement; and those who entered into [it] did not, he dared say, see what would be a compromise; and he hoped that the members

---

one am prepared to give it my warm support in the hope that many others also may give their hearty co-operation.' *Scotsman* 2 November 1871.

20. Forsyth, Mary, Ed. *The Cowans At Moray House*. Edinburgh: T. & A. Constable, 1932. 18.

21. It is surprising, given the number of marriages between cousins and within such a tight family circle, that there was not more evidence of difficulty.

of Council would do their best to restore peace to Edinburgh, to bury the weapons of warfare, and to go on together in amity and goodwill.'[22]

The election of the Lord Provost was the first item of business for the new Town Council. It was clear that James Cowan was the man who could, as was said, 'Throw oil on troubled waters,' as he was not a party man. At the first meeting of the Town Council on 8 November 1872, Baillie Marshall nominated James to be the new Lord Provost, stating that 'Mr. James Cowan is thoroughly well-known in Edinburgh, and is as highly esteemed as the other members of his family; and I have no doubt that his appointment will give universal satisfaction.' Treasurer James Colston, in his seconding speech, declared that '[b]y none are the Cowan family more respected than by those who are the emloyes [*sic*] of the firm, and those are a very large number indeed. But I consider it my duty on this occasion to say that Mr. Cowan is a member of a family whose hands and hearts have been open to the call of humanity and benevolence.' Their comments were punctuated by 'Hear, hear.' James Cowan was then elected by acclamation as Lord Provost of Edinburgh.

Because of his office as Lord Provost, James now, ironically, presided over meetings of the Water Trust, and during his tenure he set about resolving the city's recurring water shortages. A second reservoir was created along the White Clough Burn, which went west from Logan Cottage (a short distance up from Logan House), and from there, it linked up with Threipmuir, which had been built in the late 1840s by the well-known civil engineer James Jardine.[23]

Negotiations about the 'scandal of the Glencorse log' could proceed. With water at a dangerously low level, one of the first things James asked his brother was to restore the log. Charles placed it as before and thus increased the amount of water in the reservoir by five per cent. Subsequently arrangements were made to regularize and legalize the log, the issue being who would pay for the road repairs alongside the reservoir, which was damaged through flooding when the water was high.

---

22. 'Edinburgh Town Council' *Scotsman* 13 March 1872..

23. James Jardine FRSE FSAScot (1776–1858) one of the first to call himself a civil engineer. He was responsible for much of the landmark railway bridges and tunnels in Scotland.

At the September 1873 meeting of the Edinburgh and District Water Trust, James had an awkward moment in the chair as he was called upon to recount what had happened and read a memo from his brother. He stated that 'Mr. Chas. Cowan and himself had been held up before the public as if he had been trying to favour Mr. Charles Cowan and put money in his pocket, and as if they were trying together to take advantage of the Trustees.' It seemed eminently fair since the road had been corroded by flooding to pay for repairs, particularly since the water overflowed because the log had been positioned to bring water from Charles' property, water which he was giving to the city.

James served just over a year as Lord Provost, and his time in office was marked by two significant achievements. First, the widening of North Bridge, which kept his name in public view until the brass plaque honouring his contribution was recently removed. His second accomplishment was the passage of the Moorfoot Water Bill in May of 1874, which finally resolved Edinburgh's reservoir rage: the £19,000 levy against the former Trustees was paid by the Water Trust and the Glencorse log uncertainties were removed through legislation that was created '[t]o ratify and confirm an Agreement entered into with Charles Cowan, Esq., of Logan House, and others, holding from or under him for continuing in perpetuity the raising One Foot, or thereabout, of the Weir of the Reservoir of the Trustees known as the Glencorse Reservoir, situated in the Parishes of Glencorse and Penicuik, both in the Co[unty] of Edinburgh, by means of a Timber Log or substituted Masonry Work, of other material, and to legalise such raising and the impounding of water in the said Reservoir to an additional height of One Foot, or thereabout, consequent upon the raising of the said Weir by the means aforesaid.'[24]

By the time the Moorfoot Water Bill was passed, James was already in London, sitting as a Member of Parliament. Gladstone may have been turned out of office, but Liberals James Cowan and Duncan McLaren were sent to Westminster by the voters of Edinburgh. The General Election on 2 February 1874 marked several firsts: the campaign lasted ten days, the labour unions were involved, and the

24. *Scotsman* 12 September 1873.

secret ballot was used. In Scotland more Tories were returned than had been since 1832. By teaming up with Duncan McLaren, much more experienced and mature, the younger Cowan provided a curious combination. Cowan was the candidate of the Whig (Aggregate) Liberals. McLaren's partner since 1868 (when he was unopposed), John Miller of Leithen,[25] having become 'left of the extremist Left' according to one report,[26] no longer shared 'the same platform'[27] as McLaren. One paper, while favouring Miller, said that James Cowan would become 'a good average member of Parliament'.[28] So he was.

Though short, it had not been a pleasant campaign: James Cowan, not the most religious of the three Cowan brothers, was accused of desecrating the Sabbath, then a grave charge against a politician. The final vote came in at McLaren 11,431, Cowan 8,749, Miller 6,281, and Macdonald (the Tory) 5,713. Though victorious, McLaren was not happy at being teamed with a Whig instead of an Independent Liberal. James' career in Parliament was undistinguished: 'Of a quiet and retiring disposition, Mr. Cowan did not often speak in Parliament, though he did occasionally take part in Scottish debates.'[29]

*****

The water struggles over, what was it all about, this conflict that aroused public opinion more than any event since the Disruption? In a way, Charles Cowan's sparring partner David Lewis represented what Charles Cowan had once identified with, but which now seemed less important to him. For all his unctuous piety, Lewis was a devout believer seeking, as a Radical, to exercise his active social conscience wherever it led him: alcohol abuse or water was what he regarded as his civic responsibility to all his constituents. To the very end he maintained, in almost Biblical terms, 'the assurance

25. John Miller of Leithen (1805-1882) Obituary in *Scotsman* 9 May 1883.

26. *Scotsman* 3 February 1872

27. *Scotsman* 9 May 1883.

28. Pickard, Willis *The Member for Scotland*. Edinburgh: Birlinn, 2011. 223. quoting the *Daily Review*.

29. 'The Late Mr James Cowan,' *Scotsman*, 25 November 1895.

of the righteousness of his cause.'[30] Though Lewis was described as 'McLaren's loyal lieutenant', Duncan McLaren, now an MP in London, did not get involved in the scrap, which is surprising given his active participation in the 1840 debate. Willis Pickard, McLaren's recent biographer, sees the polarities as being between old-style radicals such as Lewis and 'middle-class Whigs and Tories.'[31]

Both sides claimed to be motivated by a concern for the poor. In a 9 June 1871 letter to Alexander Russel, Editor of the *Scotsman*, Dr. Alexander Wood specifically exempted Charles Cowan and Russel as 'incapable of an ungenerous thought towards their poorer brethren, and whose liberality towards them is well known and justly appreciated.' He claimed that the real issue could be summarized in a single word: 'caste.' Opponents of the St Mary Loch proposal were asking, he claimed, 'Are we to be led by a shoemaker like Bailie Lewis, or a coffee-dealer like the Lord Provost?'[32]

The municipal 'shopocracy' was a sitting target for the rising middle-class. Charles Cowan, on the other hand, was a man remarkably free of social pretensions. Indeed he may have thought that he was maintaining a family tradition, providing cheap water for the working classes. As a businessman he appears to have thought the amount required to bring water from St Mary's Loch was indefensible. But why so much passion? Now over seventy, Cowan could afford to rest on his laurels. Indeed throughout the debate he was generally treated, even by his opponents, with great deference. As he aged – and before he actually became aged – he was increasingly outspoken and irascible and appears to have enjoyed sparring even with friends (as we will see with John MacGregor McCandlish). Besides, the controversy kept him, in spite of his age, in the public eye, showing he could not be easily written off.

As Charles Cowan's political radicalism faded so did his earlier intense religious radicalism. In that development he reflected the transformation of the Free Church of Scotland from its early revivalist intensity into bourgeois respectability and spiritual complacency, especially in the Lowlands.

---

30. Lewis, David *Edinburgh Water Supply* Edinburgh: Andrew Elliot, 1908. 375.
31. Pickard, Willis *The Member for Scotland*. Edinburgh: Birlinn, 2011. 216.
32. *Scotsman*, 8 June 1871.

Chapter 20

Intellectual Inquiries

The Free Church of Scotland has been described 'as well-educated a church as any in history, laity as well as clergy.'[1] Its reputation as a 'cerebral communion'[2] can be traced back directly to Thomas Chalmers. As a polymath, Chalmers had a broad range of interests and accomplishments, including mathematics, astronomy, economics, and the new science of sociology. His thirst for knowledge was typical of leaders in the Free Church of Scotland, with its demanding academic standards and rigorous scholarship. As a new denomination, without its own traditions and experience, the Free Church could prove open to theological innovation and intellectual speculation. And the nineteenth century was no time, if there ever has been one, for theological uncertainties and ambivalence. Scientific inquiry was very much a feature of nineteenth century Scotland. As Richard Sher has shown, the Scottish Enlightenment of the previous century was succeeded by what he called 'a rush to science' in the next[3].

---

1. Riesen, R. A. *Criticism and Faith in Late Victorian Scotland: A. B. Davidson, William Robertson Smith and George Adam Smith*. Lanham, MD: University Press of America, 1985. 221.

2. MacLeod, J. L. *The Second Disruption: The Free Church in Victorian Scotland and the Origins of the Free Presbyterian Church*. East Linton: Tuckwell Press, 2000.7.

3. Sher, Richard. *Church and University in the Scottish Enlightenment: The Moderate Literati of Edinburgh* Princeton: Princeton University Press, 1985.310.

Encyclopaedia Britannica, Edinburgh Journal of Science and David Brewster

That so-called 'rush to science' was a gradual transformation: the *Encyclopaedia Britannica* began appearing in 1768 and was a catalyst. David Brewster's *Edinburgh Journal of Science* started publication in 1824. Brewster, who went into the Free Church in 1843, was a leader in the new direction and served as a reminder that intellectual vitality and achievement were no longer the exclusive property of the Moderates who had led the Scottish Enlightenment a hundred years earlier.

In addition to Thomas Chalmers, David Brewster[4] was a decisive intellectual influence on Charles Cowan. Principal of the United Colleges of St Andrews University and later of Edinburgh University, his research in optics was path breaking and earned him a fellowship in the Royal Society as well as a knighthood. In his scientific interests David Brewster closely collaborated with Thomas Chalmers after 1808, the year he asked Chalmers to contribute the article on Christianity in Brewster's *Edinburgh Encyclopaedia*.

In 1843 when he joined the Free Church, the Church of Scotland Presbytery of St Andrews sought to deprive Brewster of his principalship at the university. Cowan came to his defence, telling the Commons that it was an 'honour and a privilege' to call Sir David a friend. In reality Brewster was much more than that: a man whom Charles Cowan admired and identified with, not only because of his experiments, but even more his robust and outspoken evangelical faith. Brewster had an impressive list of scientific discoveries: the kaleidoscope, the law of double refraction, the polarization of biaxial crystals, and optic mineralogy.

Charles Cowan, Prince Albert, and the *Encyclopaedia Britannica*

In 1851 Charles Cowan was summoned to Buckingham Palace to explain to Prince Albert recent advances in the science of paper

4. Sir David Brewster (1781-1868) was destined for the ministry but instead at the age of 20 became an editor. In 1838 he went to St Andrews and in 1861 to the University of Edinburgh until his death. He was a regular contributor to *The Witness* and *The North British Review*. An active churchman, elder, and Evangelical, he opposed Darwin. Ironically it was a debate in Brewster's British Association for the Advancement of Science in 1860, pitting Huxley against the Bishop of Oxford, that established Darwin's reputation.

manufacture. He produced 'several specimens of paper made of materials not previously used' and the Prince took a great interest.[5] However the Prince wisely refused to be drawn into a discussion Cowan tried to initiate about the paper excise. The next year he was a judge and exhibitor at the Crystal Palace, being present when Prince Albert opened the Great Exhibition in Hyde Park, London, on 1 May, 1851. It was a triumph for Prince Albert but also for David Brewster. In a speech to the Commons on 25 June 1851 Cowan noted the fact that David Brewster had made a substantial contribution to its success and 'was at that moment engaged in unremitting labours from morning to night in the Crystal Palace, one who was always most willing as he was able to impart valuable scientific information from the rich stores of his mind.'[6]

Brewster was also a substantial contributor to the sixth, seventh, and eighth editions of the *Encyclopaedia Britannica*. The eighth edition, with twenty-two volumes appearing between 1852 and 1860, was edited by Thomas Stewart Trail[7], who taught medical jurisprudence at the University of Edinburgh. Charles Cowan, as a friend of Brewster and known to Traill, was assigned the section on 'Paper.' It is not clear how much this owes to the 1798 article on the same subject, though classical references (to which the *Scotsman* took exception[8]), have been largely omitted. 'Paper' extends for seventeen pages and, after providing historical and international background, focuses on the present-day manufacture of paper, a subject in which Cowan was fully versed. He started with an extensive discussion of ancient Egyptian papyri then being discovered. With the recent opening up of China and Japan to the West he was able to go on to cite previously unknown varieties, explaining the differences between the papers of the two countries. A lengthy description of the manufacture of paper followed, starting with the process of making paper by hand. This provided a segueway, using his expertise,

5. *Reminiscences*, 446.

6. *Reminiscences*, 483.

7. Thomas Stewart Trail (1781-1863) from Orkney, clergy son, medical graduate of Edinburgh University who, after 30 years in Liverpool, returned there as Professor of Medical Jurisprudence.

8. As in chapter 10, page 171.

to promote his industry's 'prodigious advancement which it has attained in Great Britain during the last thirty years [due] to the ingenious and successful application of machinery' which he went on to describe fulsomely.[9]

Charles' social conscience as a papermaker was apparent. 'The women engaged in the rag-house cut on an average about three quarters of a hundredweight of home rags (that is, rags collected in Scotland and England) in the day of ten working hours, and about one hundredweight and a half of foreign rags in the same time.' Their wages averaged between ten pence to a shilling per day. Doctors had suggested that because of the dust and fibrous matter circulating, each worker should have a sponge over their nose and mouth but Cowan stated firmly that this was not necessary for their health. Regarding one technique he states, 'To attain this method perfectly requires a long apprenticeship, simple as it may seem.'[10] The new steel pen introduced a further recent complication: its introduction had served to complicate the last stage of the process (the toughness or sizing of the paper), since a high gloss was now required. Among other innovations, new since 1798, was the introduction of the Fourdrinnier cutting machine which allowed manufacturers to produce any dimension of paper that customers desired and made it possible for newspapers such as the *Times*, to measure two feet by three, in contrast to the earlier allowable measurement, 22 by 32 inches.

'The manufacture of paper,' he concluded, 'has immensely increased in Great Britain and Ireland within the last twenty-five years, consequent upon the penny postage, the repeal of the newspaper stamp and of the restriction of the dimension of newspapers formerly prescribed by law, and also from the greatly increased amount of our manufactures and exports. This will appear from a comparison of the account of the duty charged twenty-five years ago, and what it has amounted to since.' He used figures to demonstrate 'the marvellous fact that the quantity produced is as nearly as possible three times as great in 1858 as it was twenty-five

9. *Encyclopaedia Britannica*, 250.

10. *Encyclopaedia Britannica* 256.

years previously.'[11] It appears that all the while he was attempting to shake off the charge of plagiarism by referring to advances in the past half-century that could not possibly have been covered in the 1798 article.

The Learned Societies:

Charles Cowan was a member of three of the new societies formed for scientific and intellectual inquiry: the British Association for the Advancement of Science, the Society for the Encouragement of Useful Arts in Scotland (later the Royal Scottish Society of Arts), and the National Association for the Promotion of Social Sciences. They were, in different ways, among the more significant and intellectually challenging organizations of Victorian Britain. All three were established during Charles' most productive years and brought him into contact with a large circle of stimulating people in the realm. Edinburgh was a veritable hive of exploration, inquiry, innovation, discovery, and experimentation that maintained its reputation as the Athens of the North. Rarely has such a galaxy of luminaries been concentrated in one city.

1. The British Association for the Advancement of Science

The British Association for the Advancement of Science, founded in 1831 in York, came out of a discussion David Brewster had with the Rev William Vernon Harcourt. Brewster felt the need a society less intellectually snobby than the Royal Society. Harcourt picked up on the idea. The Association's purpose was stated 'to give a stronger impulse and a more systematic direction to scientific inquiry; to promote the intercourse of those who cultivate Science in different parts of the British Empire with one another and with foreign philosophers; to obtain more general attention for the objects of Science and the removal of any disadvantages of a public kind that may impede its progress.'[12]

The Association met in various locations, even in Niagara Falls in 1897. In 1850 they chose Edinburgh as the venue for their annual

11. *Encyclopaedia Britannica* 260.

12. http://www.britishscienceassociation.org/about-british-science-association/our-history (accessed 27 August 2013).

meeting. On a beautiful summer's day, Charles Cowan hosted an outing to Penicuik as a part of the programme. Delegates left Edinburgh by omnibus on Saturday morning, 3 August, stopped by briefly to see the reservoirs in the Pentland Hills where they were met by Charles and then taken to Valleyfield. 'The rest of the day,' it was reported, 'was spent in viewing the different operations connected with the manufacture of paper, and in an examination of the various objects of interest in the neighbourhood of Penicuik.' The visit was regarded by those who went on the excursion as highly successful, providing much knowledge of the science of paper making. It is not known how comitted Charles Cowan continued to be in the Association, given his two other involvements in learned societies.

2. *Society for the Encouragement of Useful Arts in Scotland*

The Society for the Encouragement of Useful Arts in Scotland was another organization started by David Brewster. Established in 1821, it was committed to 'the promotion of invention and enterprise.' Melville Bell was among the Society's members, and he addressed the group once, describing his Visible Speech system. He subsequently took that invention to Brantford in the Canadian province of Ontario, where he emigrated with his family, including his son Alexander Graham. Thomas Stevenson also presented a paper to the Society – on his specialty, the holophotal system of illuminating lighthouses.

Cowan joined the Society in 1836 (to be followed by his father two years later) and gave his first paper on 23 January 1854. Titled 'Sketch of various changes and improvements in the Manufacture of Paper during the last thirty years,' it was an anticipation of his later *Encyclopaedia Britannica* article. 'There were twelve or fourteen processes,' he stated, 'in the old vat mill, requiring a period of three weeks to produce the paper, whereas now it was manufactured in almost as many minutes.' He explained both the Fourdrinnier machine and an even more recent advance, as it could now produce "laid" or ribbed paper, preferred by artists. Charles passed around specimens of different papers and told the audience that if the twenty-four machines in operation produced at an average rate of thirty-six feet per minute (some could do fifty feet) and worked fifteen hours a day the result would be 147 miles of paper five feet broad.[13]

In 1864, Cowan allowed his name to stand for office as president because he 'could not find it in his heart to refuse, for he always held it as part of his social creed that when anyone was called to discharge a public duty which he might be considered worthy of, it was his duty to comply.' The question has been asked as to why it took so long for him to be asked, but presumably this was because previously he had been occupied with both business and political office. On 28 January 1865, as president, he gave a paper titled 'Our Sewage and Soapy Waters: What can be done with them?' After a brief and witty apology for the subject, he started: 'For many years the attention of medical men, philanthropists, and of Parliament, has been beneficially directed to the prevention of diseases eminently dangerous and destructive to human life, and clearly traceable to defective drainage.'[14] While improvements had been made, particularly in the introduction of the water-closet, he was disappointed that better use had not been made of sewage and its beneficial effects on agriculture, if used properly. William Napier was spending £2 million on the London project because he valued the sewage of the city at £ 1.5 million. Could Edinburgh not make similar use of its sewage, perhaps by fertilizing 'the hundreds of acres of sand on the shores of the Firth of Forth to the east of the town of Portobello, left dry at low water'? Edinburgh sewage, he concluded, could certainly net an annual amount of £10,000. His concept would raise serious concerns today about its impact on the environment.

The second part of his talk, about soapy water, was more personal and controversial. The topic would explode in the courts two years later as a result of a longstanding lawsuit by the Duke of Buccleuch and Lord Melville against the paper makers along the Esk River described in more detail in Chapter 15. River pollution, he explained, was the result of seismic changes that had taken place in the past because of the exponential growth of the paper-making

13. 'Appendix: Proceedings of the Royal Scottish Society of Arts' in *Transactions of the Royal Scottish Society of Arts*, Vol. 4. Edinburgh: Adam and Charles Black, 1856. 183.

14. *Proceedings of the Royal Scottish Society of Arts*. Vol. 6. 22.

industry, the realities of climate change (drought in summer and frost in winter), and changes in agriculture (deforestation on high ground). Surely, Charles declared, the Duke of Buccleuch would not want to throw thousands of people out of work, and he added that the manufacturers were 'desirous to conduct … [their] business and wash … [their] raw materials in such a way as to produce as little annoyance or discomfort as possible.'

'Can science in its advanced state, whether chemical or mechanical, do anything to help in solving the problem?' he asked the Society, promising a premium of £50 for information about the best way of 'transmitting the water used in the paper manufacture as pure and innocuous as possible.' The answer he proposed was installing a drain, something his son-in-law civil engineer Charles Wahab suggested. That drain could be either iron, clay, or open and would carry foul water from Penicuik to Musselburgh and the North Sea. Additional storage would be created by raising the height of Fairliehope reservoir, which was owned by paper millers on the north Esk River. However, the cost of the entire installation would be £70,000 or £80,000, not an insubstantial amount.

The discussion that followed, according to the minutes, was of a high order. Comments were made by a galaxy of engineering greats: Thomas Stevenson, Stevenson Macadam (son of the road paver and professor of chemistry at Edinburgh University), Robert William Thomson (inventor of the pneumatic tyre), James Falshaw (associated with Stephenson as one of the great railway engineers of the day), and James Leslie (a famous water engineer). 'A cordial vote of thanks to Mr Cowan was unanimously adopted, for his interesting Paper and liberal offer of a Premium [the £50 reward].'

On 13 November 1865, towards the end of his term in office, Cowan delivered a forty-eight-page presidential address,[15] summarizing many engineering achievements of the past half-decade. His survey began with drainage in the city of London whose population was now over three million. The Metropolitan Main Drainage Scheme had been approved six years earlier, at a time when

15. Cowan, Charles. *Address to the Royal Scottish Society of Arts November 1865*. Edinburgh: Neill and Company, 1865.

fifty-two million gallons of raw sewage had gone directly into the Thames. The improvement was dramatic and had been adopted widely. He went on to advances in the production of steel rails, now replacing iron rails. Henry Bessemer's invention of a process to turn pig iron into steel had revolutionized the industry a decade earlier. Armaments were also being improved such as the new nine-ton, wrought-iron Mackay gun. There were also experiments in gun powder. He noted that these advances in technology only improved the potential for human self-destruction. How little he knew the future. Reliability and safety in rail travel was another concern, and Charles stated that the UK railway system was 'on the eve of a great change.'[16] As was communication: amazing technological advances signified by the recent attempt to lay a cable across the Atlantic. As he drew his lengthy presentation to a close the improvement in ale did not escape his notice. A new method of cooperage made possible the production of four hundred barrels a day. Perhaps the lecture adjourned with a pint.

3. *The National Association for the Promotion of Social Sciences*

Charles Cowan was also an active member of the National Association for the Promotion of Social Sciences. Sociology, pioneered by Auguste Comte in the 1830s, was a very new discipline, combining history, economics, and philosophy, in an attempt to understand the dynamics of social relationships. Along with other luminaries, Charles was present at the London residence of Lord Brougham in 1857, when the Association was founded, its stated objective being 'to aid legislation by preparing measures, by explaining them, by recommending them to the community, or it may be, by stimulating the legislature to adopt them.'[17] It would have a major impact, affecting many areas of society and making significant social progress. In 1861 an Edinburgh branch was formed and the Cowan brothers were involved from the outset: Charles was appointed to the

16. Cowan, Charles. *Address to the Royal Scottish Society of Arts November 1865*. Edinburgh: Neill and Company, 1865. 33.

17. Quoted in Goldman, Lawrence. *Science, Reform and Politics in Victorian Britain: The Social Science Association, 1857–1886*. Cambridge: Cambridge University Press, 2002. 1.

education subcommittee, and his brother John was made convener of the reformation subcommittee, charged with scrutinising the existing policies for the incarceration of lawbreakers.

The Social Science Association held its national gathering yearly at different places around the country, and according to a recent study. '[I]ts annual meetings ... were a focus for social and institutional reform in mid-Victorian Britain.'[18] In 1862 a deputation from Edinburgh including Charles Cowan travelled to London to invite the Association to meet in Edinburgh the nest year. The delegation guaranteed the Association's governing Council all local expenses, with a surplus (if any) to go to the work of the Edinburgh chapter. Unfortunately that provision was not followed through, creating a 'feeling of great irritation' among the sponsors after the event, according to a letter from Charles Cowan to George Hastings,[19] secretary of the Association, published in the *Scotsman.*[20] Faced with an outraged Charles Cowan, Hastings beat a hasty retreat, and the Edinburgh committee kept their money.

Aside from that squabble over money, the October 1863 Edinburgh meeting of the Association was a great success. The programme ran in parallel 'departments,' covering the topics of jurisprudence, education, punishment and reformation, public health, social economy, and trade and international law. Trade and international law were regarded by Cowan as his personal *métier* and so he claimed the sixth section as his own. Judge Mountiford Longfield, [368] Dublin academic and Irish land reformer, was in the chair, and Cowan, along with the head of the Merchant Company and the head of the Edinburgh Chamber of Commerce, were vice-presidents. That department dealt with patents, Scottish trading, international law, and assessing the value of ships. For an entire week, a thousand of the brightest minds in Britain were in Edinburgh,

18. Goldman, Lawrence. *Science, Reform and Politics in Victorian Britain: The Social Science Association, 1857–1886.* Cambridge: Cambridge University Press, 2002. 1.

19. Warren Hastings was the first governor general of Bengal and his seven year trial for 'high crimes and misdemeanours' by the Commons eventually resulted in his acquittal in 1795.

20. *Scotsman,* 15 December 1863. 4.

interacting through creative thinking. At the Presidential Dinner[21] held in the Music Hall Charles Cowan was seated behind the Edinburgh-born eighty-five-year-old Lord Brougham. Described as being 'in full working harness', Edinburgh's Lord Provost toasted him for his leadership in the organization, noting that 'scarcely any man will deny the necessity for the principles and reforms which it seeks to establish.' As the guests departed Cowan and Lord Brougham were left alone. The bitter days of the Disruption appear to have been forgotten: in a symbolic gesture Charles Cowan extended his hand to the aging Brougham. As the two descended the long flight of steps Brougham remarked on the welcome Edinburgh had given him.[22] Five years later Brougham was dead.

The Association did not meet in Edinburgh again until 1880, and attendance that year was less than half what it had been when the Association previously met there.[23] Charles Cowan, by then a senior statesman, was on the platform for the opening ceremonies with other supernumeraries. Charles' brother James, then an MP, was nominated to the section dealing with jurisprudence and amendments to the law. Women's rights were high on the agenda, and 132 women were present. After the meeting, the Association had another six years of life. In its time the Association was in the vanguard of progressive thinking in Victorian Britain.

Faith and Scientific Discovery

As the pace of scientific discovery quickened, as new inventions proliferated, and as scientific knowledge expanded, there were new challenges in relation to science and religion, particularly the orthodoxies of the Free Church of Scotland. Charles Cowan wanted to hear more from the clergy about 'the light which has in recent years been shed upon the works of creation by researches into the domains of earth, water, air, and sea, teeming with proofs of the beneficent design and infinite power and skill of the Almighty.'[24] He

21. *Scotsman*. 14 October 1863. 3.

22. *Reminiscences*,167.

23. *Scotsman*, 8 October 1880.

24. *Reminiscences*, 352.

particularly recommended *Reflections on the Works of God in Nature,* a classic eighteenth century text by the German Pietist pastor Christoph Christian Sturm.[25] This he had read from childhood and he commended its approach to the natural world because it was written in a 'humble, pious, grateful spirit.'[26] It provided for every day of the year a meditation on the natural world.

Two preachers in the Free Church exemplified the way in which Cowan wished science to be dealt with by people of faith: his 'dear friend'[27] William Arnot[28] of the Free High in Edinburgh, and the botanist Hugh MacMillan, minister at Kirkhope Ettrick Free Church in the Borders. Arnot was known for his homespun aphorisms and illustrations and spoke of his 'desire to lay the Christian System along the surface of common life without removing it from the doctrines of Grace.'[29] MacMillan[30] was best known for his books such as *Bible Teachings in Nature.* At his installation as President of the Scottish Cryptogrammic Society in 1887 he declared that 'Theologians are now beginning to realize, far more than their predecessors did, that the word from above includes, in addition to the things primarily necessary for salvation, all in the natural as well as in the mental and spiritual worlds that can furnish the soul with food convenient for its high capacities and boundless appetites.'[31] Both Arnot and the younger MacMillan represented what for Cowan was a way out of the conundrum of how to integrate scientific truth and Scriptural narrative. The focus on 'Nature,' which sometimes barely avoided

---

25. Christoph Christian Sturm (1740–1786) graduate of Jena and Halle universities and a popular preacher in Halle, Magdeburg and Hamburg. He was accused of universalism, a charge which appears to have broken his spirit.

26. *Reminiscences,* 352.

27. *Reminiscences,* 372.

28. William Arnot (1808-1875) trained as a gardener but went on to Glasgow University. Best known for his writing, he visited America for the Free Church three times. He refused honourary degrees from NY and Glasgow.

29. Arnot Wm. *Illustrations of the Book of Proverbs* London: Thomas Nelson 1858, v.

30. Hugh MacMillan (1842-1930) D,D,, Ll.D., FRSE, author of many books and articles such as *The True Vine; Or, the Analogies of our Lord's Allegory* Cryptogrammic is a particularly Scottish botanic expression.

31. MacMillan, Hugh 'Inaugural Address 4 Oct 1887' *The Scottish Naturalist* vol 9, 196-7.

pantheism made it possible to evade hard questions and maintain an uneasy truce.

What Charles Cowan did not realize was that in this climate of intellectual inquiry – and the intellectual pride that accompanied it – were the very seeds of the undoing of the Free Church's early faith and confidence in Biblical revelation. The excitement of new discovery would soon have to be weighed against the possibility that such inquiry could be both unsettling and disturbing to a church which had so prided itself on its intellectual prowess.

Chapter 21

Changing Certainties

In the 1870s Scotland was experiencing severe social and cultural stress. Charles Cowan was not immune to these pressures. The Free Church of Scotland also seemed in danger of losing its way during that decade. The abandonment of union negotiations with the United Presbyterian Church in 1873 and the disestablishment debate were both causes of wide discontent and an anxious awareness of an old order changing. 'The heroes of the Disruption have now almost all passed away,' Charles Cowan noted at the General Assembly of 1877. Charles Cowan was being challenged to adapt to a rapidly changing environment. He did not find it easy.

Loss of a Wife

Just at the time that Charles' own earlier certainties were being challenged, his wife, always a bulwark of traditional faith, was gradually withdrawing from the family. Catharine Cowan, Charles' remarkable life-time partner, was failing. A biographical journal handwritten by her childless daughter and namesake, Catharine or Kate Wahab, records Catharine struggling with ill health and increasing worries about her family as they scattered.

The beginning of the end for Catharine Cowan occurred suddenly. Her oldest and first married, Jeanie Chalmers, lived nearby. With her six children she was a frequent and favourite visitor to 37 Royal Crescent' the city home where her parents lived at the time. Jeanie and the six grandchildren were staying with her parents while her home 'Longcroft,' Linlithgow, was being renovated when on 8 May 1864 she died suddenly. Two days later, in shock, Catharine wrote: 'The blow has been sudden and stunning, and not easily realized. She was so blooming, hearty, active and energetic.'[1] Kate Wahab reflected in retrospect that 'It was a crushing blow to all who loved her, and especially so to her Mother whose joy and pride her first born had always been.' Visiting Longcroft that autumn Catharine wrote, 'I don't think I ever fully felt what a *terrible* loss a mother was to her children till I went there.' The oldest child, Isabella, was only eleven at the time. Catharine Cowan was devastated and for her, with increasing physical challenges, life was never the same again.

The event cast a long shadow on Charles and Catharine's Ruby Wedding celebration on 19 October 1864. 'Uncle John,' Catharine reported to her namesake daughter in India, 'made a feeling little speech after dinner referring to all our happy life with the mingling of trial and sorrow and the recent one with its deep shadow still pressing upon us. Papa was too full hearted to say even one word but we were all able to sing the XXIII Psalm.'[2] At a subsequent anniversary celebration the honours fell to Uncle James as 'spokesman and was most kind and tender about the shadows that were year by year falling over the pleasure of the meeting. Yes that is true,' Catharine added quickly, 'but how the mercies abound.' Charles again was emotional: 'Papa's heart is very tender whenever we speak of Kate [their first grandchild, Jeanie's firstborn, who died at thirteen months] and Jeanie.'[3]

Catharine's rheumatism, as well as the precarious health of

1. Wahab, Catharine. 'Catharine Menzies' handwritten memoir in the possession of Judith A MacLeod. 19.

2. Wahab, Catharine. 'Catharine Menzies' handwritten memoir in the possession of Judith A MacLeod. 22.

3. Wahab, Catharine. 'Catharine Menzies' handwritten memoir in the possession of Judith A MacLeod. 24.

daughter Maggie, sent the family to the baths in Germany in 1865 and in 1868 to a closer spa at Buxton, Derbyshire. Her rheumatism steadily got worse and her confinements to her room longer. A decision was made to settle permanently in Edinburgh, so property in Murrayfield was bought, and Catharine's niece's husband Campbell Douglas was engaged as architect.[4] There was to be a suite downstairs so that she would not have to climb stairs. Her daughter wrote: 'We had dreaded [the final removal from the dear old home at Valleyfield] for our Mother for her associations were so tender with all who had lived & died there and with the burying ground where rested the bodies of her departed children, but God gave strength for this trial.'

Her time at Wester Lea, the new home, was not long. On 1 February 1872 she slipped on a rug, was in great pain, and died twenty-six days later. Kate Wahab provided a detailed account of her final days as was expected by Victorians fascinated by deathbed scenes. She concluded: 'Her life was a happy, useful, unselfish one. She walked humbly with her God, trying to do good to all as she had opportunity and looking to heaven as her home. Her chief desire of her children was that they might be *God's children* and that she might meet them all at His right hand, an unbroken family.'[5] The recurring nightmare for pious Victorian parents was that their children, faced with increasing attacks on religious belief, supernaturalism, and Biblical veracity, would lose the faith in which they had been raised. She had cause for worry.

Her youngest child, as an old man, remembered her with awe: 'I have no hesitation in saying that the most important part in my education was the religious teaching given to me by my mother, who had been brought up in the Manse of Lanark, and I simply accepted

---

4. Campbell Douglas (1828–1910) son of the parish minister at Kilbarchan who came out at the Disruption. In 1856 he married Elizabeth Menzies, daughter of Professor Allen. After Pilkington left for England he was the Cowans' architect of choice, designing the Cowan Institute, Penicuik (1893). Best known for his Scots Baronial North Leith Church and his Italianate Kelvinside Free Church, a Glasgow landmark.

5. Wahab, Catharine. 'Catharine Menzies' handwritten memoir in the possession of Judith A MacLeod. 37-8.

as gospel everything that she taught me. My father backed her up, but his teaching led me by degrees to look at things from a broader point of view.'[6] It was apparent to the more perceptive that Charles Cowan had become detached from his wife's simple acceptance of earlier certainties.

The Changing Role of Women

Change was inevitable but there was much anxiety about how much would be lost in the process. And change was affecting not just the church: it was being felt in society. Women's position in society was very much a part of the conversation and forms part of the context in which long-standing cultural identities were being challenged. With all of his strong-minded and independent daughters it was predictable that progressive Charles Cowan would be caught up in the early debates about women's rights.

In Edinburgh the issue focussed on whether women should be allowed to become doctors, given the possibility of immodesty and impropriety while treating male patients. In 1869 Sophia Jex-Blake, along with four other qualified women later known as 'the Edinburgh Five', signed the matriculation roll at the University of Edinburgh to begin training in medicine. In reaction, the 1870 *Regulations for the Education of Women in Medicine in the University of Edinburgh* stipulated that they would receive tuition in all classes separate from men, thus necessitating higher fees. Professors were *permitted* but not *required* to conduct classes for women.

Opposition to mixed classes was led by the distinguished Professor, Sir Robert Christison, Bt., aged 70, who felt women's role was to be housekeepers and mothers. If they sought otherwise, midwifery was always an option. So in spite of more enlightened university personnel such as Dr Masson, and on-going agitation in their favour, the women continued in separate classes. Matters came to a head on 18 November 1870 when the Edinburgh Five attempted to enter Surgeon's Hall to take their anatomy examination under a sympathetic professor, Dr Handyside. There was a riot, the women forced their way in, took the exam successfully, in spite of a sheep

6. J. J. Cowan. *From 1846 to 1932* Edinburgh: Pillans and Wilson, 1932. 103-4.

being let loose in the room as a distraction. 'The riot at Surgeons' Hall became a landmark in the history of the medical women's campaign.'[7]

The Cowan family had long had a financial interest in the Royal Infirmary, the teaching hospital for the University of Edinburgh. Charles as a donor had considerable clout at the Annual Meeting of Contributors where, at the beginning of January, thirty-four Directors were appointed. As the 1871 meeting approached, the rhetoric became rancorous: 'circulating among the subscribers to the Infirmary [were] documents descriptive of scenes in dissecting-rooms and in the operating theatres, grossly prurient in spirit and elaborately indecent in language.'[8] Usually the meeting was held in the Edinburgh Council Chambers but with heightened interest the venue shifted to St Giles Church. Sophia Jex-Blake, who was now a contributor and thus eligible to speak, made a spirited defence of her position and got involved in a confrontation with Dr Christison over whether his assistant had been intoxicated during the Surgeon's Hall riot. Charles Cowan, described at the meeting as 'everyone's friend',[9] was elected a manager, as was Dr Masson who was noted for his empathy for women in medicine.

The debate continued at the 1872 meeting. Two panels of Managers were nominated, one opposed to women in medicine and the other, put forward by Charles Cowan, was favourable. Charles' panel was elected by a vote of 177 for, 168 against. Dr Masson moved that all registered medical students be given the educational opportunities of the Infirmary and when that motion was about to be carried those opposed to women in medicine walked out, making the vote unanimous.

At the 1873 Annual Meeting of Contributors 550 were present. James Cowan as Provost was in the chair and referred to 'both sides of the present question'. Charles Cowan, at his side, then addressed the packed and agitated crowd producing an alternate slate than the one proposed. He began with a reference to the 'hereditary interest

---

7. Robers, Shirley *Sophia Jex-Blake A Woman's Pioneer in Nineteenth Century Medical Reform* London: Routledge, 1993. 103.

8. *Scotsman,* 16 December 1870.

9. *Scotsman,* 3 January 1870.

he took in this venerable and noble institution.' He went on to say that 'He voted last year with the ladies, for he thought they had been somewhat ungenerously treated.' But his view had changed. He now thought 'it was premature to advocate the extension or perpetuation of facilities for female students beyond what was necessary for the present ladies to complete their medical education'. He felt assured that 'if it was promulgated now that young people of both sexes were to be educated medically together and in the same classes it would create a feeling of insuperable aversion – he might say repulsion – throughout the whole families of every rank and degree. He thought that if the object was good it might be attained by means of a medical female college and to the institution, if it appeared to be based upon proper principles, he would be most happy to contribute liberally.' He then referred – somewhat condescendingly it appears – to 'his friend Miss Jex Blake for whom he had great respect – who knew but that that accomplished lady might become Principal of the institution or possibly the professor of military surgery?' Three new managers were up for election: 'Mr Cowan's slate,' equivocating over the admission of women to the medical faculty, was elected by a vote of 279 to 271. The Infirmary, it was argued, could not go against their contributors.

Cowan's attempt at cheap humour was not appreciated. A subsequent leader in *The Scotsman* was scathing. His ingenuous claim that he did not know what the position of the three whom he had nominated was in regards to women studying at the Infirmary was mocked. 'Alone, of all men in Edinburgh, or indeed in Scotland, he knew nothing of the matter, and sought to commend himself to his audience by the preliminary statement that he had not the least idea what he was about.' The editorial went on 'From this it clearly appears that, if Mr Charles Cowan is not blind, he never reads; and that, if he is not deaf, he never hears ... this decay, or utter extinction, of two of Mr Cowan's senses, is the more remarkable as it must have taken place since this time last year when he voted for election of managers favourable to the admission of ladies and yet claims he doesn't know whether he is voting consistently or in contradiction to last year.'[10]

10. *Scotsman*, 8 January 1873.

Soon after this donnybrook, a ruling by James Cowan as Provost was supposed to have settled the issue as it affirmed the right of the Edinburgh Five to do rounds on Sunday mornings with a sympathetic professor. Sabbatarian scruples were raised as a red herring, but James reminded the agitators that there was good precedent in the Gospels for healing not being contrary to the Sabbath. Then the Court of Session legally barred women from studying medicine in Edinburgh. With that decision the Edinburgh Five, led by Sophia Jex-Blake, decamped. Four years later she received her MD at Basle and gained the License of the King's and Queen's College of Physicians. She returned to Edinburgh, set up a practice, and in 1886 founded the Edinburgh School of Medicine for Women.

Charles Cowan does not come out of the Sophia Jex-Blake imbroglio with great credit. His ear seems to have been close to the ground, assessing the public mood and, always the compromiser, trying to bring two irreconcilable positions together. Meanwhile his daughter was moving ahead with the times. Charlotte Wilson, as a colleague of Josephine Butler,[11] served on the Central Council of Women and fought for women's rights, particularly those in the sex trade, enlisting other family members in the cause. She was regarded as even better on the stump than her pacifist husband Henry Joseph Wilson, for twenty-seven years the fiercely independent minded and courageous MP for Holmforth.[12]

---

11. Josephine Butler (1828–1906) a radical Victorian feminist and Christian was a campaigner against the Contagious Diseases Act which regularized prostitution. In her *A Victorian Feminist Christian* (Milton Keynes: Paternoster, 2004) Lisa Nolland states that Henry Wilson was a Congregationalist (227, 286) which belies his strong Quaker commitments. Quakers were early allies with Butler in her activism.

12. Henry Joseph Wilson, MP (1833–1914) graduate of University College, London. Farmed from 1853-1867, married Charlotte Cowan 23 Nov. 1859. Charlotte's sister Elizabeth after a visit shortly after the wedding warned: 'I think a husband will always respect his wife more when he sees that she has an opinion of her own, and if need be, gives it up for his.' Anderson, Mosa. *Henry Joseph Wilson: Fighter for Freedom 1833–1914*. London: James Clarke & Co, 1953. 14. Charlotte never became a Quaker, worshipping in Queen St Congregational Church, Sheffield, where she conducted a mother's meeting. In 1867 Henry joined brother Wycliffe Wilson in the family business, Sheffield Smelting Co. MP for Holmforth and a Home Ruler 1885–1912. In 1895 he went to India as a member of the Royal Commission on Opium Traffic. Six children, one died as a child. Oldest son was Cecil Henry Wilson (1862–1945). MP for Sheffield

Charlotte and Henry's daughter, Helen Mary Wilson,[13] Charles Cowan's granddaughter, was a true pioneer among women in medicine. She was an 1891 graduate of the London School of Medicine for Women, which had been set up by Sophia Jex-Blake after her Edinburgh rejection and before returning to Edinburgh. At the age of twenty-eight Dr. Helen Wilson became House Surgeon at the London Temperance Hospital. She went on to set up her own practice in Sheffield and campaigned with her parents against the state regulation of prostitution. She was Honourary Secretary and President of the Association for Moral and Social Hygiene, President of the Sheffield Women's Suffrage Society, and an early suffragette. She and Sophia Jex-Blake were kindred spirits.

Three of Charles' other daughters were likewise women of great courage and individuality, each making a life East of Suez. 'I have contributed three daughters to India, one to each of its three Presidencies, and their husbands, all Government officers, are respectively Irish, Scotch, and English. I doubt if anyone else can say the same thing.'[14] It was said with paternal pride. Each daughter had inherited their father's risk-taking sense of adventure.

A threefold challenge to the Free Church

Callum Brown dates what he calls 'The Decay of Evangelicalism' from 1880, but evidence in the Free Church demonstrates that the signs were already present in the previous decade. 'From within the churches,' Brown states, 'evangelical certainty was dissolving because of the cumulative effect of the liberalisation of presbyterian

---

Attercliffe 1922-31, 35-44 See Fowler, W.S. *A Study in Radicalism and Dissent: the Life and Times of Henry Joseph Wilson 1833-1914.* London: Epworth Press, 1961. Other Wilson historical material includes: Wilson, Helen Mary; 'The Osgaathorpe Family and Its Descendants' (monograph dated 25 May 1937); 'Cecil Henry Wilson (1862-1945)' 16 pp monograph; 'Alexander Cowan Wilson (1866-1955) Testimony, London Yearly Meeting, May 1955.

13. Helen Mary Wilson (1864-1951) was born in Mansfield, Nottinghamshire, educated at Sheffield High School for Girls, Bedford College London, and the London School of Medicine for Women. Her papers are held in London Metropolitan University: The Women's Library, 25 Old Castle Street, London E1 7NT. Reference: GB 106 10/29.

14. *Reminiscences*, 374.

standards, the modernisation of worship, and most crucially because of the inexorable advance of biblical criticism.'[15]

(1) Liberalisation of Presbyterian standards

As we have seen, just eight years after the Disruption Charles Cowan in the 1851 debate about the Universities (Scotland) Bill had referred to the Westminster subordinate standards, the historic creed sworn by all clergy and elders of the Church on their ordination, as a 'volume of dogmatic theology, containing many abstruse points with which none but accomplished theologians could well be expected to grapple.' William Lockhart, MP for Lanark and a member of the Established Church, had expressed consternation at Cowan's denigration of the Confession of Faith. When union with the United Presbyterians was deliberated Cowan had little patience with scruples raised about its perceived laxity in its subscription requirement.[16] As events unfolded, it appeared that the Established Church of Scotland had greater concern for doctrinal orthodoxy and less desire for theological novelty or intellectual respectability than the Free Church.

(2) Modernisation of worship: Moody and Sankey

The modernisation of worship, Brown's second evidence for the decay of evangelicalism, is a complex issue. In their worship historically many Presbyterians and Reformed Christians have traditionally followed the 'regulative principle' which meant that only those elements specifically stated in the Bible, or drawn out of it by good and necessary inference, are permissible in the public worship of Almighty God. Traditionally, in Scottish Presbyterianism, the exclusive and unaccompanied use of metrical psalms was regarded as the only Biblically authorized means of praise. The precentor with his tuning fork and the preacher with his Bible were the mark of Scottish

---

15. Brown, Callum *Religion and Society in Scotland since 1707*. Edinburgh: Edinburgh University Press,1997.125

16. There is a useful recent summary of the United Presbyterian culture in Pickard, Willis. *The Member For Scotland* (Edinburgh: Birlinn, 2011). 95-6. He says: 'The well-to-do [United Presbyterian] laity held much power in these churches of a 'polite' character, and it was claimed that ministers were chosen more for their oratory or social connections than for religious zeal.' (96)

Presbyterianism after the Reformation. With the rise of paraphrases and then the occasional use of hymns, exclusive psalm singing was under some threat. Now all that was to be openly challenged by two young Midwestern American evangelists.

When the Cowans moved to Murrayfield in 1870 they cast about for a local Free Church. Charles would retain his membership in Penicuik, where he was a founding elder, but a church in the city was important to the family. A variety of Free Churches were on offer, though the young Disruption pulpit luminaries in the city, such as Robert Candlish of Free St George's and Thomas Guthrie of Free St John's, were coming to the end of their careers. Candlish's successor, thirty-five year old Alexander Whyte, typified the change.[17] Whyte, born to an unwed mother in Kirriemuir, flagged a new era in the pulpit style of the Free Church: literary, urbane, ecumenical ('catholic' was the word used – he was a friend of Cardinal Newman), at times sentimental, and more topical and thematic than expository in his sermons. For forty years Whyte was the iconic Free Church preacher.

The Cowans however settled on Barclay Free Church of Scotland, not their nearest but chosen for its unique quality of life and particularly for its minister, James Hood Wilson, who not only impacted the Cowan family but also the direction of the Free Church. Wilson, who grew up in the secession church, entered New College in 1848 and on graduation was appointed a home missionary to 'The Chalmers Territorial Church, Fountainbridge.' There, as a devoted pastor, mesmerizing preacher, and creative evangelist, he succeeded in building up a congregation of over a thousand. His 'services for men in working clothes' became legendary. Home mission work 'has been my meat and my drink, my sleep, my study, my recreation, my very life' he told the 1866 General Assembly.[18] As Charles Cowan soon discovered, he was a remarkable man.

The Ulster revival of 1859-60 profoundly impacted Wilson. Returning from Ireland, where he had seen 'God's river in spate', he was approached about a bequest of £10,000 from a Miss Barclay. She had designated the money for building a new Free Church. Would

17. Alexander Whyte (1836–1921) served at St George's Free, later UF, for fifty years. From 1909 he was also Principal of New College, University of Edinburgh.

18. Wells, James. *James Hood Wilson* 2nd Ed London: Hodder and Stoughton, 1905. 72.

Wilson move from Fountainbridge to the more affluent area in a site carved out of The Meadows, an Edinburgh park? Frederick Thomas Pilkington, a close friend of John Cowan,[19] was engaged as architect and he created a striking Franco-Venetian Edinburgh landmark: the 250 foot steeple still dominates the Edinburgh skyline and the heart-shaped sanctuary with three balconies seated 1200. Wilson, styling himself an 'evangelical Calvinist', quickly filled the church.

At Charles Cowan's funeral James Hood Wilson described his relationship to Barclay church: 'He kept a formal connection as member and elder with his old congregation at Penicuik, but in 1869, when he came to reside in this neighbourhood, he became a frequent worshipper in the Barclay Church, and for many years he has been constant in his attendance at the ordinary services and especially at the dispensation of the Lord's Supper.' Wilson held services in Westerlea and was a frequent visitor to the home.

James Hood Wilson was a warm-hearted, passionate and pastoral man. 'His theology could not be of a hard, a controversial, or a legal type; and he was in no danger of putting the subordinate standard [i.e., the Westminster Confession of Faith] in the place of the supreme, for he lived and had his being in the Bible,' his biographer wrote. Moderator of the Free Church in 1895, Wilson stood on the sidelines during the theological controversies then engulfing the Free Church. 'He greatly disliked the process of lightening the ship by minimising the creed,' his biographer noted.[20] 'He believed that public controversy was no particular part of his calling, and that he had neither the time, nor the scholarship, nor the training needed for interposing with good effect ... He therefore did not turn aside from the white harvest field into the heated arena of controversy.'[21] That was an approach that appealed to Charles Cowan.

---

19. John Cowan *Diary 18 November 1860 – 24 November 1869* On 4 June 1861 John Cowan and Pilkington left for Germany (Cologne) on to Pyrenees, returning 29 July. Diary in the possession of Elizabeth and Jane Errington, Elie, Fifeshire, Scotland, and used by kind permission.

20. Wells, James. *James Hood Wilson* 2nd Ed London: Hodder and Stoughton, 1905. 177-178.

21. Wells, James. *James Hood Wilson* 2nd Ed London: Hodder and Stoughton, 1905. 183.

Wilson saw revival in the Free Church as a way out of the rancour that had attended the negotiations with the United Presbyterians and a sense that the denomination was becalmed. Not that he wanted a shallow emotionalism: he sought lasting spiritual well-being and health for the church. He longed for another Pentecost 'when intense religious feeling became electric.'[22] The news of the arrival of the American evangelist Dwight Lyman Moody in England in the summer of 1873 seemed the answer to his longing. Wilson, along with John Kelman of the North Leith Free Church, invited Moody to lead a series of evangelistic meetings in Edinburgh that November.

Moody was an unordained Chicago shoe salesman with minimal education, who spoke ungrammatically in a flat New England twang but who had developed a reputation: 'When Moody speaks, everybody listens. Even those who do not like him,' stated a reporter visiting his Chicago church.[23] He was bringing with him his accompanist and singer, Ira David Sankey. When they arrived at Waverley Station they failed to connect with Wilson who later found them on Princes Street looking for a hotel. When the news of their arrival began spreading, Edinburgh was appalled. University students nominated Moody to be rector of the university at their traditional nominating meeting accompanied by boisterous laughter.

On 23 November 1873, a Sunday evening, in Edinburgh's Music Hall Moody and Sankey began their historic city-wide mission. Disaster struck immediately: Moody lost his voice, James Hood Wilson had to preach as a fill-in, and Sankey's melodeon was nowhere to be seen. The carriage carrying it, hurrying through the streets of Edinburgh, had overturned, and as Sankey remembered, 'The kist was in a sadly demoralized condition and its appearance now strangely suggestive of its Scotch name [bagpipes].' Moody regained his voice and Sankey his harmonium for the next day's meeting in Barclay Church, which soon was completely inadequate for the crowds as hundreds had to be turned away each night. The

---

22. Wells, James. *James Hood Wilson* 2nd Ed London: Hodder and Stoughton, 1905. 214-5.

23. George, Timothy. *Mr Moody and the Evangelical Tradition* London: T & T Clark International. 2004. 3.

Music Hall was soon engaged, and then, as numbers swelled, the Free Church Assembly Hall. Nothing had been seen like it in Scotland for generations and the story was repeated in Glasgow to even larger crowds.

Moody's appeal to someone like Cowan was immediate: he was a self-made businessman, a gifted salesperson, a no-nonsense raconteur with engaging stories and a minimum of theological gobbledygook. He had a special cachet for the wealthy. A friend said that Moody's weakness was his 'Ambition to lead and influence Rich Men.'[24] At the 1884 dedication of the Carrubber's Close Mission – James Hood Wilson was a board member for fifty years – Moody announced that the building had a deficit. He then turned to Charles Cowan and five other businessmen on the platform, 'who would help him to complete the £1000 (Laughter and applause).'[25]

As Ira Sankey played the third night of the Moody Edinburgh meetings, hymn-writer Horatius Bonar sat next to the harmonium placed in front of the imposing high pulpit.[26] At the end of the service, he leaned over and said, 'Well Mr. Sankey, you sang the gospel tonight.'[27] Music was an integral part of the Moody-Sankey meetings. With catchy tunes and simple lyrics Sankey put a new song on the lips of many Scots, particularly in the Free Church. James Hood Wilson was in that vanguard: 'Very largely through his influence,' his biographer states, 'the Free Church was gradually brought to recognise the great store of spiritual power that is treasured up in hymnology.'[28] Wilson compiled hymnbooks for Sunday School use 'and paved the way for the more extensive use of hymns in the ordinary services'.

---

24. D. W. Whittle in Bebbington, David. 'Moody as a Transatlantic Evangelical' in George, Timothy. *Mr Moody and the Evangelical Tradition* London: T & T Clark International. 2004 . 85-6.

25. *Scotsman* 5 March 1884.

26. Horatius Bonar (1808–1889) hymn and devotional writer was married to Jane Catharine Lundie who predeceased him in 1884.

27. *Sankey's Story of His Own Life* Christian Biography Resources http://www.wholesomewords.org/biography/biosankey3.pdf. Accessed 27 February 2012.

28. Wells, James. *James Hood Wilson* 2nd Ed London: Hodder and Stoughton, 1905. 132.

Charles Cowan's daughter, Elizabeth Lundie, was deeply affected by Moody's ministry. Her husband, Rev. Robert Henry Lundie of Birkenhead, a member of the first New College graduating class, heard Moody in Chicago during his 1867 visit to North America. He invited Moody and Sankey to Liverpool. Lundie reported after the first week of meetings that '[a] prestige has gathered around the names of "Moody and Sankey" which collects vast audiences in any town in England, and certain it is that those who assemble hear the Gospel plainly and earnestly spoken.' What impressed Lundie was Moody's ability to reach out to 'persons of different classes – workers, non-church-goers, women only, and men professing anxiety about their souls.'[29] At Elizabeth's funeral in 1921 it was said that 'Dr. and Mrs. Lundie threw themselves into that movement.... Many who were strangers to the faith of Jesus Christ were led to confess Him. Many Christian people, too, received spiritual quickening. I venture to suggest our friend did.' As for many others, Moody and Sankey's visit was a highlight of her long life.

Elizabeth's brother-in-law, Horatius Bonar, defended Moody from a complaint by John Kennedy of Dingwall, a leading Free Church conservative confessionalist, that he was indulging in hyper-evangelism. '[T]he harmonium and the hymn-singing ought not to commend themselves to some; but still, discounting these "blots," as some will call them, did there not remain enough of excellence behind to warrant our rejoicing in the work as genuine?'[30] Kennedy did have a point: Sankey's melodeon playing challenged the worship of the Free Church, Moody's communication of the good news arguably reflected McLeod Campbell's emphasis on universal salvation[31]

29. Lundie, R. H. 'Messrs Moody and Sankey in Liverpool–I' *The Messenger and Missionary Record* (1 March 1875), 56. Archives of the United Reformed Church, Westminster College, Cambridge, UK.

30. Bonar, Horatius. *Evangelism A Reformed Debate*. Trowbridge, Wilshire: James Begg Society, 1997. 78. Bonar was replying to John Kennedy of Dingwall's *Hyper-Evangelism*.

31. Campbell, John McLeod (1800-1872) C of S minister, Row, Dumbartonshire from 1824 until deposed by GA in 1831 for heterodox views on the atonement. Joined the Congregationalists. His classic The Nature of the Atonement rejected penal substitution and any 'legalism,' and emphasized the love of God the Father, verging on universalism.

rather than John Calvin's particular redemption.[32] 'Historically the judgement of Bonar,' one recent commentator has noted, 'that Moody's teaching was thoroughly Calvinistic may well seem naive since the campaign now appears to have been a turning point in the transition from the old Calvinism to a less doctrinal Evangelicalism with quite different emphases.'[33] Charles Cowan was caught up in this transformation and felt comfortable with it and particularly with one of its leading proponents, his own minister and friend, James Hood Wilson.

Some in the next generation were not so impressed. John James, Charles' youngest son who lived on in Westerlea after his marriage on 19 August 1869 to Sophy Gillespie, thought otherwise. He chafed under the three-quarter-hour sermons of 'a very earnest man with a very large congregation'. 'I must admit,' he added, 'that although I had a great admiration for Dr. Wilson, I was really happier when not in his presence.' Three years later John James and Sophy, who was Episcopalian, left Barclay Church. They joined others who were abandoning the Free Church of their parents in the 1870s.[34]

(3) Biblical criticism: William Robertson Smith

A third indication that evangelicalism was declining – what Brown called 'the inexorable advance of biblical criticism' – followed from the other two. Much of Moody's appeal was his folksy style of popular preaching with its use of stories and humour, a far cry from pulpit fare at the time of the Disruption. Unlike another travelling evangelist George Whitefield a century earlier, it was neither specifically doctrinal nor intellectually rigorous, appealing more to the heart than the head. Moody's great gift was his ability to communicate and in this he was superb.

32. Cf Carnegie Simpson about Moody 'His preaching of a 'a free Gospel' to all sinners did more to relieve Scotland generally–that is to say, apart from a limited number of select minds–of the old hyper-Calvinistic doctrine of election and of what theologians call 'a limited atonement' and to bring home a sense of the love and grace of God towards all men, than did even the teaching of John Macleod Campbell.' *The Life of Principal Rainy*. London: Hoder and Stoughton, 1909, Vol 1, 408.

33. Ross, Kenneth R. 'Calvinists in Controversy: John Kennedy, Horatius Bonar and the Moody Mission of 1873-74' *Scottish Bulletin of Evangelical Theology* Vol 9, No 1, 61.

34. Cowan, J. J. *From 1846 to 1932* (Edinburgh: Pillans & Wilson, 1933). 106.

Not that there was unanimity among the Disruption patriarchs on the subject of Biblical inspiration. John James Cowan recalled his father sending him an article on inspiration by Robert Candlish,[35] while he was in Switzerland studying in 1863, in order to have it translated into French. 'He told them they must use their brains in their search of the Scriptures and that verbal inspiration was not to be thought of.'

Charles Cowan, a man of personal and traditional piety, with intellectual curiosity and a thirst for new discovery, was open to the new Biblical scholarship. Julius Wellhausen and other scholars on the Continent had challenged the historical credibility and reliability of the first five books of the Old Testament. The development of the four gospels had already been questioned in Tűbingen by Bruno Bauer and David Strauss. This was impacting Scottish divinity students: for instance, John James Stevenson, Campbell Douglas' partner, went into architecture after two years at Tubingen, giving up on parish ministry.

The saintly but disorganized and eccentric 'Rabbi' Duncan, the first Old Testament professor at New College, had been too detached to provide much ballast for the approaching conflict. 'It is unmistakable,' one recent analysis states, 'that he failed as a teacher to pass on his own faith and theology.'[36] Duncan was followed by Andrew Bruce Davidson who, after a summer in Gottingen, found the new critical views irresistible.[37] He, in turn, greatly influenced

35. The argument started in the 1863 General Assembly over the inclusion of the Apocrypha in editions of the Bible. Candlish's *Reason and Revelation* then appeared. The Colenso affair escalated matters. One letter to the *Scotsman* (signed TSG) ended 'if Colenso ought not to be a Bishop of the Church of England, neither ought Dr Candlish to be a clergyman of the Free Church of Scotland, or the Principal of its college in Edinburgh. Certain if we are to uphold verbal inspiration at all, I think the attitude of the Confession of Faith the best.' *Scotsman* 18 February 1864. Vide Nicholas Needham's *The Doctrine of Holy Scripture in the Free Church Fathers*. Edinburgh: Rutherford House, 19911. 120-124.

36. Finlayson, Sandy *Unity and Diversity: The Founders of the Free Church*. Fearn: Christian Focus Publications, 2010. 233.

37. Andrew Bruce Davidson (1831–1902) succeeded 'Rabbi' Duncan as Professor of Hebrew and Old Testament at New College in 1863. He was an early devotee of Julius Wellhausen and was opposed to aspects of the Westminster Confession. He was primarily a brilliant linguist.

his student William Robertson Smith, a most attractive and devout individual. It seemed that each generation was more susceptible to the new continental approach, although retaining the original warm piety of the Disruption. The Free Church of Scotland was moving toward a showdown.

This was provided on 7 December 1875 when an article titled 'Bible' appeared in the ninth edition of the *Encyclopaedia Britannica*. Written by William Robertson Smith, now Professor of Hebrew at the Aberdeen College of the Free Church, it called for the Bible to 'be tested by the evidence which the books themselves offer to the judicious critic.'[38] As a judicious critic, it was claimed, Robertson Smith found little in the Old Testament to inspire confidence in the veracity of the sacred text or the trustworthiness of Jesus as its interpreter.

Robertson Smith was the son of a Free Church minister. He had impressive credentials, and as a multitalented scholar he excelled both in Biblical studies and in scientific and mathematical subjects. He had been greatly influenced by Andrew Bruce Davidson, his Old Testament Professor, who opened him to the new scholarship. At the age of twenty-four, after two sessions of study in Germany, Robertson Smith was appointed by the Free Church to an academic position at its Aberdeen theological college. Youth and inexperience would be factors in the ensuing tragedy.

It was a Church of Scotland minister, Archibald Hamilton Charteris, Professor of Biblical Criticism and Biblical Antiquities at the University of Edinburgh, who first flagged Smith in an anonymous review which appeared on 16 April 1876 in the *Edinburgh Evening Courant*. 'We regret that a publication which will be admitted without suspicion into many a religious household, and many a carefully guarded public library, should upon so important a matter as the records of our faith, take a stand – a decided stand – on the wrong side. We hope that the publisher and the editor will look after the contributors – or after each other – and cease to pass off rationalistic speculations as ascertained facts.'[39]

38. Black, John Sutherland and Chrystal, George. *The Life of William Robertson Smith*. London: Adam and Charles Black, 1912. 186.

39. Black, John Sutherland and Chrystal, George. *The Life of William Robertson Smith*. London: Adam and Charles Black, 1912. 189.

A blizzard of articles, pamphlets, and sermons soon appeared. Smith's encyclopaedia contribution was referred to the Free Church's College Committee, which indicated its unhappiness with Smith's views, particularly on the authorship and composition of the book of Deuteronomy. The Presbytery of Aberdeen became involved and raised the matter at the General Assembly of 1877. Under Smith's own prodding (because he wanted vindication), the issue came up as a 'Libel' charging him with a breach of the Westminster Confession's statement on Scripture. Smith was quoted seven times implicitly (or explicitly) denying this. Smith's position of influence and responsibility in a divinity faculty made the offence more egregious.

'I attended all the morning sittings of the General Assembly of the Free Church, 1877,' Cowan wrote shortly thereafter, 'but owing to my age and the state of my health, I was never present in the evening.' That Tuesday evening, 29 May 1877, two competing motions were brought: a recommendation from the Colleges Committee, moved by Dr Wilson of Dundee, that the Smith article contains 'statements of a dangerous and unsettling tendency', the other from James Stuart Candlish, son of Robert and a proponent of the new Biblical criticism, that the Presbytery trial be allowed to take its course, in effect to do nothing. The vote was 491 to 113 in favour of the Wilson motion, 106 abstained or did not vote, among them Charles Cowan. 'I had to leave the Assembly, owing to the dense crowd and the closeness of the atmosphere,' he explained. 'Professor Smith,' he stated, 'is not an ordinary man, whose talent and piety I trust are to be blessed to the young men under his charge and to the people of Scotland.' Alexander Whyte had invited Smith to preach at St George's the previous Sunday and Cowan was impressed.

The case went on to appeals, and the 1879 Assembly, by a single vote, 321 to 320, served the libel on Smith. Had Charles still been a commissioner the vote would have been tied. The libel was an admonishment of Smith, taking his professorship from him, but allowing him to remain a minister. The following year's General Assembly, after a lengthy debate which lasted into the early hours of the morning, William Robertson Smith was officially admonished by the church but allowed to retain his appointment. He responded with contrition: 'I feel that, in the providence of God, this is a very weighty lesson, to one placed, as I am, in the position of a teacher, and I hope that by His grace I shall not fail to learn by it.'[40]

Ten days after the Assembly adjourned, a further incriminating article written by Smith titled 'Hebrew Language and Literature,' appeared in the *Encyclopaedia*'s eleventh volume, directly challenging the historicity and credibility of much of the Old Testament. This further exacerbation of the conflict led to a Commission being appointed that summer. In October, subject to confirmation by next year's General Assembly, Smith was dismissed from his post, on the grounds that his approach 'demonstrated a singular lack of sympathy with the reasonable anxieties of the Church as to the bearing of critical speculations on the integrity and authority of Scripture.'[41]

After that decision was released, Cowan leant his name and reputation in a last ditch attempt to rescue Smith. His name headed a list of eleven elders on a circular summoning a conference of 'elders connected with the congregations in the Free Presbytery of Edinburgh who are dissatisfied with the recent action of the Commission of Assembly in regard to the Aberdeen College Case.' Approximately one hundred people attended a meeting on 10 December 1880 in the YMCA on St Andrew Street. Dr Benjamin Bell chaired the meeting.[42] He combined a commitment to the most up-to-date science with a deep piety and opened the meeting with a Bible reading and prayer. He then made clear that 'the meeting was intended exclusively for those office-bearers of the Church who were dissatisfied with the recent action of the Commission of Assembly in the case of Professor Smith (Applause).'[43] The meeting was described

40. Black, John Sutherland and Chrystal, George. *The Life of William Robertson Smith*. London: Adam and Charles Black, 1912. 360.

41. Black, John Sutherland and Chrystal, George. *The Life of William Robertson Smith*. London: Adam and Charles Black, 1912. 425.

42. Benjamin Bell FRCSE (1810–1882) was connected with the surgical department of the Royal Infirmary, opened two years before, and generously endowed by the Cowans. He was grandson of the pioneer surgeon of the same name, and father of Joseph Bell, Conan Doyle's inspiration for Sherlock Holmes.

43. *Scotsman*, 11 December 1880.

as private, and reporters withdrew, as did an elder who had not understood the tenor of the meeting. After two hours of discussion, a committee was appointed who were to report back.

It was too late. Robertson Smith was stripped of his academic post at the 1881 General Assembly. The two Cowan commissioners were sharply divided. Charles William voted as his father would have, siding with those who wanted to exonerate Robertson Smith, His uncle John cast his ballot the other way. Their votes cancelled each other out, but the tally was 423 against and 245 voting for Alexander Whyte's motion to retain him.

Robertson Smith may have lost the final vote, but the importance of his case in dramatically changing the Free Church of Scotland cannot be denied. The victory that those anxious to put to rest once and for all the questions raised by Robertson Smith proved to be a Pyrrhic one, as the next generation of Free Churchmen were of a different breed. Laymen such as Charles Cowan could not see that the drift was an indication of just how far he (and others like him) had gone in their zeal for what they were assured was the latest scholarship. After all, in the close-knit fraternity that was the Free Church of Scotland – men like Robertson Smith, Marcus Dods, and James Stuart Candlish with their scholarly innovations – were children of Evangelicals well known to Cowan. Robertson Smith was the son of William Pirie Smith of Keig, an Aberdeenshire cleric who had come out at great personal cost during the Disruption in 1843. Cowan, as was mentioned earlier, had picnicked on the Pentland Hills with Marcus Dods senior. How could their sons be that destructive to the unity and future of the Free Church?

At the centenary of the birth of Robertson Smith, Principal Carnegie Simpson[44] said that the case 'touched to the quick the nerve of Scottish piety'.[45] Robertson Smith continues to resonate. Professor F. F. Bruce, a leading twentieth century Evangelical Biblical scholar and a member of the Brethren, found in Robertson Smith's

44. Patrick Carnegie Simpson (1865–1947), Professor of Church History, Westminster College, Cambridge (1914–1938) and biographer of Principal Robert Rainy.

45. Smith, Carnegie, 'The Robertson Smith Controversy: Some Personal Recollections' *British Weekly*, October 1946.

writings help 'as a student in wrestling with the implications of Biblical criticism'.[46] Bruce is summarized at the end of this recent biography, as 'a believing critic' just like Robertson Smith.[47]

'In 1875,' J. R. Fleming, a Scottish church historian of the next generation, stated, 'the ideas of a static Revelation and a verbally infallible Bible held the field almost without question. By the end of the century, all that had changed.'[48] Charles Cowan, who as a young man had spent four hours a day reading his Bible, who noted carefully in his diary the text of every sermon he heard in the 1830s and was critical if the preacher strayed from it, was now, with his church, in a different space. He failed to see that biblical criticism was indeed the crux of the matter. The deposition of Robertson Smith actually hastened, according to Alex Cheyne, 'the ultimate triumph of his approach in the Free Church and its sister Churches of the Presbyterian order in Scotland.'[49] All that Charles Cowan could hardly have anticipated, but it was utterly predictable.

---

46. Glass, Tim. *F F Bruce A Life* (Milton Keyes: Paternoster, 2011). 93.

47. Glass, Tim. *F F Bruce A Life* (Milton Keyes: Paternoster, 2011). 227.

48. Fleming, J. R. *A History of the Church in Scotland 1875–1929* (Edinburgh: T & T Clark, 1933). 16.

49. Cheyne, Alex *The Transforming of the Kirk* Edinburgh: St Andrew Press, 1983. 51.

Chapter 22

Partner No More

Charles Cowan's retirement in April 1875 from the company did not mean that he was slowing down. Greater freedom meant that he could work on his memoirs, which were published two years later as his *Reminiscences*. It was a time for reflection as other changes occurred: conclusion of his forty years at General Assembly and the end of his time at Scottish National Insurance Company because of a merger. It also brought new stresses both in his investments and in some time-honoured relationships. At his time of life old friends died. His brothers' on-going involvement in politics meant that he was called on to be a senior statesman. And those years for the Cowans would be dominated by William Ewart Gladstone.

During the previous year Charles had become identified with one final cause, the Scottish Disestablishment Association. The disestablishment of the (Anglican) Church of Ireland in 1871 was the catalyst for ensuing conversations in Wales, England and Scotland where the United Presbyterians were committed to disestablishment on the basis of principle and because of their heritage and history. The 1874 Free Church General Assembly had been divided with a majority in favour of disestablishment of the Church of Scotland. It took thirty years, in spite of the concerns of Thomas Chalmers, to win a plurality in favour of Voluntaryism.

Charles Cowan was one of three[1] who called a meeting on 26 October 1874 to organize the Scottish Disestablishment Association. A circular had previously been sent out to discover how much support such a group would have and it was now reported that: 'It is the general opinion of Nonconformists that it is now become an imperative duty to call for the disendowment and disestablishment of the present Scottish Ecclesiastical Establishment.'[2] Because of changes recently made in education now was the time to redirect the church's teinds[3] and endowments to local school boards, but emphasizing all the while that such a change which would provide relief for the rates should be done gradually. Cowan's health kept him from attending a second meeting. He got into trouble in a speech promoting disestablishment when he quoted a bishop of the Established Church of England who, he claimed, supported baptismal regeneration thus demonstrating the unreliability of expecting a religious establishment to protect orthodoxy.[4]

At the 1877 Free Church Assembly, Charles spoke to a motion by Robert Rainy, successor to Robert Candlish as Principal of New College, calling on the government 'to terminate the connection of the State with the existing Established Church.' Cowan supported Rainy's motion and said he was in favour of disestablishment, but also 'expressed sympathy with the work which the Established Church was carrying on in the country.' He referred to the apathy and ignorance that he experienced in the House of Commons during debates on ecclesiastical questions. 'It would be better if Parliament had nothing to do with such questions.'[5]

In June 1878 Parliament debated disestablishment of the Church of Scotland for the first time. A Paisley MP asked for a select committee to be formed to discuss the issue but the debate was adjourned and never resumed. Meanwhile a Church Defence Association was formed from the Established Church, comprised of

1. Along with James Morton and John Greig.
2. *Scotsman.* 26 October 1874.
3. Scottish word for tithes, 10% of income.
4. *Scotsman.* 9 March 1875 and 1 April 1875.
5. *Scotsman.* 1 June 1874.

people 'resolved no longer to be under the imputation of coquetting with the Disestablishment party'.[6] Although it was a cause dear to the heart of many Liberals (and to Charles Cowan), Gladstone refused to make it an issue at the 1880 election because international concerns took precedence. It would be more than a generation before Scottish disestablishment was enacted. Cowan saw disestablishment as ensuring his wider goal: the reunion of the three Presbyterian denominations in Scotland.[7] It would not come in his lifetime.

*****

On Charles Cowan's retirement there was a reorganization of the family business. It was part of a strategy, only completed the year Charles died, to make the company a limited partnership. Senior partners, his brothers James and John, were each allocated 4/20 shares. The four junior partners each received 3/20 of the shares: Charles' sons Charles William and John James, Charles William's son Alexander (Charles' grandson, aged 12), and Charles' half-brother George Cowan. The business was also restructured: the three existing partnerships of Valleyfield Mills, the sales and distribution office in Edinburgh, and the sales and distribution office in London, were now merged into a single operation.[8]

Charles Cowan chose the thirtieth anniversary of Thomas Chalmers' funeral to make his final speech to his last General Assembly. He spoke so softly and with such effort that, as the minutes record, he could only be heard 'with difficulty'. As he had for years it was his personal response to the report of the Sustentation Committee. 'He was understood,' the recorder stated apologetically, 'to give an account

6. I. G. C. Hutchison *A Political History of Scotland, 1832-1924* Edinburgh: John Donald, 1986. 148.

7. *Reminiscences,* 330.

8. For this information I am indebted to the PhD thesis of Ying Yong Ding, *A Business History of Alex. Cowan & Sons Ltd., Papermakers, Penicuik, 1779-1965* University of the West of Scotland, 2011. 85. See also her 'Alex. Cowan and Sons, Papermakers, Penicuik, 1779-1975: A Historical Sketch, with Implications for Chandler's Theories' *Scottish Business and Industrial History*. Business Archives Council of Scotland. Vol. 24, Series 2, July 2009. The partnership agreement is with the Penicuik Historical Society, to whom I express my appreciation.

of meetings of the eldership, held at the time of the Disruption, to consider means by which the ministry could be supported in the crisis.' As old men do, and young men tolerate, he reminisced before the Assembly: '[t]hey had much to be thankful for in the wonderful flow of blessings upon their Church within the last thirty years.' It was his last hurrah in the counsels of the Free Church of Scotland.

*****

That was the same year Charles Cowan left the insurance business. Since 1848, he had been a Director of the Scottish National Insurance Company. At its final board meeting on 27 January 1877, Cowan, in the chair, proposed amalgamation with the Scottish Union Insurance Company, 'to unite so as to constitute one wealthy & powerful corporation.' Four days later, the Scottish Union and National Insurance Company came into being. The merger was opposed by two other major Scottish insurance companies,[9] but an act of Parliament approving the amalgamation received royal assent in May 1878 and the merger went ahead.[10]

Charles Cowan, however, was not totally free of the insurance business. Details of a court case are murky, motives are unclear, and the final resolution unknown. It went back to 1848, when fresh from his victory over Macaulay, Charles Cowan was approached by John MacGregor McCandlish to serve on the board of the Scottish National Insurance Company.[11] Twenty-five year old McCandlish, a lawyer, had joined the board as secretary two years previously. Son of the Receiver-General of Taxes for Scotland, McCandlish was one of the earliest actuaries and wrote the definitive book on the subject,

9. North British and Mercantile Insurance Company and the Edinburgh Life Assurance Company.

10. http://www.aviva.com/about-us/heritage/companies/union-insurance-company/

11. John MacGregor McCandlish, FRS, JP, FFA (1821–1901). On his retirement in 1890 from SUIC he became President for two years of the Faculty of Actuaries Edinburgh. Besides his *Encyclopedia Britannica* article he authored *Contributions to the story of insurance, fire and life as a science and an art* Papers read to professional societies and printed with their transactions, 1866-1895. Faculty of Actuaries, Edinburgh. See *Leading Insurance Men of the British Empire* London: Index Publishing, 1892. 130.

as well an article on 'Fire Insurance' in the reputation-shaping (or breaking) *Encyclopedia Britannica*. McCandlish had come out at the time of the Disruption and was an ardent Free Churchman for the rest of his life. In his later years he was the Financial Agent of the Free Church of Scotland, writing a useful summary of its finances at the time of the golden jubilee.[12]

After almost a quarter century of a working relationship the ties between Charles Cowan and John McCandlish began to fray. In 1871, court documents later attested, 'some differences arose among the officials of the Scottish National Insurance Co.' Their ability to work together amicably had been seriously challenged. A committee was appointed and a report made to the whole Board. Resolutions were passed but were kept out of the ordinary Minute Book of the company. Instead they were entrusted to a responsible employee, James Cunningham. It is clear from subsequent disclosures that the matter was between McCandlish and Cowan. The only item in the public minutes that year referring to Charles Cowan may or may not be related: he recused himself as the board agreed to provide him with a personal loan for £6,000 at 3.5% interest. Given the amount involved (and even making allowance for inflation since then), it seems highly unusual for him to seek such a sum unless he was trying to avoid public disclosure.

There the matter rested for four years when there was a quarrel between Charles Cowan and another unnamed individual. McCandlish, as an old friend of Cowan's, was asked to negotiate, though the subject had nothing to do with the Scottish National. It would appear that Cowan did not appreciate McCandlish's subsequent arbitration. Meanwhile Cunningham, the trusted employee of Scottish National, retired and died. In 1878 Cowan went to his widow and asked for a copy of the secret 1871 minutes, claiming his right as a member of the board at the time. She went to the directors of the new company. On learning about Cowan's intention to have them published in a way 'calculated and intended to injure the feelings and reputation' of John

12. Ryley, George Buchanan and McCandlish, John M.; *Scotland's Free Church: An Historical Retrospect And Memorial of the Disruption* London: Arnold Constable and Co., 1893.

McCandlish, which would also be prejudicial to the company, they went to court requesting an interdict against Cowan, to stop him from publishing the incriminating minutes. The 1871 minutes contained, it was claimed, 'false and libelous statements' about McCandlish. It was noted in court documents that McCandlish had made 'repeated and earnest endeavours to adjust the said misunderstanding' but Cowan adamantly refused. McCandlish had not vindicated Cowan in the 1875 arbitration, and somehow publishing the 1871 minutes, which would destroy his reputation, was to satisfy a need either for justice or for revenge.

The ruling of the judge came down on 3 January 1881: 'He regrets exceedingly that parties should have found it necessary to present the Note of Suspension and Interdict and he hopes that by the mediation of neutral friends it will not be necessary to proceed any further therein. He thinks there has been misunderstanding between old friends which mutual explanations tendered and received in frankness would obviate and remove and he cannot suppose that Mr Cowan wishes for a moment to give pain to, or to hurt the feelings of those with whom he has had intimate business and other relations for so long a period of time.' He called for 'an absolute and amicable settlement' 'to which the Lord ordinary cannot too strongly urge.'[13]

There is no indication as to whether there was indeed reconciliation between McCandlish and Cowan. One can only hope there was. The whole case reads like a whodunit and, after a century and a quarter it is difficult to reconstruct what actually happened, either in the 1871 meeting or in the failed arbitration of 1875. Presumably the two are related. It does provide insight into an aging Charles Cowan. It is ironic that at that very moment, Cowan and McCandlish came together to ask for a vindication of William Robertson Smith from the libels that the Commission had recommended and would be ratified by the 1881 General Assembly

*****

13. 'Note of suspension and Interdict for the Scottish Union and National Insurance Co. and John Macgregor McCandlish as a Manager and an Individual against Charles Cowan by A. D. M. Black, Writer to the Signet.' West Record Office, Edinburgh.

Troubles continued to assail Charles Cowan. On 2 October 1878 the collapse of the City of Glasgow Bank impacted him as a major shareholder. The devastating effects of the crash were felt on both sides of the Atlantic. When the Bank had been organized in 1839 much of its initial capitalization of £656,250 had been raised from the rising Scottish middle class. The name 'Bank of the City of Glasgow' was chosen for its similarity to the City Bank of New York, founded in 1812. The Glasgow bank had substantial assets in the United States – investments which, it turned out, they did not understand well and handled poorly. At the centre of the collapse was William John Menzies, Charles Cowan's 1867 travelling companion.

Without today's social assistance safety net, the devastation caused by the failure of the City of Glasgow Bank was widespread and for many irremediable. Widows were left on the street, trust funds were wiped out, and the general misery was appalling. A City of Glasgow Bank Shareholders Relief Fund was set up in Edinburgh and collected £870,397 within the first year, most of it raised in Scotland.

At a meeting of the Edinburgh Association for Improving the Condition of the Poor that December, chairman Charles Cowan noted 'the calamitous character of the year now closing.' 'Mr Cowan remarked that in Scotland, through misplaced confidence in men who apparently – though of course they were entitled to be considered innocent till they were tried – had proved themselves a gang of swindlers and robbers – (applause) – hundreds and thousands of families were involved in penury and ruin; and he was sure that one of the duties of our common religion, perhaps too much neglected hitherto in Scotland, was to consider intelligently and practice earnestly and prayerfully the duty of caring for the poor.'[14]

The ripple effect was felt across the Atlantic. The City of Glasgow Bank's substantial American assets were mostly in railroad stocks, the value of which was, shockingly, largely unknown. John Stewart Kennedy was still the American agent of the Scottish American Investment Company, which Charles Cowan had set up as a result of his North American tour. From his office in New York, Kennedy

14. *Scotsman*, 10 December 1878.

helped William John Menzies sell off all of those railway shares on favourable terms as the stock market started to improve.[15] Kennedy, who acted with great integrity, received little remuneration for his brilliant parlaying of the City of Glasgow Bank's American assets into favourable terms for the liquidators. The blustery and mercurial Menzies, who went to the United States to deal with the situation first-hand and who persistently came between the liquidators and Kennedy, did not come out of the crisis well.

Meanwhile, Charles Cowan, as a shareholder of the Bank, responded to all calls. At the end of 1880, he was one of 123 individuals and 54 trusts that had met every one. Total calls amounted to £2,750 per £100 of stock, so his personal obligation was just over £100,000. He tried unsuccessfully to keep the depositors from pursuing their claims in the judiciary. The Court of Session heard 'the question as to the remuneration of the liquidators of the City of Glasgow Bank' on 16 March 1880. Cowan was singled out as a shareholder 'who entertained moderate and conciliatory views' and 'might be a great aid to the court.'[16] A judge subsequently commended his Christian attitude in the face of the substantial losses he had sustained. His father's attitude toward wealth sustained him. By the time his will was probated nine years later, his estate had been halved as a result of the failure of this bank.

*****

Politics was never far from Charles' view and he took an active role in the formation of the Midlothian Liberal Association in April of 1878 when his brother John was appointed chairman of the Executive Committee. John had little idea at the time that that new responsibility would thrust him into the national spotlight, dominate the last years of his active life, and win him a baronetcy. The new Association spent the first months assessing the strength of the Liberal vote in the constituency and determined that it

15. See Engelbourg, Saul. 'John Stewart Kennedy and the City of Glasgow Bank' *Business and Economic History*, Second Series, Volume Fifteen, 1986. 69–83.

16. *Scotsman* 17 March 1880. 5.

was strong. Thus reassured the Association passed a motion to 'Cordially invite the Right Honourable William Ewart Gladstone to become a candidate for the representation of the county at the first election, and beg to offer the assurance of an enthusiastic and united support.' Gladstone, defeated by Disraeli in the election of 1874, had gone into 'retirement', though retaining his seat in Parliament.

Their invitation was fortuitous. Gladstone had been roused by Disraeli's political machinations and what he regarded as an amoral foreign policy, sentiments with which the Cowan brothers very much agreed. As Ewen Cameron points out, Gladstone's whole subsequent Midlothian campaign (despite its innovation) was based on a recovery of Britain's moral imperative.[17] His campaign speeches would represent an attack on novelty and a return to the old values with which seventy-eight year old Charles Cowan could identify. Cameron quotes a 30 June 1879 letter from Gladstone to John Cowan ('a leading Liberal in Midlothian') in which he states that, should he return to active politics, he would challenge the electorate with 'one comprehensive question, the question whether or not this is the way in which the country wishes to be governed.'[18] For John and his brothers the answer was an emphatic 'No'.

Plans for Gladstone to contest the forthcoming election proceeded apace. All the time John involved his older brother as a veteran politician. Gladstone wrote John Cowan on 4 November, thanking him for his 'loving words' and adding characteristically, 'I have much cause to desire a better strength than my own for the effort that is before me.'[19] He told Cowan his only concern was not to schedule any speech before the main event of the evening 'because physical freshness in such cases is essential.' He inquired from him, and from William Adam, 'what are the particular <u>Scottish</u> subjects to which it would be expedient for me to refer in the course of this

17. Cameron, Ewen A., *Impaled Upon a Thistle: Scotland Since 1880*. Edinburgh: Edinburgh University Press, 2010. 55.

18. Cameron, Ewen A., *Impaled Upon a Thistle: Scotland Since 1880*. Edinburgh: Edinburgh University Press, 2010. 54, quoting BL, Add. MS 44137, fo. 389.

19. WEG to John Cowan, 4 Nov 1879, in the possession of Elizabeth and Jane Errington, Elie, Fifeshire, Scotland, and used by kind permission.

series of speeches.' And he concluded: 'I am sure my friends will understand that they ought not to occupy the foreground while on the other hand practical assurance should be given that they will not be neglected.'

In mid-December the answer was given: if John Cowan and the Executive Committee could guarantee a decided majority he would accept. An immediate canvas was made and 'the grave responsibility of inviting Mr Gladstone to become a candidate' was entrusted to John Cowan. On 30 January it was announced that Gladstone would be their man and was prepared to let his name stand as the Liberal candidate for Midlothian. Teamed with John Cowan on the organizing committee were the fifth Earl of Rosebery, the brilliant twenty-nine year old Archibald Primrose, and the Liberal Chief Whip, William P. Adam.

It is impossible to recapture the excitement generated by the Midlothian campaign of 1879-1880, often described as the first modern political campaign.[20] Gladstone entered it with the fervour of an Old Testament prophet waging a holy war against 'Beaconsfieldism,' Disraeli's cynical and amoral foreign policy *realpolitik*. At seventy-one, his was the vigour of a man utterly convinced of the rightness of his position, seeking to restore Britain's stature after a series of morally ambivalent attempts by Disraeli to prop up the Turks and wage a futile war in Afghanistan and a morally ambivalent one in Zululand. Gladstone, as David Bebbington says, was now engaged in a 'campaign against the government's foreign policy'.[21]

'Remember,' he told a rapt audience of Midlothian electors in November 1879, 'that the sanctity of life in the hill villages of Afghanistan, among the winter snows, is as inviolable in the eye of Almighty God as can be your own. Remember that He who has united you as human beings in the same flesh and blood, has bound you by the law of mutual love; that that mutual love is not

20. Contemporary biographer of Sir John A. Macdonald, Richard D. Gwyn recently claimed this honour for the Canadian nation-builder's campaign of 1876-8. *Nation Maker Sir John A. Macdonald: His Life, Our Times* Vol 2: 1867-1891. Toronto: Random House Canada, 2011. 276.

21. Bebbington, David *William Ewart Gladstone: Faith and Politics in Victorian Britain* Grand Rapids: Wm Eerdmans, 1993, 171 quoting Gladstone's diary.

limited by the shores of this island, is not limited by the boundaries of Christian civilisation; that it passes over the whole surface of the earth, and embraces the meanest along with the greatest in its unmeasured scope.'[22] The Free Church electorate connected with Gladstone's Christian faith and piety, even though he was by now a high church Anglican.

The election was called in early March. Gladstone made his way north by rail, at each stop being greeted by rapturous crowds. John Cowan met him at the station with a formal welcome and he made his way out to Dalmeny House, the Scottish residence of Arthur Primrose, the fifth Earl of Rosebery. Edinburgh Music Hall was filled to capacity on 18 March 1880, with 1,590 ticket-holding electors, 70 reporters, and 180 recipients of platform tickets. A cheer went up when Charles Cowan took his seat on the platform, followed by one for his brother James, as junior MP for Edinburgh. Duncan McLaren, as senior MP, was in the chair. 'The instant the well-known face was visible,' the press reported, 'the whole assembly sprang to their feet and cheered and waved their hats with all the lustiness and goodwill of a parcel of boys, but also with the evident earnestness of feeling of sober-minded men welcoming their chosen leader in a great political struggle.'[23]

Charles Cowan escorted Gladstone to the platform at Corstorphine, near his home in Westerlea, two days after his great Music Hall speech. On 26 March, Gladstone visited Penicuik for 'a reception rivalling in the warmth of its enthusiasm any previous demonstrations connected with his remarkable progress.' The bunting festooning the main street of the village said it all: 'Peace on earth and goodwill to men,' 'Good laws and fair taxes,' 'A fair field for the plough.' Gladstone lunched at Charles William's home and, together, the Cowan family made their way to Penicuik's United Presbyterian Church. There Charles Cowan introduced Gladstone to the crowd, as recorded in the local press the next day: 'Though from Liverpool (accident of birth) [he is] a true Scotsman – [it is]

22. As quoted by John Morley *Life of Gladstone* Vol II London: MacMillan, 1902. 595.

23. *Scotsman* 18 March 1880.

nineteen years since the tax on paper was repealed and we owe it to Gladstone alone. (Cheers) Sorry some papermakers in the country were opposed to Mr. Gladstone, considering the universal blessings which had resulted from the abolition of the tax on paper; he thought any opposition from papermakers was very ungracious and ungrateful (Hear hear) not only blessing this country but upon humanity by his exertions on behalf of the oppressed nationalities of the south of Europe.'

Gladstone then made 'one of the most telling addresses he has made in the course of the memorable campaign,' making a geographic sweep through Austria, Cyprus, and Afghanistan and criticizing 'the acts, at once cruel and impolitic, for which this country has been made responsible.' On 5 April 1880 Gladstone was elected and his party formed the government, with the electors of Midlothian giving him a narrower affirmation than elsewhere. James Cowan was also returned, along with Duncan McLaren, in the constituency of Edinburgh, Portobello, and Musselburgh. Gladstone had replaced Disraeli, who sat at home stoically accepting his defeat.

*****

The Mid-Lothian campaign and the election of 1880 was the first in which international issues were at the forefront. The moral outrage that swept Gladstone, and James Cowan, to the House of Commons was unprecedented in British electoral history. The conscience of the Free Church, nurtured over two generations by a commitment to foreign missions, was enflamed by Gladstone. At the Disruption all the overseas missionaries of the Church of Scotland had thrown their lot into the Free Church. One of them, Alexander Duff of Calcutta, further mobilized their enthusiasm, a man who, as Charles Cowan said, 'inculcated the duty of all classes in society to do what they can to save the lives of the perishing.'[24]

It was David Livingstone that made all Scotland identify with his moral outrage about the elimination of slave trafficking in Africa. Cowan wrote that 'I cannot refrain from expressing my hope and

24. *Reminiscences*, 441.

prayer that the labour and life-sacrifice of David Livingstone, that chief of missionaries in modern history, may issue in an earnest and judicious continuance on behalf of down-trodden Africa.'[25] John Cowan had been a heavy financial backer of Livingstone's expeditions, receiving an elephant's tusk with a brass inscription of gratitude from the great explorer. When Livingstone's body was returned from Africa in 1874 for burial in Westminster Abbey it was a national event. The funeral cortege consisted of twelve carriages. In the seventh Charles Cowan rode with Duncan McLaren MP.

Four years later the Edinburgh Medical Missionary Society dedicated the Livingstone Memorial Missionary Training Institute (for medical interns going overseas) in the Cowgate, Edinburgh. Charles Cowan was a major contributor. As a doctor Livingstone was a great inspiration for the Society, the first interdenominational organization devoted exclusively to medical missions that remained for three generations a Cowan family cause.[26] Dr John Coldstream, who had established in 1829 a medical practice in Leith for the poor, and was married to Catharine Cowan's sister Margaret, was one of three secretaries appointed in 1841, the year the society was founded. The other two men quickly dropped out and for the next twenty-two years Coldstream was at the helm. Surgeon Benjamin Bell (whom we met in chapter 11) teamed with Coldstream and remained as secretary for forty-one years. The Mission inspired deep loyalties.

Charles Cowan invited two hundred of his business associates to an 1860 *conversazione* featuring a presentation by his brother-in-law on 'The Merchant as the Public Benefactor'.[27] John Coldstream's theme that evening was 'the mutual benefits necessarily flowing from mercantile transactions, when conducted in a fair, honest, and Christian spirit.' Trade, he said, could advance 'the progress of Christianity and civilisation' in Africa and help put a final end to the slave trade. As example, he cited Livingstone whose explorations in Africa were being supported at the time generously (and anonymously) by John Cowan. In 1877 the Edinburgh Medical

25. *Reminiscences*, 405.

26. See Wilkinson, John *The Coogate Doctors* Edinburgh: EMMS, 1991.

27. *Scotsman* 30 March 1860.

Missionary Society dedicated in Cowgate the Livingstone Memorial Missionary Training Institute, largely funded by the Cowan family.

*****

The election of 1880 marked the end of Charles Cowan's active involvement in politics. He was, at eighty, no longer physically up to the challenge of electioneering. But in his brother John he had a surrogate and confidant. His other brother James left Parliament two years later, without having distinguished himself. Gladstone's government was a disappointment as many contentious issues went unresolved. Internationally, situations that had aroused his righteous wrath proved more challenging than his powerful oratory had previously led the electorate to believe. In the British Isles there were more immediate matters: the perennial dilemma represented by Ireland, the unsuccessful attempt to silence agitation for Scottish disestablishment, rising social concerns over temperance, all proved as intractable as ever. Gladstone, soon known as the Grand Old Man, often appeared (at least to his critics) becalmed, a victim of his own rhetoric and popularity. Through it all he could always count on the loyalty of John Cowan, with Charles Cowan not far behind. The last chapter of Charles' life would see the brothers divided and their loyalties sorely tested.

Chapter 23

Graceful Goodbyes

'Our opponents have stated that the declarations of the Mid-Lothian campaign have been forgotten,' Gladstone stated at the Edinburgh Corn Exchange on 20 August 1884. John Cowan was in the chair on that occasion, but his eighty-four year old brother Charles sent regrets. Gladstone had not returned to Edinburgh since the tumultuous days of 1879 and 1880 because of ill-health as he told his audience. This was Gladstone's Third Midlothian campaign and the crowds were, if anything, even more enthusiastic. 'Scotland has stood true to him these many years; and during the few days he has been amongst us at this time, enough has surely been done to tell once more to the onlooking world that he lives in the hearts of the Scottish nation.'[1]

It had been a bruising four years for Gladstone. In 1881 Charles Cowan, as president of the West St Cuthbert's Liberal Association, resolved 'unbounded confidence in our worthy representative, the Right Hon W. E. Gladstone, especially at the present crisis in Irish affairs.' It expressed confidence that Gladstone would 'remove the grievance of the Irish people, having every confidence that they

1. *Scotsman* 1 September 1884.

will, according to their traditional policy, be on the side of liberty and justice.' Two months later the Secretary for Ireland, Frederick Cavendish (married to Gladstone's niece), along with Thomas Burke, the permanent undersecretary, were murdered in Phoenix Park, Dublin by the Irish National Invincibles. This challenge was followed by an Egyptian insurrection led by the firebrand Urabi and the subsequent bombardment of Alexandria, which compromised Gladstone's defence of international morality. But it was the turndown of the extension of the franchise by the House of Lords the previous month that particularly annoyed Gladstone. As he said in his Corn Exchange speech: 'What we want is, gentlemen, a national expression of opinion in the constitutional modes familiar in this country upon this great question whether two millions of your fellow subjects are to be admitted to a share in political and Parliamentary power.' In December, after considerable politicking, Gladstone got his Representation of the People Act. The Third Reform Act raised the eligibility threshold in Scotland: three in five males were now entitled to vote.

On 10 February 1886 John Cowan nominated Gladstone as candidate in the Midlothian constituency for the forthcoming election 'and as there was no other candidate he was duly elected'.[2] The Liberal Party was breaking up over the question of Home Rule for Ireland and the Cowan brothers were divided. John maintained loyalty to Gladstone. At a 21 April 1886 meeting it became clear that James was of a different mind, Charles no longer able to participate in the conversation. James called the gathering to hear a report from a delegation that had gone to London to meet with the Marquis of Hartington. Two weeks earlier Hartington had declared his opposition to Gladstone's Irish Home Rule Bill, and a week previously, he had appeared on the same platform with Lord Salisbury, the Tory leader. There was treason in the ranks.

On 1 May 1886, a great rally 'in favour of the legislative unity of the United Kingdom' was held in the Edinburgh Music Hall. The Marquis of Hartington and George Goschen, MP for the city of London, both leaders in the anti-Home Rule Liberal secession, were

2. *Scotsman* 10 February 1886.

the orators of choice for the evening. James Cowan was very much in evidence: he led the Earl of Stair to the chair. Lord Hartington, after flattering the Scots, immediately referred to Gladstone. 'I do not disparage for one moment the authority of one who is held in such respect among you and has rendered such services to his country.' But, he went on: 'there is no party in this country, and most of all the Liberal party, who ought to take its opinions or shape its policy, simply in deference to the opinion of one man, however eminent he may be.' He concluded with a prescient comment that the fate of Ireland and of the Empire for generations to come was in the balance.

Ninety Liberal MPs identified themselves with Lord Hartington and George Goschen as Whigs, conservative Liberals, and in June, the first Irish Home Rule Bill was defeated by a majority of thirty. The following month there was a second 1886 election. Gladstone was defeated, though again returned by acclamation in Midlothian. Henry Campbell Bannerman, who had served as Chief Secretary for Ireland from 1884 to the first 1886 election and then as Secretary for War for six months, wrote on War Office stationery to John after the defeat: 'It was very kind of you to send me a congratulatory note.... On the whole, Scotland has done well – and this is what I (and I imagine you also) am most concerned about. The only exception, as often before, is the South West.... But even beaten as we are, we are more to be envied than our opponents, and especially the Liberal backsliders, whose troubles and difficulties are now beginning.'[3]

As he was leaving office Gladstone wanted to honour his loyal friend John Cowan. When Cowan declined, Gladstone's private secretary, W.P. Primrose, wrote on his behalf: 'Mr Gladstone has received your letter and desires me to say that he appreciates your reasons for wishing to decline the honour which he had proposed for you, and will not press you to do what is contrary to your decision because he had felt that the distinction which it was proposed to confer on you would have given so much genuine satisfaction to your friends and his in Midlothian.'[4] It was to John Cowan that

3. Henry Campbell-Bannerman to John Cowan, 15 July 1886, in the possession of Elizabeth and Jane Errington, Elie, Fifeshire, Scotland, and used by kind permission.

4. H. W. Primrose to John Cowan, 31 July 1886, in the possession of Elizabeth and Jane Errington, Elie, Fifeshire, Scotland, and used by kind permission.

Gladstone, as he left Parliament after sixty-two years, sent his letter of withdrawal in 1894. He is described in John Morley's great biography as being 'so long the loyal chairman of his electoral committee'.[5] As a final gesture, and in deference to the man he revered, John Cowan accepted a baronetcy and would be known for the last six years of his life, as Sir John Cowan of Beeslack.

The Irish situation would continue to fester for the next century and beyond. Meanwhile, with Gladstone gone, Britain under Joseph Chamberlain followed a different, arguably less moral foreign policy. The Boer War (which Charles' son-in-law, the MP Henry Joseph Wilson, strongly opposed), the arms race, and ultimately the First World War, provided a mixed legacy for a new generation. Of the sixteen grandchildren of Charles Cowan who served in the Great War, seven paid the supreme sacrifice.[6]

*****

There were several jubilees in the 1880s that evoked nostalgia for Charles Cowan as a survivor whose life had started with the century. There was the fiftieth anniversary of the Great Reform Acts, already cited, and two years later his picture was the frontispiece of the *Annual* of the Royal Caledonian Curling Club 'as a becoming tribute to its oldest member'.[7] Five years later at the club's jubilee dinner celebration, months before his death, his greetings were read out. The greatest jubilee was that of Queen Victoria's accession to the throne. On Tuesday, 21 June 1887, fifty years to the day after she had become Queen, the entire United Kingdom and its Empire were caught up in celebration and self-congratulation. As the bells pealed, church services extolled the glory of her reign and the blessings of monarchy. After a beautiful day, bonfires were lit across the whole

---

5. Morley, John. *Life of Gladstone*. Vol. 3. London Macmillan & Co., 1903. 517 n3.

6. 'Cowan and Menzies Kinsmen Who Have Joined the Royal Navy or the Army Before Christmas' 1914 lists 42 men in the armed services, of whom two had already been killed in October and another drowned on the 'Bulwark' that November. (Pamphlet in possession of Judith Alison MacLeod)

7. *Annual of the Royal Caledonian Curling Club for 1884-85*. Edinburgh: Crawford & M'Cabe, 1884. ix

country. Charles Cowan was asked to light the bonfire on Carnethy Hill. He had come full circle from that day in Westminster Abbey, at her coronation, when he had initiated shouts of 'God Save the Queen!' from the balcony.

These years were also marked by the funerals of friends and contemporaries. On 15 March 1882 he watched as Rab Brown was buried in Calton Cemetery. Brown was the doctor and author whose love of animals and children helped shape the children of Victorian Scotland. His classic *Rab and His Friends* had been a delight for all the Cowans. Two months later, he was at Grange Cemetery for the interment of William Hanna, the man who had enshrined the memory of his father-in-law, Thomas Chalmers, in his biography. In April 1886, he attended the service for his own comrade-in-arms and political opponent Duncan McLaren, born just a few months before he was and active to the end. The final obsequies he attended were for the publisher William Nelson, who died suddenly at the age of sixty-one just as he was about to travel to Greece on business. Thomas Nelson and Sons had become a major customer of Cowan's firm. He was buried in Grange Cemetery on 14 September 1887.

1887 was a year of heavy losses in Charles' immediate family. Two of his daughters, Catharine ('Kate') Wahab and Mabel Cleghorn, predeceased him: Kate at the age of fifty-five on 19 November and Mabel at forty-nine, three days before Christmas. News came from India that summer that Anna's husband, Lt Col. Edward George Newnham, Sixth Prince of Wales' Bengal Cavalry, had succumbed at Naini Tal. After his death, Anna returned to Scotland, and lived in Auchindinny House outside Penicuik and was with her father at the end.[8]

*****

8. Anna's older daughter, Catharine 'Kate' (1866-1948) was for 45 years companion to Dr Minnie Gomery (1875-1967). Gomery, one of the earliest female medical students in Canada, graduated from Bishops Medical School with the Wood Gold Medal in 1898 eight years after it was opened to women. Only one hospital, the Western in Montreal, would hire her. She served in India with the CMS from 1900 to 1953. For a time she was sole physician and surgeon in the John Bishop Memorial Hospital in Islamabad. (http://freepages.genealogy.rootsweb.ancestry.com/~gomery/minnie.html)

In the records of the Penicuik Free Church, where Charles had been an elder for forty-five years, there is reference to an old man of eighty-seven emerging from his coach at the church door on the arm of his daughter, wrapped in heavy blankets. 'The June sacrament of 1888 was made memorable by the presence of the venerable Charles Cowan,' the account reads. The imminence of death, and his careful preparations for it, led him at the end to come to renewed faith.

James Hood Wilson, his Edinburgh minister, wrote: 'The latter weeks of his life were marked by a very remarkable spiritual experience. Amid great bodily weakness, and with failing faculties otherwise, his mind seemed to run almost entirely in the line of spiritual and divine things, and much of his time was spent in prayer. During one of my last visits to him, he prayed that Scotland would be kept loyal to Christ, true to her old traditions, etc. Indeed, the characteristics of his last days may be said to have been thankfulness, humility, trust, and prayerfulness. It was interesting to see the active man of business coming at the close to the simplicity of a little child, and at length passing gently away, reminding one of a serene sunset after the clouds which had intervened had passed away.'[9]

*****

Charles Cowan's long life came to an end at 6:30 on Friday evening, 29 March, 1889. The family had gathered in anticipation of the end. He was eighty-eight years of age. At noon the following Tuesday, 2 April, the Rev James Hood Wilson, as his city minister, led a service in the parlour of Westerlea. Over a hundred attended: the crowd spilled into the hall. If space allowed, funerals were often held in homes at the time. John Cowan described the service in his diary that day as 'beautiful'.[10] The cortege, consisting of a hearse, four horses, and over thirty private vehicles, made its way out to Penicuik. At the outskirts of the village, the mourners got out of their carriages and were met by over 1,500 people. Many of them were employees or

9. Wilson, J. H. 'In Memoriam–Mr Charles Cowan'.

10. 2 April 1889 entry, *Diary of John Cowan 19 January 1882 – 24 February 1895*, in the possession of Elizabeth and Jane Errington, Elie, Fifeshire, Scotland, and used by kind permission.

local residents. The mill was closed for the afternoon and all business in Penicuik ceased.

Charles Cowan was laid to rest in the family plot in the churchyard, in a tomb of three panels designed by his father. Even in death he could not escape Alexander's long reach, though Alexander himself had a towering fresco in Grange Cemetery, Edinburgh, where Cowans continue to be buried. Pallbearers were Charles' two surviving sons, two of his grandsons, four sons-in-law, and his three brothers, John, James and half-brother George. After the coffin had been placed in the tomb, Charles' son-in-law Rev. Robert Lundie gave the message, 'holding up as well worthy of emulation all that had been good, honourable, and Christlike in the life of the deceased.'[11] After prayer and helped by the Penicuik Free Church choir, Lundie led in the singing of his brother-in-law's hymn, 'I Heard the Voice of Jesus Say.' It was noted that this was the song 'the deceased had heard daily during the last three months of his life.'[12] To John the occasion was 'overpowering.'

The day after Charles Cowan's death was announced, the *Scotsman* provided a full column tribute. 'Though he has long been laid aside from public duty, he deserves to have his memory cherished by all citizens who admire a life spent in the promotion of the welfare of his fellow men. During the course of a long and active life he devoted himself with disinterestedness to whatever work of the people he was called up to perform; and in the discharge of his public functions he brought to bear great sagacity, discrimination, judgment, and ability. Few men have been more generous and hospitable; and it might be said of him as he had said of his father, "One aim that actuated him was to be of use or service in the course of each day to some person or other, however humble the individual might be." Not many years ago, Mr. Cowan frequently contributed letters on public questions to our columns. They were always marked by thorough knowledge of the subject and charitable appreciation of the efforts and motive of those from whom he might differ. He was a kindly, genial man,

11. *Peeblesshire Advertiser*, 6 April 1889. Anna Cowan's newspaper clipping scrap-booke.

12. Quoted by the *Peeblesshire Advertiser*, 6 April 1889.

whose friendship was warmly to be desired. He is mourned by two sons and four daughters, a large number of grandchildren and a wide circle of relations and friends.'[13]

Ten months after the death of Charles Cowan, Alexander Cowan and Sons was incorporated with limited liability under the Companies Act of the year before. That arrangement continued for seventy-six years until in 1965 the company was bought out by Reed Paper. The family's hold on the business was loosened with the death of Alexander, Charles William's son, in 1943. Eight years later the company was floated on the Edinburgh Stock Exchange, further weakening the family's stake in the business. By regulation a listed company could only have a third of its stock held by family members. By the time of the 1965 takeover the Cowan family business legacy was all but gone. Alexander Cowan's great enterprise had slipped from the family's grasp.

13. *Scotsman* 30 March 1889.

Vale

The Charles Cowan who emerges from his letters, diaries, family lore, and particularly his *Reminiscences,* was an engaging figure, a raconteur, gregarious and generous, if somewhat impulsive, with a big heart and amazing stamina. His life spanned eighty-eight years of the nineteenth century, an era of rapid change in Scotland. He personified and epitomized what was taking place, providing a unique insight from an observer who moved with events rather than shaped them.

Best known for his 1847 electoral triumph over Macaulay, he was not a great parliamentarian but served his constituents with a dogged commitment to their Scottish – and Edinburgh – identity. Neither was he a great intellect, but he had a restless curiosity and a willingness to explore the new frontiers of knowledge breaking out at the time with dizzying rapidity. His métier was that of a successful businessman who, in his lifetime, made a lot of money that he used generously for the good of society and shared with his large family. As he aged, he became a fixture at charitable and political events, his longevity providing a first-hand witness to a past that would otherwise have been obliterated from collective memory. On occasion, and with someone lacking his gravitas, his quickness to speak might come across as tiresome and predictable, but the elderly Charles Cowan was usually heard with the respect his years demanded.

Comparison with his near contemporary Duncan McLaren, the so-called 'MP for Scotland', who finally made it to the House of Commons at the age of sixty-five, six years after Charles Cowan had stood down, illuminates the careers of both men. McLaren differed from Cowan because, without family wealth behind him, he made his own way in business, prospering first as a shopkeeper on the Edinburgh High Street, and then through canny investments in railways and insurance. Though returned to Parliament four times, he was never as popular as Cowan, coming across (particularly in his early years) as abrasive and devious, hence his sobriquet 'the Snake'. The quintessential back-room politician, unlike Charles Cowan, he played that game with gusto.

As a parliamentarian, be it said, Duncan McLaren was more effective than Cowan and maintained a consistency in his radicalism that owed much to his third wife Priscilla, the sister of John Bright. Both Cowan and McLaren were free-traders, aggressive in their commitment to social causes such as female empowerment. They were one in the long and bitter campaign against the Edinburgh annuity tax. They joined hands in the mid-1850s for the vindication of Scottish rights. Together they became, in old age, fixtures on the Edinburgh social scene, throw-backs to the bitter political controversies of the 1840s and 50s. It was the long shadow of Thomas Chalmers that divided them. Duncan McLaren was quintessentially United Presbyterian, a denomination dominated by up-and-coming urban businessmen whose concern, in reaction to their Secession roots, was the respectability of prosperity and culture. McLaren, though a churchman with in-laws and nephews who were clergy, never strikes one as having the same religious passion that motivated the young Charles Cowan. And the contrast in this regard between the Quaker Priscilla and the Evangelical Catharine could not be more striking. Cowan was shaped by an intense religious experience as a youth about which we know little, though the evidence that such occurred appears everywhere in his early diaries. McLaren had no such epiphany.

Both born at the turn of a new century, McLaren and Cowan each impacted Scotland during their lifetime as rapid and accelerating change took place. When the first Charles Cowan arrived in Edinburgh in 1756 he came to a city with a population of just over 50,000 with narrow streets, unsanitary conditions, and few amenities. The New Town was in the early planning stage and soon a beautiful city, the envy of Europe for its culture and sophistication, emerged. Some Cowans took up residence on Royal Crescent, a jewel of the new Edinburgh. By the time of Charles Cowan's majority the population had soared to 138,000 and continued to grow, imposing strains on the social fabric of the city to which the Cowans responded with beneficent and practical concern. Hence their controversial obsession over water rights for the burgeoning city.

With this accelerating urbanization, however, the family's links with an earlier, rural Scotland still remained strong. Charles' father, the infant Alexander, was sent back to the country for a more salubrious environment until early childhood vulnerabilities, due to the lack of sanitation and the pollution of the city, could be withstood. From 1791 on, for five generations, the family maintained concurrently a strong Penicuik identity. Their rootedness in rural Fife, where they continued to summer, was a matter of pride. Strong family connections there provided ballast in the fierce competition of the city. Hence the close links between Alexander Cowan and his son Charles and Alexander's first cousin, Thomas Chalmers of Anstruther.

Lowland Scotland, particularly in the circles in which the Cowans mixed, became increasingly impacted by the wider world. In an earlier generation young Marjorie Fidler was educated by nuns of Dunkerque where she spent her childhood with her exiled parents. Her grandson Charles Cowan as a boy at Valleyfield encountered soldiers from all over Europe when the mill was commandeered as a repository for prisoners of the Napoleonic Wars. His time in Geneva as a sixteen-year-old, and the facility with French that he gained there, gave him an awareness of a wider world. Later the family were drawn to Germany, perhaps because it was there that Sandy, Charles' gifted brother, died and was buried.

Later in life, after retirement from the House of Commons, Charles traveled widely. He visited Russia, where his company had an interest in the rag trade, and then ventured further afield in the year of Canadian confederation to North America to explore firsthand wider investment opportunities. The family business developed strong affiliates overseas, particularly in Australia. Missionary appeals were a powerful incentive to add an international dimension to the Cowans' benefactions: Charles' brother John was an early sponsor of David Livingstone and Charles himself was a great admirer of Alexander Duff of Calcutta. Three of Charles' daughters gravitated to India as their husbands were enlisted in serving the British raj. John James, his youngest son, having married a woman born in Montreal, circled the globe in the 1870s.

The passage of the Scottish Reform Act of 1832 was a harbinger of social as well as political change. As Lord Advocate Francis Jeffrey stated, the Bill 'left not a shred of the former system'. The political landscape changed: some Whigs became increasingly radicalized. Charles' mentor Thomas Chalmers might be a Tory, but there was no question where his own allegiance lay. The emotional and passionate Charles Cowan identified himself, as a member of the entrepreneurial middle class, with those opposed to what they saw as the arbitrary use of power. The elimination of first the excise tax on paper, the so-called 'tax on knowledge', and then the hated Edinburgh annuity tax became his *causes célèbres*. Charles Cowan was the essential democrat and for over half a century he played a vital role on the Scottish political scene.

Eleven years after the Scottish Reform Act the other great event that shaped Cowan's life occurred. The interconnection between the Reform Act and the Disruption is a matter for debate: did having a greater voice in London also make the Scots less willing to submit to arbitrary and insensitive interference in their religious life? When Charles Cowan marched with the come-outers from St Andrew's Church Edinburgh to Tanfield Hall on 18 May 1843, as a facilitator of the Disruption, he was a witness both to a heroic protest but also the fracturing of Scottish society. The Evangelical ascendancy in the Church of Scotland for the previous decade ended with their departure. As so often in their history, Evangelicals self-immolated. It was a heroic measure, ultimately more costly than any of them could imagine.

Chalmers' death three years later created a vacuum of leadership in the Free Church. By the 1870s the momentum that had propelled the so-called 'angry boys' of the Disruption was exhausted. After the collapse of negotiations with the United Presbyterians in 1873 following six years of discussion, Charles Cowan lost some of his enthusiasm for the Free Church. By that time, as studies have shown,[1] Thomas Chalmers' vision of Scotland as a Christian commonwealth was being claimed by Norman MacLeod of the Barony and others in the Established Church. In 1876 that kirk found itself the exposer of heterodoxy in the Free Church. For a layman who had facilitated the Disruption it was all puzzling. As we have seen, Charles Cowan rose at his final of forty General Assemblies in 1877 to remind other commissioners of the glory days when his business savvy in the setting up of the Sustentation Fund had made the Disruption financially viable. He found solace in the warm and uncomplicated piety of Dwight Lyman Moody and his own minister, James Hood Wilson, a welcome reprieve from complex theological questions.

The three Cowan brothers formed a powerful family compact as business partners in their late father's business. Contrasts between them highlight their separate identities. Each made a considerable contribution to the political life of Victorian Scotland. Charles, considerably older, led the way by becoming a Member of Parliament over their father's misgivings. Charles' brother John, fourteen years younger, was a widower for the last thirty-nine years of his life. He was steadier, more thoughtful, but also less colourful.[2] As Gladstone's manager he made his own historic contribution in the background,

---

1. Brown, Stewart J. 'Thomas Chalmers and the Communal Ideal in Victorian Scotland' in Smout, T.C. Ed. *Victorian values : a joint symposium of the Royal Society of Edinburgh and the British Academy* Oxford: Oxford University Press for the British Academy, 1992. 61 – 77.

2. 'Sir John Cowan did not come so prominently before the public of Edinburgh as his brothers, though in a quiet and unobtrusive way he took an active part in the affairs of many of the benevolent institutions of the city and district.' ("The Late Sir John Cowan, Bart' *Scotsman* 27 October 1900, 8.)

providing loyalty during the political turbulence of Gladstone's later years. In contrast James, with less than two years between them, bailed out over the Irish question, joining the new Unionists. Not for nothing was he nicknamed 'Chattie'. Even his restoration after his bankruptcy, when twenty years later he first became Edinburgh Provost and subsequently a lacklustre MP, could not dispel that aura of delightful unpredictability that surrounded him. At the end, childless, he left generous bequests to various nieces and nephews.[3]

If as businessmen the brothers were representative of a burgeoning Scottish middle class, it was the tone of the business that set Charles, John and James Cowan apart from others. As senior partner after his father's death, Charles Cowan set the bar high and his brothers followed him on a path already marked out by their father. The firm Alexander Cowan and Sons was a byword for probity and integrity, carefully practising Christian principles in their conduct of a business that grew exponentially in mid-century and provided a very generous return on investment. As an alternative to the anti-religious rhetoric and ethic of Robert Owen, they demonstrated a similarly enlightened approach to employer-employee relations based instead on Christian convictions nurtured by their Free Church culture. To this day, in Penicuik , even though the name "Cowan Institute" has been chiselled off the façade of the Town Hall, there remains a strong loyalty on the part of now aging former employees. Charles Cowan never distanced himself from his men, skipped alongside of them at the bonspiel, and took a personal interest in the welfare of the 1500 who worked for him, providing practical employee benefits and assistance unusual in that day.

True to his Christian convictions, as a good steward, and following his father's example, Charles Cowan was a remarkably giving and

3. James died on 24 November 1895 at his country estate in Glengorm, Tobermory, where he had been confined for the final two years of his life. His tenantry and neighboring proprietors at Tobermory gathered for a first funeral, followed by one at his home at 35 Royal Crescent, Edinburgh, conducted by his minister, Rev. R. J. Sandeman, Free St. Andrew's. After the 1871 Education Act James Cowan was first chair of the Edinburgh School Board. Like Charles he was heavily involved in charity, particularly the Blind Asylum and the Infirmary Board. A long-time member of the Association for the Promotion of the Fine Arts in Scotland, 'he was always regarded as a man of artistic taste, and was a liberal supporter of the fine arts.' ("The Late Mr James Cowan' *Scotsman* 25 November 1895, 7; 'Funeral of Mr. James Cowan' *Scotsman* 30 November 1895, 8.)

generous man. His charities, however, were not done with the anonymity that Alexander insisted on. In the press he was often cited for his gifts and he was a sure (if not soft) touch for many needy Edinburgh causes. He exemplified his father's attitude toward money and refused to be embittered by the collapse of the City of Glasgow Bank in 1878. He died leaving an estate of £85,344, considerably less than he had at one time been worth.[4] In contrast, his brother John, initially the junior partner, left £118,252. Charles was not mercenary or avaricious, a feature of some of his more successful and prosperous contemporaries. He never flaunted his wealth or position.

In his *Reminiscences,* thirty years after his electoral triumph over Thomas Babington Macaulay, Charles Cowan reflected over the upset victory that advanced him to national attention. 'I did not expect to be returned,' he modestly admitted, 'and had I known it was to be otherwise, I would have shrunk from the responsibility of accepting such a trust.' His standing for office was a protest against 'the treatment which Scotland had experienced from the Government and Legislature in ecclesiastical matters.'[5] Charles Cowan was a protagonist in the struggle for Scottish identity and justice. He was no narrow nationalist but rather one who wanted to avoid, by asserting the rights of his country, another 'great national blunder' such as the one that had created the Disruption. To do this he sought to ensure that Scotland had a voice in London and that her rights and faith would be acknowledged and respected. For that cause he would always be known as 'the man who beat Macaulay'.

4. In a news article 'The late Mr Charles Cowan's will' the *Scotsman* noted that 'It is said that Mr Cowan lost £100,000 in the City of Glasgow Bank.' *Scotsman* 6 April 1889.

5. *Reminiscences,* 212.

Appendix

The Member's Wife (Thought to be written by Thos Constable)

Air – "there's nae luck aboot the house"

And are ye sure the news is true.
    And are ye sure he's in?
Gae up and speir at Provost Black,
    As fast as ye can rin!
They said my Charlie was sae blate
    He wouldna speak ava',
And little thocht was in their heads
    That he wad ding them a'!
        Oh there's nae luck aboot the House,
        The Commons House, ava'
        There's little pleasure in the House,
        When my gudeman's awa'.

And am I then a Member's wife?
    Are thae a Mrember's weans ?
Is my gudeman in Parliament ?

I wonder what it means! –
I'm sure there's no a better man
In a' big London toun;
And I would never chynge him wi'
The Queen that wears the croun !
Oh there's nae luck aboot the House …

He taught the Provost, Adam Black
That muckle ill-faur'd loon
That his auld Whigmaleery pack
Nae longer ride the toun.
He's shewn them he can twist their Craig,
And send Macaulay home,
To try and mak' anither lay –
A lay of auncient Rome!
Oh there's nae luck aboot the House …

The neebours think that noo I'll haud
My head aboon them a';
But better wisdom tells me that
Pride goes before a fa'.
And sall I see him tak' his seat?
And sall I hear him speak?
My head grows dizzy at the thocht
In truth I'd like to greet.
Oh there's nae luck aboot the House,

But daur'd I tell my sober mind,
And could I ha'e my will, --
For a' the honour's very great,
He'd never left the Mill.
And were he in the House o' Lords
A Marquess or a Duke,
I'd rather ha'e him back again
At bonny Penicuik!
Oh there's nae luck aboot the House

Primary Sources and Bibliography

Primary Sources

Charles Cowan original publications:

Under pseudonym 'Head of a family in communion with the Church of Scotland,' '*The Analogy Which Subsists Between the British Constitution in its Three Estates of Queen, Lords, and Commons, and That of the Church of Scotland in the Mutual Relations of Patron, Presbytery, and People, Shortly Considered, Being a Letter Respectfully Addressed to the Scottish Representatives in Parliament by the Head of a Family in Communion with the Church of Scotland.* Edinburgh: Fraser & Crawford. 8 January 1840.

'Paper,' *Encyclopaedia Britannica* 8th Edition. Vol. 9. Edinburgh: A & C Black, 1854. 246-261.

Address to the Royal Scottish Society of Arts November 1865. Edinburgh: Neill and Company, 1865.

Reminiscences. Published privately, 1877. 524pp.

Aviva archives, Norwich

Minutes Scottish Union Insurance Co., 1848 – 1878 (one volume missing)

Isabel Buckoke, Lymington, Herts

Edited and photocopied privately in 2000 as *The Cowan Letters*

Edinburgh City Library

'A Journal of Travel to and Residence at Geneva' transcribed by Charles Boog-Watson *Diary, 10 April 1842 – 6 May 1846*

Elizabeth and Jane Errington, Elie, Fifeshire, Scotland.

George Cowan *Report book/Diary 30 May 1819 – 27 Nov 1819*

John Cowan Diary *19 Jan 1882 – 24 February 1895*

Numerous correspondence, pictures and memorabilia of John Cowan

London School of Economics Archives

Cowan family collection COLL MISC 0343:

Business book for Charles Cowan, Melville Mill, Edinburgh 1818-1819.

Personal account book for Charlotte Wilson, 1849-1862.

Judith A MacLeod collection

Cowan, Catharine *'My dear girls'* Memories of her son Alexander Handwritten notebook 34 pp 16 March 1840

'Cowan and Menzies Kinsmen Who Have Joined the Royal Navy or the Army Before Christmas 1914.'

Diary of Charles Cowan 27 January 1833 – 31 December 1836

Newspaper clipping scrapbook, 1887 – 1909 by Anna Thompson [Cowan] Newnham

'Record of the Services of Lt. Col. Edward George Newnham' 1 February 1881.

Wahab, Catharine. 'Catharine Menzies Cowan' handwritten memoir. 28 pp nd

Wilson, J H. 'In Memoriam – Mr Charles Cowan.'

Letters and correspondence and memorabilia

National Archives of Scotland

GD45/14/690 Fox Maule (Dalhousie) papers

GD310 To the Parliamentary Commission of Revenue Inquiry 4 Nov 1824

GD69/7/69/2-4 Minute book of partners A C & Sons

GD311/2/1 Letter book General – 30 July 1827 – 21 June 1828

GD311/2/2 Letter book – General – 19 October 1832 – 31 December 1833

GD 311/2/37 Correspondence 1813 - 1818

GD311/2/39 – Letter box 4 Jun 1820 – 3 Aug 1822

GD311/2/42 – 25 Aug 1828 – 1 Mar 1830 Fr Balerno Mill – small note book

GD311/2/41 – 16 Dec 1823 – 7 Jun 1825 Letter books

In the former West Registry Office, NAS

CS228/B/20/8 Outer House 30 August 1852 – *Summons of Relief* J. Balfour Esq against James Cowan and Cautioners

Note of suspension and Interdict for the Scottish Union and National Insurance Co. and John Macgregor McCandlish as a Manager and an Individual against Charles Cowan

Report of Jury Trial - The Duke Buccleuch, Lord Melville, and Sir James Drummond, Pursuers, against Alexander Cowan & Sons, Wm Somerville & Son, James Brown & Co., Archibald Fullerton Sommerville, and Wm Tod & Son Defenders. Edinburgh: R. Clark, 1866.

New College Library, University of Edinburgh

Thomas Chalmers correspondence

United Reformed Church archives, Westminster College, Cambridge

R. H. Lundie file

Family and Local History Bibliography

Boog-Watson, Charles. *Alexander Cowan of Moray House and Valleyfield*. Perth: D. Leslie, 1915.

Buckoke, Isabel. Ed. *The Cowan Letters (1800-Circa 1850) & Chalmers, Menzies, McFarlan, Meryon, & Other Letters & Memoirs*. 82 pp. Printed privately, 2000.

Cowan, Alexander (Sandie). *Remains of Alexander Cowan consisting of his verses and extracts from his correspondence and journals*. Edinburgh: Thomas Constable, 1839.

Cowan, J. J. *From 1846 to 1932*. Edinburgh: Pillans and Wilson, 1932.

Forsyth, Mary. *The Cowans at Moray House*. Edinburgh: T & A Constable, 1932.

'History of Penicuik' 4 vols. 55 pp each. n.d. Penicuik Historical Society.

Martin, J. C. *Alexander Cowan, His Kinsfolk and Relations*. Revision to 1948. Binder, 32 pp, July 1949.

Menzies, William John. 'America as a Field for Investment: a Lecture Delivered to the Chartered Accountants Students' Association 18 February 1892.' Edinburgh: William Blackwood, 1892.

Reid, Thomas. *The Lanark Manse Family - Narrative Found in the Repositories of the Late Miss Elizabeth Bailie Menzies of 31 Windsor Street Edinburgh*. Lanark: D. A. V. Thomason, 1901.

Wilson, John J. *Annals of Penicuik*. Edinburgh: T & A Constable, 1893.

Bibliography

Anderson, Mosa. *Henry Joseph Wilson: Fighter for Freedom 1833 - 1914*. London: James Clarke & Co, 1953.

Annual of the Royal Caledonian Curling Club for 1884-85. Edinburgh: Crawford & M'Cabe, 1884.

Battiscombe, Georgina. *Shaftesbury the Great Reformer (1801-1885)* Boston: Houghton Mifflin, 1975.

Bebbington, David 'Moody as a Transatlantic Evangelical' in George, Timothy. *Mr. Moody and the Evangelical Tradition*. London: T & T Clark International. 2004.

Bebbington, David. *William Ewart Gladstone: Faith and Politics in Victorian Britain*. Grand Rapids: Wm. Eerdmans, 1993

Black, John Sutherland & Chrystal, George. *The Life of William Robertson Smith*. London: Adam and Charles Black, 1912.

Bonar, Horatius. *Evangelism A Reformed Debate*. Trowbridge, Wilshire: James Begg Society, 1997.

Boyd, Kenneth. *Scottish Church Attitudes to Sex, Marriage and the Family, 1850-1914*. Edinburgh: John Donald Publishers, 1980.

Brown, Callum. *Religion and Society in Scotland since 1707*. Edinburgh: Edinburgh University Press, 1997.

Brown, Stewart J. 'Beliefs and Religions,' chapter 4, *A History of Everyday Life in Scotland, 1800 to 1900* (Griffiths and Morton, Eds.) Edinburgh: Edinburgh University Press, 2010.

Brown, Stewart J. 'Religion and Society to c.1900' in Devine, T. M. and Wormald, Jenny, Eds. *The Oxford Handbook of Modern Scottish History*. Oxford: Oxford University Press, 2012. 78 – 98.

Brown, Stewart J. and Fry, Michael, Eds. *Scotland in the Age of the Disruption*. Edinburgh: Edinburgh University Press, 1993.

Brown, Stewart J. *The National Churches of England, Ireland, and Scotland 1801-1846*. Oxford: Oxford University Press, 2001.

Brown, Stewart J. 'Thomas Chalmers and the communal ideal in Victorian Scotland' in Smout, T. C. Ed., *Victorian Values: A Joint Symposium of the Royal Society of Edinburgh and the British Academy, December 1990.* Oxford: Oxford University Press, 1992. 61-80.

Brown, Stewart J. *Thomas Chalmers and the Godly Commonwealth.* Oxford: Oxford University Press, 1982.

Buchanan, Robert, *The Ten Years Conflict: History of the Disruption of the Church of Scotland.* (4 vols.) Glasgow: Blackie and Son, 1863.

Cameron, Ewen A, *Impaled Upon a Thistle: Scotland Since 1880.* Edinburgh: Edinburgh University Press, 2010.

Caverly, R. B. & Nugent-Bankes, George. *Leading Insurance Men of the British Empire.* London: Index Publishing, 1892.

Checkland, Olive. *Philanthropy in Victorian Scotland.* Edinburgh: John Donald, 1980.

Cheyne, Alexander, *The Ten Years' Conflict and the Disruption.* Edinburgh: Scottish Academic Press, 1993.

Cockburn, Henry. *Journal of Henry Cockburn; being a continuation of the memorials of his time, 1831-1854* Edinburgh: Edmonston & Douglas, 1874.

Colston, James. *The Edinburgh and District Water Supply* Edinburgh: Colston Printers, 1890.

Devine, T. M. *The Scottish Nation 1700 – 2000.* London: Allen Lane, 1999.

Dickson, J. N. Ian. *Studies in Evangelical History and Thought: Beyond Religious Discourse* Carlisle: Milton Keynes 2007.

Ding, Ying Yong. *A Business History of Alex. Cowan & Sons Ltd., Papermakers, Penicuik, 1779-1965* University of the West of Scotland, 2011.

Ding, Ying Yong. 'Alex. Cowan and Sons, Papermakers, Penicuik, 1779-1975: A Historical Sketch, with Implications for Chandler's Theories' *Scottish Business and Industrial History.* Business Archives Council of Scotland. Vol. 24, Series 2, July 2009.

Donnachie, Ian and Hewitt, George. *Historic New Lanark* Edinburgh: Edinburgh University Press, 1993.

Dyer, Michael. *Men of Property and Intelligence: The Scottish Electoral System prior to 1884*. Aberdeen: Scottish Cultural Press, 1996.

Engelbourg, Saul. 'John Stewart Kennedy and the City of Glasgow Bank' *Business and Economic History*, Second Series, Vol. 15, 1986.

Fairley, John A. *Agnes Campbell, Lady Roseburn – A Contribution to the History of Printing in Scotland* Aberdeen: D. Wyllie & Son, 1925.

Finlayson, Sandy, *Unity and Diversity: The Founders of the Free Church of Scotland*. Fearn: Christian Focus Publications, 2010.

Fleming, J. R. *A History of the Church in Scotland* Edinburgh: T & T Clark, 1927.

Fowler, W. S. *A Study in Radicalism and Dissent: The Life and Times of Henry Joseph Wilson, 1833 - 1914*. London: Epworth Press, 1961.

Fraser, W. Hamish and Morris, R. J. Eds. *People and Society in Scotland II, 1830-1914*. Edinburgh: John Donald with the Economic and Social History Society of Scotland. 1990.

Fry, Michael. *Edinburgh: A History of the City*. London: Macmillan, 2009.

Fry, Michael. *Patronage and Principle*. Aberdeen: Aberdeen University Press, 1987.

Gillespie, Alastair. *Made In Canada: A Businessman's Adventures in Politics* Montreal: Robin Brass Studio, 2009.

Goldman, Lawrence. *Science, Reform and Politics in Victorian Britain: The Social Science Association, 1857 - 1886*. Cambridge: Cambridge University Press, 2002.

Hanham, H. J. *Scottish Nationalism*, Cambridge, MA: Harvard University Press, 1969.

Hanna, William. *Memoirs of Dr Chalmers D.D. LLD.* 3 vols. Edinburgh: Fullerton & Co., 1852.

Hutchison I. G. C. *A Political History of Scotland, 1832-1924.* Edinburgh: John Donald, 1986.

Kerr, John. *The History of Curling*. Edinburgh: David Douglas, 1890.

Lee, C. H. 'Scotland, 1860-1939: growth and prosperity' in Floud, R. and Johnson P. *The Cambridge Economic History of Modern Britain.* Volume2: *Economic Maturity, 1860-1939.* Cambridge: Cambridge University Press, 2004.

Lewis, David. *Edinburgh Water Supply* Edinburgh: Andrew Elliot, 1908.

Machin, Ian.'Charles Cowan' *Oxford Dictionary of National Biography.* vol. 13, 747-8.

MacLaren, A. Allan; *Religion and Social Class: The Disruption Years in Aberdeen.* London: Routledge & Kegan Paul, 1974.

MacLeod, James Lachlan. *The Second Disruption: The Free Church in Victorian Scotland the Origins of the Free Presbyterian Church.* (Scottish Historical Review Monograph No. 8). East Linton: Tuckwell Press, 2000.

Mechie, Stewart. *The Church and Scottish Social Development.* London: Oxford University Press, 1960.

Morley, John. *Life of Gladstone.* Vol. 2. London: MacMillan, 1902.

Morrison-Low, A. D. and Christie, J.R.R., eds. *'Martyr of Science': Sir David Brewster 1781-1868. Proceedings of a Bicentenary Symposium 21 November 1981.* Edinburgh: Royal Scottish Museum Studies, 1984.

Morton, Graeme. *Unionist Nationalism.* East Linton: Tuckwell Press, 1999.

Needham, Nicholas. *The Doctrine of Holy Scripture in the Free Church Fathers.* Edinburgh: Rutherford House, 1991.

Oxford Dictionary of National Biography. 'Cowan, Charles'. 'Cowan, John'. 'Menzies, William John'.

Pentland, Gordon. *Radicalism, Reform and National Identity in Scotland, 1820-1833.* Woodbridge, Suffolk: The Boydell Press, 2008.

Pentland, Gordon. *The Spirit of the Union: Popular Politics in Scotland 1815-1820.* London: Pickering and Chatto, 2011.

Pickard, Willis. *The Member for Scotland, A Life of Duncan McLaren.* Edinburgh: Berlinn, 2011.

Pitzer, Donald. *New Harmony Now and Then.* Evansville, IN: Indiana University Press, 2012.

Robers, Shirley. *Sophia Jex-Blake: A Woman's Pioneer in Nineteenth Century Medical Reform* London: Routledge, 1993.

Ross, Kenneth R. 'Calvinists in Controversy: John Kennedy, Horatius Bonar and the Moody Mission of 1873-74,' *Scottish Bulletin of Evangelical Theology* Vol. 9.1 (1986).

Ross, William C. A. *The Royal High School.* Edinburgh: Oliver and Boyd. 1934.

Ryley, George Buchanan & McCandlish, John M; *Scotland's Free Church: an Historical Retrospect and Memorial of the Disruption* London: Arnold Constable and Co., 1893.

Scott, Hew, Ed. *Fasti Ecclesiae Scoticanae.* Vol. 1 – Synod of Lothian and Tweedale. Edinburgh: Oliver and Boyd, 1915.

Scott, John and Hughes, Michael. *The Anatomy of Scottish Capital.* London: Croom Helm, 1980.

Sher, Richard B. *Church and University in the Scottish Enlightenment: The Moderate Literati of Edinburgh.* Princeton: Princeton University Press, 1985.

Simpson, Carnegie, *The Life of Principal Rainy.* London: Hodder and Stoughton, 1909.

Smail, Peter. 'A Study of Economic and Social History in 19th Century Scotland: Comparison of the Philosophies of Cowan vs. Owen' *The Quarterly* No. 53 (January 2005) 1-5.

Smith, Carnegie 'The Robertson Smith Controversy: Some Personal Recollections' *British Weekly*, October 1946.

'Some Contributions to Scottish Paper Trade History: III The Valleyfield Mills of Messrs. Alex Cowan and Sons Ltd, Penicuik' *The World's Paper Trade Review,* Vol 58, No. 2 (12 July 1912).

Spencer, Herbert. *Railway Morals & Railway Policy*. London: Longman, Brown, Green & Longmans, 1855.

Spicer, A. D. *The Paper Trade: a Descriptive and Historical Survey of the Paper Trade from the Commencement of the Nineteenth Century*. London: Methuen, 1907.

Stevenson, Sara. *Facing the Light: The Photography of Hill & Adamson*. Edinburgh: National Portrait Gallery, 2002.

Sullivan, Robert E. *Macaulay: The Tragedy of Power.* Cambridge, MA: Harvard University Press, 2009.

Thomson, Alistair. *The Paper Industry in Scotland*. Edinburgh: Scottish Academic Press, 1974.

Turner, A. Logan *Story of a Great Hospital: The Royal Infirmary of Edinburgh, 1729 – 1929*. Edinburgh: Oliver and Boyd, 1937.

Watson, Nigel. *Last Mill on the Esk*. Edinburgh: Scottish Academic Press, 1988.

Wells, James. *James Hood Wilson* 2nd Ed London: Hodder and Stoughton, 1905.

Wilkinson, John *The Cowgate Doctors*. Edinburgh: EMMS, 1991.

Wilson, William. *Memoir of Robert Smith Candlish, D. D.* Edinburgh: Robert and Charles Black, 1880.

Index

Cc

Dd

Ee

Ff

Gg

Hh

Jj

Kk

Ll

Mm

Nn

Oo

Pp

Rr

Ss

Tt

Vv

Ww

Unity And Diversity
The Founders of the Free Church
Sandy Finlayson

It has been many years since there has been a popular level book, which has looked at the life and ministry of some of the 'fathers' of the Free Church of Scotland. This book looks at the life and ministry of a number of the key figures in the Disruption era and late 19th Century Free Church. Beginning with Thomas Chalmers, each chapter has a biographical sketch of a key figure with an emphasis on why these men mattered in their time and what they still have to say to us in the 21st century. All of the men portrayed were committed to the advancement of the Gospel in Scotland and further afield. While they shared a commitment to the Confession of Faith and reformed theology, this was expressed in unique ways by each of these men. Hence both unity and diversity is on view in these fascinating pages.

At this moment in church history the people of God sorely need to be reminded that following Christ means being willing to part with cherished denominational identities and connections, church buildings, and even houses and secure salaries. This welcome book includes a picture of each of these founding fathers of the Free Church of Scotland and - to a man - they all look as sober as hot, black coffee in a styrofoam cup. As we are in no danger of overdoing their earnestness, spending a few hours with such steely-eyed men can safely serve to remind us of what it means to stake one's life and livelihood on the lordship of Jesus Christ. Sandy Finlayson has written a clear, lively book that concedes when these churchmen were wrong without thereby obscuring their passionate stand for the Gospel.

Timothy Larsen
McManis Professor of Christian Thought,
Wheaton College, Wheaton, Illinois

ISBN 978-1-84550-550-9

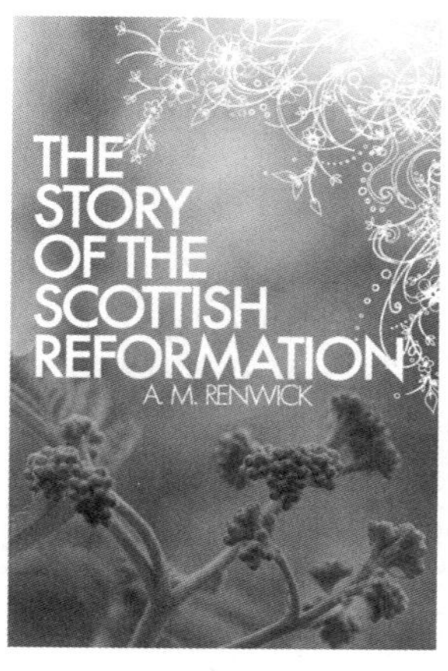

The Story of the Scottish Reformation
A M Renwick

The Reformation had a radical effect on Scotland not just spiritually but also politically and socially. Given its spiritual decadence in the lead up to this, it was in much need of reformation. A contributor to that success was the old Celtic Church who revered the Bible as the supreme standard and hence placed an emphasis on the preaching of the Word. Renwick considers the character and the experiences of the leader of the Scottish Reformation John Knox. Secularly it was to have an influence on the Scottish Parliament e.g. the importance of education for all as a result of the principles they had built. It also considers the protagonists of the reformation such as the nobles and the place of Mary of Lorraine the Queen Mother and Queen Mary. As well as looking at the Scottish Reformation it gives its historical context not forgetting what was happening elsewhere. It is clear that for those who were involved in the Scottish Reformation it was costly but they considered it important to defend the reformed faith. An opportunity to read of lives that were transformed as they became convicted of the gospel truth which in turn led them to serve God.

"Increasingly our people are interested in their roots, whether geneaological or spiritual. Here in this little book A. M. Renwick provides us with a way to trace where we've come in such a way to help us know where the church needs to go. Get out your shovel and dig into the history of the Scottish Reformation!"

Sean Michael Lucas
Senior Minister, First Presbyterian Church, Hattiesburg, Mississippi

"A. M. Renwick's small book on the Scottish Reformation is the best introduction to the period. I am delighted that on the 450th anniversary of the Scottish Reformation this superb book is being reissued."

David Robertson
Pastor, St Peter's Free Church of Scotland, Dundee

ISBN 978-1-84550-598-1

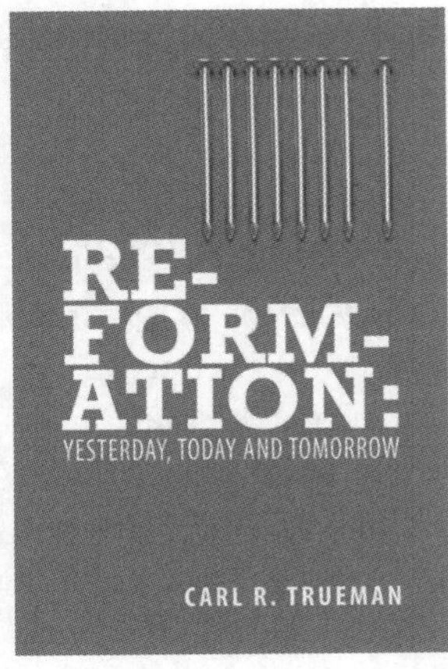

Reformation

Yesterday, Today and Tomorrow

Carl R. Trueman

Dr. Trueman examines the origins of contemporary Reformed theology in the Reformation world of the sixteenth and seventeenth centuries. After tracing how this heritage shaped and transformed the intervening period, he then describes some of the major challenges being faced by the evangelical church at the present time and suggests ways of responding which remain faithful to the Scriptures and the theology of the Reformers drawn from it and points towards a future that embraces and disseminates these wonderful doctrines of grace.

> "With knowledge, wit, and clarity, Carl Trueman brings key insights from the Reformation on Christ, Scripture, and our appropriation of both to bear on the life of the modern evangelical church."
>
> *Michael Lawrence*
> *Senior Pastor, Hinson Baptist Church, Portland, Oregon*

ISBN 978-1-84550-701-5

Churches, Revolutions And Empires
1789-1914
Ian J. Shaw

1789 to 1914 was a time of momentous and often violent change religiously, socially, politically and economically in the western world. The revolutions in the churches and the powerful empires of the day were to have a profound effect upon society at large both then and in the years that followed. In this detailed yet fascinating study, Ian Shaw gives context and understanding to this legacy which has been passed on from that era by providing an expert analysis of the period with a focus on the key leaders, influences and issues.

"...capably and confidently charts the course of the western church through this era of upheaval and change. Shaw's grasp of primary and secondary sources is impressive, as is his ability to synthesize. This is history on the big scale and an excellent example of such."

Michael A. G. Haykin
Professor of Church History and Biblical Spirituality,
The Southern Baptist Theological Seminary, Louisville, Kentucky

"I think this is a most impressive book. A book like this should become a standard work in the way that Alec Vidler's Church in an Age of Revolution used to be."

Ian Randall
International Baptist Theological Seminary, Prague, Czech Republic

"The book is clear, well arranged and up-to-date in its absorption of recent research. It covers the full range of denominations across the globe, setting religion firmly in its socio-political context and so addressing central historical issues such as empire and national identity. It is likely to command a wide readership in universities, theological colleges, ministers' studies and private homes."

David Bebbington
Professor of History, University of Stirling, Stirling

ISBN 978-1-84550-774-9

Christian Focus Publications

Our mission statement –

STAYING FAITHFUL
In dependence upon God we seek to impact the world through literature faithful to His infallible Word, the Bible. Our aim is to ensure that the Lord Jesus Christ is presented as the only hope to obtain forgiveness of sin, live a useful life and look forward to heaven with Him.

Our Books are published in four imprints:

CHRISTIAN FOCUS

popular works including biographies, commentaries, basic doctrine and Christian living.

CHRISTIAN HERITAGE

books representing some of the best material from the rich heritage of the church.

MENTOR

books written at a level suitable for Bible College and seminary students, pastors, and other serious readers. The imprint includes commentaries, doctrinal studies, examination of current issues and church history.

CF4•K

children's books for quality Bible teaching and for all age groups: Sunday school curriculum, puzzle and activity books; personal and family devotional titles, biographies and inspirational stories – because you are never too young to know Jesus!

Christian Focus Publications Ltd,
Geanies House, Fearn, Ross-shire,
IV20 1TW, Scotland, United Kingdom.
www.christianfocus.com